CANNOT BE CHECKED OUT

An Encyclopedia
of African American
Christian Heritage

An Encyclopedia of African American Christian Heritage

Marvin A. McMickle

Forewords by
Cain Hope Felder
and
J. Alfred Smith Sr.

Judson Press
Valley Forge

An Encyclopedia of African American Christian Heritage
© 2002 by Judson Press, Valley Forge, PA 19482-0851
All rights reserved.

Judson Press has made every effort to trace the ownership of all quotes.
In the event of a question arising from the use of a quote, we regret any error
made and will be pleased to make the necessary correction in
future printings and editions of this book.

Bible quotations in this volume are from The New King James Version.
Copyright © 1972, 1984 by Thomas Nelson Inc.

Library of Congress Cataloging-in-Publication Data

McMickle, Marvin Andrew.
   An encyclopedia of African American Christian heritage / Marvin A. McMickle.
        p. cm.
Includes bibliographical references and index.
ISBN 0-8170-1402-0 (alk. paper)
1. African Americans—Religion—Encyclopedias. I. Title.

BR563.N4 M353 2002
200'.89'96073—dc21   2001050411

Printed in Canada

08 07 06 05 04 03 02

10 9 8 7 6 5 4 3 2 1

Dedication

This book is dedicated to Dr. Lawrence N. Jones, dean emeritus of Howard University Divinity School in Washington, D.C. For more than thirty years you have been a mentor, a friend, and a model of Christian manhood. You will never know how much your guidance and counsel meant to me when I was a student at Union Theological Seminary in New York City and you were the dean and interim president. The many hours I spent in your office, in your apartment, and in your classes were decisive in my own spiritual and intellectual formation. Your heart was as open to your students as was your door.

You read and critiqued my Master of Divinity thesis. You helped to install me at my first pastorate in Montclair, New Jersey, in 1976. You then traveled to Cleveland in 1987 to share in my installation at my present pastorate. However, I am especially delighted to dedicate this book to you, because you and the other African American members of the faculty at Union Seminary are responsible for my eagerness to contribute to the ongoing study and discussion of the African American religious experience. You have helped to produce a generation of scholarly pastors and teachers who are now carrying on the work that each of you pursued with such passion. I am honored to be numbered among your intellectual descendants.

My indebtedness to you extends beyond the realm of professional concerns. The greatest blessing in my personal life was meeting Peggy Lorraine Noble, who since 1975 has been my wife. As you will no doubt remember, I met her on a blind date that you arranged on Valentine's Day, 1975. Less than four months later you, along with Dr. Samuel D. Proctor, officiated at our wedding ceremony. I later found out that we were not the first couple you had brought together.

It is appropriate that there be an entry in the section on Scholars and Teachers that covers your professional career. There is no one known to me who has made a greater contribution than you have to theological education, especially as regards the preparation and placement of men and women in black churches across the country. However, for the direct and personal impact you have had upon my life, I will be eternally grateful.

Your spiritual son,
Marvin

Contents

◉-◉-◉

A Foreword

BY CAIN HOPE FELDER

Professor of New Testament Studies • Editor, *The Journal of Religious Thought*
Howard University, School of Divinity, Washington, D.C.

For the past quarter century, many African American church leaders and scholars have not only recognized the need for more substantial treatment of their rich and diverse religious heritage, but they also have been attempting to do something about it. Courses in black church history and black religious studies began to appear in departments of religion and religious studies programs of American institutions of higher education. Also, significantly larger numbers of African Americans have enrolled in black studies courses that have inevitably identified the prominent role of religion. Indeed, over this same period, the ranks of African Americans earning advanced degrees and producing books in these areas have been measurably augmented. All of these certainly are encouraging developments, except for one sad paradox. Despite the fact that a great variety of specialized resources on the black religious experience now exist, they have remained out of reach, in a readily digestible form, for the masses of African Americans—many of whom regularly attend church. Yet, these are precisely the people who would benefit most from such information.

With the publication of Marvin A. McMickle's *An Encyclopedia of African American Christian Heritage,* we have collectively taken a major step in closing the gap between the academy and the pew in acknowledging and celebrating the great cloud of African American witnesses who have defined and sustained the black church in America. All of us owe a debt to Marvin McMickle for this important, comprehensive survey of a largely neglected legacy in American religion. This volume is a bold undertaking, especially for someone who already has demanding, multiple responsibilities as pastor of a large urban church, professor of homiletics at a school of theology, and community activist. An encyclopedia such as this would be a near impossible task for anyone with less vision, energy, and discipline of the mind. Evidently, Marvin McMickle has all three attributes, and as a result he deserves our kudos for this achievement. As one who has followed his career of service for many years, I can attest to his fine intellectual range, research skills, and deep religious commitments.

McMickle's encyclopedia blends biography, story, and commentary on a host of prominent and less well-known people in African American religious history. He shows sensitivity for the old and the new names; he balances the tributes and testimonies of heroes with those of heroines of the faith; furthermore, he envisions African American Christian heritage as fundamentally ecumenical. The author organizes this reference book by identifying eight rubrics: Denominational Founders and Leaders, Preachers, Teachers and Scholars, Political Leaders, Prophets, Nationalists, Cult Leaders, and Singers and Songwriters. In each instance, his aim is not merely to report on the respective significance of notable individuals. Rather, in each category, McMickle often allows persons to speak for themselves. Readers can thereby hear the virtual voice of select African American religious leaders through reading excerpts of their own writings. In addition, the encyclopedia offers helpful updated bibliographies that can serve as a basis for further study. Finally, this resource provides information on a number of African American religious organizations and institutions that are often overlooked by the majority culture, although the listing is not meant to be as comprehensive as some of the more exhaustive works with which the author and compiler is obviously familiar.

The author is well aware that some will dispute the personalities that he has selected to include in this encyclopedia. Those of us who labored hard to produce the recently published *African American Jubilee Bible* and *The Jubilee Legacy Bible* know how difficult it is to decide who is to be included and what set of criteria is to be used in a historical survey of a people's religious tradition. I am quite impressed with the list of names that McMickle has selected. Indeed, it is a double honor to find that I myself am among that number! Other contemporary figures who are included in this volume will no doubt share that sentiment. Together, we take note of the positive changes that are under way, despite all of the negatives of our socioeconomic and political circumstances as a people in America. This encyclopedia provides sufficient documentation that while all is not well in Zion, we as a people are justified in our hope that "trouble don't last always!"

A Foreword

BY J. ALFRED SMITH SR.

Professor of Preaching and Church Ministries, The American Baptist Seminary of the West, Berkeley, California, and Senior Pastor, Allen Temple Baptist Church, Oakland, California

In 1983 a study group from Allen Temple Baptist Church visited Israel and followed our young Jewish tour guide to the summit of Mount Hermon. Our visit to that historical place evoked from our academic and critical reflections a symbiosis of reverential scholarship. Our young guide marvelled at our responses and he said to us, "When we Jews come to this place, we study our history. When you Christians come to this place, you express your religion." He did not realize that our faith is rooted not only in the history of the Hebrew Bible, but in the continuing holy history of God's deeds as recorded in the tremendous efforts of Dr. Marvin A. McMickle in *An Encyclopedia of African American Christian Heritage*.

Dr. McMickle has produced another work that will enrich the academy and enlighten the church. Not every scholar prepares manuscripts that have reading appeal for diverse and divergent audiences. As busy as Dr. McMickle is in his work as pastor, professor, and prophetic voice to public policy creators in the fields of social services and government, he has found the time to compile and compose a well-written book that is long overdue in terms of the hungering need for its publication.

The shakers and movers, the innovators and improvisers of historical progress are always asking the following questions:

1. Who are we?
2. What is our source?
3. What values and instructions have been bequeathed to us?
4. What sacrifices have been made for us?
5. What was the nature of our elders' spirituality?
6. What information must we collect and preserve about our elders?
7. How shall we transmit our history to others, especially to our youth?

The research of Dr. McMickle provides the *sine qua non* needed for addressing the issues raised in these questions. The answers are not in abstract thoughts about the historical past, but they are embedded in the narratives of the persons, past and present, who used their talents as contributors and not consumers of human good.

This particular contribution of Dr. McMickle is an important extension of the historical scholarship that originated with Dr. Carter G. Woodson, who established the Association for the Study of Negro Life and History and who for many years edited *The Journal of Negro History*. Scholars such as C. Eric Lincoln, James Washington, James H. Cone, Gayraud S. Wilmore, Henry H. Mitchell, Larry Murphy, James Evans, Evelyn Brooks Higginbotham, Cheryl J. Sanders, Albert Raboteau, Juanita Evans Leonard, M. Shawn Copeland, Randall Burkett, and Manning Marable, are a few of those in academia who are helping to close the conspicuous gap in the literature on black American religious history.

In this historical handbook, you will join hands with Cheryl J. Sanders in meeting persons who understood the meaning of *Ministry at the Margins*. You will discover the saintly faces of W. E. B. Du Bois' *Souls of Black Folk*. You will be introduced to significant personalities that James Baldwin made reference to in *Nobody Knows My Name*. You will encounter those persons who passionately and prophetically championed the cause of freedom with the courage of Richard Wright in *White Man Listen*. And in these pages you will find illustrated in flesh and blood the message of C. Eric Lincoln's *Race, Religion, and the Continuing American Dilemma*.

In sum, Dr. McMickle presents to the reader an excellent list of black church leaders whose heads and hearts merged their personalities into what Prof. Luther D. Ivory calls a "theology of radical involvement," which grows out of one's search for self-discovery, meaning, and purpose, often in response to a negative experience. I am 100 percent confident that, in this survey of African American religious history, weary seekers of self-discovery, meaning, and purpose will come to discover and be encouraged in God's will for their own lives' commitment and investment.

The illustrious persons so appropriately presented in this wonderful encyclopedia stand majestically upon the strong shoulders of many anonymous African Americans throughout history whose sacrifices cannot be measured and whose sorrows cannot be weighed. Our gratitude to both our oral and written traditions is such that, in the words of Psalm 78:4:

We will not keep them from our children; we will tell the next generation about the Lord's power and his great deeds and wonderful things he has done. (Good News Bible)

Introduction

Hebrews 12:1 says, "Since we are surrounded by so great a cloud of witnesses, let us lay aside every weight, and the sin which so easily ensnares us, and let us run with endurance the race that is set before us." The writer of Hebrews was referring to the heroic men and women whose lives and deeds had been recorded in Hebrews 11, all the way from Abel and Enoch to the Christians of his generation who were being killed for the cause of Jesus Christ. Most of them were now dead and were looking on while the next generation carried forward the work of the kingdom of God. The challenge to those presently involved was to do their best, because those who had run before them were either looking down from heaven or looking on from the sidelines. They were surrounded by "so great a cloud of witnesses."

This book, like Hebrews 11, is a roll call and listing of the faithful men and women whose words and deeds gave life and shape to the African American religious experience. With only one exception, the book focuses on persons and events from the eighteenth century forward. For the most part, the people listed here are Christians, but not all of them, because non-Christian movements have played an important role in shaping the religious experience of African Americans.

This is a listing of the various movements and messages that were present within African American communities over the last several hundred years. This is a listing of denominational founders and leaders, preachers and scholars, and social prophets who attempted to alter the national landscape through their advocacy for issues and ideas.

Here are political leaders who blended together the pulpit and public policy. Here, too, are nationalists and cult leaders who gave up either on America or on the Christian faith or both. Finally, here are the singers and composers whose music has stirred our hearts for the last one hundred years. Here is a modern cloud of witnesses of the historic struggle within the African American community for faith and faithfulness. Read their stories and discover that like the characters described in Hebrews, many of the people discussed in the book were persons "of whom the world was not worthy" (Hebrews 11:38).

There is another comparison between the people listed in Hebrews and the people listed here. Neither is an exhaustive list of every name that could have been included. In Hebrews there is mention of Abraham, Joseph, and Moses but not Joshua, Jeremiah, or John the Baptist. We hear of Sarah and Rahab but not Ruth or Rachel, Mary or Martha, or Priscilla or Phoebe. This book, like Hebrews, is not a list of all the people who made historic contributions to the African American religious experience. However, it is a representative sample of that "great cloud of witnesses," based largely upon their having made some singular contribution or their having received some singular recognition for their life's work.

There was some method involved in the selection process of who would be included. The compiler assembled an initial list of one hundred names of persons who had made a singular contribution to the religious expressions found within the various African American communities across the country. That list was shared with Judson Press, whose idea it was to assemble and publish this encyclopedic reference. Judson Press then sent out the initial list to a group of distinguished scholars and pastors for their review. That panel was free to add to or take from the list, with the expectation that a final list would be assembled that represented as wide a range of people and movements as possible. I am especially indebted to J. Alfred Smith Sr., Henry Mitchell, Martha Simmons, Jeremiah Wright Sr., and Harold Dean Trulear for their willingness to provide assistance and invaluable contributions to this project. Each of them is part of my personal "cloud of witnesses."

The purpose of this book is to offer a longer and more personalized entry on each person than might be the case in some other reference works. It was important not only to provide biographical information but also to place that information in a historical context. Whenever possible, it was also deemed important to allow the people to speak for themselves; thus quotes by many of these persons appear as part of their entry. Each entry is also followed by the bibliographic sources from which the information was drawn. In addition to the persons who received an entry on their life and work, a glossary of terms and movements is found at the end of the book as a way of covering events and activities that are not identified with any single individual.

The book is not organized in simple alphabetical order. Instead, it is organized according to eight areas of activity. First are Denominational Founders and Leaders. These are the people who gave birth to many of the historically black denominations or made significant contributions to their growth and development. Next come the Preachers, those heralds of the gospel who have been widely celebrated by their peers as the best in their generation. They are followed by Teachers and Scholars, those who shaped our theology, trained our clergy, and wrote the books that gave voice to our faith and gave vent to our frustrations. Then come the Politicians who served in the government as a way of advancing the kingdom of God.

One of the great legacies of the African American religious community has been the angry cry of the voice of the Prophets. Whether the issue was abolition, black codes, enfranchisement, antilynching, women's rights, the end of segregation, or the demand for equal protection under the law, their voices are echoed on these pages. Next come the Nationalists, men and women who advocated separation from white society, whether as an isolated community within America or as émigrés back to Africa.

One of the legacies of the Great Migration of the nineteenth and twentieth centuries is the rise of the Cult Leaders. Most of their groups did not grow large in number. Few of them lasted in their original form to this day, typically because cults rarely outlive the death of the founder. But at the time in history when they were functioning, they were an important lens through which to view and consider African American life. Something else was swept up into the North with the Great Migration, and that was the music of the South, be it blues, spirituals, or jazz. All of those rich musical sources, coupled with the struggle of living as a black person in America, gave birth to gospel music. The contribution of these Singers and Songwriters gives new meaning to the phrase "Lift every voice and sing...."

I have no doubt that many persons may debate the names that are and are not included in this book. Again, this book was not meant to be the definitive, exhaustive listing of every significant person in the long history of African American religion. Such exhaustive treatments have already been compiled, most notably *The Encyclopedia of African American Religion* by Larry G. Murphy, J. Gordon Melton, and Gary L. Ward. The faculty of Howard University School of Religion has compiled a similarly exhaustive listing of denominations and religious movements in the *Directory of African Ameri-*

can Religious Bodies. The present study has made great use of those excellent resources, and if certain entries are not found here, I urge readers to consult these and many other excellent resources.

It may also happen that another writer will feel compelled to create another listing of persons who they feel deserve to be included in such a volume as this. It is neither my interest nor intention to end the discussion on a who's who in African American religious history. Rather, I want to highlight the lives and contributions of some of the most notable and some of the most overlooked people and movements within that arena.

The purpose of this book is to provide a quick and easily accessible reference for any person wishing to learn more about many of the leading figures in African American religious life. This book is also designed to provide additional bibliographic references where the reader can turn to learn more about each person and movement. This study is designed to be helpful for students doing research, as well as for teachers, whether in college or seminary, who want to provide additional historical information for their classes. The lay reader will find that each entry is clearly written so that no theological training is required to read or understand anything that is included. It is hoped that each entry is sufficiently thorough in what is included so that scholars will count this book as one of the tools available to them as they study the African American religious experience.

The compiler was determined to be faithful to the diversity within the African American religious experience. Black evangelicals such as Tom Skinner and

Howard O. Jones appear alongside womanist theologians such as Katie Cannon and liberation theologians such as James Cone. Black Muslims, black Jews, and Moors appear with a nineteenth-century black Roman Catholic priest and a nineteeth-century AME woman evangelist. An attempt was made to include persons who lived and/or worked in all regions of the country. To that end, the ministry of Jessie Jai McNeil of California is listed along with the rise and fall of Henry Lyons of Florida.

Lemuel Haynes, a Congregationalist who fought for freedom at the Battle of Lexington and Concord in 1775, is listed here, as is Nat Turner, a Baptist who fought a different kind of battle for his freedom in Southampton County, Virginia, in 1831. Jarena Lee is here to embody the limitations that were placed upon women who aspired for a place in the ministry of the African American churches. Vashti McKenzie is here as a celebration of how women have prevailed over the years and finally broken through what she calls the "stained-glass ceiling."

Some intriguing family connections can be found within these pages. Elijah Muhammad and the Nation of Islam are discussed here, and so too is his son Warithuddin Muhammad, who refused to walk in his father's footsteps. Here, too, can be found the whoop of C. L. Franklin and the moan of his daughter Aretha. The pulpit oratory of Adam Clayton Powell Sr. can be contrasted with the political accomplishment of his son, Congressman Adam Clayton Powell Jr.

There are rivalries that can be studied, as between J. C. Austin and L. K. Williams, two giants within the National Baptist Convention who were also pastors of neighboring churches in Chicago at the same time. There are other rivalries as between Joseph H. Jackson and those Progressive National Baptist Church pastors like Gardner C. Taylor and T. M. Chambers, who wanted to see the black church become more supportive of Martin Luther King Jr. and the civil rights movement.

There was more about each person discussed here that could have been said, just as there were other persons who could have been included. However, what is here will serve as a broad, general introduction to the people and movements that helped shape the religious experience of African Americans. Many of them are still alive. Most of them are watching from heaven. Taken together, they serve as "so great a cloud of witnesses" for those who are continuing the work they began.

Denominational Founders and Leaders

⊙–⊙–⊙

⊙ Adams, John Hurst

(1929–) As pastor, academician, bishop, and ecumenical leader, John Hurst Adams has been one of the great black church leaders of the twentieth century. He has served as pastor of several congregations in the **African Methodist Episcopal (AME) Church** and as professor at two AME colleges. He was a founding member of the National Committee of Negro Churchmen and the founder and first chairman of the **Congress of National Black Churches (CNBC)**, an ecumenical partnership involving seven historically black denominations.

Adams was born on November 27, 1929, in Columbia, South Carolina. He graduated from Johnson C. Smith University in North Carolina with a bachelor of arts degree in 1948. He later earned bachelor and master of theology degrees from Boston University and did additional graduate study at Harvard University and Union Theological Seminary in New York City.

Adams began his pastoral career in an AME church in Lynn, Massachusetts, from 1950 to 1952. He served on the faculty of Wilberforce University and Payne Theological Seminary in Ohio from 1952 to 1956. He served as president of Paul Quinn College, another AME-related institution in Waco, Texas, from 1956 to 1962. He then returned to pastoral ministry in Seattle, Washington, from 1963 to 1968, and Los Angeles, California, from 1968 to 1972. He was elected a bishop of the AME church on the first ballot at the general conference meeting in Dallas, Texas, in 1972.

In 1966 Adams joined with Gayraud S. Wilmore in founding a black ecumenical group now known as the **National Conference of Black Churchmen (NCBC)**. In 1978 he was the founder and first chairman of the Congress of National Black Churches (CNBC). That movement is still in operation, and its mission is well described by **C. Eric Lincoln:**

The goal of CNBC is to build cooperative institutions—for example, insurance, banking, purchasing and publishing that will serve to empower African Americans in pragmatic and structural ways. CNBC is the institutional embodiment of the black consciousness movement, representing as it does, a creative effort to merge the radical social vision of black theology and the older liberation tradition of reform, self-help, and economic uplift.

Adams has also been widely acclaimed for his preaching. He was listed among the top fifteen black preachers in America in the September 1984 and November 1993 issues of *Ebony*.

"America's Fifteen Top Black Preachers," *Ebony*, September 1984; C. Eric Lincoln and Lawrence W. Mamiya, *The Black Church in the African American Experience*; W. Augustus Low and Virgil A. Clift, eds., *The Encyclopedia of Black Americans*; "The Top Fifteen Black Preachers," *Ebony*, November 1993.

☙ Allen, Richard

(1760–1831) Born a slave in Philadelphia, Pennsylvania, on February 14, 1760, Richard Allen and his family were sold to another family residing in Kent County, Delaware. Through a process called gradual manumission, Allen worked for six years to pay for his freedom at a price of $2,000 in 1786. He had experienced

an emotional conversion to the Christian faith and had become a Methodist preacher to other blacks in the places where he was hired out to work. After attaining his freedom, he was invited by the St. George Methodist Church to preach to its black members.

Allen's belief in the need for blacks to own and operate their own institutions first took shape through the Free African Society, which he cofounded in Philadelphia with **Absalom Jones** and William White in May 1787. This group was organized as a mutual aid society, assisting members with the cost of funeral arrangements and other financial needs. It also offered instruction in moral living and character development.

He was offered an opportunity to travel with Bishop Francis Asbury, the famous Methodist preacher, but Allen decided against doing so. He objected to the conditions that would have been imposed upon him as a black man traveling and appearing in public with a white man, especially when traveling through slaveholding states. He would have to sleep in Asbury's carriage, because no inn or hotel would accept him. He would also receive no salary or payment beyond food and clothing.

As a result of Allen's efforts at St. George Methodist Episcopal Church, the black membership of that church increased dramatically. White members of the church often could not find a seat on the main floor of the sanctuary, so a policy was established relegating black members to standing around the walls of the sanctuary on the first floor or sitting in the balcony. Allen wished to build a separate sanctuary for the black members, but that idea was initially met with stiff resistance from black and white members.

Allen's belief in an all-black place of worship became more pressing when he and several other black members of St. George's walked out of that church in November 1787. The walkout occurred when they were pulled from their knees while praying one morning because they were in a section of the sanctuary reserved for whites. Forced racial segregation in churches was the order of the day in Philadelphia, the same city and in the same year in which the United States Constitution was being ratified.

Allen was the prime mover in the construction and consecration of the Bethel African Church, which was dedicated by Asbury on April 9, 1799. Similar groups of black Methodists in Maryland, Delaware, New Jersey, and other areas of Pennsylvania came to Philadelphia and laid the foundations for the first black denomination, the **African Methodist Episcopal (AME) Church.** On April 11, 1816, Allen was consecrated the first bishop of the AME Church, but only after **Daniel Coker** of Maryland declined the honor in favor of Allen.

As a former slave, Allen wrote and spoke against slavery. He sheltered fugitive slaves in his home and in the basement of the Bethel Church. He had once been captured by a slave catcher who attempted to sell him into slavery on the grounds that he was a fugitive slave. Only the willingness of a white man to vouch for Allen's identity saved him from that fate. Allen then sued the slave catcher, who was forced to spend three months in jail for making that false charge. He was an outspoken critic of the American Colonization Society (ACS), which sought to return free blacks to Africa or establish colonies in various Caribbean locations.

Hard work and thrift were marks of Allen's private life and public example. After purchasing his freedom and that of his wife, he owned and operated several businesses in Philadelphia; his enterprises included a blacksmith shop, shoemaking, and chimney sweeping. Upon his death, he left his family an estate valued at $80,000.

In 1830 Allen was elected president of the American Society of Free Persons of Color, a convention designed to improve the lives of free blacks living in the United States and Canada. His rise from a hired-out slave to a bishop, entrepreneur, founder of America's first black church denomination, and president of a national convention ended with his death in 1831 at the age of seventy-one.

Richard Allen, *The Life and Gospel Labors of the Rt. Rev. Richard Allen;* Carol V. R. George, *Segregated Sabbaths;* Albert J. Raboteau, "Richard Allen," in *Black Leaders of the Nineteenth Century,* ed. Leon Litwack and August Meier.

☻ Borders, William Holmes

(1905-1993) Known as "the Prophet of Wheat Street," William Holmes Borders made his mark in ministry in many important areas. He was the pastor of a five thousand member congregation in Atlanta. He was a civil rights activist even before the advent of his Atlanta neighbor, **Martin Luther King Jr.** Perhaps most notably, he led his church in building hundreds of units of housing for the poor and the elderly.

Borders was born in Macon, Georgia, on February 24, 1905. He was the seventh child born to Rev. and Mrs. James Buchanan Borders. He managed to graduate from Morehouse College in Atlanta in 1929, even though he had been told to leave the campus because he could not pay the tuition. But he continued to attend classes, and his professors continued to allow him to participate.

Borders won a scholarship to attend Garrett Theological Seminary in Evanston, Illinois, earning a bachelor of divinity degree in 1932. He earned a master of arts degree in 1933 from the University of Chicago. He then served the Second Baptist Church of Evanston, Illinois, from 1932 to 1937. He married Julia Pate in 1931, while he was still a student at Garrett. They had two children, both of whom became physicians. Borders left Evanston to return to Morehouse College as an instructor in 1937. On Novem-

ber 17, 1937, he was called to be the pastor of Wheat Street Baptist Church in Atlanta, where he remained for the balance of his career.

Borders's impact on Atlanta was immediate and impressive. He led the church in the construction of a new building by 1939, and a Christian education wing was added in 1957. He led a voter registration drive in 1946 that generated fifteen thousand new black voters. He then took that list of voters to the mayor of Atlanta and demanded that the city hire black policemen. With that level of political clout, the mayor's response was, "How many black police officers do you want, Reverend?"

In 1957 Borders led a group called the Triple L Committee (love-liberty-loyalty) that successfully desegregated the buses in Atlanta. He had challenged the practice of requiring blacks to enter and exit from the back door, using the front door of a bus as early as 1946. That was still against the law, and the law was not changed until the movement in 1957. Borders hosted a radio program in Atlanta that regularly challenged the white power structure of that city to treat black citizens with respect and to extend to them equal opportunity in all areas of the life of the city.

In 1945 the **National Baptist Convention, USA, Inc. (NBCUSA)**, met in Atlanta, and Borders and Wheat Street served as the official hosts. Borders was expelled from that convention in 1959 following his opposition to the attempts of **Joseph Harrison Jackson** to hold the office of convention president beyond the agreed-upon term of office. Borders then became a charter member of the

Progressive National Baptist Convention (PNBC), which was organized in 1961, largely over the question of the tenure question that had divided the NBCUSA. He hosted a session of PNBC in Atlanta in 1966.

Borders is best known, however, as a leader in the area of church-sponsored housing projects. In the neighborhood that surrounds the church, housing units include high-rise apartments and garden units. The building projects began in the 1950s, when people were being uprooted from their homes in order to make room for an interstate highway. From that beginning on 22.5 acres of land, the projects went on to include the 280 apartments called the Wheat Street Gardens (1963) and the fourteen-story Wheat Street Retirement Home (1972).

Much of the land was purchased with money that Wheat Street received after its attempt to buy a farm in 1959 about twenty miles outside of Atlanta. Borders had a vision of black people not only working on the 287-acre farm but also growing food that could be sold in the city. Thus he was engineering a genuine economic opportunity plan. However, white neighbors fiercely objected to the presence of blacks in that area. Several buildings were burned, and it was assumed but never proven that the neighbors were responsible. The church sold the property to a neighborhood group for twice the purchase price.

C. Eric Lincoln wrote about the economic development effects of the ministry of Borders and Wheat Street Baptist Church:

Wheat Street had the largest property holdings of any black church in the United States, infusing the surrounding community with more than $15 million worth of development. The church had built a middle-class apartment building, Wheat Street Towers, rented out a number of storefronts along Auburn Avenue, and owned fifteen acres of property in downtown Atlanta. Borders had also set up the first federal credit union sponsored by any church and is considered one of the pioneers in church-sponsored public housing.

Borders ran for the Georgia state legislature in 1965 as a Republican and came within ten thousand votes of being elected. In 1954 he was selected by *Ebony* as one of the nation's ten best black preachers. He was the recipient of three doctor of divinity degrees and two doctor of laws degrees from Atlanta University and Howard University. Borders coined the phrase "I am somebody," which would later be popularized by **Jesse Jackson.**

Borders retired from Wheat Street Baptist Church in 1989 and died in 1993.

Juel Pate Borders Benson, "The Eulogy of William Holmes Borders," in *The African American Pulpit* (winter 2000–2001); James W. English, *Handyman of the Lord;* funeral program for William Holmes Borders; W. Augustus Low and Virgil A. Clift, eds., *The Encyclopedia of Black America.*

☉ Boyd, Richard Henry

(1843–1922) No single person in the history of the **National Baptist Convention, USA, Inc. (NBCUSA)** has made a greater contribution and at the same time contributed to a more divisive conflict than Richard Henry Boyd. He was born into slavery in Mississippi on March 5, 1843, and some scholars argue that his name at birth was Dick Gray. The family by whom he was owned moved to Texas, and many of them were killed while fighting for the Confederacy during the Civil War.

After emancipation he changed his name to Richard Henry Boyd and enrolled in Bishop College in Marshall, Texas, in 1869. Although Boyd did not receive a degree, his call to ministry became clear, and he was ordained as a Baptist preacher. By 1870 he had organized the African American Baptist Association in Texas. When the NBCUSA was formed in 1895, Boyd was appointed general secretary of the Home Mission Board.

When the Southern Baptist Convention objected to black preachers being allowed to contribute articles to the American Baptist Publication Society, Boyd led in the effort to establish the National Baptist Publishing Board in 1897. Having already moved to Tennessee to oversee the work of the Home Mission Board, Boyd incorporated the Publishing Board under the laws of Tennessee, and the convention agreed to place the Publishing Board under the supervision of the Home Mission Board.

A facility was eventually built on land that was owned by Boyd, and all of the material that was produced was copyrighted under his name. By 1905 a feud had developed about whether the Publishing Board was an affiliate of the National Baptist Convention and answerable to its leadership or an independent business operation run by Boyd. The convention attempted over a period of ten years to separate the Publishing Board from the Home Mission Board, but Boyd and many others in the convention resisted that effort. The convention attempted a legal maneuver to gain control of the Publishing Board, but since the convention was not legally incorporated in Tennessee it could not own land as a business in that state.

During a contentious annual session of the convention held in Chicago in 1915, the so-called Boyd faction walked out of the convention, rallied at the Salem Baptist Church of Chicago, and organized the **National Baptist Convention of America.** Beginning in 1924, an alliance was formed so that the **Lott Carey** Baptist Foreign Mission Convention became the foreign mission arm of the National Baptist Convention of America. However, by the early 1940s that relationship ended, and the convention sponsored its own foreign mission program.

The National Baptist Publishing Board has remained under the control of the family of Richard Henry Boyd to this day. Upon his death in 1922, his son Henry Allen Boyd took over. Between 1959 and 1979 the board was run by a nephew, T. B. Boyd Jr. In 1979 it came under the control of T. B. Boyd III. In 1989 another feud erupted over control of the Publishing Board within the National Baptist Convention of America. As a result, another black Baptist convention was formed by yet another Boyd faction. The new group is called the National Missionary Baptist Convention. The National Baptist Convention of America has often been referred to as the Boyd convention, but no member of the family, including Richard Henry Boyd, ever served as its president.

Boyd was an entrepreneur in areas beyond the Publishing Board. He also owned and operated the National Negro Doll Company, which began selling black dolls in 1911. He formed the National Baptist Church Supply Company, which sold pulpit furniture and other items needed by local churches. His climb from slavery to head of several national business operations is worthy of note and affirmation. However, the worth and significance of his achievements have long been obscured by the controversy attached to his name.

Theodore S. Boone, *The Split of the National Baptist Convention;* Leroy Fitts, *A History of Black Baptists;* Joseph H. Jackson, *A Story of Christian Activism;* C. Eric Lincoln and Lawrence W. Mamiya, *The Black Church in the African American Experience;* Larry Murphy, J. Gordon Melton, and Gary Ward, eds., *Encyclopedia of African American Religions;* James M. Washington, *Frustrated Fellowship;* Joseph R. Washington Jr., *Black Religion.*

☾ Brown, Morris

(1770–1849) A slave insurrection was set to occur in Charleston, South Carolina, on June 16, 1822. The leader of that planned uprising was a former slave named Denmark Vesey, but the uprising was called off on the day it was to have gone into motion because Vesey suspected that white authorities had been alerted by another black person who was part of the original planning. Much of that planning took place in the **African Methodist Episcopal (AME) Church** in Charleston where Morris Brown was the pastor.

Brown was born of free parents in Charleston in 1770 and was apprenticed

to become a shoemaker. Early in his life he sensed a call to ministry, and he was ordained by the Methodist Episcopal Church. In 1817 he led a group of black worshipers out of the Methodist Episcopal Church in Charleston and organized the Hampstead African Church, which later joined with **Richard Allen** and the African Methodist Episcopal (AME) Church. He was ordained an elder in the AME Church in 1818. He continued in that role in Charleston until 1822, when he was forced to flee due to his suspected involvement in the Vesey uprising.

It could never be proved that Brown or the Hampstead AME Church were involved in or even aware of the uprising. However, Bishop **Daniel A. Payne** would later say that the AME church was fully aware of what Vesey was planning and fully supportive of his efforts. Brown was out of the city on June 16, 1822, when the rebellion was uncovered. Vesey was later caught and hanged, along with forty other conspirators.

Dozens more were whipped and released. Brown, while officially acquitted of playing any part in the insurrection, nevertheless left the city and sailed to Philadelphia, Pennsylvania, for his own safety. Peter Prioleau, the slave informant who alerted white authorities, was given his freedom by the South Carolina legislature.

As a result of the uprising, the Hampstead church was permanently closed, leaving its three thousand members with no place to assemble. A brutal set of black laws placed tight restrictions on almost every aspect of life for blacks, slave and free, in Charleston. More than five blacks could not gather at a time in the absence of a white person. It became illegal to teach any black to read under severe penalties for the teacher and the student. Restrictions were placed on the ability of black preachers to move throughout the region. The growth of the AME church halted, not to resume until after the Civil War. As an example, there were 15,000 AMEs throughout the Deep South in 1860, but by 1880 that number had swelled to 450,000.

Upon his arrival in Philadelphia, Brown resumed his work as a shoemaker. He also joined the Bethel AME Church and became an assistant minister by 1825. By 1826 he became the assistant to the bishop, Richard Allen. In 1828 Brown was consecrated as the second bishop of the AME church. He and Allen served in the episcopacy together until Allen's death in 1831. Brown then served alone until 1836, when Edward Waters was consecrated as the third bishop.

Brown is credited with encouraging and overseeing the expansion of the AME Church west into Ohio, Indiana, and Kentucky. He also helped establish an AME conference in Canada. Like a true nineteenth-century Methodist circuit rider, Brown traveled primarily on horseback through untamed wilderness and in intemperate weather. The rigor of his life may have contributed to his suffering a stroke in 1844 from which he never fully recovered. Paralyzed and afflicted with other physical problems, Brown died on May 9, 1849. The AME Church established Morris Brown College in Atlanta, Georgia, in 1881 in honor of its second bishop.

Lillie J. Edwards, *Denmark Vesey: Slave Revolt Leader;* Carol V. R. George, *Segregated Sabbaths;* Harry V. Richardson, *Dark Salvation;* Gayraud S. Wilmore, *Black Religion and Black Radicalism.*

☻ Bryan, Andrew

(1737–1812) Born in Goose Creek, South Carolina, in 1737, Andrew Bryan was among the first black men in American history to be ordained to the ministry and assigned to a congregation. He was born into slavery and was converted to Christianity under the preaching of another pioneer black preacher, **George Liele,** in 1782. Bryan began his preaching ministry around Savannah, Georgia, and for several years carried on this unofficial ministry, preaching to white and black audiences.

In 1788 Bryan was officially licensed to preach as a Baptist minister by a white Baptist pastor named Abraham Marshall. Bryan's followers were also officially organized into the First African Baptist Church of Savannah, with Bryan as pastor. His work met with great success among blacks but with stiff resistance from whites who believed that slaves who had organized for worship could easily use that organization to plot rebellion against the slave regime. Bryan and his followers were frequently, and on occasion brutally, whipped in an attempt to break their spirits. Bryan was once publicly whipped. However, he took the flogging in the spirit of the martyrs of the early church, and in so doing he won the admiration and sympathy of his former tormentors.

Through the intervention of his master, Jonathan Bryan, the followers of Andrew Bryan were allowed to meet in the barn on his plantation three miles outside of Savannah. However, as a concession to the lingering fear about slave insurrections, they could assemble only between sunrise and sunset. By 1794, however, the church had moved from the barn into its own building in the city. The continuing fear of having large numbers of blacks gathered together resulted in whites sitting in every service to be sure nothing was said that could fuel a slave uprising or plant seeds of discontent among the slaves.

Under Bryan's leadership the church grew to more than seven hundred members, at which time he urged that a Second African Baptist Church be formed. The growth continued, and soon a Third African Baptist congregation was formed in Savannah.

Following the death of his owner, Bryan bought his freedom for fifty pounds from those who held title to his owner's estate. His personal industry and frugality allowed him to acquire a home in

Savannah, a fifty-acre farm with many buildings that he rented out for additional income, and ownership of eight slaves, concerning whom he said, "For whose education and happiness I am enabled through mercy to provide."

Bryan died in 1812. On his death he was honored by the all-white Savannah Baptist Association, which wrote: "This son of Africa, after suffering inexpressible persecutions in the cause of his divine Master, was at length permitted to discharge the duties of the ministry among his colored friends in peace and quiet, hundreds of whom, through his instrumentality, were brought to a knowledge of the truth as it is in Jesus."

E. Franklin Frazier, *The Negro Church in America;* Albert J. Raboteau, *Slave Religion;* Gayraud S. Wilmore, *Black Religion and Black Radicalism;* Carter G. Woodson, *History of the Negro Church.*

☻ Burgess, John Melville

(1909-) At a time when the rest of the United States was attempting to respond to the pressures of the **civil rights movement**, the Episcopal Diocese of Massachusetts made history on December 8, 1962, when John Melville Burgess was elected to be suffragan (assistant) bishop of that diocese.

Burgess was born on March 11, 1909, in Grand Rapids, Michigan. He earned a bachelor of arts degree (1930) and a master of arts degree (1931) from the University of Michigan. Responding to a call to ministry and looking for a way to improve human relations in the country, he enrolled in the Episcopal Theological Seminary in Cambridge, Massachusetts. He earned a bachelor of divinity degree in 1934 and was ordained into the Episcopal priesthood that year.

Between 1934 and 1946 Burgess served as rector to parishes in Michigan and in Ohio. From 1946 to 1956 he was chaplain at Howard University in Washington, D.C. Between 1952 and 1956 he also served as canon at the National Cathedral in Washington. From 1956 to 1962 he served on the diocesan staff in Boston with oversight of the Episcopal city mission work. From that position he was elevated to the office of suffragan bishop. He became the first black person ever elected a bishop with responsibility over a primarily white diocese. On January 17, 1970, he was elected to the office of presiding bishop of that same diocese, once again becoming the first black person ever elected to that position in a primarily white diocese.

Burgess served as bishop until his retirement in 1976. After that he served on the faculty of Yale Divinity School. In 1982 he edited a book of sermons by various Episcopal clergy entitled *Black Gospel/White Church*. During his years as a bishop he was active in ecumenical affairs, attending various sessions of the World Council of Churches and the National Council of Churches.

John M. Burgess, *Black Gospel/White Church;* W. Augustus Low and Virgil A. Clift, eds., *The Encyclopedia of Black America.*

☻ Burroughs, Nannie Helen

(1879-1961) At a time when black women were expected to support the church but never presume to exercise leadership within it, Nannie Helen Burroughs was a courageous and outspoken advocate for the role of women in the church and in the wider society.

Burroughs was born May 2, 1879 (perhaps 1878 or 1883), in Orange, Virginia. After her graduation from high school she moved to Philadelphia and began working as a secretary for a black newspaper. She wanted to become a teacher, but she could not find a job in the public school system because she was black. Even the all-black schools would not hire her because her skin was presumed to be too dark. She was therefore the victim of a double caste system.

By 1900 Burroughs had become actively involved in the **National Baptist Convention, USA, Inc. (NBCUSA)**, but she bristled at the restrictions that were placed upon women who wanted to be involved in the life of the black Baptist convention. In that year she joined other women, including Virginia Broughton, in organizing the Women's Convention as an auxiliary of the NBCUSA. She also delivered the inaugural address, "How the Sisters Are Hindered from Helping," at that convention. She devoted her life to this convention and to the work of the black Baptist church. She would serve as corresponding secretary of the Women's Convention from 1900 to 1948.

Burroughs did not limit her time and influence to church work. She was also active in women's and black suffrage, anti-lynching campaigns, temperance, improved working conditions and fair wages for working women, and the banning of segregation statutes in public accommodations, most notably on trains and buses.

In 1902 Burroughs wrote an open letter entitled "An Appeal to the Christian White Women of the Southland" in which she appealed to white women to use their influence within the white community to help bring an end to the segregation and other forms of discrimination being imposed upon blacks in the South. That letter said in part: "We wish to appeal to you on behalf of the thousands of mothers in this land who have suffered in silence the unchristian humiliation to which they have been subjected in the Southland since the introduction of the separate-coach law." The law to which she was referring was the result of the decision in *Plessy v. Ferguson* by the U.S. Supreme Court (1896) that allowed for separate but equal facilities for blacks and whites in all areas of public life. The facilities for blacks, and especially for black women, were separate, but they were far from being equal. Thus, more than fifty years before Rosa Parks

sparked a bus protest in Montgomery, Alabama, Nannie Helen Burroughs was standing tall on the issue of integrated buses and trains.

In 1909 Burroughs and the other members of the Women's Convention opened a school in Washington, D.C., called the National Training School for Girls. Burroughs became the president of that school, and she traveled across the country raising money, almost entirely within the black community, to support that work. The curriculum was largely designed after that of Tuskegee Institute, with a strong emphasis on domestic and household service work. However, there were some liberal arts offerings as well.

Burroughs came under federal surveillance in 1919 as a result of her verbal attacks upon President Woodrow Wilson, whom she criticized for his refusal to support any anti-lynching legislation. She also was angered that American rhetoric about defending freedom in Europe in 1918 did not translate into policies to defend the freedoms of black people living in the United States, including the black men who fought in Europe during World War I. Many of them returned home and were met with the same discrimination they had known before they left to fight in France. Many of them were lynched while still wearing their uniforms. Surveillance did not silence her criticism of the government.

In 1964 the focus of the National Training School for Girls was changed, and it became an elementary school, the Nannie Helen Burroughs School. In 1971 ownership of the school and its properties was transferred to the **Progressive National Baptist Convention (PNBC)** during the presidency of **Thomas Kilgore Jr.**

Burroughs had worked with Mary McLeod Bethune to organize a labor union for black female domestic workers known as the National Association of Wage Earners. That independent labor group existed from 1920 to 1926. However, Burroughs's advocacy for the rights and dignity of working women lasted for the rest of her life. Burroughs never married. She remained an active member of Nineteenth Street Baptist Church in Washington until her death in 1961.

Evelyn Brooks Higginbotham, *Righteous Discontent;* C. Eric Lincoln and Lawrence W. Mamiya, *The Black Church in the African American Experience.*

☻ Carey, Lott

(1780–1828) Today the name of Lott Carey is associated with a black Baptist foreign mission convention that has done evangelism and outreach on four continents. However, the man behind the name lived in relative obscurity for more than half of his life. Carey was born a slave in Charles City County, Virginia, in 1780. It is known that he was the property of William A. Christian and that he was reared in the home of a devout father and grandmother. However, as was the case for the vast majority of slaves during that period, the events that surrounded his life went largely unrecorded. Nothing is known about his life until 1804, when he moved to Richmond to work as a hired slave laborer whose wages went in part to purchase his freedom and as income to his owner.

For three years Carey was caught up in street life that involved drunkenness, rowdiness, and profanity. However, he was converted and baptized in 1807 in the First Baptist Church of Richmond and was subsequently licensed to preach by that congregation. He quickly became a preacher of great renown, especially to a large congregation of blacks that met in the First Baptist Church, even though he had no formal theological training and had only recently learned how to read and write. As a result of gaining literacy skills, Carey was able to earn more money, and in 1813 he purchased freedom for himself and his three children for a sum of $850.

William Crane, Carey's teacher at the school for blacks in Richmond, was the first to interest him in the possibility of extending his preaching ministry beyond the Richmond area and to consider sailing to Africa to evangelize on that continent. In 1815 Carey helped to form the Richmond African Baptist Missionary Society, which immediately began to raise funds for a mission venture in some suitable location in Africa. On January 23, 1821, Carey and a group of followers set sail for Sierra Leone. He was not the first American-born black preacher to make that trip; David George had led an earlier group to the same country in 1792. In 1820, the year before a Baptist presence arrived, **Daniel Coker** had led a delegation to Sierra Leone on behalf of the **African Methodist Episcopal (AME) Church.** However, Carey's presence was to have the greatest and longest-lasting effect.

Two motivations led Carey to make the trip to Africa. On was a sense of religious zeal that caused him to want to share the gospel with people in Africa who had never heard the story of Jesus. Thus he said, "I long to preach to the poor Africans the way of life and salvation. I don't know what may befall me, whether I may find a grave in the ocean, or among the savage men, or more savage wild beasts on the coasts of Africa; nor am I anxious what may become of me. I feel it my duty to go."

However, the second reason involved Carey's sense that he would never be able to fully develop as a man in the United States because of slavery, race relations, and prejudice. "I am an African," he said, "and in this country, however meritorious my conduct, and respectable my character, I cannot receive the credit due to either. I wish to go to a country where

I shall be estimated by my merits, not by my complexion; and I feel bound to labor for my suffering race."

The group arrived in early March 1821, and the first communion was observed on March 22. Carey's first wife had died while they were still living in slavery. His second wife died soon after their arrival in Africa. Thus he had three distinct areas of responsibility. He was pastor of the church for the colonists, he oversaw the missionary work among the Mandingo people of that region, and he had to rear his three children alone.

In 1822 the colonists relocated to the newly formed nation of Liberia, and that is where Carey spent the balance of his life and labor. Their presence was never fully accepted by the Bassa people, who were the dominant indigenous group in that region of West Africa. However, after several skirmishes between the colonists and the natives, Liberia began to grow into a thriving and productive colony.

Among the things that developed were a school system and the concept of compulsory education for young people. Carey became the president of that school. In 1826 he was elected vice regent of Liberia. He became acting governor in 1828, when the governor became ill and returned to the United States for treatment. On August 25, 1828, Carey became governor of the colonial nation of Liberia following the death of the former governor. However, his time in office would not last long. Attacks against the colony by the native population resumed in 1828. On November 8, 1828, while preparing cartridges to use in the defense of the colony, Carey was killed in an accidental gunpowder explosion.

In 1840 black Baptists from New England and the Middle Atlantic states met at Abyssinian Baptist Church in New York City to organize the American Baptist Missionary Convention. That was the first black Baptist convention with a national purpose. This convention would be merged into the **National Baptist Convention, USA, Inc. (NBCUSA)**. In 1897, as a result of several doctrinal and operational differences, a new convention was formed, the Lott Carey Baptist Foreign Mission Convention, headquartered in Louisville, Kentucky. Since its founding, that convention has sponsored missionary efforts in Liberia, Russia, Haiti, South Africa, Zaire, India, Nigeria, and Guyana, South America.

Leroy Fitts, *Lott Carey;* C. Eric Lincoln and Lawrence W. Mamiya, *The Black Church in the African American Experience;* Gayraud S. Wilmore, *Black Religion and Black Radicalism.*

☟ Chambers, Timothy Moses (T. M.)

(1895-1977) This preacher, known for his power and intonation, was most noted for being the first president of the **Progressive National Baptist Convention (PNBC)**. That body split from the **National Baptist Convention, USA, Inc. (NBCUSA)** in 1961 over the issue of tenure for the president and over how black Baptist conventions should respond to the leadership of **Martin Luther King Jr.** and the **civil rights movement**. The new convention was organized in response to a call from Rev. L. Venchael Booth of Zion Baptist Church in Cincinnati, Ohio.

Chambers served as PNBC president for six years, from 1961 until 1967, when he was succeeded by **Gardner C. Taylor**. Chambers's leadership was important, first because of his national standing within the NBCUSA and also because of his unquestioned excellence as a preacher. That combination of reputation and stature was essential for the fledging convention, because it shifted the focus of the convention away from the more controversial personalities of Taylor and King. Taylor would have been a controversial choice as the first president, because he had been an unsuccessful candidate for the presidency of the NBCUSA the preceding year. His selection as the first president would have given the impression that the split was only in service to his aspirations rather than the larger philosophical questions of tenure and civil rights.

While PNBC was formed in order to provide a support base for King and the civil rights movement, it would not have been feasible for King to assume much of a leadership role, given the rigors of his schedule with the **Southern Christian Leadership Conference (SCLC)**. Chambers was the perfect choice, because he possessed all of the abilities required of a president of a national religious body, and his tenure allowed for time to pass after the initial break from the NBCUSA. After his presidency, PNBC instituted a tenure policy that limited the president to a maximum of two years in office. The effects of that policy were eventually felt, and the tenure policy was changed to two consecutive two-year terms.

Chambers was born June 18, 1895, in Mt. Pleasant, Texas. He attended Forth Worth I&M Institute and graduated from Bishop College in Marshall, Texas, with a bachelor of theology degree in 1920. His ministry was centered in Texas, and he served as president of the Baptist State Convention from 1945 to 1950.

In 1950 Chambers was called to the Zion Hill Baptist Church of Los Angeles. Having already established a national reputation as a preacher and leader in the NBCUSA, he was elected president of the Baptist State Convention of California/Nevada. This combination of being state president in Texas and California over a period of many years was key to Chambers's eventual selection as president of PNBC.

Chambers left Zion Hill and founded the Roger Williams–True Love Baptist Church in Los Angeles in 1966. He remained there for the rest of his career, and he died in November 1977.

Thomas Kilgore Jr. and Jini Kilgore Ross, *A Servant's Journey: The Life and Work of Thomas Kilgore;* C. Eric Lincoln and Lawrence H. Mamiya, *The Black Church in the African American Experience;* Larry Murphy, J. Gordon Melton, and Gary Ward, eds., *Encyclopedia of African American Religions.*

☺ Coker, Daniel

(1780-1846) Born in 1780 in Maryland to an English indentured woman and an African slave, Coker escaped to freedom in New York. There he joined the Methodist Church and became associated with Francis Asbury. Coker returned to Maryland, worked to purchase his freedom, and then became active among the African Methodists in Baltimore. They

had experienced the same treatment at the hands of the white Methodist Episcopal Church as had the followers of **Richard Allen** in Philadelphia some years earlier.

In 1810 Coker published a pamphlet, "A Dialogue Between a Virginian and an African Minister," believed to be the first published document by a black man in America. He led the Maryland delegation that met with Allen's followers in Philadelphia on April 9, 1816, to organize the **African Methodist Episcopal (AME) Church,** the first denomination organized by blacks in America.

On April 10, 1816, Coker was elected to serve as the first bishop of the church but declined the honor in favor of Allen. The reasons given for his decision vary widely, ranging from an impropriety that might have come to light to criticism that he was too light-skinned to be the first bishop of an African church.

Coker worked with Allen to produce the first hymnal and book of discipline for the AME Church in 1817. In 1818 he was expelled from the church for one year for undisclosed reasons. Following his restoration as an AME minister, Coker emigrated to Liberia and then to Sierra Leone under the sponsorship of the Maryland affiliate of the American Colonization Society (ACS). Accompanied by eighty-eight other émigrés, Coker began to establish AME churches in Africa. He also sought to implement the philosophy of Christianization and Westernization that would be adopted by such later émigrés as **Henry Highland Garnet, Henry McNeil Turner,** and **Alexander Crummell.** He died in 1846 in Sierra Leone, having never returned to America.

Carol V. R. George, *Segregated Sabbaths;* C. Eric Lincoln and Lawrence W. Mamiya, *The Black Church in the African American Experience;* Leon Litwack and August Meier, eds., *Black Leaders of the Nineteenth Century;* Daniel A. Payne, *Recollections of Seventy Years;* Harry V. Richardson, *Dark Salvation.*

☯ De Porres, Martin

(1579–1639) In many African American communities across the United States, one is likely to find a Roman Catholic church or parochial school that bears the name of St. Martin de Porres. He was the first person of African ancestry to become a Dominican priest when he took his vows in Lima, Peru, in 1603.

More importantly, he was the first person of African origin to be made a saint in the Roman Catholic Church when he was canonized by Pope John XXIII in May 1962.

In 1579 Martin de Porres was born in Lima, Peru, to a former slave girl and a Spanish nobleman named Don Juan de Porres. His father arranged to have Martin trained as a barber-surgeon, and he also began working as a servant in the Dominican abbey in Lima. Although he was reared to be a devout Roman Catholic, the Dominicans had a policy that would have excluded de Porres from joining. The policy states: "who are begotten on the side of either one of their parents of Indian or African blood … may not be received to the holy habit or profession of our order."

Instead, de Porres raised alms from passersby on the streets of Lima and then wisely distributed those funds to persons in need. The Dominicans placed him in charge of their infirmary, and he is reported to have shown great power in prescribing cures and in showing compassion. At the age of twenty-four he finally was allowed to take priestly vows and become a Dominican brother.

Martin de Porres practiced a rigorous form of humility that included fasting and self-flagellation. Upon his death in 1639, and as a result of his devotion to the poor and needy of Lima, the process for canonization began. It began with his beatification in 1837 under Pope Gregory XVI. In 1926 Pope Pius XI began the next phase of the process that would result in canonization. Proofs of miracles that were variously associated with persons who had prayed to Martin de Porres led to canonization. Part of the citation read: "He made it clear that every race and nationality has the same dignity, the same equality, because we are all sons of one heavenly Father and redeemed by Christ the Lord."

Russell T. Adams, ed., *Great Negroes Past and Present;* "Mulatto Saint," *Time,* May 11, 1962.

☻ Evans, Clay

(1925–) Denominational leadership can take many forms. For some it is a matter of seeking and holding a high office within a church body. For others, it is taking the lead in terms of ideas and initiatives that move the church in new directions. Clay Evans has been that kind of denominational leader.

Evans was born in Brownsville, Texas, on June 23, 1925. He moved to Chicago in 1945 to attend mortuary school, but he soon sensed a call to ministry. He was ordained in 1950, and that year he founded the Fellowship Missionary Baptist Church, remaining at that church for the next fifty years. He was educated at Chicago Baptist Institute, Northern Baptist Theological Seminary, and the University of Chicago Divinity School.

In 1952 Evans began a radio broadcast called *What a Fellowship.* He added a television broadcast of the same name in 1977. In 1954 he ordained a woman, Consuella York, to the Christian ministry at a meeting of the **National Baptist Convention, USA,**

Inc. (NBCUSA), decades before such a thing had become common. Rev. **Clarence LaVaughn (C. L.) Franklin** of Detroit also participated in that ordination service.

In 1965, when **Jesse Jackson** first came to Chicago to head Operation Breadbasket, an affiliate of the **Southern Christian Leadership Conference (SCLC)**, Evans was one of the few black Baptist clergy who embraced him. In that same year, Evans gave strong support to **Martin Luther King Jr.** coming to Chicago for a civil rights demonstration. In doing so, he lost the support of Chicago Mayor Richard J. Daley. That resulted in Evans not receiving approval for various building permits needed for a new church he had hoped to erect. However, he held to his convictions and remained supportive of King and Jackson.

In 1968 Evans broke ranks with many of the clergy in Chicago and ordained Jackson to the ministry. From 1971 to 1976 he served as the founding national chairman of Operation PUSH (People United to Save Humanity), a group formed by Jackson after his departure from SCLC. Evans's association with Jackson continued into the political arena; in 1988 he served as a delegate from Illinois to the Democratic National Convention for Jackson's presidential campaign.

In addition to the impact of his preaching and pastoral ministry, Evans has been a major force in **gospel music.** He has recorded thirty-nine albums with the Fellowship Mass Choir and with the African American Religious Connection Mass Choir.

Clay Evans, *From Plough Handle to Pulpit: A Man with a Mission;* Karen F. Williams, "Salute to a Gladiator," *GOSPEL Today,* December 2000.

☙ Harris, Barbara Clementine

(1930–) History was made in February 1989, when Harris was consecrated as suffragan bishop of Massachusetts in the Episcopal Church. A suffragan (assistant or auxiliary) bishop works under the authority of the bishop of a diocese or region. The suffragan bishop serves a life tenure but is not eligible for automatic succession to the rank of full bishop. Harris became the first woman to achieve that position in the nearly two-thousand-year history of those denominations that are governed by apostolic succession. That would include such church bodies as Roman Catholic, Eastern Orthodox, and Anglican churches, of which the Episcopal Church is a part.

Harris was born in Philadelphia, Pennsylvania, in 1930 and was reared within the Episcopal community of that city. After being among the early advocates for the ordination of women to the priesthood of the Episcopal Church, she was ordained a priest in that church in 1980. She served as rector of St. Augustine of Hippo Episcopal Church in Norristown, Pennsylvania. She also served as chaplain of the Philadelphia prison system.

It should be noted that while Harris was the first woman consecrated as bishop in the Episcopal Church, she was not the first African American woman ordained as an Episcopal priest. That distinction fell to **Anna Pauline (Pauli) Murray,** who was ordained a priest on January 8, 1977, at the age of sixty-seven, after a distinguished legal career.

Harris's ordination to the priesthood and her consecration as bishop were unique not only because she was a

issues of justice and empowerment for marginalized groups in American society.

In one of her sermons, Harris wrote, "No one expects us to eliminate all of the evils of the world, nor to liberate all those who are oppressed, nor to feed all who are hungry, or to house the millions who are homeless. But when the oppressed see one who fights for liberation, their burden is lightened because they know that somebody stands with them."

From her involvement in the voter registration drives in the South in the 1960s to her elevation to the office of bishop in the Episcopal Church, Harris has lived a life in solidarity with the oppressed.

Bettye Collier-Thomas, *Daughters of Thunder;* J. D. Douglas, ed., *Dictionary of the Christian Church;* Richard Newman, "Barbara Harris," in *The African American Century,* ed. Henry Louis Gates Jr. and Cornel West.

Haynes, Lemuel

(1753–1833) Among the militiamen gathered to fight for the colonial cause at the battle of Lexington and Concord (April 19, 1775) was a slave named Lemuel Haynes. He also served as a volunteer at the battle of Fort Ticonderoga in western Massachusetts on May 10, 1775. After a distinguished record in the regular colonial army, Haynes went on to establish an even more admirable record as a Congregational pastor in the New England states of Massachusetts, Vermont, and Connecticut, and finally in the state of New York.

Haynes was born in West Hartford, Connecticut, on July 18, 1753. He was born out of wedlock from the union of a

woman. She also lacked any of the traditional theological training usually required by the Episcopal Church. In fact, she was not even a college graduate. However, as Episcopal Church polity allows, she did study privately in preparation for her ordination as a priest. She responded to her critics by saying that her experience in the business world gave her a unique preparation and education that would serve her well in ministry.

In 1984 Harris was appointed executive director of the Episcopal Church Publishing Company. While in that position she published and wrote for the journal *The Witness.* Her regular column was entitled "A Luta Continua" ("The Struggle Continues"). In that spirit of continuing the struggle and breaking down barriers, she entered upon her consecration as a bishop. She has devoted herself to the

black father and a white mother. His mother abandoned him at birth, and he was taken in by a family named Haynes, who kept him until he was five months old. Later he was made a servant in the household of David Rose in Granville, Massachusetts. Haynes's life was cloaked in the obscurity of slavery until 1774, when he suddenly appeared as a member of the Massachusetts militia, popularly known as the minute men because they could be assembled to fight at a moment's notice. It is probable that Haynes, like many slaves, served in the militia as a stand-in for one of the sons of his owner, with the promise of emancipation from slavery when his military service had been completed.

Haynes had learned how to read mainly by reading the Bible, and he had exhibited a wonderful natural gift for preaching. He was ordained and assigned

to a Congregational church in Middle Granville, Massachusetts, in 1780. He was the first black person ever ordained to ministry by that denomination. He married a white woman named Elizabeth (Bessie) Babbit in 1783, and very little seems to have been said about it.

After five years as a pastor in Granville, Haynes moved to Connecticut, where by 1804 he had become employed by the Connecticut Missionary Society to labor among destitute people in remote sections of Vermont. He remained in Vermont in various ministry positions until 1822. While he was in Vermont, Haynes became the first black person to receive an honorary degree (M.A.) from Middlebury College.

Despite the fact that he had fought for liberty and freedom, Haynes quickly discovered that black people, even free blacks, would not share in the benefits of American society as it then existed. He did hold to the faith, however, that those blacks who were willing to enter the Northwest Territory that had opened up in 1787 might find a brighter future. To that end he spoke these words in a speech given in Rutland, Vermont, in 1801, on the occasion of the twenty-fifth anniversary of the Declaration of Independence: "Explore every corner of the globe for an equal asylum, tired in the fruitless chase, you would most eagerly seek the refreshing shades of happy Columbia. Still it is a land of improvements; we are not to conclude that the fair tree of liberty hath reached its highest zenith; may we not add to its lustre?"

In 1822 Haynes took a pastoral position in Granville, New York, where he spent the last eleven years of his life.

Remarkably, his fifty-three-year ministry was largely devoted to white congregations and listeners. His biographer captured the meaning of his life: "So lived and died one of the noblest of the New England Congregational ministers of a century ago. Of illegitimate birth, and of no advantageous circumstances of family, rank or station, he became one of the choicest instruments of Christ. His face betrayed his race and blood, and his life revealed his Lord."

Haynes died in Granville, New York, in 1833.

William Loren Katz, ed., *Eyewitness: The Negro in American History;* Benjamin Quarles, *The Negro in the American Revolution;* Carter G. Woodson, *History of the Negro Church.*

☙ Healy, James Augustine

(1830–1900) At a time when most black people were affiliated with Baptist and Methodist churches, the ministry of Father James Healy is a reminder of the strong influence of the Roman Catholic Church within the black community in America. He was born in Macon, Georgia, in 1830, the son of an Irish immigrant planter and a slave woman. His early education was in Quaker schools. Healy graduated first in his class from Holy Cross University in Massachusetts in 1849, and after studying for the priesthood in Montreal, Canada, and in Paris, France, he was ordained in the Cathedral of Notre Dame in 1854.

In that same year Healy was assigned as an assistant pastor to St. James parish in Boston, which was a largely Irish parish. He was also an assistant to the

bishop of that diocese from 1854 to 1866. He was not initially accepted in that role due to racial animosity, but when he continued to serve his flock through a series of typhoid and influenza epidemics, he won the hearts of his congregants. He was appointed the pastor of that parish in 1866.

In 1875 Pope Pius IX named Healy to be bishop of Portland, Maine. This made him the first black person ever appointed to be a bishop in the history of the Roman Catholic Church in the United States. During his tenure as bishop the diocese built sixty-five missions stations, eighteen parochial schools, and sixty-five new church buildings. His diocese was also increased to include all of New Hampshire and parts of Massachusetts.

Healy achieved an even higher honor

in 1900, when Pope Leo XIII made him an assistant to the papal throne, an office just below that of cardinal in the hierarchy of the Roman Catholic Church. Healy died just two months after being named to that position.

Bishop Healy's brother, Patrick Francis Healy, was also a distinguished member of the Roman Catholic clergy, serving in the Jesuit order. He was the first black American ever to be awarded a doctor of philosophy degree, which he earned in 1865. He went on to become president of Georgetown University in Washington, D.C., from 1873 to 1882. However, since Georgetown did not admit black students at that time, it may be that Patrick Healy passed as white.

Russell L. Adams, ed., *Great Negroes Past and Present;* W. Augustus Low and Virgil A. Clift, eds., *The Encyclopedia of Black America;* Harry A. Ploski and Ernest Kaiser, eds. and comps., *The Negro Almanac.*

☯ Jackson, Joseph Harrison

(1900–1990) This Baptist preacher is one of the most revered and one of the most controversial names in the history of the **National Baptist Convention, USA, Inc. (NBCUSA).** He was the convention's longest-serving president (1953–1982). The issue of his tenure in office led to a split within the convention and the formation of the **Progressive National Baptist Convention (PNBC)** in 1961.

Jackson was born in Rudyard, Mississippi, on January 11, 1900. He was ordained into the ministry in 1922. In 1927 he graduated with a bachelor of arts degree from Jackson College in Mis-

sissippi; he received a bachelor of divinity degree from Colgate Rochester Divinity School and a master of arts degree from Creighton University in Nebraska. He married Maude Thelma Alexander in 1927, and they had one child. Jackson served as pastor of churches in Mississippi, Nebraska, and Pennsylvania before being called as the successor to **Lacey Kirk Williams** at the Olivet Baptist Church of Chicago in 1941.

Jackson had already been elected as executive secretary of the Foreign Mission Board of the convention, a position he held from 1934 until 1953. That position, coupled with his being the successor of Williams, who was convention president when he died, assured Jackson's election as president of the NBCUSA in 1953.

Although Jackson continued to be a successful pastor, his reputation and standing were largely the result of his work within the convention. It was widely acknowledged that the president of the NBCUSA, with a membership estimated at between five and seven million members nationwide, was the most influential black person in America. However, with the emergence of **Martin Luther King Jr.** and the **civil rights movement,** that status was no longer unrivaled. Tensions between those two men would mark their lives in significant ways.

Jackson was an outspoken opponent of King's use of civil disobedience tactics and of his leadership in direct-action initiatives in the battle against racism. Jackson preferred to work through the courts and through the political process. However, there was growing sentiment within the convention that black Baptists should play a more supportive role in the civil rights movement. As Jackson blocked such efforts, tensions within the convention increased.

Those tensions were heightened by Jackson's refusal to abide by what he called an unconstitutional requirement that the convention president be limited to a certain number of years in office. That rule was to go into effect in 1956, and the result would have been that Jackson could not serve beyond 1960. When he would not step down from the presidency in 1961, and after a challenge by **Gardner C. Taylor** of New York at the convention meeting in Kansas City, Missouri, a group of activist pastors led by L. Venchael Booth of Cincinnati, Ohio, organized the PNBC.

The two main tenets of PNBC were tenure in office and active support of King and the civil rights movement. Even though King's grandfather, A. D. Williams, had been national treasurer of the NBCUSA, and Martin Luther King Sr. had been an active member of the convention, King also joined PNBC in 1961. His father also severed his ties with Jackson and NBCUSA.

Jackson strongly opposed the 1966 civil rights campaign for open housing that King led in Chicago, believing that King's tactics of civil disobedience were illegal and un-Christian. The feud between King and Jackson continued even after King's assassination in 1968. **Jesse Jackson** returned to his home in Chicago from Memphis, where he was present when King was killed, and called for the city to honor King's memory in a significant way. It was decided that the main street through the black community on the city's south side would be

changed from South Park Way to Martin Luther King Jr. Drive. The Olivet Baptist Church was located at 3100 South Park Way; thus the change in name would require Olivet's name, stationery, and other official documents to bear the name of the chief rival of its pastor, Jackson. To avoid that possibility, Joseph Jackson had the official address of the church changed to East 31st Street.

While his role in the formation of PNBC was controversial, other aspects of Jackson's career, especially his work as convention president, deserve attention. As early as 1953 he served as a member of the executive committee of the Baptist World Alliance. He attended Vatican II in Rome in 1962 as an official Protestant observer. He helped write some campaign literature for John F. Kennedy in his 1960 campaign for president of the United

States. In 1954 *Ebony* named him one of the ten best black preachers in the country.

Jackson began a program to cultivate one hundred thousand acres of land in Liberia that would not only create jobs and a food supply but also revenue that could be used to expand missionary work in Africa. For his efforts he was awarded the title of Royal Knight of the Republic of Liberia. This was a program similar to the one planned by **Henry Highland Garnet** in 1858.

Jackson also opposed **black theology** as set forward by **James H. Cone** and others. He was concerned that such a term could breed further divisiveness in the church and make ethnicity more important than salvation and faith in Christ. He expressed his views on that topic in *A Story of Christian Activism,* in which he states, "Just as we have often been victimized by the white historian who refuses to acknowledge our existence, so also we have been misunderstood by those among our own people who attempt to reduce all of theology to a matter of color…. When we call to the bar of religious thought and opinion these so-called supporters of 'Black Theology' they bring some beautiful theories and philosophies that may encourage sincere minds devoted to civil rights and to the struggle of the race, but this has nothing to do with the theological notion of God as Spirit."

Jackson left the presidency of NBCUSA in 1982, after twenty-nine years in that position. He was succeeded by **Theodore Judson Jemison** of Louisiana. However, he continued at Olivet until his death on August 18, 1990.

Helen Hobbs, "Who Speaks for America's Blacks?", *Christian Herald,* August 1969; Joseph Harrison Jackson, *A Story of Christian Activism;* C. Eric Lincoln and Lawrence W. Mamiya, *The Black Church in the African American Experience;* W. Augustus Low and Virgil A. Clift, eds., *Encyclopedia of Black America;* Larry Murphy, J. Gordon Melton, and Gary Ward, eds., *Encyclopedia of African American Religions.*

Jones, Absalom

(1746–1818) Born into slavery in Sussex County, Delaware, in 1746, Jones purchased his freedom and that of his wife and moved to Philadelphia, Pennsylvania. He eventually became associated with **Richard Allen** and was present when Allen and several other black people were forcibly removed from the St. George Methodist Episcopal Church in September 1787. Jones was a cofounder

of the Free African Society in Philadelphia. Organized on May 17, 1787, the society was a nonsectarian benevolent organization that provided financial services and moral guidance to the free black population of the city.

Jones worked with Allen in the founding of the Bethel Church, spiritual home for free blacks in Philadelphia after their departure from St. George's. However, Jones and Allen parted company soon after, when Jones decided to seek membership in the Protestant Episcopal Church, while Allen went on to organize the **African Methodist Episcopal (AME) Church.** In 1795 Jones was the first black person to be ordained a deacon in the Episcopal Church. He subsequently became the first black person ordained to be an Episcopal priest in 1804.

Jones became rector of the all-black St. Thomas African Episcopal Church in Philadelphia, which he had helped to organize in August 1794. In 1809, along with Allen and James Forten, who was a vestryman at St. Thomas, Jones organized the Society for the Suppression of Vice and Immorality in Philadelphia. This society, a precursor to the temperance movement in American society, sought to warn free blacks against the dangers of the consumption of alcoholic beverages. In 1814 Jones agreed to help recruit blacks to fight the British should they seek to invade Philadelphia during the War of 1812.

In 1800 Jones signed a petition calling for an end to the slave trade and for changes in the laws concerning fugitive slaves. He was also an outspoken critic of the American Colonization Society (ACS). Jones died in 1818.

Richard Allen, *The Life and Gospel Labors of the Rt. Reverend Richard Allen;* Carol V. R. George, *Segregated Sabbaths;* C. Eric Lincoln and Lawrence W. Mamiya, T*he Black Church in the African American Experience;* Harry V. Richardson, *Dark Salvation;* Carter G. Woodson, *The History of the Negro Church.*

Jones, Charles Price (C. P.)

(1865-1949) The name of **Charles Harrison (C. H.) Mason** is most closely associated with the formation of **The Church of God in Christ (COGIC).** However, the cofounder of that movement in its pre-Pentecostal form in 1897 was Charles Price Jones. Mason and Jones were leaders in persuading black Baptists to embrace the teachings of the holiness movement in the 1890s. That partnership would end in a court case in 1909, the result of Jones's disapproval of the Pentecostal emphasis that Mason had brought from the **Azusa Street revival,** which Jones did not attend.

Jones was born near Rome, Georgia, on December 9, 1865. He was reared as a Baptist and, having migrated to Arkansas, he was licensed to preach by a Baptist association there in 1887. He graduated from Arkansas Baptist College in 1891. In 1893 he embraced the holiness movement, and he claimed sanctification in 1894. In 1895 he became pastor of Mt. Helm Baptist Church in Jackson, Mississippi. However, Jones was removed from his church and from the Baptist fellowship because of his persistence in teaching holiness doctrines about sanctification. He eventually became allied with Mason, with whom he had much in common, and in 1902 Jones organized Christ Temple Church, which he quickly brought under the COGIC banner.

An irreparable schism was created between the two men over Mason's insistence, following his Azusa Street experience, that sanctification was not sufficient for the certainty of salvation. Instead, Mason insisted on the baptism of the Holy Spirit as evidenced by speaking in tongues, or glossolalia. This new doctrine created a conflict in the church body that was not resolved until Mason and Jones parted company after a court ruling gave Mason the right to continue to use the name Church of God in Christ. Jones took those COGIC members who objected to the new Pentecostal focus, and with them he organized The Church of Christ (Holiness) USA. He became the church's first bishop.

The group that followed Jones established its headquarters in Jackson, Mississippi. However, it was never able to match the growth of COGIC. Today The Church of Christ (Holiness) USA has fewer than fifteen thousand members in 170 congregations across the country. COGIC membership now exceeds five million worldwide.

Jones died on January 9, 1949.

Ithiel C. Clemmons, *Bishop C. H. Mason and the Roots of the Church of God in Christ*; C. Eric Lincoln and Larry H. Mamiya, *The Black Church in the African American Experience.*

☻ Kelly, Leontine T. C.

(1920–) Leontine Turpeau Current Kelly was born on March 5, 1920, in Washington, D.C. Her initial link to the leadership of the church was through her father, Rev. David Dewitt Turpeau, who was pastor of United Methodist churches in Washington and then in Cincinnati, Ohio. She was married twice, and both of her husbands were United Methodist pastors. She did not pursue a career in ministry for herself until she was fifty years old. She spent ten years in parish ministry, and in 1984 she became the first African American woman and only the second woman ever to be elected a bishop in the United Methodist Church.

Kelly attended West Virginia State University between 1938 and 1941. However, she did not remain to receive a degree, because she married Gloster Bryant Current and began a family. They had three children, but the marriage ended in divorce. In 1956 she married James David Kelly, who encouraged her to become a

certified lay speaker and urged her to finish her degree. She did so at Virginia Union
University in Richmond (1960).

While her husband served churches in
Virginia and Tennessee, Kelly was a public school teacher. When he died in 1969,
Kelly was invited to be the interim pastor.
She knew instantly that she had found
her niche. She enrolled in Wesley Theological Seminary in 1970 and then transferred to Union Theological Seminary in
Richmond, Virginia. While continuing to
serve at the Galilee United Methodist
Church, she was ordained a deacon in
1972, and she earned her master of divinity degree in 1976. She was ordained an
elder in the United Methodist Church in
1977 and appointed as pastor of the
Asbury–Church Hill United Methodist
Church in Richmond. She also served a
four-year term on the Richmond Board
of Education.

With the support of the clergywomen
of the United Methodist Church, Kelly
was elected a bishop of the church on
July 19, 1984, at a session of the Western Jurisdiction of the church meeting in
Boise, Idaho. The Western Jurisdiction
was chosen, because even by 1984 the
Methodist church in the Southeastern
Jurisdiction, which included Virginia,
was not prepared to support a black
woman for the office of bishop. Following her consecration, Kelly was assigned
to the San Francisco Episcopal Area,
where she served until her retirement.

Kelly was an activist bishop, involved
in such issues as HIV/AIDS, the rights of
farm workers, and civil rights in general.
No African American Methodist denomination elected a woman as a bishop for
another twenty years: **Vashti McKenzie**

by the **African Methodist Episcopal
(AME) Church** in 2000.

In 1999 Kelly was awarded the doctor
of divinity degree by Emory University.
The citation read in part: "You made a
second career in middle age, bringing to
the work of the church critical wisdom,
winning humor, undaunted faithfulness.
You have opened important dialogues on
critical issues—violence, poverty, racism,
sexuality, illiteracy—building bridges
between those with power and those without. Your strong prophetic life inspires
young people to serve, women to minister,
the powerless to claim their authority,
and schools and universities to see more
clearly the way to moral leadership."

Norman E. Borlaug, "Five Receive Honorary
Degrees," *EMORY Magazine,* summer 1999; Larry
G. Murphy, J. Gordon Melton, and Gary L. Ward,
eds., *Encyclopedia of African American Religions.*

Kilgore, Thomas, Jr.

(1913–1998) This pastor and civil rights activist was one of the major black leaders of the twentieth century. He served as the first black president of American Baptist Churches (1969–1970) and as president of the **Progressive National Baptist Convention** (PNBC, 1976–1978). At the same time, he was one of the major strategists of the **civil rights movement.** No one played a larger role in shaping the civil rights or the ecumenical agenda of the nation during the critical years of the 1950s through the 1970s than did Kilgore.

Kilgore was born in Woodruff, South Carolina, on February 20, 1913. He graduated from Morehouse College in 1935. He was elected to that college's board of trustees in 1966 and served as

chairman from 1974 to 1991. His theological studies at Howard University School of Religion were interrupted in 1945 so that he could accept the position of executive secretary of the General Baptist State Convention of North Carolina. He earned his bachelor of divinity degree from Union Theological Seminary in New York City in 1957.

Kilgore was licensed to preach in 1930, at the age of seventeen, by the Bethel Baptist Church of Brevard, North Carolina. The same church ordained him to the ministry on August 15, 1935. He then served as pastor of New Bethel Baptist Church of Asheville, North Carolina, from 1936 to 1938. Between 1938 and 1947 Kilgore took on three overlapping responsibilities with the Friendship Baptist Church of Winston-Salem, North Carolina, the Rising Star Baptist Church of Walnut Cove, North Carolina, and chaplain at Winston-Salem State University. He served as pastor of the Friendship Baptist Church of New York City from 1947 to 1963. He concluded his pastoral career serving at the Second Baptist Church of Los Angeles, California, from 1963 to 1985. While in Los Angeles he also served as director of Special Community Affairs on the campus of the University of Southern California.

Much of Kilgore's work was done behind the scenes, but his administrative and organizational skill was unmatched. While serving at the Friendship Baptist Church of New York City, he and Bayard Rustin planned the 1957 March on Washington called "A Prayer Pilgrimage for Jobs and Freedom." These men also were responsible for planning the 1963 March on Washington, where **Martin**

Luther King Jr. delivered his now famous "I Have a Dream" speech. Kilgore was director of operations for the **Southern Christian Leadership Conference (SCLC)** in New York and in Los Angeles. In that role, he remained one of the closest advisors to King.

In his autobiography, *A Servant's Journey,* Kilgore writes about his involvement in the funeral of his friend: "My family and I traveled to Atlanta to attend the funeral and memorial service for Dr. King. I offered the prayer at the service held on the campus of Morehouse College, which was attended by some seventy-five thousand persons, after helping to guide the mule cart that carried his body from Ebenezer Church, where the funeral was held, to the Morehouse campus for the mass service afterward. As we marched to Morehouse, the wheel on my side of the mule cart became loose, and I had to keep pushing it back on its axle to prevent it from falling off. Somehow this seemed a fitting metaphor for the instability that arose in our country following Dr. King's assassination."

On February 20, 1992, Kilgore presided at the ribbon-cutting ceremony for the new Thomas Kilgore Jr. Campus Center at Morehouse College, a tribute to his lifelong commitment to that school as student and trustee. At his side was his wife, Jeanetta, whom he married in 1936. They had two children, Lynn Elda and Jini Medina (now Rev. Jini Kilgore Ross). Thomas Kilgore died on February 4, 1998.

Taylor Branch, *Parting the Waters;* Thomas Kilgore, "The Black Church: A Liberating Force for All America," *Ebony,* August 1970; Thomas Kilgore Jr. with Jini Kilgore Ross, *A Servant's Journey;* C. Eric Lincoln and Lawrence H. Mamiya, *The Black Church in the African American Experience.*

☯ Liele, George

(1750–1820) The first black Baptist church to be organized in the United States (1773–1775) was located in Silver Bluff, South Carolina. It was located on the plantation of George Galphin, who allowed his slave, George Liele, to serve as the preacher to that congregation. Thus Liele may have been the first black preacher to an organized congregation in America.

Liele was born in 1750 in Virginia. His master, Henry Sharpe, moved to Georgia prior to the Revolutionary War. While attending church with his master, Liele was converted and baptized. Soon thereafter it was discovered that he had great gifts as a preacher, and his owner allowed him to travel freely throughout the region so that he could exercise his gifts. He traveled along the Savannah River as far as the Yamacraw region, where massive rice plantations made use of thousands of slaves.

Liele was eventually freed by his owner so that he could devote himself to preaching the gospel among slaves and before some white audiences. However, when the Revolutionary War erupted, Liele's work was interrupted. His owner was killed in the war, and the heirs to the estate tried to reenslave Liele, but a British army officer intervened to save him. In July 1778, when the city of Savannah fell to the patriot forces and the British fled to Jamaica, Liele went with the British as an indentured servant. He had to work for the governor of Jamaica until the cost of his transport had been covered. That was accomplished by 1784.

Before leaving Savannah, Liele baptized **Andrew Bryan** and his family. Bryan would go on to establish the African Baptist Church of Savannah. Thus Liele was largely responsible for establishing the black Baptist church in South Carolina and Georgia before the end of the Revolutionary War. After his departure, the Silver Bluff church continued under the leadership of David George. After migrating in 1782 to Nova Scotia, where he established several Baptist churches, David George led a group of freed slaves to Sierra Leone in West Africa in 1792. There they organized a new colony, and George organized the first Baptist church in Africa. In light of this, it could be said

that Liele's ministry resulted in the establishment of black Baptist congregations in those two countries.

Following his period of indentured service, Liele went to work and quickly organized a church in Kingston, Jamaica. That congregation quickly grew to more than five hundred members, despite the fact that Jamaica was a British colony that was dominated by the Anglican Church. He also started and supervised a school for the children in the community. His success was due in part to his industrious nature. He was also well-connected to members of the Jamaican Assembly, one member of which did some fund raising on Liele's behalf from supporters in England.

Through his efforts in Jamaica, Liele became the first American-born missionary to another country. His influence in South Carolina before the war and his influence on the life of David George mean that Liele was responsible for evangelizing many parts of the world.

White people were willing to support Liele's ministry because they were convinced that his efforts resulted in making their slaves less inclined to resist or challenge the authority of their owners. For instance, he would not allow any slave to attend one of his services who did not have the permission of his or her master. He also sought the approval of the local authorities for any literature or instruction he was going to share. Unlike preachers like **Nat Turner, Morris Brown,** and many others who used religious gatherings as an occasion to plot rebellion, slave owners were sure that no such thing would occur at any meeting held by Liele. One owner said that he did not need an overseer or a whip, because Liele's effect on his slaves had made them more industrious and obedient.

Liele died in 1820.

Leroy Fitts, *A History of Black Baptists;* C. Eric Lincoln and Larry H. Mamiya, *The Black Church in the African American Experience;* Carter G. Woodson, *The History of the Negro Church.*

☯ Lyons, Henry J.

(1942–) In the history of the **National Baptist Convention, USA, Inc. (NBCUSA),** several sad events have damaged the strength and witness of that community. The 1915 split over the Publishing Board that resulted in the birth of the **National Baptist Convention of America,** the so-called Boyd convention, was one such event. The battle over tenure that resulted in the accidental death of Rev. A. G. Wright of Detroit at the 1961 session held in Philadelphia and the subsequent formation of the **Progressive National Baptist Convention (PNBC)** is another such event. A third event is the 1999 conviction of the convention president, Henry Lyons of Florida, who was sentenced to five and a half years in prison on charges of racketeering. From the time his conduct became a matter of public knowledge in July 1997 until the present, the work of the convention has been overshadowed by the scandal that surrounded its former president.

Lyons was born on January 17, 1942, in Gainesville, Florida, to a seventeen-year-old unmarried mother. He never knew his father, but his paternal grandparents reared him. The influence of his grandfather, Booker T. Lyons, made Henry Lyons decide to enter the ministry.

Lyons earned a bachelor of arts degree from Bethune-Cookman College in Daytona Beach, Florida, in 1964. He earned a theology degree from the **Interdenominational Theological Center (ITC)** in Atlanta, Georgia, in 1968. In a 1995 interview in *Ebony,* Lyons stated that during his second year at ITC, God had revealed to him that he was destined to be the president of the convention. It seems that from that time on, Lyons did everything he could to bring that vision to reality.

Lyons's pastoral ministry began with the Abyssinia Baptist Church of Brunswick, Georgia, in 1964. In 1966 he moved to the Macedonia Baptist Church of Thomaston, Georgia. He temporarily left the pastoral ministry and the South to become academic dean at the Cincinnati Baptist Bible College and Seminary in 1970. However, in 1971 he was called to be the pastor of Bethel Metropolitan Baptist Church in St. Petersburg, Florida. He was thirty years old, and his climb to power and prominence was about to begin.

In 1977 Lyons became the first vice president of the Florida General Baptist Convention. In 1982 he was elected the president of that state convention, the youngest person ever to hold that office. In that year, he and five other presidents of large Baptist state conventions were recruited by **Theodore Judson Jemison** to help him in his bid to replace **Joseph Harrison Jackson,** who had been the president of the NBCUSA since 1953.

That effort was successful, and Jemison served two terms as president; Lyons was given a prominent role in Jemison's administration. When Jemison announced that he would not seek a third term, Lyons campaigned across the country for the position, and in September 1994 Lyons was elected to that position.

Always a businessman, Lyons began trading on the estimated 5.5 million membership of the convention. He made arrangements to give various companies access to the convention mailing list or access to the members at convention sessions from year to year for purposes of solicitation. He became a broker for such services as insurance, cemetery plots, and credit cards. However, having accepted fees from these companies, Lyons was never able to deliver what he had promised them. That would be the basis for racketeering charges.

In 1996 Lyon also accepted $200,000 from the Anti-Defamation League, a contribution that was meant to help rebuild black churches in the South that had been targets of arson. It was later discovered that Lyons had pocketed all but $30,000 of that money. None of this might ever have come to light had Lyons's third wife, Deborah, not set fire to a home that she believed he was sharing with a mistress, Bernice Edwards. An investigation into the fire revealed that Lyons was living the most lavish lifestyle imaginable, paid for either through convention funds or through monies fraudulently acquired through bogus business deals.

Lyons was eventually forced to resign from the office he had been pursuing for so long. He did so even though many members of the convention earnestly sought to retain him in that position, blaming the events not on any wrong that he had done but on the attempt of unnamed "white racists" to destroy another black leader. No less a figure than Dr. E. V. Hill, a well-respected

pastor and convention leader from California, argued that Lyons was the real victim. However, when Lyons stepped down in 1998, Hill was one of the persons who campaigned to replace him as president.

At the 1998 session meeting in Tampa, Florida, in an election campaign that resembled a national political campaign, William Shaw, pastor of the White Rock Baptist Church of Philadelphia and president of the Pennsylvania Baptist Convention, was elected the new president of the NBCUSA.

The racketeering trial for Lyons was held in April 1999. He was convicted, sentenced, and began serving his prison term in June of that year.

Edward Gilbreath, "The Redeeming Fire: The Ambition and Avarice of Henry Lyons Could Save the National Baptists," *Christianity Today,* December 6, 1999; "The Struggle for the Soul of Henry Lyons," a series of articles in *The St. Petersburg (Florida) Times* (1999).

☻ Mason, Charles Harrison (C. H.)

(1866–1961) In a life that spanned nearly a century and that was influenced by Reconstruction, Jim Crow laws, and the civil rights movement, Mason became one of the monumental figures in African American religious history. He was born on September 8, 1866, in Shelby County, Tennessee, near Memphis. His parents, Jerry and Eliza, lived as slaves until the year before he was born.

Mason's father died from yellow fever in 1879, and Charles seemed to be near death at the same time from the same disease. However, he credits his survival to a miraculous healing that occurred in 1880. That healing played an instrumental role in his spiritual development. Following his healing he was baptized at Mt. Olive Baptist Church near Plumersville, Arkansas. For the next ten years he served as a lay preacher in the Baptist church.

In 1891 Mason was ordained to the ministry. His wife, Alice Saxton, disapproved of his decision to enter the ministry, and Mason delayed doing so for two years. They were divorced in 1893, and in November of that year Mason enrolled at Arkansas Baptist College to begin training for the ministry. However, he dropped out of school by February 1894 and never resumed formal theological training.

Mason's decision to withdraw from school was driven by two factors. First, he objected to the emphasis that was placed on biblical criticism, which he thought called into question the authority of the Bible. He also believed that formal training might dampen the enthusiastic form of preaching and worship that he had learned from and experienced among former slaves in the South. Preserving that authentic religious enthusiasm of his youth would be among Mason's primary concerns for the rest of his life.

Although Mason had abandoned theological training, one book had a profound impact upon his life. That book was *An Autobiography: The Story of the Lord's Dealing with Mrs. Amanda Smith, the Colored Evangelist.* Amanda Smith (1837?–1915) was a black evangelist in the rapidly spreading **holiness movement** in the United States. As a result of reading that book, Mason acknowledged that he received the spiri-

tual gift of sanctification. The emphasis of holiness is that persons who have been converted and baptized must also manifest a life of holiness made possible by being sanctified. That message became the center of Mason's preaching beginning in 1893.

In 1895 Mason met **Charles Price (C. P.) Jones,** who became his friend and colleague in preaching the holiness message. As they spread that message they cofounded a new religious movement, **The Church of God in Christ (COGIC),** in Memphis (1897). Initially Mason and Jones remained within the Baptist church. However, both were expelled from the National Baptist Convention in 1899, because Baptist leaders objected to their insistence that conversion must be followed by sanctification. At that point, COGIC became an independent denomination within the holiness movement. The inspiration for the name Church of God in Christ was found in 1 Thessalonians 2:14 and 2 Thessalonians 1:1.

In 1907 Mason traveled to Los Angeles to attend the **Azusa Street revival,** which was being led by another black preacher, **William Joseph Seymour.** That revival stretched from 1906 to 1909 and was the pivotal event in the emergence of the Pentecostal movement in the United States. Under the influence of Seymour's preaching and its emphasis on being baptized in the Holy Spirit and speaking in tongues, Mason had a Pentecostal experience on March 7, 1907. As a result, he reshaped his core beliefs to include not only holiness as a lifestyle but also speaking in tongues as a sign of the baptism in the Holy Spirit.

Jones did not attend the Azusa Street revival, and he objected to the new Pentecostal emphasis that Mason was introducing to COGIC. That disagreement eventually led to a split between the two men and their followers in 1909. Those who remained loyal to Mason and who embraced the new doctrine of **Pentecostalism** continued under the name The Church of God in Christ. Those who agreed with Jones and who resisted the Pentecostal influence organized a new group called The Church of Christ (Holiness) USA.

From 1907 until 1914, Mason was the only Pentecostal preacher in the United States with a legally incorporated denominational structure that allowed him to ordain other ministers into the Pentecostal church. As a result, more than three hundred white clergy were ordained by Mason and served within COGIC. That marvelous interracial fellowship ended in 1914, when the white clergy withdrew from COGIC and formed the Assemblies of God. It would appear that America's racial policies in 1914 would not allow either for an interracial church or for a black preacher to be in authority over whites.

Mason was arrested during World War I because of his pacifist views. He was also placed under Federal Bureau of Investigation (FBI) surveillance, perhaps because of his continuing interracial following and popularity.

Mason married three times. After his divorce from Alice Saxton (1893), he married Lelia Washington in 1903. Following her death, he married Elsie Washington in 1936. He died on November 17, 1961.

Before his death Mason had transformed COGIC from a rural Southern movement to a vibrant religious movement that stretches across the United States and into many places around the world. The Pentecostal movement is the fastest-growing segment of the African American church. COGIC alone includes five million members.

The legacy of Mason continues in two distinct forms. One is Mason Temple in Memphis, the headquarters of COGIC. It was from the pulpit of Mason Temple that **Martin Luther King Jr.** delivered his last sermon ("I've Been to the Mountaintop") on April 3, 1968. The other legacy is the Charles Harrison Mason Theological Seminary, one of the member institutions of the **Interdenominational Theological Center (ITC)** in Atlanta, Georgia. That is a remarkable tribute to a man who initially rejected formal theological training.

Ithiel C. Clemmons, *Bishop C. H. Mason and the Roots of the Church of God in Christ;* Corrie Cutrer, "COGIC Presiding Bishop Ousted," *Christianity Today,* January 8, 2001; C. Eric Lincoln and Larry H. Mamiya, *The Black Church in the African American Experience;* Elsie W. Mason, "Bishop C. H. Mason, Church of God in Christ," in *African American Religious History: A Documentary Witness, 2d ed.,* ed. Milton C. Sernett.

☻ McKenzie, Vashti Murphy

(1947–) Vashti McKenzie became the first woman elected to be a bishop of the **African Methodist Episcopal (AME) Church** on July 11, 2000. A graduate of the University of Maryland, she received a master of divinity degree from Howard University Divinity School in Washington, D.C., and a doctor of ministry degree from United Theological Seminary in Dayton, Ohio. She also served as a mentor for a group of doctor of ministry students at United.

Prior to her election as bishop, McKenzie had served as pastor of Payne Memorial AME Church in Baltimore, Maryland. The first church to which she was assigned following seminary had only seven members, but during her ministry in Baltimore, Payne became one of the fastest-growing churches in the AME fellowship. Following her election as bishop, McKenzie coined the phrase, "The stained-glass ceiling has been broken." That was a reference to the fact that capable and qualified women had long been prevented from rising to that level of leadership due to gender prejudice in the church.

McKenzie is the author of the best-selling book *Not Without a Struggle,* which offers leadership strategies and encouragement to women in ministry. She serves on the advisory board of *The African American Pulpit,* a quarterly journal that focuses on sermons and scholarly articles by black preachers. She also serves on the board of Wilberforce University in Ohio.

Prior to entering the ministry, McKenzie worked in journalism. Her grandfather, John H. Murphy Sr., founded the *Afro-American* newspaper in Baltimore in 1892. She worked as a writer for that newspaper and for the *Arizona Republic.* She also worked as a radio broadcaster for a **gospel music** station.

During McKenzie's ten-year tenure, Payne Memorial AME Church grew

rapidly and expanded its ministries to include a school, a catering service that employs persons who had received welfare, and a community center that provides support for persons living with HIV/AIDS. All the while, McKenzie emerged as a preacher in great demand. The October 1997 issue of *Ebony* named her one of America's top fifteen black women preachers. She was invited by President Bill Clinton to give the closing prayer at the Democratic National Convention in 1996.

She has been assigned as bishop to the eighteenth district of the AME Church, which includes the African nations of Mozambique, Lesotho, Botswana, and Swaziland. McKenzie is the national chaplain of Delta Sigma Theta Sorority. Her grandmother is credited with being one of the founders of that group.

David Briggs, "First Woman Bishop Elected by AME," *Cleveland* (Ohio) *Plain Dealer*, July 12, 2000; Laurie Goodstein, "After Reluctant 'Yes' to Ministry, Confident Climb to Top," *New York Times*, July 15, 2000; "An Interview with Vashti M. McKenzie," *The African American Pulpit* (winter 1999–2000); Vanessa Williams Snyder, "The Explosion of Women in Ministry," *Gospel Today*, September–October 1999; "Woman Returns to Her Church, Carrying the New Title of Bishop," *New York Times*, July 17, 2000.

☙ Miles, William Henry

(1828-1892) The origins of the **Colored (Christian) Methodist Episcopal (CME) Church** can be traced to a gathering in Jackson, Tennessee, in December 1870, when the predominantly white Methodist Episcopal Church, South, agreed to establish a new charter for its black members, most of whom had recently been freed from slavery and wanted to remain Methodist Episcopal but in an independent church. The first person elected to be a bishop in the newly formed Colored Methodist Episcopal Church was William Henry Miles.

Miles was born into slavery in Kentucky in 1828 but was freed upon the death of his owner in 1854. However, the heirs delayed his release in a dispute over the provisions of the will. That fact, coupled with restrictions against free blacks living in many parts of Kentucky, resulted in Miles not becoming fully free until 1864. However, he joined the Methodist Episcopal Church in 1855; showing gifts for ministry, he was licensed to preach in 1857 and ordained as a deacon in 1859.

With the end of the Civil War and the end of slavery, more than half of the black members of the Methodist Episcopal Church, South, left that denomination because of continued segregation and second-class status. Most of them affiliated either with **African Methodist Episcopal (AME)** or **African Methodist Episcopal Zion** churches; both groups began to evangelize throughout the South immediately after the end of the war in 1865. The blacks who remained were organized into the CME Church. Unlike the groups that followed **Richard Allen** in 1816 and **James Varick** in 1821, those who went with Miles into the CME Church were not leaving in protest. Rather, they asked the senior bishop of the Methodist Episcopal Church, Robert Paine, to preside at their organizational meeting and to consecrate their first bishops.

Two bishops were elected in 1870, Miles and James H. Vanderhorst. Bishop Vanderhorst, who was fifteen years older than Miles and in failing health, died less than two years after taking office. Unable to oversee the rapidly growing church by himself, Bishop Miles convened a general conference in March 1873 at which three more bishops were elected. They were Joseph Beebe of North Carolina, Lucius Holsey of Georgia, and Isaac Lane of Tennessee.

One of Miles's concerns was to reduce illiteracy within his church. He worked tirelessly to raise money to open and provide support for church-run schools. The first one to be opened was Lane College (named in honor of Isaac Lane) in 1882 in Jackson, Tennessee, the church's birthplace. In 1898 Miles College (named in honor of William H. Miles) opened in Birmingham, Alabama. The church also organized colleges in Mississippi and Texas. The denominational seminary, Phillips School of Theology, is part of the **Interdenominational Theological Center (ITC)** in Atlanta, Georgia.

In 1954 the church changed its name from Colored to Christian Methodist Episcopal Church. The CME Church has stretched beyond its Southern roots to every section of the country. However, it remains the smallest of the three black Methodist bodies.

Miles died in 1892.

C. Eric Lincoln and Lawrence W. Mamiya, *The Black Church in the African American Experience;* Harry V. Richardson, *Dark Salvation;* Carter G. Woodson, *The History of the Negro Church.*

☻ Morton, Paul S., Sr.

(1950–) One of the fastest-growing church ministries in the world is the Full Gospel Baptist Church Fellowship, whose founder and presiding bishop is Paul S. Morton Sr. He is the pastor of the 18,000-member Greater St. Stephens Full Gospel Baptist Church in New Orleans, Louisiana. Out of that church, the Full Gospel Baptist Church Fellowship has grown to include more than 2,500 congregations.

Morton was born in Windsor, Ontario, Canada, on July 30, 1950, one of the children born to Bishop C. L. Morton and Evangelist Matilda Morton. His early life was spent within the Pentecostal environment of **The Church of God in Christ (COGIC)**, in which his father was one of the bishops. Morton's grandfather had been among the founders of COGIC under the leadership of **Charles Harrison (C. H.) Mason.** Even as a youth it was assumed that Morton would follow his father into the COGIC ministry. He acknowledged his calling in 1967.

Morton graduated from St. Clair College in Windsor. In 1972 he was led of the Lord to leave all that was familiar to him in Canada and the church of his upbringing and go to New Orleans, Louisiana, where he became the assistant pastor of Greater St. Stephens Missionary Baptist Church. The pastor was Percy Simpson, and when he died in a tragic accident in 1974, Morton was installed as pastor of Greater St. Stephens in January 1975. The growth of the church was phenomenal, and the congregation had to construct a 2,000-seat sanctuary that was completed in 1980.

By 1988 the congregation was operating out of two locations on both sides of New Orleans. By 1992 the east side affiliate had constructed a 4,000-seat auditorium and was offering a wide array of social and economic development programs as well. The size of the congregation requires that Morton preside at five services throughout the day each Sunday.

The key to his success, Morton believes, is the added emphasis of the work and gifts of the Holy Spirit that he brought to the Baptist church from his Pentecostal upbringing. He says, "We believed the basics of the Bible that you needed to be saved. We believed in the death, burial and resurrection of Jesus Christ. But growing up in the Pentecostal church, I knew that God had another level for us as it related to the fullness of the Holy Spirit, as it related to casting out demons, laying hands on the sick, speaking in a heavenly language. So what God did, He said to transition the traditional Baptist church I had into the fullness of the Holy Spirit.... And God began to bless Greater St. Stephens in such a mighty way."

The growth that Morton experienced did not remain limited to one church in one city. On March 19, 1993, following what he considered a mandate from God, Morton founded the Full Gospel Baptist Church Fellowship, and he was consecrated bishop and named presiding bishop. At the first annual session of the fellowship, more than thirty thousand delegates from across the country were in attendance. That number grew to forty thousand in 1994. Since then, more than fifty thousand delegates have packed into the New Orleans Super Dome each year for the annual convocation. In addition to the Fellowship, Morton is also president of Greater St. Stephen Full Gospel Baptist College and Theological Seminary in New Orleans.

A gifted musician since his youth, Morton has recorded many gospel albums that have reached the top of the Billboard charts. He records on the Gospo-Centric label and has collaborated with such stars as **Kirk Franklin,** Yolanda Adams, Donnie McClurklin, **Shirley Caesar,** and Vanessa Bell Armstrong. He has also written three books, *It's Time for the Outpouring, Why Kingdoms Fall,* and *What Is the Full Gospel Baptist Church?* The church sponsors a daily radio broadcast called *Striving for Excellence.* Worship services from Greater St. Stephens Full Gospel Baptist Church can be viewed every Sunday morning on the Black Entertainment Television (BET) network.

While the work of the Holy Spirit accounts for much of the growth that Morton's church and denomination have experienced, one cannot underestimate the musical talent of Morton. An interview with Morton by the Internet magazine Gospelcity.com makes this point clear: "Want to try out church for the first time (in a long time)? How about finding a seat among twenty thousand other eager church folks. The music is kickin'. The congregation is dressed down. And the minister...well he looks like he's about to deliver what the multitude came to find ...some food for the soul. But before he sets the Holy Ghost loose, the preacher shows why he's signed to the biggest gospel label today and sings the church right off its foundation."

Morton has built an entire community around the grounds of Greater St.

Stephen. It is called St. Stephen's City and includes seventy-five single-family homes and a commercial mini-mall.

Morton married Debra Brown in 1977, and they have three children. Together Bishop Morton and Elder Morton preside over a church that has come to be known as Crescent City Fire.

www.gospelcity.com, October 23, 2000; www.greaterststephen.org; www.thewordnetwork.org/newsletter/december2000.

☾ Muhammad, Warithuddin Deen

(1933–) Following the death of **Elijah Muhammad** in 1975, the question of succession to leadership of the **Nation of Islam** was quickly resolved. Wallace D. Muhammad, the seventh child of the Messenger, was unanimously confirmed into that position by twenty thousand members of the Nation at the 1975 Savior's Day celebration in Chicago. Although Wallace D. Muhammad may have followed in his father's footsteps in terms of leadership within the Nation, once installed he began to lead the movement in a different direction.

Wallace D. Muhammad was born on October 30, 1933, in Chicago. He grew up within the various branches of the Nation of Islam. He graduated from the University of Islam, a parochial school operated by the Nation. He then joined the paramilitary group known as the Fruit of Islam, a security force that protected leaders of the Nation. He was appointed leader of Muhammad's Temple in Philadelphia in 1953.

In that year he was drafted into the armed forces but sought conscientious objector status on the grounds of being a minister. When he refused the alternative service assignment in a state hospital, he was indicted on charges of draft evasion. After a protracted court battle he was convicted, and after a denial of an appeal he was sentenced to three years in federal prison beginning on April 21, 1960.

That time away from the movement had lifelong consequences for Muhammad. He began to read about orthodox Islam and soon came to doubt most of the teachings of his father. Upon his release from prison Muhammad began to voice those disagreements, and on three different occasions he defected from the movement to form other groups. However, each time he would reunite with the movement, perhaps because he feared that what happened to **Malcolm X** might also happen to him.

When Muhammad became the leader of the Nation of Islam, he was able to act on those areas of concern, and he did so almost immediately. In an effort to move his followers into an orthodox observance of Islam, he dropped the nationalist and separatist ideology of his father. He opened the community to white members. He disbanded the Fruit of Islam, largely to prevent them from being used in a coup d'etat against his leadership. In 1976 he changed the name of the organization from Nation of Islam to World Community of Al-Islam in the West. He changed it again in 1978 to the American Muslim Mission. All of Muhammad's temples were referred to first as mosques and later as masjids. *Muhammad Speaks* newspaper became the *Bilalian News* and later the *Muslim Journal*. He also urged his followers to adopt names found in the Qur'an, and in January 1976 he took the new name of Warithuddin Muhammad. He also refused to refer to himself as the Messenger of Allah, as his father had done. Instead, he referred to himself as the Mujeddid, or one who watches over the new Islam.

In an attempt to reduce rancor from hardliners in the Nation of Islam, Muhammad sought to justify his changes by saying that all of them were the fulfillment of his father's wishes. That explanation was not sufficient for more than half the members of the movement. In reaction to these dramatic changes, many members of the Nation of Islam broke away from Muhammad, and on November 8, 1977, under the leadership of **Louis Farrakhan,** returned to much of the separatist and race-conscious ideology that had been taught by Elijah Muhammad. They kept the original name of the organization, so the Nation of Islam and the American Muslim Mission began a tense coexistence. By 1987 Warithuddin Muhammad disbanded the American Muslim Mission and urged his followers to affiliate with any local Sunni Muslim mosque. He then became the imam of a mosque in Chicago, where he continues to work.

In 1978 Muhammad was named as the sole consultant for the distribution of private funds from oil-rich Persian states to various causes in the West. He was also allowed to make the hajj to Mecca, Saudi Arabia, one of the four requirements for an orthodox Muslim. He had received what had always eluded his father, universal acceptance by Muslim leaders from around the world.

In 1984 Farrakhan urged his followers to support the presidential campaign of **Jesse Jackson,** but Muhammad opposed Jackson's bid. Instead, he told his followers to support Ronald Reagan, saying "his leadership had been good for the country." In 1986 he was elected to the Supreme Council of Masajid of the Muslim World League, with responsibility for the American mosques. In November 1992, Muhammad became the first imam to deliver the prayer at the opening session of the United States Senate.

Within a two-year period, Warithuddin Muhammad had transformed his father's organization. He had abandoned the demonization of whites and the deification of blacks. He had dropped the creation mythology of Yakub. He had ended the racial separatism with such statements as, "There is no black Muslim or white Muslim, all are Muslims, all children of God." What had begun in his prison cell between 1960 and 1963 had come to fruition. He had taken all the necessary steps to create a nonradical, depoliticized Sunni Muslim community. It is estimated that in 2001 Warithuddin Muhammad has one hundred thousand followers.

E. U. Essien-Udom, *Black Nationalism;* Mattias Gardell, *In the Name of Elijah Muhammad: Louis Farrakhan and the Nation of Islam;* C. Eric Lincoln, *The Black Muslims in America;* C. Eric Lincoln and Lawrence W. Mamiya, *The Black Church in the African American Experience.*

☻ Payne, Daniel A.

(1811–1893) Born to free parents in Charleston, South Carolina, on February 24, 1811, Payne went on to become one of the leading figures in the growth and expansion of the **African Methodist Episcopal (AME) Church.** Most of his career centered around his desire to improve the educational level of black people in general and of black clergy in the AME Church in particular.

Payne began his education at the Miner's Moralist Society in Charleston. In 1830, when he was nineteen years of age, he opened a school for free blacks in Charleston. That school was forcibly closed when the South Carolina legislature passed a bill in April 1835 making it illegal to teach blacks how to read or write. That action was taken in the aftermath of the **Nat Turner** rebellion in 1831. Payne left the South in 1835 and migrated to Philadelphia, Pennsylvania, to further his education and to open a school for black children in that city.

Upon his graduation from the Lutheran Theological Seminary in Gettysburg, Pennsylvania, in 1838, Payne spent three years in the Lutheran ministry before joining the AME Church. He became an AME preacher in 1841, serving at Bethel AME Church in Philadelphia, the church that had been founded by **Richard Allen** in 1799 and that was the mother church of the denomination. His service as a minister resulted in his being elected a bishop of the church in 1852. He also served as the first historiographer of the AME Church, traveling throughout the United States and into Canada to chronicle and observe the growth and development of the church. That resulted in *The History of the AME Church* (1891).

While in Philadelphia Payne founded and served as president of the Vigilance Committee, which sheltered runaway slaves from those who were seeking to capture them and return them to their owners. He was also active in the Philadelphia temperance movement. His service to the church was marked by two emphases: education and music. He urged AME ministers to seek as much training as possible. To that end, he wrote five "Epistles on the Education of the Ministry." He also roundly condemned much of the music he heard in AME churches. He especially objected to the slave songs or "Negro spirituals," which he called "cornfield ditties." He urged the inclusion of choral and instrumental music in the worship life of the AME Church. Both of

his emphases were resisted at first but over time became the accepted norm.

Payne was an outspoken abolitionist who earned the respect of such notables as Frederick Douglass and William Lloyd Garrison. Douglass referred to Payne as "this life without a flaw, and this name without a blemish." On April 14, 1862, Payne became the first black person in United States history to receive a private audience with the president of the United States when he met with Abraham Lincoln. The meeting was meant to urge Lincoln to sign a bill that would outlaw slavery in the District of Columbia, which at that time was home to more than three thousand slaves. Payne told Lincoln that with three thousand slaves living in the federal city, failure to sign the bill would make Lincoln the largest slave owner in the nation. Lincoln signed the bill several days after the meeting.

In 1856 Payne led the AME Church in acquiring a college and grounds near Xenia, Ohio, that would later become Wilberforce University. He became the first black person in the United States to serve as a college president when he was appointed president of Wilberforce in 1863, a position he held for thirteen years. This bivocational ministry, bishop of the AME Church and president of an AME-owned university, made him one of the most influential clergymen in the country. It also helped him advance his chief concern, which was to improve the educational level of AME clergy. He died in 1893.

Daniel A. Payne, *Recollections of Seventy Years;* Harry V. Richardson, *Dark Salvation;* Henry J. Young, *Major Black Religious Leaders, 1755–1940.*

☻ Seymour, William Joseph

(1870–1922) The Pentecostal movement in the United States can arguably be traced to one man and one event. The man was William Joseph Seymour, and the event was the **Azusa Street revival** in Los Angeles (1906–1908). The major Pentecostal denominations in the world, including the Assemblies of God and **The Church of God in Christ (COGIC)**, trace their origins to Seymour and Azusa Street.

Seymour was born in Louisiana on May 2, 1870. He relocated to Indianapolis, Indiana, in 1895 and then to Cincinnati, Ohio, in 1900. He encountered a former Methodist minister named Martin Knapp who had founded a holiness movement, and Seymour joined, eventually associating with the Church of God (Anderson, Indiana) in 1902. He was ordained by the Church of God.

In 1903 Seymour relocated to Houston, Texas, and there he encountered Charles F. Parham, who had developed the idea of **Pentecostalism** as an act of the Holy Spirit beyond sanctification. Seymour sought to attend classes with Parham, but prevailing racial segregation and Parham's hostility toward interracial events required that Seymour sit outside the classroom and listen to what was being said inside. Seymour accepted the argument of Pentecostalism and came to believe that the final mark of salvation is speaking in tongues (glossolalia) and being baptized in the Holy Spirit.

After a year of informal study with Parham, Seymour was called to a small holiness church in Los Angeles in 1906. He began preaching about the necessity of being baptized by the Holy Spirit and speaking in tongues (Acts 2:4), and within a short time he was locked out of the church. He then began holding meetings in a house in Los Angeles, and next began to meet in the building that had formerly housed the First African Methodist Episcopal (AME) Church. The date was April 12, 1906, and the church was located at 312 Azusa Street. The rest is history.

Seymour became the central figure of a revival that was eventually felt all over the world. People from across the country and around the world came to Azusa to share in that outpouring of the Holy Spirit. Despite the prevailing policies of racial segregation, an interracial church was being birthed. Seymour said, "We are on the verge of the greatest miracle the world has ever seen." He called his new movement The Azusa Street Apostolic Faith Mission of Los Angeles. He also began a periodical entitled *The Apostolic Faith,* which carried his sermons and teachings to locations across the country.

Charles Harrison (C. H.) Mason traveled to Los Angeles to share in the revival. He was baptized in the Holy Spirit and returned to Memphis to spread the Pentecostal teachings within COGIC, which he had cofounded with Charles Price (C. P.) Jones. When Jones, who did not attend Azusa Street, rejected the new emphasis on Pentecostalism, he and Mason parted. Mason remained with COGIC and led that group into Pentecostalism. Jones formed The Church of God (Holiness) USA.

Almost as quickly as the movement began, it ended. By 1909 Clara Lum, a white follower of Seymour, had taken the mailing list for The Apostolic Faith and

relocated to Portland, Oregon. She ceased to carry any messages from Seymour, and thus the movement lost its outreach to the rest of the country. In 1911 a white minister named William Durham withdrew from Seymour's movement and took more than six hundred white persons with him. He probably left over racial and doctrinal issues. Durham embraced Pentecostalism but rejected Seymour's equal emphasis on holiness. As would later happen with Mason and COGIC, it was not possible at that point in history for white ministers to accept the spiritual leadership of a black person. The miracle that Seymour thought might occur never developed because of America's preoccupation with race relations.

Seymour's popularity and following dropped off rapidly after these events. He continued to preach but never again approached the earlier level of appeal he had experienced during the Azusa Street revival. He died in 1922.

Ithiel C. Clemmons, *Bishop C. H. Mason and the Roots of the Church of God in Christ;* C. Eric Lincoln and Lawrence W. Mamiya, *The Black Church in the African American Experience;* Elias Morris, "Bishop C. H. Mason and COGIC," in *African American Religious History,* ed. Milton C. Sernett; Gayraud S. Wilmore, *Black Religion and Black Radicalism.*

☻ Smith, J. Alfred, Sr.

(1931–) The city of Oakland, California, is home to every social malady and economic disadvantage imaginable. One resource that works to address and correct those problems is the ministry of the Allen Temple Baptist Church and its pastor, J. Alfred Smith Sr.

Born on May 19, 1931, Smith began his ministry as a field representative for the Ministers and Missionaries Benefits Board of American Baptist Churches. Since being installed in 1971 by **Thomas Kilgore Jr.,** Smith has stood in the pulpit of the four-thousand-member Allen Temple Baptist Church, where his son, J. Alfred Smith Jr., now serves as copastor. In addition, Smith has carried on an active ministry in the academic world; he teaches in two theological schools. He has been an ecumenical leader as well, serving as the president of the **Progressive National Baptist Convention (PNBC)** and president of American Baptist Churches of the West.

Smith earned a bachelor of science degree at Western Baptist College in Kansas City, Missouri. He earned bache-lor of divinity and master of theology degrees at Missouri School of Religion in Columbia. He also earned a master of arts degree from the American Baptist Seminary of the West and a doctor of ministry degree from Golden Gate Baptist Theological Seminary. In addition to his pastoral duties as senior minister at Allen Temple Baptist Church, he is professor of preaching and Christian ministries at the American Baptist Seminary of the West. He also teaches at the Graduate Theological Union in Berkeley, California.

Smith is the author of sixteen books, including *The Overflowing Heart, Making Sense of Suffering, Preach On,* and *No Other Help I Know.* He edited *Outstanding Black Sermons,* in which one of his sermons also appears. As a tribute to his ability as a preacher, he was listed in the November 1993 issue of *Ebony* as one of the top fifteen black preachers in the country. He also serves on the advisory board of *The African American Pulpit,* and his articles and sermons regularly appear in that journal.

From 1982 to 1986 Smith served as president of the PNBC. In 1993 he was designated as the Outstanding Citizen of Oakland, California, an honor given in recognition of his leadership in creating housing and job services for the poor in Oakland. More recently he led Allen Temple in opening a hospice for persons dying of HIV-related infections.

In a 1992 conference at Vanderbilt Divinity School, Smith spoke about his philosophy of ministry: "I believe that the church in the world is to continue the work agenda of our Lord in a servant ministry to a world in need of healing and reconciliation. I believe in the ability of the parish church to incarnate the heart and mind of Jesus Christ, in action to humanize and personalize its life in a dehumanized and depersonalized environment."

The ministries of Allen Temple are featured in "Nourishing Soul and Body," in *African American Voices of Triumph: Leadership,* a four-volume series edited by Henry Louis Gates of Harvard University. The preaching philosophy of Smith is well discussed in an interview in *The African American Pulpit* (winter 1998–1999).

"An Interview with J. Alfred Smith Sr.," *The African American Pulpit* (winter 1998–1999); Thomas Kilgore Jr. and Jini Kilgore Ross, *A Servant's Journey; Outstanding Black Sermons,* ed. J. Alfred Smith Sr.; "Top Fifteen Black Preachers," *Ebony,* November 1993; web page of Vanderbilt Divinity School.

☺ Varick, James

(1750-1828) In 1796 a group of black members withdrew from the John Street Methodist Church in New York City. Like the followers of **Richard Allen** in Philadelphia, this group objected to the discrimination they faced in the church. Chief among their concerns was the fact that black and white communicants could not kneel side by side at the communion rail. Black members had to be served separately, because whites objected to their presence.

The group first organized a separate congregation, which they called the Zion Church, still affiliated with the white Methodist Episcopal Church. Like the black Methodists in Philadelphia, it took decades before the members of the Zion Church in New York City evolved into an independent denomination.

Instrumental in that process was Varick. Although he was not listed among the charter members of this congregation, he was ordained a deacon of the Zion Church in 1806. His biographer, B. F. Wheeler, dates Varick's birth in 1750 in Newburgh, New York. He received little formal education but was reputed to be a teacher and a shoemaker.

On August 11, 1820, that body in New York decided not to affiliate with the Allenites in Philadelphia and not to continue membership in the John Street Church. Thus the groundwork was laid for another independent black church, which was called the African Methodist Episcopal Church in New York City. Almost a year later, on June 21, 1821, joined by other black Methodists in the New York City area numbering 1,410, they changed their name to the African Methodist Episcopal Church of America. Varick, who had been elected a local elder by the Zion Church in October 1820, was among the first three persons to be ordained an elder within this new denomination on June 17, 1822. Later that year he was elected to be the first bishop of the new church. He served as bishop until his death in 1828.

Early conflicts existed between the Allenites and Zionites over areas of expansion and growth. The followers of Varick focused on New York City and the rest of New York State and New England. Following the Civil War, a similar scramble for areas of influence occurred when both bodies sought to expand among the newly freed slaves in the South. The word *Zion* was not officially added to the formal name of the denomination until it was voted in a general conference gathering in 1848. That happened while Christopher Rush served as the bishop, having succeeded Varick and serving from 1828 to 1852. Much of the early growth of the denomination was a result of his energetic leadership.

In 1898 the **African Methodist Episcopal Zion (AME Zion) Church** became the first denomination in America, black or white, to extend full clerical rights to women. That was consistent with its reputation as "the freedom church," which it acquired as a result of claiming among its members such persons as **Sojourner Truth,** Frederick Douglass, and Harriet Tubman. The church was deeply involved with abolitionist efforts, and many of its congregations served as locations for the Underground Railroad. Paul Robeson was also a member of the AME Zion Church; his brother, Benjamin, served as the pastor of the mother church in New York City from 1936 to 1963.

Varick never received the kind of attention given to Allen, and the AME Zion Church has never matched the size of the AME Church. Nevertheless, Varick's leadership in the AME Zion movement is of equal importance to that of the efforts of black Methodists in Philadelphia. Today the AME Zion Church has approximately 1.2 million members worldwide.

Carol V. R. George, *Segregated Sabbaths;* C. Eric Lincoln and Lawrence W. Mamiya, *The Black Church in the African American Experience;* Calvin Marshall, "The Black Church: Its Mission Is Liberation," in *The Black Experience in Religion,* ed. C. Eric Lincoln; Harry V. Richardson, *Dark Salvation;* Gayraud S. Wilmore, *Black Religion and Black Radicalism;* Carter G. Woodson, *History of the Negro Church.*

☻ Williams, Lacey Kirk (L. K.), Sr.

(1871–1940) In 1930, when race relations in America were defined by lynch mobs and Jim Crow laws, a white Christian wrote: "Reverend Lacey K. Williams, A.B., B.Th., D.D., LL.D., is the leading colored leader of the Christian world. He is president of the National Baptist Convention of the U.S.A., the largest organized group of Negroes in the Christian world…. Situated in America, probably no living man is in a better position than the president of the National Baptist Convention to serve the darker races of the world by creating a favorable public opinion through the white and colored churches of America."

The man whose influence and prominence was being described was born on July 11, 1871, on the Shorter Plantation, a sharecropping plantation in Eufaula, Alabama. He was one of several children born to parents who had lived as slaves on that plantation. They remained there even after emancipation, believing there was more security for them on that familiar soil than would have been the case if they had gone elsewhere to begin life anew as freedmen. Their one concession to their new status was to change their last name from Shorter, the name of their former owner, to Williams. It is not known why that name was chosen.

At the age of five or six, Lacey Kirk Williams was enrolled in a school operated by a white New Englander, Mr. Jordan, who had come to work with former slaves. In 1880 Williams was converted and baptized in the Thankful Baptist Church of Eufaula, and by 1884 he had sensed a call to ministry. The family eventually relocated to Texas, and as economic conditions worsened for them, Lacey was encouraged to launch out on his own. He settled in Belton, Texas, working at a variety of odd jobs, including picking cotton for seventy-five cents per hundred pounds.

Williams earned a teaching certificate with the help of a mentor/tutor and taught second grade in an all-black school in Hookersville, Texas, for $60 for a three-month term. He married one of his former pupils, Georgia Lewis, and they had two children, one of whom died in infancy. The other child, Lacey Kirk Williams Jr., followed his father into a career in the ministry. In 1893 the elder Williams sought to further his education by enrolling in Hearne Academy, one of three schools operated by black Baptists in Texas for the education of their people. He preached his trial sermon and was licensed to preach in December 1894, and he was ordained into the ministry on February 11, 1895.

Within one year, Williams was serving as pastor of three congregations simultaneously: Washington Chapel, Pleasant Grove, and Thankful Baptist churches. He continued to add congregations to his charge, and the resulting stress ended in a three-month period of convalescence in a Denver, Colorado hospital.

Following his release from the hospital, Williams's career began to take on an ever-widening circle of influence. He first went to Macedonia Baptist Church of Dallas, Texas. Today it is known as Good Street Baptist Church, where **Caesar Clark** has served since 1950. While there Williams enrolled in Bishop College. He graduated in 1912 with a bachelor of theology degree. He also edited two black newspapers in the Dallas area, the *Dallas Express* and the *Western Star.* He was elected president of the black Texas Baptist Convention and vice president of the National Baptist Convention. From that position began a series of interracial dialogues with the members of the all-white Texas Baptist Convention, which was allied with the Southern Baptist Convention (SBC).

Williams then went to the prestigious pulpit of Mount Gilead Baptist Church in Fort Worth. His preaching was so popular and so powerful that on any given Sunday there were as many white people in attendance as there were members of his all-black congregation. That was a remarkable achievement in the South in 1909, when he went to Fort Worth. However, Williams's greatest fame would come with his next and final move, when he accepted the pastorate of the Olivet Baptist Church in Chicago, Illinois. The man from a sharecroppers' plantation in Alabama was now the pastor of the oldest and most prominent black church in the second-largest black community in the United States. The year was 1916, and Williams was on his way to becoming "the leading colored Christian in the world."

In 1916 Olivet Baptist had thirty-nine hundred members, but by 1930 Williams had increased that number to more than twelve thousand. Olivet in Chicago and Abyssinian Baptist Church in New York City were rivals for the title of the largest Protestant congregation in the world. In addition to overseeing the normal array of church programs and ministries, Williams turned the church into a full-service social agency for the tens of thousands of black people who were migrating to Chicago from the South during 1895 to 1945. Olivet became the place to turn for help with housing, employment, day care, job training, and education. Williams was also involved in helping black workers gain standing with organized labor groups in the meat packing and steel industries. The growth of Olivet, and hence of Williams's influence, was driven both by his singular abilities and by the effects of the Great Migration on the black population of Chicago.

Williams attended his first session of the National Baptist Convention in 1902, when he was serving his churches in Texas. By 1922 he had been elected president of that organization, vaulting him into the leadership of the largest black organization in the world. He would serve in that position for nineteen years. He regularly expressed a desire to step down from that position during all of those years, but he was reelected by popular demand.

Williams served the convention and the black church most ably. In 1928 he addressed the Baptist World Alliance meeting in Toronto, Canada. That year he was elected vice president of that body. He addressed the attendees at the New York World's Fair in 1939. In 1940 he became the second black person ever to preach before the faculty and students at the Divinity School of the University of Chicago; **Mordecai Wyatt Johnson** was the first.

Williams also worked to maintain good relations with the Southern Baptist Convention, and with its help managed to construct a seminary and a headquarters building for the National Baptist Convention in Nashville, Tennessee (1924–1925). His greatest disappointment, given his success in working across racial lines, was his inability to ward off a division within his convention that took place in 1915 and was led by **Richard Henry Boyd**. The group that left over a feud concerning control of the Publishing Board organized under the name **National Baptist Convention of America**. That split was a wound not only to Williams but also to the strength of the black Baptist witness to this day.

Williams was killed in an airplane crash in November 1940 while traveling from Chicago to Flint, Michigan, as part of his Goodwill Tour, in which the president of the **National Baptist Convention, USA, Inc. (NBCUSA)** would visit somewhat remote locations across the country. At the time of his death, he was still "the leading colored Christian in the world."

Black Metropolis; Lillian B. Horace, *Crowned with Glory and Honor: The Life of Rev. Lacey Kirk Williams,* ed. L. Venchael Booth; J. H. Jackson, *A Story of Christian Activism.*

◉ Williams, Peter, Jr.

(1780-1849) Born in 1780 in New York City, Williams was the son of one of the founders of the **African Methodist Episcopal Zion (AME Zion) Church**, Peter Williams Sr. The younger Williams, deciding not to remain with his father in the black Methodist movement, instead entered the ministry of the Episcopal Church. In 1818 he organized St. Philip's Episcopal parish in New York City. He

was ordained a deacon in 1820 and a priest in 1826. He became the second black Episcopal priest in America following **Absalom Jones**. However, Williams was the first black priest in the diocese of New York.

Williams was a leading figure in the black community of New York City. He worked closely with **Samuel Cornish** and John Russworm in the founding of the first black newspaper, *Freedom's Journal,* in 1827. He was on the executive committee of the American Antislavery Society when it was founded in 1833. He was also an outspoken opponent of the efforts of the American Colonization Society (ACS) to resettle America's black population in Liberia.

On July 4, 1830, Williams delivered a scathing address condemning America's rhetoric about freedom and liberty while allowing black people to be held in slavery. This was more than twenty years before the famous Fourth of July speech given by Frederick Douglass. In his speech Williams said, "We are natives of this country; we ask only to be treated as well as foreigners. Not a few of our fathers suffered and bled to purchase its independence; we ask only to be treated as well as those who fought against it. We have toiled to cultivate it, and to raise it to its present prosperous condition; we ask only to share equal privileges with those who come from distant lands to enjoy the fruits of our labor."

Williams became so outspoken in his antislavery and anticolonization views that his bishop threatened to have his church closed and to have him defrocked if he did not cease and desist. Much to the disappointment of many in New York's black community, Williams complied with that demand. He never spoke out as forcefully as he once had done.

On September 15, 1830, Williams joined with Bishop **Richard Allen** in convening the inaugural session of the National Negro Convention in Philadelphia, Pennsylvania. He would collaborate with other leaders in New York's black community to organize a self-help organization known as the Phoenix Society, whose purpose it was to "promote the improvement of the colored people in morals, literature and the mechanic arts."

Williams remained as the rector of St. Philip's until his death in 1849. The St. Philip's Episcopal Church was not admitted into the Diocese of New York City as a full member until 1853. His willingness to conform to the wishes of the bishop was due in large measure to ensure that his parish would not be excluded from admission to full standing in the diocese.

Carol V. R. George, *Segregated Sabbaths;* Peter Williams Jr., "A Plea for Help," in *Black Gospel/White Church,* John M. Burgess; Carter G. Woodson, *The History of the Negro Church.* ▣

Preachers

◉-◉-◉

◉ Adams, Charles G.

(1936–) In 1984 and again in 1993, Adams was listed in *Ebony* as one of the top fifteen black preachers in America. Popularly known as "the Harvard whooper," Adams has long been one of the most intellectually stimulating and emotionally stirring preachers in the country. Over the course of a forty-year career in ministry, he has earned an honored place among the royalty of the black pulpit.

Adams was born in Detroit, Michigan, on December 13, 1936. He graduated from the University of Michigan in 1958 with a bachelor of arts degree. He earned a bachelor of divinity degree from Harvard Divinity School in 1964. From 1962 to 1969 he was the pastor of Concord Baptist Church in Boston, Massachusetts. During that period he began his affiliation with the **Progressive Baptist National Convention (PBNC).** He has serving as the editor of the *Baptist Progress,* which is the official journal of the PBNC. He also served two terms as president of the convention in the 1990s.

Since 1969 Adams has been pastor of Hartford Memorial Baptist Church in Detroit. That congregation has led the nation in the establishment of economic development programs that help to revive inner-city neighborhoods. Through his connections with Harvard University, he has organized economic development seminars on that campus for other pastors from around the country. At the same time, like most of the founding pastors of PBNC, Adams has maintained an active involvement with the **civil rights movement.** He has held leadership positions in the city of Detroit and in the state of Michigan with such groups as the **Southern Christian Leadership Conference (SCLC),** the National Association

for the Advancement of Colored People (NAACP), and Operation PUSH (People United to Save Humanity). He also wrote a weekly column for the *Michigan Chronicle*, a newspaper that reports on events in black communities throughout that state.

Adams is the master of the use of a manuscript in preaching. He literally reads his sermons but does so with such passion and precision that there is never a sense of being disconnected from the hearers. His use of language is so sophisticated and his perfectly turned phrases are so central to his preaching content that the use of the manuscript allows him to retain and deliver all that he has written. Nevertheless, his effect upon an audience is nearly mystical. He teaches, then preaches, then, as his honorary title would suggest, he whoops. That is the use of rhythm, repetition, tonality, volume, spiritual celebration, and cultural expression that has long been the trademark of so many great black preachers.

Adams has lectured, taught, and preached at conferences, conventions, and schools around the world. The list of schools includes Andover Newton Theological Seminary, Harvard Divinity School, Boston University, Howard University, Tuskegee University, and Vanderbilt University. He has also served as chair of the board of trustees at Shaw University in North Carolina. He has also preached throughout the nation of South Africa. Indeed, his anti-apartheid activities helped secure the release of Nelson Mandela from prison. In tribute to Adams's leadership, Mandela appeared in Detroit as part of a national tour in 1991 at Tiger Stadium, and

Adams stood at his side and introduced Mandela to that audience of more than fifty thousand persons.

Adams can become so intensely engaged in the preaching act that he has been known to come out of the pulpit, walk through the aisles, and even leave the sanctuary and return to the pastor's study while preaching. His mind may have been molded at Harvard, but his soul and spirit have "just come from the fountain."

"America's Top Fifteen Black Preachers," *Ebony,* September 1984; "The Top Fifteen Black Preachers," *Ebony,* November 1993.

Austin, Junius Caesar (J. C.)

(1878-1968) "For sheer power, I never heard anyone to compare with J. C. Austin of Chicago." Those words were spoken by **Gardner C. Taylor** about a man who was one of the leading figures in the **National Baptist Convention, USA, Inc. (NBCUSA),** when Taylor was beginning his distinguished preaching ministry. That is high praise indeed for a man who was undoubtedly one of the greatest preachers, pastors, and church leaders of the twentieth century.

Austin was born in Buckingham County, Virginia, in 1878. He acknowledged his call to preach at the age of eleven. He earned a bachelor of arts degree (1905) and a bachelor of divinity degree (1908) from Virginia Seminary in Lynchburg. He also received an honorary doctor of divinity degree in 1910. He was called to the Ebenezer Baptist Church of Pittsburgh, Pennsylvania, in 1915, and by 1925 that congregation had grown from two hundred to five thousand members. He became the president of the Pennsylvania Baptist State Convention in 1924, and in that year he was appointed chairman of the Foreign Mission Board of the NBCUSA. In that position he pursued an active agenda of sending missionaries and money to various locations on the African continent. He even lent support to **Marcus Garvey**'s back-to-Africa movement between 1920 and 1925, because he saw it as an opportunity to transport missionaries to Africa.

In 1926 Austin was called to the Pilgrim Baptist Church of Chicago. That placed his ministry in the center of the Great Migration of black people moving out of the South in search of better employment, decent housing, and relief from racial hostilities. As Randall Burkett observes, Austin turned Pilgrim Baptist Church into a "classic Black Diaspora church." The enormous numbers of persons moving into Chicago at that time were in search of a new church home. The many educational, social, job training, and welfare programs offered by Pilgrim helped attract people to that congregation. As a result, by 1930 Pilgrim Baptist Church, with ten thousand members, had become the third largest church in the NBCUSA, behind Olivet of Chicago and Abyssinian of New York City.

Preaching was the key to Austin's success. The church could seat twenty-five hundred persons, and he preached to packed houses twice, sometimes even three times, every Sunday. More importantly, his sermons could regularly be heard over the national radio broadcast called "Wings over Jordan." Austin preached every year at the annual session of the National Baptist Convention and throughout the country as a popular evangelist.

Austin was the first pastor of a leading congregation to fully embrace the new musical genre called **gospel music.** He invited **Thomas A. Dorsey** to form a gospel chorus at Pilgrim in 1932, and that church remained Dorsey's spiritual home for the rest of his life. Michael W. Harris notes that Austin's support was essential in the acceptance of gospel music in the black churches of America: "One can assume that had Austin not organized a chorus at Pilgrim, the advent of gospel blues in old-line churches would have stagnated in derision and for want of serious regard from the old-line establishment.... Only an old-line preacher and church of the stature of Austin and Pilgrim could have imparted respect to gospel blues." Thus Austin is to be credited not only for his contributions to preaching but also for his invaluable contribution to the emergence of a new genre of music in the black church.

Austin was a pioneer in seeing the black church as an engine of economic development. He organized the Home Finders' League, a group that worked with Chicago's two black-owned banks to provide homes for worthy customers at discounted finance rates. While in Pittsburgh he also helped to organize the black-owned Steel City Bank. His close political ties with the mayors of Pittsburgh and Chicago helped in his attempts to meet the needs of recent arrivals from the South.

Austin can only be called a rival to **Lacey Kirk (L. K.) Williams**, who was then serving as president of the NBCUSA. Not only did they work in the same city, but also their churches were less than one mile from each other. The two men frequently clashed over many issues in Chicago's political, social, and religious life. However, it was in the life of the convention that their rivalry reached its most extreme forms. Williams dismissed Austin as chairman of the Foreign Mission Board, allegedly because he wanted to limit his stature in the convention. Austin frequently ran against Williams for the office of president of the convention.

The term "Progressive Baptists" does not originate with the group convened by L. Venchael Booth in 1961 to protest the leadership in the convention of **Joseph Harrison Jackson.** Instead, that term is traceable to 1931, when Austin led a group of disgruntled ministers who wanted a change from Williams's leadership style. After Williams's accidental death in 1941, more than one thousand ministers answered a call by Austin, who was once again seeking the presidency, and they formed the Progressive Baptists of the NBCUSA.

However, Austin and Williams agreed that the black church could not simply offer sermons and Bible studies to the community. The church had to offer a comprehensive outreach ministry that speaks to the whole person: body, mind, and soul.

After seventy-years as a preacher, Austin died in 1968.

Randall Burkett, "The Baptist Church in Years of Crisis: J. C. Austin and Pilgrim Baptist Church, 1926–1950," in *African American Religion: Interpretive Essays,* ed. Timothy E. Fulop and Albert J. Raboteau; Michael W. Harris, *The Rise of Gospel Blues: The Music of Thomas Andrew Dorsey;* Allan H. Spear, *Black Chicago: The Making of a Negro Ghetto 1890–1920;* James M. Washington, *Frustrated Fellowship;* Carter G. Woodson, *History of the Negro Church.*

☻ Clark, Caesar

(1914–) If any one preacher could be called the modern preserver and practitioner of the black folk tradition of preaching that dates back to the slave era, it would be Caesar Clark. He has been preaching for nearly seventy-five years since his conversion and call to preach (1927). Since that time, he has thrilled and inspired congregations and convention audiences across the country and around the world. His rhythmic and melodic intonations, his use of repetition and alliteration, and his manner of building his sermons from a slow beginning to a fast-paced and dynamic conclusion puts him in the tradition of **John Jasper** and the black preachers of the nineteenth-century rural South.

Clark was born on December 13, 1914, in Shreveport, Louisiana. An only child, he was reared on a tenant farm in Clarence, Louisiana. During his early years he was able to attend school only three months out of the year. The balance of the time he was required to work in the cotton and cane fields.

At the age of fourteen Clark preached his first sermon. He was called to be the pastor of Israelite Baptist Church of Longstreet, Louisiana, at the age of nineteen. He furthered his education first at Coleman College of Gibsland, Louisiana. He graduated from Bishop College in Marshall, Texas, in 1946. That college honored him with an honorary doctorate in 1960. As was common among preachers in the rural South, he served as pastor of several small congregations at the same time, serving them on alternate Sundays or at morning or evening services.

In 1950 Clark was called to the Good Street Baptist Church of Dallas, and his service at that church continues to this day. From that church he became one of the most sought-after preachers in the country. He has averaged thirty week-long revivals for the last forty years. He is possessed of a high-pitched voice and a deliberate pacing when he preaches. However, when he begins to conclude his sermon he takes on another spirit, almost as if possessed by the Holy Spirit, and he moves audiences to shouts and tears in equal measure.

Clark may be most noted for his service to the **National Baptist Convention, USA, Inc. (NBCUSA)**. He has served as a board member and as a vice president at large and has been the editor of the convention journal, *The National Baptist Voice*. He has also been regularly featured as lecturer and preacher to the Ministers' Division at the annual sessions. His power as a preacher and the affection he has enjoyed among other preachers is enormous. He also served as a member of the board of trustees of Bishop College.

Clark was listed among America's fifteen greatest black preachers in *Ebony* (1984, 1993). He has twenty-two sermons available on record and tape. Clark once said of preaching, "All of your life, preaching will tease you and taunt you. And when you come to the end you will have to say that your

preaching has been an embarrassed stammering." That humility is part of the greatness of Clark's preaching.

"America's Fifteen Greatest Black Preachers," *Ebony*, September 1984; David Gray and Helen Gray, *Dr. Caesar Clark: The Man, the Preacher, the Pastor, the Evangelist;* "An Interview with Henry Mitchell," T*he African American Pulpit* (winter 1997–1998); "The Top Fifteen Black Preachers," *Ebony*, November 1993.

Cook, Suzan D. Johnson

(1957-) If ever an African American woman preacher could be called a trailblazer, that woman would be Suzan D. Johnson Cook. She became the first African American woman to be elected senior pastor of an American Baptist Church when she was called to Mariner's Temple Baptist Church in New York City in 1983. She served there for thirteen years, and the membership increased from fifteen to more than five hundred.

Cook became the first woman to be elected an officer of the historic Hampton Ministers' Conference, the largest gathering of African American clergy in the country. She was the first woman named to be a chaplain of the New York City police department. She is also the only woman named in the Baylor University survey of the most effective preachers in the English-speaking world. As a result of that designation, she is one of an elite group of preachers featured in a video series released by the Odyssey Television Network.

In 1993 Cook was chosen to be a White House fellow and served as a domestic policy advisor to President Bill Clinton. In 1997 Clinton selected her as one of seven members of his President's Initiative on Race and Reconciliation, a panel that studied race relations in the United States and made recommendations to the president. That designation and visibility established her as a leader of national importance.

Cook was born in the Bronx, New York, in 1957. She received her bachelor of fine arts degree from Emerson College in Boston. She received a master of arts degree from Columbia Teachers College and a master of divinity degree from Union Theological Seminary in New York City. Her doctor of ministry degree is from United Theological Seminary in Dayton, Ohio. She is married to Ron Cook, and they have two sons, Christopher and Samuel. She is the founder and pastor of the Bronx Christian Fellowship Church, located not far from where she was born.

Cook was involved with Presbyterian and Baptist churches while growing up in New York City. As a result of her Presbyterian connection, she was greatly influenced in her decision to pursue a career in ministry by **Katie Cannon,** a Presbyterian minister and theologian. Cook speaks eloquently and forcefully about her call: "I make no apologies for being a woman. And I make no apologies for being a woman in ministry. If God didn't want me to be in the ministry, he would not have called me. If he didn't want me to preach, he would not have shut this fire up in my bones. If I couldn't preach, I believe I would spontaneously combust. I even preach in my dreams. That's one of the ways I knew God was calling me into the ministry in my early twenties; I would be sound asleep and wake up preaching."

Cook is the editor of the widely acclaimed book, *Sister to Sister: Devotions for and from African American Women*. She is the author of *Too Blessed to Be Stressed*, editor of *Wise Women Bearing Gifts*, and coauthor with William D. Watley of *Preaching in Two Voices*. In addition, she has served on the editorial board for *The African American Pulpit*; her sermons can regularly be found in that journal.

Suzan D. Johnson Cook, *Too Blessed to Be Stressed*; "An Interview with Suzan Johnson Cook," *The African American Pulpit* (spring 1998).

◉ Forbes, James Alexander, Jr.

(1935–) Two nationally known black preachers have publicly discussed their struggle to be faithful to their Pentecostal upbringing and responsive to their present standing as Baptist preachers. The two men are **Paul Morton Sr.** and James A. Forbes Jr. Their common struggle has led them in different directions. Morton formed the Full Gospel Baptist Church movement, thus creating a new denomination within which to blend these two traditions. Forbes has walked a different path that has led him to become the first African American senior minister at Riverside Church in New York City.

Forbes was born on September 6, 1935, in North Carolina. He is the son, grandson, and nephew of preachers within the United Holy Church of America, a Pentecostal group that was founded in 1886. He graduated from Howard University in 1957. Against the advice of many within his denomination who feared that he might lose his Pentecostal fervor, he attended and graduated from Union Theological Seminary in New York City in 1962. That exposure to liberal theology began what would be a lifelong quest to blend a religion of the head and the heart. Forbes received a doctor of ministry degree from Colgate Rochester Divinity School in 1975. He was in the

first group of Martin Luther King Jr. Fellows in a program headed by **Henry Heywood Mitchell.**

In 1976, after serving with a consortium of seminaries in the Washington, D.C., area, Forbes was appointed as an associate professor of preaching at Union Theological Seminary in New York City. He was awarded an endowed chair and became the Joe R. Engel Professor of Preaching. In 1984 and again in 1993 he was listed among the top fifteen black preachers by *Ebony.* In 1986 Forbes was invited to deliver the Lyman Beecher Lectures on Preaching at Yale Divinity School. And on February 5, 1989, he was elected to be the senior pastor at the historic Riverside Church.

By going to Riverside, a congregation dually aligned with the American Baptist Churches and the United Church of Christ, Forbes was officially moving beyond his Pentecostal roots. But his preaching in the church and beyond has maintained that fervor. Forbes continues a legacy of great preaching at Riverside that began with Harry Emerson Fosdick and included Robert McCracken, Ernest Campbell, and William Sloan Coffin.

However, as the first black senior pastor, Forbes has brought some new constituencies to the church. The black and Hispanic membership at Riverside has grown tremendously in response to his presence and preaching. He created a considerable debate within the national black church community over his decision to affirm and even be the celebrant at same-sex unions within the Riverside Church family.

In *The Holy Spirit and Preaching,* Forbes writes about his desire to merge his Pentecostal upbringing with his theologically liberal training and perspective on many issues. Reflecting on the three United Holy Church congregations in North Carolina he had served after finishing seminary, he writes: "I came to characterize our style of ministry as 'progressive Pentecostalism'—a strong emphasis on spirit, but deep commitment to transformative social action. This has been a continuing emphasis for me, both in congregational leadership and in seminary teaching."

In his attempt to offer a philosophy of preaching that takes his Pentecostal background into consideration, Forbes tells his students that "the anointing makes the difference." A sample of his anointed preaching that touches upon the spirit and upon transformative social action can be read in "The Battle of Bethlehem," in *Outstanding Black Sermons* (vol. 3). Forbes is also featured in a video as part of the Great Preachers series produced by the Odyssey Television Network. That series is based upon a survey by Baylor University that names the most effective preachers in the English-speaking world.

"America's Fifteen Greatest Black Preachers," *Ebony,* September 1984; James A. Forbes Jr., *The Holy Spirit and Preaching;* "Forbes Called to Riverside," *Christian Century,* February 22, 1989.

☙ Franklin, Clarence LaVaughn (C. L.)

(1915–1984) Born in Sunflower County, Mississippi, on January 22, 1915, Franklin went on to become one of the most celebrated and imitated black preachers of the twentieth century. He was reared on a sharecropping plantation near Cleveland, Mississippi, and received his early education during those breaks in the agricultural year when blacks were allowed to attend school. He became a migrant farm worker traveling throughout Mississippi, Tennessee, Missouri, Kentucky, and Michigan.

During his years as a migrant worker, he began to preach, and he was ordained in Cleveland, Mississippi, at the age of eighteen. He left farm work and began preaching full time, pastoring churches around Clarksdale. He pastored several churches at one time, because no one church was able to provide an adequate salary for a full-time pastor during those Depression years.

Franklin furthered his education when he moved to Greenville, Mississippi, and enrolled at Greenville Industrial College. He followed the same pattern when he went to pastor a church in Memphis, Tennessee, and enrolled at LeMoyne College, and when he went to serve a church in Buffalo, New York, and studied at the University of Buffalo. He was called to pastor New Bethel Baptist Church of Detroit, Michigan, in 1946. During his ministry in Detroit, New Bethel Baptist Church once occupied a building that had been used by the black cult leader Prophet Jones. However, the ministries of the two men had nothing in common.

Central to his ministry wherever Franklin served was the use of a radio broadcast that greatly expanded the reach of his sermons. He began that radio ministry in 1951 and continued for the balance of his ministry. People would arrive at the church one hour before the

broadcast just to be in the audience for that evening service. The choir at New Bethel was especially trained for the radio broadcast ministry by the noted gospel singer **James Cleveland.**

Beginning in 1953, those radio broadcast sermons were recorded and distributed by Chess Recording Company of Chicago. Record sales across the country exceeded one million copies, causing Franklin to be known as "the Million Dollar Voice." His records resulted in his being in demand as a preacher in places where people who had heard him on a record wanted to see and hear him in a live service. He began traveling with the Clara Ward Singers, preaching at programs held at civic auditoriums, schools, and churches across the country.

Franklin eventually left Clara Ward and traveled with his daughter Aretha serving as musical soloist. He and his daughter frequently sang together. Their most requested selection was "Going Up the Rough Side of the Mountain." He continued that schedule of preaching appearances for fifteen years and then focused his remaining years on his ministry at New Bethel in Detroit. **Aretha Franklin** went on to become the most popular and successful female rhythm and blues singer of all time.

Franklin was a great supporter of **Martin Luther King Jr.** In 1963 he and King led a march through the streets of Detroit that rivaled the size of the March on Washington earlier that year. He supported King's efforts to improve conditions for sanitation workers in Memphis. He also preached during the Poor People's Campaign in Washington, D.C., in the summer of 1968.

The preaching style of Franklin defined a generation of black preachers who were influenced either through his recordings or his personal appearances. His mastery of the form that blends speaking and singing, no doubt adapted from the sermons he had heard in rural Mississippi, can still be heard in black churches and many white Pentecostal churches. The form is variously known as "whooping" or "intoning." He was most noted for a single sermon, "The Eagle Stirreth Her Nest."

One of Franklin's sermons appears in a recent anthology of great sermons, *Tongues of Angels/Tongues of Men.* In the introduction to that sermon, **Jesse Jackson** says about Franklin, "He is the most imitated soul preacher in history, a combination of soul and science and substance and sweetness."

Franklin's wife, Barbara, died in 1952, leaving him to rear their four children: Cecil, Erma, Carolyn, and Aretha. C. L. Franklin died in 1984 as a result of gunshot wounds sustained during an attempted robbery in his home on June 10, 1979. He survived his wounds but remained in a coma without life support for five years.

Commentary by C. L. Franklin on the album "Amazing Grace," Aretha Franklin; *Give Me This Mountain: Life History and Selected Sermons of Reverend C. L. Franklin,* ed. Jeff Todd Titon; Hettie Jones, *Big Star, Fallin' Mama;* John F. Thornton and Katherine Washburn, *Tongues of Angels/ Tongues of Men.*

☯ Gomes, Peter J.

(1942–) In 1979 *Time* listed those persons the staff thought to be the seven most influential preachers in the United States. Among that elite group of pulpiteers was Peter J. Gomes. He has been, since 1974, the Plummer Professor of Christian Morals and Pusey Minister in the Memorial Church at Harvard University.

Gomes, born in Boston, Massachusetts, in 1942, earned a bachelor of arts degree from Bates College in 1965 and a bachelor of sacred theology degree from Harvard Divinity School in 1968. After a short term as an administrator at Tuskegee University in Alabama, Gomes joined the staff at the Memorial Church at Harvard in 1970, and he became the senior minister in 1974.

Gomes rocketed to international prominence with the release of two books. *The Good Book: Reading the Bible with Mind and Heart* was on the *New York Times* bestseller list in 1996. That was followed by a collection of his *Sermons: Biblical Wisdom for Daily Living* (1998). That year he delivered the Lyman Beecher Lectures on Preaching at Yale Divinity School.

In the foreword to his collections of sermons, Henry Louis Gates Jr., Gomes's colleague at Harvard and a member of the Memorial Church, wrote about his pastor's preaching technique: "To my astonishment I now attend the Memorial Church at Harvard whenever Peter preaches, where each week he delivers witty and urbane sermons to standing-room only congregations representing the diversity of society itself. I love the timbre of his voice, an uncanny blend of high-toned old New England with the biblical cadence of the King James Version of the Bible filtered through the black Baptist tradition. Peter's sermons do not much address such large and vexed questions as the virgin birth or an eternal afterlife as they do how thoughtful and intelligent people, determined to be citizens of a multicultural, cosmopolitan, secular world, maintain a sense of deep spirituality and social justice within a highly competitive, often brutally irrational and grossly unfair existence."

This American Baptist minister has earned twelve honorary degrees. He offered the prayer at the second inaugural for Ronald Reagan in 1985 and preached the sermon prior to the inaugural of George H. W. Bush in 1989. In 2000 he delivered the university sermon before Cambridge University (England) and preached the Millennial Sermon in Canterbury Cathedral. In addition to his preaching and teaching duties, Gomes has served on the advisory board for several preaching journals, including *The Living Pulpit*, *Preaching*, and *The Pulpit Digest*. He has also been a frequent contributor to each of those journals for the last twenty years.

Gomes has been profiled in *The New Yorker* and has been interviewed on *60 Minutes*. David Gergen, editor at large of *U.S. News and World Report*, conducted an interview with Gomes that focused on *The Good Book*. In that interview Gomes spoke about the meaning of living a spiritual life: "The spiritual life is not an alternative to the life you are living. The spiritual life is the only life worth living, and it begins to provide the basis for your thinking and feeling and your being. And it will be with you from this life into the next one."

The Bates Student, September 5, 1997; Peter J. Gomes, *The Good Book and Sermons;* Harvard Divinity School Faculty Profiles; "An Interview with Peter J. Gomes," *Pulpit Digest* (September/October 1998).

☙ Grimké, Francis J.

(1850-1937) No black preacher of the last 150 years has been more effective at using the Christian faith as the perspective from which to attack the evils of racial prejudice than Francis J. Grimké. **Carter G. Woodson** observed that Grimké was "decidedly outspoken" on the sufferings of blacks in America, and he spoke at a time when race relations had reached what Charles Chestnutt called "the nadir," or the darkest and lowest, period in American history between the years of 1895 and 1925.

Grimké was born in Charleston, South Carolina, on November 4, 1850, to a white father and his slave mistress. Along with his brother Archibald, who became a lawyer and civil rights leader, Francis attended Lincoln University in Pennsylvania and graduated in 1870. He briefly studied law at Howard University but then felt called into the ministry. He graduated from Princeton Theological Seminary in New Jersey in 1878 and was then called to the Fifteenth Street Presbyterian Church in Washington, D.C. While in Washington he also became a trustee of Howard University.

Grimké's appeal was largely to the black elite of Washington, D.C., and his sermons were directed more to the head than to the heart. However, there was great power in his preaching as he tackled the difficult issues of race and social class in late nineteenth-century and early twentieth-century America. In a sermon delivered in 1902, Grimké spoke about the justice that God will surely visit upon America for its history of abuse of black people: "God is not dead,—nor is he an indifferent onlooker at what is going on in this world. One day he will make requisition for blood; he will call the oppressors to account. Justice may sleep, but it never dies. The individual, race, or nation which does wrong, which sets at defiance God's great law of love, of brotherhood, will be sure, sooner or later, to pay the penalty. We reap as we sow. With what measure we mete, it shall be measured to us again."

In 1909 Grimké was among the founding members of the National Association for the Advancement of Colored People (NAACP). He also received critical acclaim as a poet and teacher. In 1878 he married Charlotte Forten, the daughter of James Forten, a wealthy black leader in the antebellum era. His brother Archibald won the Spingarn Medal of the NAACP in 1919. His sister, Angelina, was also a noted poet and writer. Francis J. Grimké died in 1937.

Marcus Boulware, *The Oratory of Negro Leaders;* Cleophus LaRue, *The Heart of Black Preaching;* Gayraud S. Wilmore, *Black Religion and Black Radicalism;* Carter G. Woodson, *The History of the Negro Church.*

☙ Hall, Prathia Laura Ann

(1940-) When *Ebony* offered its first list of the outstanding black women preachers in the country (1997), the first name on the list was that of Prathia Hall. Not only has Hall been among the best preachers in the country, male or female, for the last twenty-five years, but also she has been an outspoken advocate of the right of women to stand in the pulpit of black Baptist churches and preach the gospel of Jesus Christ.

Born in Philadelphia, Pennsylvania, in 1940, Hall is a graduate of Temple University. She went on to earn her master of divinity in 1984 and a doctor of philosophy degree from Princeton Theological Seminary in 1997. She served as pastor of the Mt. Sharon Baptist Church of Philadelphia from 1978 to 2000. However, she maintained a full schedule of preaching and teaching across the country. She has been the dean of the African American studies program and a lecturer at United Theological Seminary in Dayton, Ohio. She has also taught at the **Interdenominational Theological Center (ITC)** in Atlanta, Georgia. In 2000 she was appointed the Martin Luther King Jr. Associate Professor of Social Ethics at Boston University.

During her college years, Hall was a member of the Student Nonviolent Coordinating Committee (SNCC). In 1961 she was one of the Freedom Riders who challenged segregation in interstate bus service in the Deep South. She was arrested for her activities and continued to work for the cause of civil rights in Georgia and Alabama.

Hall is an ordained American Baptist minister who serves on the denomination's advisory council on the Women in Ministry Project. She is also actively involved in the program committee of the **Progressive National Baptist Convention (PNBC)**. She is an avid proponent of womanist theology, which reflects upon the implications of biblical faith from the unique perspective of African American women, unlike the feminist perspective, which is perceived to be sensitive to issues of gender but not to issues of race and racism.

Hall's commitment to a womanist theology is apparent in her preaching and public addresses. In a 2001 address at Boston University, Hall took the occasion of a Martin Luther King Jr. memorial service to remind the audience that "the movement was so much more than Dr. King.... It was largely women. If there'd been no women, there would've been no movement." In a 1996 article in *Sojourners*, in which she commented favorably upon the Million Man March, she also offered this poignant insight: "I must make it abundantly clear that while as a black woman I could understand and support the March of Men on October 16, the survival and liberation of our community requires the equal partnership of black men and black women in the family, in the church, and in the community. There is no place in our forward movement for the

misogyny often demonstrated by some march organizers."

Her dissertation at Princeton, "The Religious and Social Consciousness of African American Baptist Women," also helped Hall spell out her womanist perspective on theology. In an interview in *InSpire,* she spoke about her sense of call and vocation: "Like Jeremiah, I have always had a sense that my life wasn't mine to simply do with as I please. My earliest memories have some spiritual character. I have always been aware of God's presence in my life, and I knew that would have something to do with how I would live my life."

"15 Top Black Women Preachers," *Ebony,* November 1997; "Prathia Hall: A Lifetime of Speaking Out," *InSpire* (summer 1998); Prathia Hall-Wynn, "Transcendent Power: A Black Woman's Perspective on the Million Man March," *Sojourners,* January–February 1996; studentadvantage.com at Boston University 2001.

☾ Jakes, Thomas Dexter (T. D.)

(1957–) In 1982, when the Union Carbide chemical plant closed in Charleston, West Virginia, twenty-five-year-old Thomas Jakes was forced to dig ditches to make ends meet. By 1992 he had helped create a powerful ministry in Charleston, and there he preached a sermon entitled "Woman, Thou Art Loosed." From that sermon was launched one of the most remarkable ministries of the twentieth century. Bishop **Paul Morton Sr.** of the Full Gospel movement calls Jakes "the black Billy Graham." As if to support that designation, the *New York Times* named Jakes as one of the five national

evangelists most likely to succeed Billy Graham as "evangelist to the world."

Jakes was born in Charleston, West Virginia, on June 9, 1957. In his early years he preached to imaginary congregations and always carried a Bible to school, earning him the nickname Bible Boy. He acknowledged his call to preach at the age of seventeen, believing the words of Jeremiah 1:7, "While you were in your mother's womb I knew you." He attended West Virginia State University, majoring in psychology, but he did not graduate. Instead, in 1980 he began a part-time ministry with Greater Emanuel Temple of Faith, a storefront church in Montgomery, West Virginia, that began with ten members. His ministry became full time in 1982. He moved from Montgomery to Charleston in 1990, and from Charleston his ministry launched him upon the world stage.

By 1993 Jakes had released his first book, *Woman, Thou Art Loosed!* That also became the name of a women's conference that Jakes sponsors across the country. In addition to his ministry focus on the brokenness of women, in 1993 he held his first Manpower Conference, a ministry to men. In 1993 he also began a weekly television broadcast, *Get Ready with T. D. Jakes.* That program was first aired on the Trinity Broadcasting Network (TBN) and Black Entertainment Television (BET).

In 1994 he established T. D. Jakes Ministries as a nonprofit organization that managed his books, conferences, and broadcast ministries. Jakes added another conference to his schedule, When Shepherds Bleed, a ministry to pastors and their spouses. By this time,

Jakes had become a bishop within the Pentecostal community of the Higher Ground Always Abounding Assemblies. This Ohio-based movement is a network of approximately two hundred Oneness Pentecostal churches. Oneness Pentecostal churches deemphasize the Trinity and focus solely upon the divinity of Jesus. They also baptize "in the name of Jesus," as opposed to using the trinitarian formula of "Father, Son, and Holy Spirit." These theological issues have created some controversy, but they have not in any way inhibited the growth of T. D. Jakes Ministries.

In 1996 Jakes moved his family and fifty other families to Dallas, Texas, and began a new church called The Potter's House (Jeremiah 18:2). This move not only brought him closer to TBN but also positioned his ministry for future growth and expansion. His ministry bought the church and grounds from The Eagle's Nest Family Church, which was headed by the jailed televangelist W. V. Grant. Within four years, Jakes had built the Potter's House into a 26,000-member multiracial congregation that moved into a $33 million facility in 2000.

Jakes has frequently been criticized for the great wealth he has amassed and for the fact that he lives in a $1.7 million home. His response is that his money has come largely through royalties from the fourteen books he has written, many of which have spent months on the bestseller lists. Rather than apologizing for his prosperity, he quips that "God allows some of his children to travel first-class as well as coach." It is clear, however, that his ministry has a heavy emphasis on marketing various products, ranging from

tapes and CDs to T-shirts and canvas bags that bear the ministry logo.

T. D. Jakes Ministries is not without substance. The Potter's House operates a homeless shelter, a soup kitchen, a clothing exchange, a tutoring program, a graduate equivalence degree program (GED), and a ministry to persons living with HIV/AIDS. The Potter's House sends tapes and books to more than six hundred prisons across the country, in addition to special conferences that Jakes beams into prisons in twenty-two states through a satellite connection. However, the heart of his ministry continues to be his conferences for women, men, and pastors, as well as his preaching at The Potter's House in Dallas.

Jakes lives in Dallas with his wife, Serita, whom he married in 1981, and their five children. It was out of his attempts to provide spiritual support for his wife that the Woman, Thou Art Loosed! concept was born.

Theresa Hairston, "A Relevant Word for Today," *Gospel Today,* September 1997; Jim Jones, "Swift Growth Shapes Potter's House," Christianity Today.com, January 12, 1998; Douglas leBlanc, "Apologetics Journal Criticizes T. D. Jakes," Christianity Today.com; Kelly Starling, "Why People, Especially Black Women, Are Talking about Bishop T. D. Jakes," *Ebony,* January 2001; "Thunder from Heaven," *Charisma,* November 1996; Lauren F. Winner, "T. D. Jakes Feels Your Pain," Christianity Today.com; www.tdjakes.org.

☻ Jasper, John

(1812–1901) Born on July 4, 1812, Jasper was the most widely known and celebrated slave preacher of the nineteenth century, and after the Civil War he became pastor of Sixth Mount Zion Baptist Church in Richmond, Virginia, from 1867 to 1901. It was said of Jasper that "he was great in his bondage and became immortal in his freedom."

Jasper's father was an exhorter who preached to gatherings of slaves with white supervision. His mother named him John after John the Baptist. Although he married three other times subsequently, Jasper and his first wife were forcibly separated by his owner because Jasper had married without permission. That experience sent him into a period of being "a wild sinner." However, on July 25, 1839, he experienced a dramatic conversion while working in a tobacco factory in Richmond.

Jasper was baptized in February 1840 and on the same day preached his first sermon, which was a eulogy at the funeral of another slave. His owner, Samuel Hardgrove, encouraged Jasper to pursue his call to preach. He was in constant demand as a preacher, especially at funerals of whites and blacks. He would frequently preach a eulogy of upwards of one hour after a white preacher had already delivered a sermon. If they knew he was scheduled to appear, people waited and wanted to hear from Jasper.

The fact that he was still a slave did not prevent Jasper from pursuing his work as a preacher. His owner allowed him to travel away from his labors in the tobacco factory on every fourth Sunday. On any other day that Jasper was requested to preach, Hardgrove had to be paid one dollar for every day that Jasper was away from the factory. Jasper could keep any additional monies offered to him beyond that one dollar.

Jasper was licensed to preach by the Old African Baptist Church of Richmond in 1840. At that time, slaves could not be ordained. Jasper was illiterate on the day of his conversion, but within fifteen months he had learned how to read and became a great student of the Bible, bringing its stories and characters alive with an unmatched imagination and zeal. When he was allowed to preach on a regular basis at a black church in Petersburg, Virginia, a Jim Crow section had to be created for the white people who crowded in to listen to his sermons. When the Civil War erupted, Jasper would regularly preach to wounded Confederate soldiers in military hospitals in Richmond and Petersburg. He was never known to have spoken against slavery or to have urged slaves to rebel or resist in any way.

Jasper remained a slave until the city of Richmond surrendered to Union forces on April 3, 1865. Freedom allowed him to pursue his lifelong goal of becoming a full-time pastor. On September 3, 1867, he organized the Sixth Mount Zion Baptist Church in Richmond. It began with nine members but by 1883 had grown to more than two thousand. His popularity as a preacher attracted large numbers of white people to his services. Jasper jokingly had to say to the throngs of white visitors, "Look heah, you all white folks, don't git in de seats uv de reg'lar customers." It must also be said that Jasper's popularity with whites and blacks created bitter resentment on the part of the other black preachers in Richmond, many of whom prided themselves on having acquired a formal education.

Jasper is noted for one sermon, "The Sun Do Move," based upon Joshua 10:12-14. He preached this sermon more than 250 times between 1878 and 1898, even preaching it before the Virginia State Legislature. It is the best example of his use of vivid imagery coupled with a firm conviction of biblical literalism. When it was announced that he was to preach that sermon, white and black people would crowd the church two hours before the service started.

Jasper offered this description of his preparation to preach. "First I read my Bible until a text gets hold of me. Then I go down to the James River and walk it in. Then I get into my pulpit and preach it out." He died March 28, 1901, in Richmond. He remained as the pastor of Sixth Mount Zion until his death at the age of eighty-nine. His obituary in the *Richmond Dispatch* read in part: "John Jasper made an impression upon his generation, because he was sincerely and deeply earnest in all that he said. No man could talk with him in private, or listen to him from the pulpit, without being thoroughly convinced of that fact."

Richard Ellsworth Day, *Rhapsody in Black;* William Eldridge Hatcher, *The Biography of John Jasper;* David L. Larsen, *The Company of Preachers;* Martha Simmons, "A Master of Making a Sermon Come Alive," *The African American Pulpit* (spring 2001).

☾ Jones, Howard O.

(1923-) Many black preachers of great power and effectiveness during the 1950s and 1960s were not household names because they were not involved in the **civil rights movement** or prominent within one of the historic black denominations. These black preachers were evangelists who typically worked under the sponsorship of a white denomination or evangelistic agency. The late evangelist **Tom Skinner** would fit into this category. So too would the internationally renowned black evangelist Howard O. Jones. He may be better known within the white community than he has been in the black communities across the country, but his contribution is worth noting.

Jones was born in Oberlin, Ohio, in 1923. His family started the Mt. Zion Baptist Church of that city. However, his initial interest was in music. He began his professional life as a jazz saxophonist in the dance clubs of nearby Cleveland. However, his wife-to-be, Wanda, persuaded him to give up that life and turn to Christ. Following his conversion he abandoned the jazz scene, and they both enrolled in Nyack College in New York. He began a career in pastoral ministry with the Christian and Missionary Alliance Church in Harlem, New York. That was followed by another C&MA pastoral work in Cleveland.

In 1957 Jones joined the Billy Graham Evangelistic Association as one of the members of the crusade team. That was the year that Billy Graham held an extended crusade in New York City. It was Jones who persuaded Billy Graham not to stay in Yankee Stadium and expect black people to come to him. Rather, argued Jones, Graham should go to Harlem and hold a series of crusades directed especially to that black community. Graham did so in 1957, and during that crusade Ethel Waters, the great black singer and actress, rededicated her life to Christ. From then until her death in 1977, she became a member of the Billy Graham team.

Jones did not always travel with Graham but also led crusades on his own in other cities as part of worldwide ministry of the Graham organization. Jones spent considerable time throughout Africa but focused on Liberia. He believed that worldwide missionary outreach was the fundamental challenge facing the black church. However, he feared that too many black churches never embraced this vision because they were preoccupied with issues of racism or improperly focused on various programs that he viewed as not being central to the mission of the church. In *Shall We Overcome?* Jones writes, "The time has come when Negro churches in America must awake and accept responsibility for worldwide missions. They must have a vision of the home and the foreign field. With John Wesley the Negro church must say 'the whole world is my parish'; it must be realized that The Great Commission of Jesus Christ is not only a positive command to white churches, but to the Negro churches as well."

With an eye on the home and the foreign field, Jones has hosted two evangelistic broadcasts in which he has concentrated on winning souls to Christ. One broadcast is done in Liberia on station ELWA. The other broadcast is called "The Hour of Freedom" and is broadcast on Christian stations throughout North America. Jones has been a popular conference speaker and has served as president of the National Negro Evangelical Association.

Jones reports that during the bloody civil rights campaigns in Birmingham, Alabama, in 1963 and in Montgomery, Alabama, in 1965, Graham was running crusades in those cities at those times. The racial violence in the streets seemed a stark contrast to the spirit of reconciliation that he reported seeing between blacks and whites in those cities under the influence of the preaching of the gospel. He wrote: "Under the preaching of the cross of Christ, Negroes and whites met together in integrated meetings which made history. The Message of the Gospel brought conviction of sin to the hearts of people, and at the evangelist's invitation hundreds came to receive Christ as their Saviour. For the first time people representing both races found Christ to be the answer to all problems, including race prejudice and hatred."

Those experiences in Alabama led Jones to conclude that while racism is a great evil, the methodology of the civil rights movement was not likely to be successful in removing racism from the human heart. Unlike the activism and nonviolent demonstrations associated with such preachers as **Martin Luther King Jr., Fred Lee Shuttlesworth, Ralph David Abernathy,** and **James Lawson,** Jones represented another group of black preachers who took a very different position. Jones said: "As I see the race problem from the Christian standpoint, I am convinced that only Christ can give us the capacity to love all men, even our enemies."

Howard O. Jones, *Shall We Overcome?;* Howard O. Jones and Wanda Jones, *Heritage and Hope.*

◉ Jones, William Augustus, Jr.

(1934–) There may be no better combination of poetry, prophecy, and power in the pulpit than can be found in the preaching of this Brooklyn, New York, pulpiteer. For the last forty years Jones's preaching has been heard and heralded by audiences in every denomination of Christendom and on nearly every continent on earth. He has taken seriously the Great Commission and has gone into all the world to preach the gospel.

Jones was born in Louisville, Kentucky, on February 24, 1934. He is the son and grandson of Baptist preachers. He served in the United States military from 1953 to 1956, reaching the rank of first lieutenant. He received his bachelor of arts degree from the University of Kentucky in 1958 and a bachelor of divinity degree from Crozer Theological Seminary in 1961. From 1959 to 1962 he was the pastor of First Baptist Church in Philadelphia (Paschal), Pennsylvania. Since 1962 he has been pastor of Bethany Baptist Church in Brooklyn. He was part of the Brooklyn-based trinity of Baptist

preachers that included **Sandy F. Ray** and **Gardner C. Taylor.**

A longtime social activist, Jones served as national president of Operation Breadbasket, an affiliate of the **Southern Christian Leadership Conference (SCLC),** in the early 1970s. At the same time, he was active within the **Progressive National Baptist Convention (PNBC),** serving as president of that body from 1978 to 1980. He was the founder and president of the National Black Pastors' Conference, an interdenominational gathering of black clergy from across the country that convened for the first time in Detroit, Michigan, in 1980. This unique conference brought together pastors and professors, Baptists, Methodists, Pentecostals, and clergy from many other religious groups.

Jones received his doctor of ministry degree at Colgate Rochester Divinity School in 1975 as a member of the first class of Martin Luther King Jr. Fellows. His dissertation in that doctoral project became the basis of *God and the Ghetto.* He also wrote *The Black Church Looks at the Bicentennial* with **Wyatt Tee Walker** and Harold Carter. Jones has taught homiletics and related pastoral courses at such schools as Colgate Rochester, Union Seminary in New York City, Princeton Theological Seminary, and Wesley Seminary in Washington, D.C. For many years he was a mentor to doctoral students, along with Carter, at United Theological Seminary in Dayton, Ohio.

However, it has been as a preacher that Jones has made his mark and his contribution. He is one of the most sought-after evangelists in the country, on the road upwards of thirty weeks per year. He is regularly scheduled to preach in the Ministers' Division at the annual session of the PNBC. He preached at the Baptist World Alliance meeting in Toronto in 1980 and is the featured preacher on *The Bethany Hour,* a television program that can be seen on cable stations across the country. In 1984 *Ebony* named him one of the top fifteen black preachers in America. In addition to his other writings, he has released a book of his sermons, *Responsible Preaching.*

Jones's preaching is as likely to intrigue a listener's mind with a quote from a lofty theological source as it is to thrill the soul with his characteristic shout of "Hallelujah, yes!"

In 1958 Jones married Natalie Brown, with whom he had four children. The number of young preachers across the country who are his sons and daughters in the ministry is much larger.

"America's Fifteen Greatest Black Preachers," *Ebony,* September 1984; William A. Jones Jr., *God in the Ghetto and Responsible Preaching.*

☻ Lee, Jarena

(1783-1855) The first black woman to achieve recognition as a preacher in the United States, Lee was born free in Cape May, New Jersey, on February 11, 1783. She was separated from her parents at the age of seven and went into domestic service in a private residence near Philadelphia, Pennsylvania. During those years she experienced a series of mystical visions that led her toward a spiritual conversion. That conversion was completed in 1804, when she responded to a sermon preached by **Richard Allen,** then the pastor of Bethel Church in Philadelphia.

After another series of visions, Lee felt a call to preach the gospel. She approached Allen in 1809 and asked him to sanction her calling and grant her ordination within the life of his **African Methodist Episcopal (AME) Church.** However, Allen refused to do so on the grounds that AME polity did not allow for the ordination of women. He suggested that she could be an exhorter as a layperson or could host and participate in prayer meetings. But of women preachers, "Our discipline knew nothing at all about it—that it did not call for women preachers."

Lee's response in her autobiography is a powerful rebuttal to those who continue to oppose the idea of women in ministry: "O how careful ought we to be, lest through our bylaws of church government and discipline, we bring into disrepute even the word of life. For as unseemly as it may appear nowadays for a woman to preach, it should be remembered that nothing is impossible with God. And why should it be thought impossible, heterodox or improper for a woman to preach, seeing the Savior died for the woman as well as the man?"

Failing to receive ordination, Lee chose to exhort without a license, and with much success. In 1811 she married Joseph Lee, who was an AME preacher, and her work as a preacher was greatly reduced. However, following his death in 1817 she returned to her desire to preach, and she resumed holding prayer meetings in her home and preaching as she received opportunity.

In 1822 Lee again approached Allen for ordination. By this time, the AME Church had been formally organized into a connectional denomination, and Allen was now the bishop. She sought to be ordained as part of that larger system. He again refused to sanction her call with the act of ordination, believing that her male colleagues would never accept her in that role.

However, Allen did urge Lee to continue in the work of exhorting and speaking at prayer meetings. He also invited her to travel with him to conferences in New York and Baltimore, where she could sit in meetings with other ministers who had been ordained. He offered her speaking engagements in churches that were directly under his jurisdiction for pulpit supply. It is reported that he allowed her to preach at Bethel Church in Philadelphia, the mother congregation and the emotional center of the AME family. In so doing, he unofficially designated her as the first black woman preacher in the nation's history.

Lee is believed to have died in the mid-1850s.

Jacqueline Grant, "Womanist Theology," in *African American Religious Studies,* ed. Gayraud S. Wilmore; Carol V. R. George, *Segregated Sabbaths;* Jarena Lee, "A Female Preacher among the African Methodists," in *African American Religious History: A Documentary Witness,* ed. Milton C. Sernett; C. Eric Lincoln and Lawrence W. Mamiya, *The Black Church in the African American Experience.*

☻ Massey, James Earl

(1929–) Born in Detroit, Michigan, in 1929, this son and grandson of preachers in the Church of God (Anderson, Indiana) acknowledged his call to preach at the age of sixteen. He was studying to become a classical pianist at the Detroit Conservatory of Music, and music continues to play a central role in his ministry. However, it would be in the pulpit and not at the piano that Massey would make his greatest contribution.

Massey graduated from Detroit Bible College with a concentration in biblical languages. He received his bachelor of divinity degree from Oberlin School of Theology and did additional graduate study at Wheaton College and the University of Michigan. As a member of the Church of God (Anderson, Indiana), a predominantly white holiness group, Massey began his ministry at the Metropolitan Church of God, where he was the pastor from 1954 to 1976. From 1969 to 1976 he also served as the campus minister at Anderson University, the denomination's college. He left both of those positions to become the weekly preacher on the denomination's international radio program, "The Christian Brotherhood Hour," which he did from 1977 to 1982. In 1982 he returned to Anderson University to be a professor of New Testament and preaching.

In 1984 Massey took his first step outside of the life of his denomination when he was appointed dean of the chapel at Tuskegee University in Alabama. He was also appointed university professor of religion and society. His presence was not limited to the campus. He maintained active ties with the Church of God pastors throughout the Deep South, most of whom had been his students at Anderson University. Many pastors in the Tuskegee area would also come to hear him preach at an early service in the university chapel before rushing off to their own 11 a.m. services. Massey was called back to Anderson University in 1990 to become dean of the School of Theology. He retired as dean emeritus in 1995.

Massey has had a productive scholarly career. He has written several books, including *The Responsible Pulpit* (1974), *The Sermon in Perspective* (1976), *Designing the Sermon* (1981), and *The Burdensome Joy of Preaching* (1998). His colleagues in the Academy of Homiletics prepared a series of lectures in his honor in *Sharing Heaven's Music: The Heart of Christian Preaching, Essays in Honor of James Earl Massey* (1995). In addition, he has served on the editorial boards of *Christianity Today, Leadership, Preaching,* and *The New Interpreter's Bible,* in which he wrote two articles on hermeneutics.

Massey has lectured at more than one hundred colleges and seminaries across the country and on four continents. **Henry Heywood Mitchell** observes that Massey has developed a "bicultural style and vocabulary" that make his preaching equally effective before a white or a black audience. Although he has not yet been invited to deliver the Lyman Beecher Lectures, two black preachers who have delivered those lectures, **Kelly Miller Smith** (1983) and **James Alexander Forbes Jr.** (1986), spoke in their lectures about Massey's contributions to the field of preaching and homiletics.

In an interview with Mitchell, Massey points to five things that make for effective preaching: a sermon must have focus and purpose, encourage people to celebrate their faith in God, help promote community within the congregation, be a radical proclamation by a faithful and fearless messenger, and result in a climax that leaves an impression on the hearers.

Barry Callen, "An Interview with James Earl Massey," in *Sharing Heaven's Music;* James Earl Massey, *The Burdensome Joy of Preaching.*

Mitchell, Ella Pearson

(1917–) Few people have done more to highlight and encourage the preaching gifts of black women or to advocate for their right to exercise those gifts than has Ella Pearson Mitchell. She is elegant in her pulpit presence, and she has been tireless in opening the doors of opportunity for the women who have come after her. She can rightly be called the "dean of black women preachers in America."

Mitchell was born in Charleston, South Carolina, in 1917. The daughter of a Presbyterian minister, she graduated

from Talladega College in Alabama in 1939. Before she departed for college, her father would allow her to preach for Youth Sunday at the Olivet Presbyterian Church, not knowing that the pulpit would eventually become as familiar to the daughter as it was to the father. She majored in religion in college, working with Joseph W. Nicholson, who had co-authored *The Negro's Church* with **Benjamin Elijah Mays** in 1933.

Following a two-year break after college, Mitchell enrolled in Union Theological Seminary in New York City. That was her second choice. She had earlier applied to Yale Divinity School, but they implied that they would be unable to place her after graduation. Yale then referred her to Union. Not only did she earn a degree in Christian education in 1943, but she also met Henry Heywood Mitchell, who became her husband in 1944 and who has been her partner in ministry ever since. There is no more delightful reading than the account of their life together found in *Together for Good: Lessons from Fifty-five Years of Marriage.*

Most of their life together saw Henry Mitchell in the spotlight as a teacher and a writer. However, with her ordination to ministry in 1978, Ella Mitchell quickly carved out an enviable reputation for herself in the same categories. Having begun her teaching career at Berkeley Baptist Divinity School (now the American Baptist Seminary of the West) in 1949, she became an associate professor of Christian education and director of continuing education at the **Interdenominational Theological Center (ITC)** in Atlanta, Georgia, from 1982 to 1986. In 1986 she

was appointed dean of the chapel at Spelman College, a prestigious black women's college in Atlanta. Her passion for preaching and teaching continues, and she and Henry Mitchell continue to team teach courses in homiletics at ITC as visiting professors.

Ella Mitchell has edited four books and contributed to many more. There have been three volumes of sermons by women preachers entitled *Those Preaching Women.* She also edited a book of essays and sermons, *Women: To Preach or Not to Preach.* Her preaching has been so widely regarded that in 1997 *Ebony* named her as one of the top fifteen black women preachers in America. However, as effective as Henry and Ella Mitchell are when preaching on their own, they have reestablished a form of preaching known as the dialogue sermon, which they refer to as "team preaching." That teamwork continued when they served together as copresidents of the Academy of Homiletics. That is not surprising, for this clergy couple has become as noted for their life together as for anything either one has done separately.

In recognition of their life's work, their faculty colleagues at ITC contributed to a book in honor of Ella and Henry Mitchell, *Born to Preach: Essays in Honor of the Ministry of Henry and Ella Mitchell.* In the introduction to that book, Samuel K. Roberts writes, "Ella Mitchell has been regarded almost universally as the dean of black women preachers. Her quiet demeanor belies a boldness when she mounts the pulpit. Ella has been hailed by countless black women preachers who have sought to find their own voice in a profession that has historically been dominated by men."

Born to Preach, ed. Samuel K. Roberts; Ella P. Mitchell and Henry H. Mitchell, *Together for Good;* Gayle White, "A Three-Way Partnership Lasts for 56 Years—with Extraordinary Results," Cox News Service, January 27, 2001.

☺ Moss, Otis, Jr.

(1935-) When your mentors are **Benjamin Elijah Mays** and **Martin Luther King Jr.**, people may be inclined to expect a great deal from you. The words of Jesus, "To whom much is given," come to mind. Otis Moss Jr. was given much in terms of early mentors and role models. It can safely be said that he has done much and given much in return.

Born in LaGrange, Georgia, in 1935, Moss graduated with a bachelor of arts degree from Morehouse College in 1956 and a master of divinity degree from Morehouse School of Religion in 1959. He also earned a doctor of ministry degree from United Theological Seminary in Dayton, Ohio, in 1990. Called to the ministry at the age of seventeen, he was pastor of Old Mt. Olive Baptist Church in LaGrange from 1954 to 1959. He was pastor of Providence Baptist Church in Atlanta from 1956 to 1961. Except for one year (1971), when he served as copastor of Ebenezer Baptist Church in Atlanta, Moss served the Mount Zion Baptist Church in Lockland (Cincinnati), Ohio, from 1961 to 1975. From there he was called to the Olivet Institutional Baptist Church in Cleveland, Ohio, where he has served since

1975. The Second Baptist Church of Los Angeles, California, extended a call to become their pastor, but after considering the offer, Moss decided to remain with Olivet in Cleveland.

Moss was listed among the top fifteen black preachers in the country in the September 1984 and November 1993 issues of *Ebony.* His sermons can also be found in *Best Black Sermons,* edited by Richard Philpot, and in various issues of *The African American Pulpit.* He delivered the Easter Sunday sermon from the chapel of Morehouse College to a national audience on CBS-TV in March 1986. He is in great demand as a preacher at conventions, on college campuses, and in churches across the country and

around the world. Moss also serves as a mentor for doctor of ministry students at United Theological Seminary.

Moss's work outside of the pulpit is equally impressive. He has consulted at Camp David with President Jimmy Carter and at the White House with President Bill Clinton. He hosted Carter at Olivet during his 1976 election campaign and did the same for Clinton in 1988. With University Hospitals, Inc., he established the Otis Moss Jr.—University Hospitals Medical Center across the street from Olivet. It is a full-service medical center bringing twenty-first-century health care into Cleveland's inner city. Since 1994 he has served as chairman of the board of trustees of Morehouse College. He has also served as a board member of United Theological Seminary, Morehouse School of Religion, and the Martin Luther King Jr. Center for Non-Violent Social Change.

Like many great preachers, Moss's life has been shaped by personal tragedy, including the death of his mother when he was four years of age, the death of his father when he was sixteen, and the death of one of his children. His experience with suffering has sensitized him in a remarkable way to the sufferings of others. From such a tender spirit great preaching can more easily flow. Great preaching has been flowing from the head and heart of Otis Moss Jr. for nearly fifty years.

"America's Fifteen Greatest Black Preachers," *Ebony*, November 1993; Thomas Kilgore Jr. and Jini Kilgore Ross, *A Servant's Journey*; W. Augustus Low and Virgil A. Clift, eds., *Encyclopedia of Black America*; "The Top Fifteen Black Preachers in America," *Ebony*, September 1984.

☉ Powell, Adam Clayton, Sr.

(1865–1953) Powell was born to an African-Cherokee woman and a German-born slave owner in Franklin County, Virginia, on May 5, 1865. In his autobiography, *Against the Tide*, he recalls that the only memories he had of the first ten years of his life were of hunger and poverty. His family lived in a one-room log cabin. His only item of clothing was an old burlap flour sack that scratched him night and day. For the first twenty years of his life, he divided his time between sharecropping and coal mining. Things did not seem promising for this illegitimate child as he struggled to survive in the face of the devastation brought upon the Old South by the Civil War.

Powell found a way to rise above the circumstances of his birth and to become one of the most prominent and successful black ministers in the nation's history. Much is known of the success of his son, Congressman and Pastor **Adam Clayton Powell Jr.** However, the father's story is just as impressive. He taught himself how to read mainly through the use of the Gospel of John. However, educational opportunities were limited for blacks in Virginia, so Powell worked most of his early life.

His family relocated to West Virginia when he was ten; Powell moved on to Rendville, Ohio, where he worked in the coal mines. He took on a raucous lifestyle, deeply engaged in gambling, drinking, and fighting. However, he was converted to the Christian faith and soon sensed a call to the ministry after a chance visit to a revival service in Rendville. Before following the call of God into ministry, Powell entertained the idea of attending Howard University Law School and aspired to serve in the U.S. Congress. However, he discovered that what little education he had received left him woefully inadequate to be admitted into a law school program. In 1888 he finally acknowledged his call and enrolled in the normal-academic-theological programs at Wayland Seminary in Washington, D.C. That school later became Virginia Union University in Richmond, Virginia. He graduated in 1892. In 1902 he received an honorary doctorate from that school.

Powell's ministry career began in 1892 at the Ebenezer Baptist Church in Philadelphia, Pennsylvania. After one year he moved on to the Emanuel Baptist Church of New Haven, Connecticut (1893–1908). While he lived in New Haven, Powell took additional courses at Yale Divinity School. He became a sought-after speaker on college campuses and in pulpits across the country. In 1900 he lectured in London at an ecumenical gathering.

On December 31, 1908, Powell was installed as pastor of the Abyssinian Baptist Church of New York City. For the next thirty years, he and that congregation grew together. His reputation as a preacher and lecturer steadily increased, and the membership swelled to more than fourteen thousand persons. When Powell retired from Abyssinian in 1937, he was the pastor of the largest Protestant congregation in the world. His was one of the most stunning reversals of fortune in the history of African Americans.

In 1923 Powell led the church in a building drive that resulted in the con-

struction of a neo-Gothic structure in the Harlem section of Manhattan. The church moved into that community at the same time that the Harlem Renaissance and the Great Migration were turning Harlem into the black mecca of the United States. It was home to the largest black population of any city in the country. Powell and Abyssinian were as much a part of that renaissance as Langston Hughes or **Duke Ellington** or the Savoy Ballroom that was just around the corner from the church.

In addition to the church building, Abyssinian built a home for the aged and a community center. The church sponsored a missionary to the French Congo and during the Great Depression operated a soup kitchen and offered

other social services. Adam Clayton Powell Jr. joined the staff in 1930 as the business manager and succeeded his father as pastor in 1937.

In 1932 Powell Sr. was a delegate to the Republican National Convention meeting in Buffalo, New York. He was active with the National Association for the Advancement of Colored People (NAACP) and the Urban League. He continued to speak on college campuses, especially black colleges in the South. Howard University, which earlier would not admit him as a student, later conferred on him the honorary degree of doctor of divinity.

Powell was approached by playwright Marc Connelly about the possibility of accepting the role of Da Lawd in the film version of *The Green Pastures*. The man who had played that role in the stage production, Richard Harrison, had died. Someone was needed who could bring dignity and stature to the role, and Powell was the man the production team wanted to use. However, he told them that he was "married to the church" and could not leave to go into motion pictures.

Powell married Mattie Fletcher Shatten in 1890, and they had two children, Adam Jr. and Blanche, both of whom were born in New Haven. Blanche died in 1926 at the age of twenty-eight. Mattie Powell died in 1945, and Powell married Inez Cottrell, a woman who was forty years his junior. They remained together until his death on June 12, 1953.

Upon his retirement from Abyssinian Baptist Church in 1937, the editorial page of the National Baptist Convention journal was devoted to Powell. Among the accolades was the following statement: "Dr. A. Clayton Powell, Sr. is one of the great spiritual leaders of this generation. There can be no question of this assertion. He has done all a Christian minister can do.... The modernity of his preaching is startling. It is down to the minute, yet it is far from sheer sensationalism. It is practical, venturesome, and, in a very true sense, devotional."

Powell attributed his success as a preacher to the fact that for fifty years of his life he devoted four hours a day to reading. That discipline filled his cup and kept him current and relevant as he went before so many different audiences. Adam Clayton Powell Jr. saw his father's success related to something quite different. Powell Jr. said, "My father was a kingdom seeker. He believed that the mere act of seeking the kingdom brought all things you need unto you."

Gilbert Osofsky, *Harlem;* Adam Clayton Powell Sr., *Against the Tide and Riots and Ruin;* Adam Clayton Powell Jr., *Adam by Adam;* Carter G. Woodson, *The History of the Black Church.*

☻ Ray, Sandy F.

(1898–1979) Ray was born on a sharecropping plantation near Marlin, Texas, on February 3, 1898, one of ten children born to Sandy and Fannie Ray. He was educated in the local school system but was allowed to attend school for only three to five months a year, because he and his siblings were needed to work on the farm during the remainder of the year. That practice was the standard for black children in the South during the sharecropping era between the end of Reconstruction and World War II.

Following the death of his father, Sandy had to leave school and take care of the family. Crop failures forced the Rays to leave the farm and resettle in Palestine, Texas, where Sandy worked a variety of jobs. He also became active in the Mt. Zion Baptist Church. There he acknowledged his call to the ministry in 1922 at the age of twenty-five. He was encouraged to resume his education, and he graduated from high school at the Arkansas Baptist College in Little Rock. He received his college degree from Morehouse College in Atlanta, Georgia.

During his student years at Morehouse, Ray was called to his first pastorate, the First Baptist Church of LaGrange, Georgia. In LaGrange he met and married his lifelong companion and wife. He went on to serve First Baptist Church in Macon, Georgia, and St. Luke's Baptist Church in Chicago, Illinois. While in Chicago he became a protégé of **Lacey Kirk (L. K.) Williams,** who was pastor of Olivet Baptist Church in Chicago and president of the **National Baptist Convention, USA, Inc. (NBCUSA).**

In 1936 Ray was called to the Shiloh Baptist Church of Columbus, Ohio. While there he began a successful radio ministry and was elected to a seat in the Ohio state legislature on November 3, 1942. At the height of his popularity and influence in Ohio, Ray surprised everyone by accepting the call to go to the Cornerstone Baptist Church in Brooklyn, New York, in 1944. At that church he established his national reputation as a preacher, church leader, and mentor of younger preachers.

In 1954 Ray was elected president of the Empire State Baptist Convention. In 1956 he was awarded an honorary doctorate from his alma mater, Morehouse College. In 1968 he was elected a regional vice president of the NBCUSA, a position which allowed him to serve as the preacher at the annual sessions of the Ministers' Division of the National Sunday School and Baptist Training Union (BTU) Congress, a branch of the national convention. Ray also appeared annually as national chairman of the Lacey Kirk Williams Ministers' Institute held every year at Bishop College in Dallas, Texas. In addition, he served as a visiting lecturer in homiletics at Union Theological Seminary in New York City. From these positions, Ray became one of the most widely heard and greatly loved preachers in America.

Ray's preaching style can only be called unique. In an era that featured the

thunderous voices of **Clarence LaVaughn (C. L.) Franklin, Junius Caesar (J. C.) Austin,** Lacey Kirk Williams, and **Gardner C. Taylor,** Ray was truly "a still small voice." He was not noted for excessive emotion (intonation or whooping). In fact, he seldom raised his voice beyond a conversational tone. But his preaching had great power. He was the master of biblical storytelling. He also made excellent use of analogies, drawn either from his boyhood in rural Texas or his experiences in the gritty urban centers of Chicago, Columbus, and Brooklyn. He was soft-spoken, but he was imaginative when it came to the use of the oratorical devices of alliteration and repetition. That oratorical skill is apparent in all of the sermons contained in his only book, *Journeying through a Jungle,* which was released shortly after his death in 1979.

During his years in Brooklyn, Ray continued his interest in politics, working closely with New York governor Nelson Rockefeller. However, that friendship did not prevent him from opening the doors of Cornerstone Baptist Church to many of the victims of the Attica Prison uprising in 1971, a riot that was put down by force by order of Governor Rockefeller. He was ahead of his time as a black Baptist pastor by establishing a church-based credit union in the early 1960s. In 1964 he led in the construction of a $1 million Christian education building for the church. That was consistent with his lifelong emphasis on the importance of education and his leadership role in focusing on Christian education within the state and national conventions.

No one better described the preaching of Sandy Ray than his Brooklyn colleague and thirty-year confidant, Gardner Taylor. As the eulogist at Ray's funeral in 1979, Taylor said, "At the height of his pulpit oratory it was hard to tell whether one heard music half spoken or speech half sung.... He was president of preaching, ambassador plenipotentiary from the imperial court of King Emanuel. He was the crown prince of the pulpit, a flaming herald of Calvary's news."

Henry H. Mitchell, *Black Preaching;* Sandy F. Ray, *Journeying through a Jungle;* Gardner C. Taylor, "The Eulogy for Sandy F. Ray," *The African American Pulpit* (winter 2000–2001).

☻ Robinson, James Herman

(1907–1972) This Presbyterian minister made history in 1955 when he became the first black preacher to deliver the prestigious Lyman Beecher Lectures on Preaching at Yale Divinity School. His lectures resulted in *Adventurous Preaching.* Six other black preachers have since delivered the Beecher Lectures: **Henry Heywood Mitchell** (1974), **Gardner C. Taylor** (1976), **Kelly Miller Smith** (1983), **James A. Forbes** (1986), **Samuel Dewitt Proctor** (1990), and **Peter J. Gomes** (1998).

Robinson was born in Knoxville, Tennessee, in 1907. He graduated from Lincoln University in Pennsylvania in 1935 and Union Theological Seminary in New York City in 1938. He was the founding pastor of Church of the Master (Presbyterian) in New York City. He also founded an international aid program called Crossroads Africa (1958), which was a forerunner of the Peace Corps and was sponsored by the federal government. His philosophy and program ideas for that program were spelled out in *Africa at the Crossroads* (1962).

Crossroads Africa was the result of Robinson's friendships with the leaders of the newly independent nations of West Africa, many of whom he met during an earlier tour of eleven sub-Sahara nations in 1954. He recognized that those emerging independent nations needed help in developing the infrastructure in terms of roads, wells, schools, and hospitals that served rural populations. Robinson's program helped to recruit and place those persons in villages throughout West Africa.

President John F. Kennedy acknowledged that Crossroads Africa was the inspiration for the much larger Peace Corps program, one of the hallmarks of his administration. Robinson served in several advisory roles within the Kennedy administration on issues dealing with Africa. Robinson resigned from pastoral ministry in 1962 in order to work full-time on Crossroads Africa.

Robinson died on November 6, 1972.

Robert T. Handy, *A History of Union Theological Seminary in New York;* Larry G. Murphy, J. Gordon Melton, and Gary L. Ward, eds., *Encyclopedia of African American Religions;* James Herman Robinson, *Road Without Turning* (1950, autobiography), *Tomorrow Is Today* (1954), *Love of This Land* (1956), *Christianity and Revolution in Africa* (1956), and *Adventurous Preaching.*

☻ Scott, Manuel Lee, Sr.

(1927–2001) From the pulpit of St. John Baptist Church in Dallas, Texas, to college campuses and church convention platforms, Manuel L. Scott Sr. has been a preacher to the world. He has appeared with the Billy Graham Evangelistic Association and has been one of the few black preachers to appear before the Southern Baptist Convention (SBC). He also has been a regular preacher within the **National Baptist Convention, USA, Inc. (NBCUSA)** and most of its state affiliates.

Born in Waco, Texas, in 1927, Scott graduated with a bachelor of arts degree from Bishop College in Marshall, Texas. In 1966 he was named Alumnus of the Year, and he received an honorary doctorate from that school in 1975. He began his ministry as pastor of Strangers' Temple Baptist Church in San Antonio, Texas. From 1950 to 1982 he was pastor of Calvary Baptist Church in Los Angeles, California. Since 1982 he has been the pastor of St. John Baptist Church. He has served as a regional vice president for the NBCUSA. He has also been a member of the general council of the Baptist World Alliance and was a preacher at the International Congress for World Evangelization in Lausanne, Switzerland. He also served on the board of trustees of Bishop College.

Recognized as one of the great preachers of the twentieth century, Scott was listed in the September 1984 and November 1993 issues of *Ebony* as among the top fifteen black preachers in America. He wrote two books of sermons, *From a Black Brother* (1971) and *The Gospel for the Ghetto* (1973). Scott died in 2001, slight of stature and unusually soft-spoken for a preacher of his reputation. But when he caught fire in the pulpit, his voice and spirit seemed to fill every inch of the sanctuary. He is survived by six children, one of whom,

Manuel L. Scott Jr., is an evangelist in the image of his father.

"America's Fifteen Greatest Black Preachers," *Ebony,* September 1984; Manuel L. Scott Sr., *From a Black Brother* and *The Gospel for the Ghetto;* "Top Fifteen Black Preachers," *Ebony,* November 1993.

☉ Skinner, Tom

(1942–1994) Powerful testimonies concerning conversion and changed lives as a result of an encounter with Jesus Christ have been an important part of the witness of the Christian church since the days of Saul of Tarsus. The story of a transformed life was central to the preaching ministry of Tom Skinner. His ministry was informed by the teaching of Paul in Ephesians 4:11, which states that some are called to be evangelists and others pastors and teachers. Skinner saw himself as being called to that vocation of evangelism unencumbered by the regular duties of pastoral ministry.

Skinner was born in New York City on June 6, 1942. While he had always been active in the church, by the age of fourteen he had also been drawn into the life of the Harlem Lords, one of the most notorious street gangs in New York City. For several years he lived a double life as preacher's kid and gang leader. However, he was saved from that gang activity as a result of a sermon he heard over the radio. After he decided to walk away from the Harlem Lords, several other gang members left and confessed their faith in Christ.

Skinner was ordained as a Baptist minister in June 1959. He quickly became disenchanted with the petty politics of the local church and with the preoccupation that so many black pastors seemed to have with money, cars, and women. As a result, he set out to organize his own ministry, and in October 1961 the Harlem Evangelistic Association had been formed. His first crusade was a weeklong evangelistic effort at the Apollo Theatre in the summer of 1962. On the strength of that crusade, Skinner led crusades in Brooklyn, New York, as well as in other parts of the United States and in the Caribbean. In 1963 he participated in the formation of the Association of Black Evangelists.

Skinner graduated from Warner College in 1963 and from Manhattan Bible Institute in 1966. By 1964 his crusades were airing over the radio. He later changed the name of the organization to Tom Skinner Crusades and later to Tom Skinner Associates. Over time the ministry moved out of New York City and settled in East Orange, New Jersey. His organization also expanded beyond evangelistic crusades and began to offer workshops to local church groups on such topics as time management and leadership development. As a result of his regular appearances before college audiences, the evangelistic work was confronted with the challenge of how to present the gospel to black groups that were being influenced by the rhetoric of the black power and black nationalist movements. To help in that effort Skinner wrote several books, including *Black and Free* (1968), *Words of Revolution* (1970), and *How Black Is the Gospel?* (1970). He also wrote *If Christ Is the Answer, What Are the Questions?* (1974).

During the 1970s and 1980s Skinner was the first black minister to serve as a chaplain and spiritual advisor to a professional sports franchise; he worked with the Washington Redskins football team. His tenure with that team was during the period when it was a perennial Super Bowl contender. Thus he could regularly be seen on the sidelines during the games that were frequently broadcast over national television. He eventually relocated to a farm in Maryland, where he started the Skinner Farm Leadership Institute.

Tom Skinner died at the age of fifty-two on June 17, 1994.

Papers of Tom Skinner in the Billy Graham Archives Collection 430 at bgcarc@wheaton.edu; Tom Skinner, *Black and Free.*

☻ Smith, Kelly Miller

(1920–) In 1960, when the sit-in movement came to Nashville, Tennessee, the student protesters found an organizing headquarters and a spiritual haven inside the First Baptist Church Capitol Hill. The pastor who welcomed them for both purposes was Kelly Miller Smith. Branch president of the Nashville National Association for the Advancement of Colored People (NAACP) from 1956 to 1959, an active participant in the **Southern Christian Leadership Conference (SCLC),** and a member of the Nashville Urban League, Smith was an ideal person to provide spiritual counsel and moral support to the students who were risking their lives every day in the sit-ins.

Smith was born in Mound Bayou, Mississippi, on October 28, 1920. He received a bachelor or arts degree in 1942 from Morehouse College and a bachelor of divinity degree from Howard University School of Religion in 1945. From 1946 to 1951 he was pastor of Mount Heroden Baptist Church in Vicksburg, Mississippi. From there he went to Nashville to become pastor of First Baptist Church. Except for a few months in 1964, when he was pastor of Antioch Baptist Church in Cleveland, Smith remained in Nashville until his death in 1984. In 1954 Smith was listed in *Ebony* as one of the ten most effective black preachers in America.

In addition to his duties as a pastor, Smith became the first black faculty member at Vanderbilt University Divinity School in 1965. In 1969 he was appointed the assistant dean of that divinity school. He had earlier taught at Natchez College in Mississippi and at American Baptist Theological Seminary, also in Nashville. On the strength of his career as preacher, teacher, and activist, Smith was invited to deliver the Lyman Beecher Lectures on Preaching at Yale Divinity School in 1983. Those lectures resulted in *Social Crisis Preaching.* One of his sermons, "Time Is Winding Up," appears in *Best Black Sermons.*

Smith's support of the sit-in movement was not only courageous at the time but also has produced a long list of black leaders, many whose work continues. The list would include **James Lawson, John Lewis,** James Bevel and Diane Bevel, and Marion Barry.

Aldon D. Morris, *Origins of the Civil Rights Movement;* Kelly Miller Smith, *Social Crisis Preaching;* William Philpot, ed., *Best Black Sermons;* Juan Williams, *Eyes on the Prize.*

 **Taylor, Gardner C.**

(1918-) Born in Baton Rouge, Louisiana, on June 18, 1918, Taylor is the son of a preacher who went on to be widely acclaimed as possibly the greatest preacher of his generation or, some say, the greatest preacher of the twentieth century. His father, Washington Monroe Taylor, was pastor of Mt. Zion Baptist Church of Baton Rouge, originally known as First African Baptist Church. He was also vice president at large for the **National Baptist Convention, USA, Inc. (NBCUSA).**

Educated at Leland College in Baker, Louisiana, Gardner Taylor did not originally intend to enter the ministry, having been accepted into the University of Michigan School of Law. However, in 1937 he was involved in an automobile accident in which two white men were killed. A white person who was an eyewitness exonerated Taylor of any wrongdoing in the accident, thus delivering him from a terrible fate that could have befallen a black man in that situation in the South during that time. From that moment, his mind turned toward the ministry.

Taylor enrolled in Oberlin School of Theology, from which he graduated in 1940. He pastored the Bethany Baptist Church of Elyria, Ohio, while still a student. He returned to Louisiana to pastor a church in New Orleans. In 1943 he returned to Baton Rouge to serve as pastor of his home church. In 1948 he was called to the Concord Baptist Church of Brooklyn, New York. Under his leadership, that congregation grew to a membership in excess of fourteen thousand. Concord sponsors an elementary school (kindergarten through sixth grade), a senior citizens' housing project, and many other programs that benefit the Bedford-Stuyvesant neighborhood in Brooklyn.

While at Concord Taylor became the second African American to serve on the New York City board of education. He was frequently encouraged to run for other political offices, but he declined in order to devote himself to his pulpit ministry. He served Concord until his retirement in 1990. He did serve as president of the Protestant Council of Churches in New York City.

A great supporter of **Martin Luther King Jr.,** Taylor was disappointed that the NBCUSA would not embrace King's efforts in the **civil rights movement.** In the 1960 session of the convention, meeting in Kansas City, he sought unsuccessfully to unseat **Joseph Harrison Jackson,** who was then serving in his eighth year as president of the convention. Following that defeat, Taylor joined with King and other activist pastors in forming the **Progressive National Baptist Convention (PNBC).** He served a two-year term as president of that body in the 1960s and remains one of its elder statesmen.

Taylor delivered the Lyman Beecher Lectures on Preaching at Yale Divinity School in 1976, which resulted in *How Shall They Preach?* Much of his philosophy of preaching is captured in an excerpt from those lectures and that subsequent book: "The power and pathos of the preacher are to be found not in volume of voice nor those patently contrived tremors of tone preachers sometimes affect, but in passionate avowals which are passionate because they have gotten out of the written word into the preacher's own heart, have been filtered and colored by the preacher's own experiences of joy and sorrow, and then are presented to and pressed upon the hearts and minds of those who hear."

His other books include *The Scarlet Thread* and *We Have This Ministry,* which he coauthored with Samuel Dewitt Proctor. A six-volume series, *The Words of Gardner Taylor,* was published by Judson Press. The first volume of that series includes sermons that Taylor preached over NBC's National Radio Pulpit in the 1950s and 1960s. That was a responsibility he shared with such noted preachers as Harry Emerson Fosdick, Ralph Sockman, and Paul Scherer.

Taylor has taught homiletics at such divinity schools as Harvard, Princeton, Union in New York City, and Colgate Rochester. He has preached and lectured at dozens more. His preaching has taken him onto almost every continent on earth and before scores of denominational gatherings and clergy assemblies. In 1980 *Time* declared that Taylor was "the dean of the nation's black preachers." **Wyatt Tee Walker** observes, "Gardner Taylor is the greatest preacher living, dead or unborn." In two separate polls undertaken by *Ebony* in 1984 and 1993, Taylor ranked first as the most popular and effective black preacher in the country. High praise indeed for someone who had initially planned to enter the legal profession, not the pulpit.

James Earl Massey compares Taylor with the giants of the pulpit in the white preaching tradition in America: Phillips Brooks, Henry Ward Beecher, and Harry Emerson Fosdick. He says, "Taylor possesses Beecher's prolix ability to spin words, Brooks' earnestness of style and breadth of learning, and Fosdick's ability to appeal to the masses and yet maintain dignity in doing so." This comparison with these white preachers may be explained by the assessment of **Henry Heywood Mitchell,** who says, "He's not only master of black preaching as such. He knows all the great white preachers and quotes them as well."

Taylor's first wife of fifty-two years, Laura Scott Taylor, died in a tragic accident in 1995. He now lives in Brooklyn with his second wife. He maintains an active preaching schedule, which included participation in the first and second inaugural celebrations of President William Jefferson Clinton in 1993 and 1997. In 2000 President Clinton awarded Taylor the Presidential Medal of Freedom, which is the highest honor the country can bestow upon a civilian.

The power and poetry of Taylor's preaching has been captured on video as part of the Great Preachers series produced by the Odyssey Television Network in conjunction with the Baylor University survey of the greatest preachers of the English-speaking world. The best description of his preaching style is found in the introduction to the first volume of *The Words of Gardner Taylor:* "In Dr. Taylor's preaching can be found a mix that includes a sort of grand nineteenth-century Victorian style, the richness of the African American folk tradition, and a unique interpretation of modern homiletical theory."

Michael Eric Dyson, "Gardner Taylor," *Between God and Gangsta Rap;* "Gardner Taylor: One of the Greatest Preachers of All Time," *ABC People,* 1997; "An Interview with Gardner Taylor," *The African American Pulpit* (summer/fall 1999); "Pulpit Laureate and Presidential Favorite: An Interview with Gardner Taylor," *Pulpit Digest,* September–October 1996; Gardner Taylor, *How Shall They Preach?;* "Introduction," *The Words of Gardner Taylor,* comp. Edward L. Taylor.

◉ Walker, Charles Thomas (C. T.)

(1858–1921) Walker was born into slavery in Hephzibah, Georgia, on February 5, 1858. From those humble beginnings he rose to become the most widely known and widely heard black preacher of his generation. When he appeared in city-wide revivals, he would draw larger crowds of white and black worshipers than did the famous evangelist D. L. Moody. Those who heard Walker began referring to him as "the black Spurgeon," comparing him with the famous English preacher Charles Haddon Spurgeon, who was believed by many people to be the greatest preacher of the nineteenth century.

Walker was one of eleven children born to Thomas and Hannah Walker. His father died of pneumonia and was buried the day before Charles was born. His mother died when he was eight. He experienced a religious conversion in 1873 and joined the Franklin Covenant Baptist Church. After receiving some basic training in reading and writing from the local Freedmen's Bureau, Walker enrolled in the Augusta Institute to begin training for a career in ministry. That school would subsequently move to Atlanta and become known as Morehouse College. He was licensed to preach in 1876 and ordained in May 1877.

In January 1878 Walker began his ministry in the Augusta area by serving four congregations simultaneously. Feeling the strain of caring for four congregations, he resigned after two years and assumed the pastorate of First Baptist Church of LaGrange, Georgia, in 1880. However, his national fame began to spread when he assumed the pastorate of the Tabernacle Baptist Church in Augusta in 1883. While serving at Tabernacle, Walker became involved with the Georgia Baptist State Convention and became one of the first regional vice presidents of the newly formed National Baptist Convention when it was organized in St. Louis, Missouri, on August 25, 1886.

Walker appeared at churches and in public auditoriums all across the South as preacher and platform speaker, and that was at a time when Jim Crow laws designed to limit the opportunities for black people were in full force. Walker's preaching, and the popularity that flowed from it, defied all of the laws and habits of segregation. When he appeared as a speaker in any Southern city, blacks and whites came out in throngs to hear him. It was not uncommon for him to speak to crowds in excess of eight thousand persons in a civic auditorium or arena.

In 1891 Tabernacle sent Walker on a trip to the Holy Land, an almost unheard of thing for a black preacher to do at that time. As another sign of his popularity and influence, the letters he sent back to Tabernacle from his three months in the Middle East were published every week in the *Augusta Sentinel*, a black community newspaper that he had founded in 1884. Upon his return he was immediately enlisted to enter upon a national speaking tour to share his reflections on "The Holy Land: What I Heard and Saw." That tour took him across the United States. Once again, Walker defied the existing racial policies of the day and openly condemned the segregation and lack of opportunity experienced by black people in America. Those practices seemed more obvious to him after he had traveled outside of the country. As a black man traveling in Europe and Israel he did not face the same prejudices that had surrounded him all of his life in Georgia.

Like Booker T. Washington in his *Atlanta Exposition* address in 1895, Walker warned against the dangers of white immigration. Both were concerned by the ease with which foreign-born

whites could blend into American society and the willingness of white employers to give even the most menial jobs to immigrants rather than blacks who had lived within that community all of their lives.

In June 1898 Walker was appointed by President William McKinley to be an army chaplain to colored troops serving in Cuba after the Spanish-American War. He was elected to be one of the five vice presidents of the International Sunday School Convention, a body representing 23 million believers in the United States, Canada, and South America.

After sixteen years in Augusta, Walker accepted the call to Mt. Olivet Baptist Church of New York City. He had first come to that church's attention when his many speaking tours after his return from the Middle East brought him to New York City. His ministry in New York met with immediate success, with the church growing from four hundred to eighteen hundred members within two years. On one Sunday in April 1899 he had to baptize 187 persons who had joined the church that month. While serving the spiritual needs of his people, he also helped to organize a Young Men's Christian Association (YMCA) inside the Mt. Olivet Baptist Church. That program experienced rapid growth, moved into a building of its own, and became the major YMCA for the black population of New York City.

Walker by no means limited himself to the four walls of the church. On May 27, 1900, he gave an address on patriotism and race relations before an audience of eight thousand people at Carnegie Hall in New York City. Excerpts from that speech were reprinted in newspapers across the country. In that speech Walker continued to challenge the social policies that impacted black people in America. He said, "The Negro is an American citizen. The amendment to the Constitution did not make us men; God made us men before man made us citizens."

At the turn of the twentieth century, Walker was the most prominent and influential black clergyman in America. From his secure and prominent position at Mt. Olivet Baptist Church in New York City, he continued to preach and deliver orations in churches and auditoriums across the country. Beyond the power of his preaching at his home church and across

the country, he was visible on the lecture circuit. He was regularly quoted in the national news media. He was a force within the National Baptist Convention. He also had the ear of many of the most powerful white people in America.

In 1904, to the shock of whites and blacks in New York City, Walker resigned from Mt. Olivet and returned to Tabernacle Baptist Church in Augusta. He remained there for the balance of his ministry, serving a total of forty-five years as pastor of that church. Many white Northerners would take winter vacations in Augusta, and when they did they would attend Tabernacle just to hear Walker. Among those who visited the church were President William Howard Taft and John D. Rockefeller.

Walker became president of the Georgia Baptist State Convention. He also became national treasurer of the National Baptist Convention. From that position he launched an unsuccessful bid for the presidency of the national body in 1910. In 1917 he was part of a committee of black clergy that met with members of the all-white Southern Baptist Convention (SBC) to discuss the possibility of a merger between the two bodies. Those talks proved to be unsuccessful, largely because of the racial climate in America at that time.

Walker's biographer, Silas X. Floyd, offered a moving tribute to his life and character: "The number of those whom he has been instrumental in saving from the jails, chain gangs and penitentiary; those he has had released from imprisonment, whose fines he has paid out of his own pocket; the number whose house rent he has paid, and furnished food, and clothing, and fuel; the number of unhappy husbands he has reconciled to unhappy wives, thereby making both happy again; the young people he has sent to school and has helped to educate; the men and women for whom he has secured employment; those he has brought to Christ by private ministrations; the number he has encouraged and cheered by a kind act or a word fitly spoken; the number he has helped and inspired in one way and another will reach far into the thousands. The number cannot be known."

Walker died in Augusta in 1921 at the age of sixty-three.

Silas X. Floyd, *Life of Charles T. Walker, D.D.;* J. D. Gallop, "Walker Was Born a Slave," *Augusta Chronicle* online, June 21, 1996; Joseph H. Jackson, *A Story of Christian Activism;* Carter G. Woodson, *History of the Negro Church.*

Wright, Jeremiah A., Jr.

(1941-) Very rarely does a preacher come along who is almost universally identified with one classic sermon. When you think of the sermon "The Sun Do Move," you think at once of **John Jasper.** When you think of "The Eagle Stirreth Her Nest," **Clarence LaVaughn (C. L.) Franklin** comes to mind. If the name B. W. Smith is mentioned, the sermon "Watch Them Dogs" is likely to be mentioned as well. So it is with the sermon "What Makes You So Strong?" by Jeremiah A. Wright Jr. The message and the messenger are inseparably wed.

Jeremiah Wright was born in Philadelphia, Pennsylvania, in 1941; his father, Jeremiah A. Wright Sr., was the pastor of Grace Baptist Church in the

Germantown section of Philadelphia for forty-two years. Wright earned degrees at Virginia Union University, Howard University, and the University of Chicago. He also earned a doctor of ministry degree from United Theological Seminary in Dayton, Ohio.

Following a stint in the United States Marine Corps, Wright entered the ministry and has been an active preacher since 1959. He is in his third decade as pastor of Trinity United Church of Christ in Chicago. The church had eighty-five members when he became the pastor. Today the membership is in excess of six thousand persons. However, his preaching ministry has taken him literally "to the uttermost parts of the earth."

As a testimony to his preaching genius, Wright was listed among the top

fifteen black preachers in America in the November 1993 issue of *Ebony.* He is also featured in a video in the Great Preachers series produced by the Odyssey Television Network. That series was based in part on a survey done by Baylor University to identify the most outstanding preachers in the English-speaking world. In addition, Wright sits on the advisory board for *The African American Pulpit,* a quarterly journal that highlights the best preaching being done by African American clergy. His sermons regularly appear in that journal, and he was afforded an interview on his approach to preaching in the spring 1999 issue.

Wright's preaching is noted for its use of Afrocentric themes, a powerful delivery, and a wonderful relevance to issues in the contemporary world. In the 1993 *Ebony* recognition, someone said of his preaching, "A Wright sermon is a four-course meal. It is spiritual, biblical, cultural and prophetic." So attractive has his preaching become, he has to hold four services at Trinity on Saturday night and Sunday to accommodate the crowds that gather to hear him. He is in constant demand across the country at churches, conferences, and college campuses.

Wright is also an accomplished author, having written four books, including *What Makes You So Strong?* (1993), in which his classic sermon appears. That sermon resonates with these questions: "What makes you so strong, black man? How is it that after all this country has done to you, you can still produce a Paul Robeson, a Thurgood Marshall, a Malcolm X (el-Hajj Malik el-Shabazz), a Martin King and a Ron McNair? What makes you so strong, black man?…What makes you so strong, black woman? How is it that after all this world has done to you, after all white women have done to you, after all white men have done to you, after all black men have done to you, you can still produce an Angela Davis, a Toni Morrison, a Barbara Jordan, a Betty Shabazz, an Oprah Winfrey, and a Winnie Mandela? What makes you so strong, black woman?"

The answer to these questions must surely be attributed, at least in part, to the encouraging and equipping sermons of preachers like Jeremiah A. Wright Jr.

Wright is married to Rev. Ramah Wright, and they have four daughters. Dr. Wright has adopted these words as his motto, both for himself and for the church: "Unashamedly Black/Unapologetically Christian!"

"Fifteen Top Black Preachers," *Ebony,* November 1993; Jeremiah A. Wright Jr., *What Makes You So Strong?;* www.tucc.org.   ▣

Teachers and Scholars

☻ Butts, Calvin O., III

(1950-) The tradition of outstanding black preachers being chosen to serve as college and university presidents began with **Daniel A. Payne,** the **African Methodist Episcopal (AME)** bishop who became president of Wilberforce College in 1863. It continues with Calvin O. Butts III, the pastor of the historic Abyssinian Baptist Church of New York City, who was installed as president of the State University of New York at Old Westbury in October 2000. From those two positions in the ecclesiastical and academic communities, Butts is one of the most influential black ministers in the country.

Butts was born in Bridgeport, Connecticut, on July 17, 1950, but he was reared in New York City and apart from his college years has always made that city his home. He graduated from Morehouse College in 1972. He earned a master of divinity degree from Union Theological Seminary in New York City and a doctor of ministry degree from Drew University in Madison, New Jersey.

In 1972 Butts began his ministerial career at Abyssinian as an assistant to **Samuel Dewitt Proctor,** and he was installed as pastor of that church in July

1989. Under his leadership the church has redeveloped housing for seniors and persons of moderate income. Through the Abyssinian Economic Development Corporation that congregation has been instrumental in helping to revive Harlem through the investment of more than $150 million in housing, retail, and commercial development. In that capacity, Butts has continued the legacy of

community involvement and leadership begun by **Adam Clayton Powell Sr.** and **Adam Clayton Powell Jr.**

Butts was among the first persons in the country to see the dangers of the musical genre called gangsta rap. He tried to convince record companies not to produce it, and he also tried to convince parents not to allow their children to purchase or listen to it because of the offensive lyrics. Butts led the Harlem community in painting over the billboards that advertise alcohol and tobacco products that are disproportionately present in minority communities.

For all of his social and economic programs and protests, Butts has always found time to remain involved in the academic world. He has taught at the City College of New York and at Fordham University in the Bronx. He also helped to establish the Thurgood Marshall Academy for Learning and Social Change, a public intermediate and high school in New York City.

Butts has served as president of the Council of Churches of the City of New York and vice chair of the board of directors of United Way of New York City. He has also served as chairman of the board of the Harlem Young Men's Christian Association (YMCA) that had been organized by another black preacher, **Charles Thomas (C. T.) Walker.** Butts has been an outspoken leader in relieving human suffering, whether it involves famine in Africa (through his leadership in AfriCare) or the spread of HIV/AIDS (through his work with the Balm in Gilead black church AIDS organization).

Butts's name has frequently been mentioned in political circles for offices ranging from mayor of New York City to being a possible successor to Charles Rangel in the U.S. House of Representatives. Given the political legacy of Adam Clayton Powell Jr. as pastor of that congregation and as a member of the New York City council and as an eleven-term congressman, the speculation about Butts's political future is not without foundation.

Butts and his family live in New York City. However, the pulpit of Abyssinian Baptist Church and the president's office at Old Westbury College have allowed Butts's influence to be felt and his voice and views to be heard across the country and around the world.

Charles M. Collins, ed., *The African Americans;* "Dr. Calvin O. Butts III: President, SUNY College at Old Westbury," *The Positive Community* 2/3 (March 2001); Eric Pooley, "The Education of Reverend Butts: Will He Become Harlem's Next Great Leader?" *New York,* June 26, 1989.

☻ Cannon, Katie G.

(1950–) This African American woman is credited with a long list of firsts and an equally long list of academic and scholarly achievements. In 1974 Cannon was the first African American woman to be ordained into the ministry of the United Presbyterian Church of the USA. In 1983 she became the first African American woman to earn a doctor of philosophy degree from Union Theological Seminary in New York City. Her degree was awarded in Christian ethics. She received her bachelor of arts degree from Barber Scotia College in North Carolina and a master of divinity degree from Johnson C. Smith School of Religion at the **Inter-**

denominational Theological Center (ITC) in Atlanta, Georgia.

Cannon was born in 1950 and was reared in Kannapolis, North Carolina. She experienced the Jim Crow oppression of the South, where racial segregation in every area of life was the order of the day. Her life story forms the opening portrait in Sarah Lawrence-Lightfoot's *I've Known Rivers: Lives of Loss and Liberation.*

Cannon's teaching career took her first to the Episcopal Theological Seminary in Cambridge, Massachusetts. She then taught at Temple University in Philadelphia, Pennsylvania. She now teaches at the School of Theology at Virginia Union University in Richmond. She is the author of two books, *Black Womanist Ethics* (1988) and *Katie's Canon: Womanism and the Soul of the Black Community* (1995). Her edited volumes include *God's Fierce Whimsy: The Implications of Feminism for Theological Education* (1985), *Inheriting Our Mother's Gardens: Feminist Theology in Third-World Perspective* (1988), and *Interpretation for Liberation* (1989).

Cannon's most notable contribution is her development of a theological perspective she calls **womanist theology** or womanism. Womanism as a social and political construct seeks to critique traditional feminism, pointing out the ways that the dual struggles of being black and female and being black, female, and poor in America have not been addressed by feminist thinkers, most of whom have reflected on feminist issues from the position of white privilege. Womanist scholars seek to reflect upon issues of oppression while using the experience of black women as the point of departure.

Womanism seeks to offer a perspective from which the interrelated issues of oppression based upon race, gender, and class can be viewed. It also wonders how so much of earlier Protestant theology managed not to make these connections any sooner. Thus womanist theology offers a sharp critique of racism within the ranks of feminism and an equally sharp critique of sexism within the black church, **black theology,** and the **civil rights movement.**

Katie Cannon, *Katie's Canon: Womanism and the Soul of the Black Community;* Jacqueline Grant, "Womanist Theology: Black Women's Experience as a Source for Doing Theology with Special Reference to Christology," *The Journal of the Interdenominational Theological Center* 13 (spring 1986); C. Eric Lincoln and Lawrence H. Mamiya, *The Black Church in the African American Experience.*

⊙ Chavis, John

(1763-1838) This Presbyterian clergyman and teacher was born free in 1763 in Granville, North Carolina, and attended the College of New Jersey, now Princeton University, as a private student of John Witherspoon, the college president and a signer of the Declaration of Independence. It is believed that Chavis's going to Princeton was an experiment to see "if a Negro could take a collegiate education." Witherspoon responded, "The experiment would issue favorably."

Chavis later attended Washington Academy, now Washington and Lee University, in Lexington, Virginia, after which he launched an extraordinary career as a teacher and preacher. He was licensed to preach by the Lexington Presbytery on November 19, 1800, and assigned to be a riding missionary to free blacks and slaves whose owners would allow them to hear a black preacher.

From 1801 to 1831, Chavis carried on a productive ministry, preaching to white and black congregations and offering educational opportunities to black and white students in separate sessions. He opened four schools offering a classical education that reflected what he had learned at Princeton. Those schools were located in Granville, Wake, Chatham, and Orange counties in North Carolina.

Chavis's schools were considered the best preparatory academies in the state, attracting large numbers of white students from leading families. They were drawn there largely because knowledge of Greek and Latin was needed to gain college admission in those days, and Chavis provided that training. Among the white students who attended his schools were W. P. Mangum, who went on to become a U.S. senator from North Carolina, and Charles Manly, who went on to become governor of North Carolina.

Chavis's schools offered the same curriculum to white students in day sessions and one hour later to black students, who remained with him until 10 p.m. He was aided in his desire to provide education to slaves and free blacks by the apprenticeship system in North Carolina that required that all apprentices be able to read and write. Many slaves in that state became literate because of that single provision in the law.

The course of Chavis's life changed dramatically in 1831. As a result of the **Nat Turner** rebellion in Virginia, North Carolina and all the other slave-holding states imposed several restrictions meant to prevent rebellions. A law was passed that forbade free blacks from preaching to slaves. That put severe limits on Chavis's ministry as a riding missionary. Over time, offering education to free blacks was resisted, because the presence of educated free blacks in the midst of a slaveholding society was deemed as too volatile. Thus Chavis seemed to be on the verge of losing yet another outlet for his aspirations to provide education to his own free people.

It did not seem to matter to slaveholders that Chavis openly and regularly spoke against slave rebellions, urged slaves to continue to serve their masters after the Turner rebellion, and even spoke against the value of emancipation within the foreseeable future. In an April 1836 letter he wrote: "That slavery is a national evil no one doubts, but what is to be done.... All that can be done, is to make the best of a bad bargain. For I am clearly of the opinion that immediate emancipation would be to entail the greatest earthly curse upon my brethren.... I suppose if they knew I said this they would be ready to take my life, but as I wish them well, I feel no disposition to see them any more miserable than they are."

Chavis persisted in his work as a preacher and a teacher. He continued to preach to mostly white Presbyterian congregations in North Carolina. He also continued to provide education to white and free black students. By 1850, more than 40 percent of free adult blacks in the areas where his schools were located had become literate, largely as a result of his efforts. He died in 1838.

Lavinia Dobler and Edgar A. Toppin, *Pioneers and Patriots;* Milton C. Sernett, ed., *African American Religious History;* Carter G. Woodson, *The History of the Negro Church.*

☻ Cone, James H.

(1940–) Born in Fordyce, Arkansas, in 1940 and reared within the segregated conditions of nearby Bearden, Cone drew from the experiences of his lifelong struggle with white racism to fashion the arguments for what came to be called **black theology.**

Cone attended Philander Smith College in Little Rock, Arkansas, and was in that city during the tumultuous efforts to integrate Central High School in 1957. He earned his doctor of philosophy degree in systematic theology from Garrett/Northwestern University in 1963. His struggle to do so is detailed in the autobiographically styled *My Soul Looks Back.*

Cone's academic career began at Philander Smith, and then he taught at Adrian College in Michigan. Since 1969 he has taught theology at the Union Theological Seminary in New York City. He is now the Charles Briggs Distinguished Professor of Systematic Theology. At Union he laid out the arguments and created much of the bibliography for black theology, beginning with *Black Theology and Black Power, A Black Theology of Liberation,* and *God of the Oppressed.*

Cone's motivation for fashioning a black theology was to challenge the kind

of theology taught by white colleagues who seemed oblivious to the realities of racism and black suffering. He was astounded to discover and determined to point out that even the most noted theologians and ethicists of the twentieth century made little if any reference to the history of black slavery or the continuing problem of white racism. He could not understand how the tumultuous events of the civil rights and black power movements could be going on during that time, yet white theologians and Bible scholars felt no obligation to give theological expression to those events.

However, all of Cone's concern was not focused on what white scholars were saying or doing. He also wanted to build upon and add further theological substance to the claims being made by another black scholar, Joseph Washington,

in *Black Religion* and *The Politics of God.* Cone also wrote about the influence of **Albert Cleage,** who had earlier introduced the concept of the black Messiah, an understanding of Jesus as sympathetic to matters of oppression. Thus Christian theology had to be made relevant to the oppression of blacks in America.

Although they met with initial disapproval in white and black church circles, the theological arguments put forward by Cone became widely affirmed and resulted in a lecture schedule that has taken him all over the world and that has seen his books translated into Dutch, German, and Japanese.

Cone did not limit his work to issues of black theology. He joined Miles Mark Fisher, **Benjamin Elijah Mays,** John Lovell, Michael Harris, Bernice Johnson Reagon, and others in studying the theological themes found in the spirituals and slave songs. His work went beyond the other works mentioned here, in that he also sought to link the study of spirituals to the message of the blues in *The Spirituals and the Blues.*

Cone was initially uneasy about the idea of studying and teaching theology while other black people were in the streets fighting against the segregation he had experienced in Arkansas. He soon came to see his role as a theologian who could shake the foundations of the white church as having as much value as anything going on in demonstrations and mass movements. Cone also made a tremendous contribution to the discussion of the leaders and lessons of the civil rights era with *Martin and Malcolm and America.*

The work of Cone paved the way for such subsequent liberation theology formulations fashioned by Latin Americans, Asians, feminists, and womanists. Cone was the driving force in an approach to thinking theologically that is now taught and practiced around the world. The German theologian Jürgen Moltmann offered a ringing endorsement of Cone's theological position when he said, "Only liberation theology is for me a theology which radically focuses on Christian hope, as it has been proposed in this country by James H. Cone" (October 17, 1971, in New York City).

James H. Cone, *My Soul Looks Back, For My People, God of the Oppressed, A Black Theology of Liberation, The Spirituals and the Blues, Martin and Malcolm and America; Black Faith and Public Talk: Critical Essays on James H. Cone's Black Theology and Black Power,* Dwight N. Hopkins, ed.; Henry J. Young, *Major Black Religious Leaders Since 1940.*

☯ Du Bois, William Edward Burghardt (W. E. B.)

(1868–1963) One of the most important essays ever written about the religious life of black people in the rural South is "Of the Faith of the Fathers," in *The Souls of Black Folk* (1903) by W. E. B. Du Bois. Of his first experience of a revival meeting in which the zeal of the worshipers seemed fully unleashed, Du Bois said, "Those who have not thus witnessed the frenzy of a Negro revival in the untouched backwoods of the South can but dimly realize the religious feeling of the slave; as described, such scenes appear grotesque and funny, but as seen they are awful. Three things characterized this religion of the slave,—the preacher, the music and the frenzy."

Du Bois was not accustomed to the religious fervor of black people in the rural South. He was born in Great Barrington, Massachusetts, on February 23, 1868. He earned a bachelor of arts degree in 1888 from Fisk University in Nashville, Tennessee. He earned a second bachelor of arts degree from Harvard University, and in 1895 he became the first black person to earn a doctor of philosophy degree from Harvard. Du Bois also studied economics and history at the University of Berlin from 1892 to 1894. He taught at Fisk, Wilberforce, and the University of Pennsylvania between 1894 and 1897. From 1897 to 1910 he taught at Atlanta University. He quickly began his career as the preeminent black social scientist of the twentieth century with the publication of *The Suppression of the Slave Trade* (1896), *The Philadelphia Negro* (1899), and *The Souls of Black Folk.*

Du Bois stood in sharp contrast to Booker T. Washington on how the uplift of the black race should occur. Washington believed in emphasizing industrial education and other programs that equipped the masses of black people to become self-sufficient through manual and domestic labor. Du Bois, however, was the architect of the "talented tenth" philosophy. By that he meant that an elite group of blacks should be trained in the liberal arts and prepared for the professions. Their example of success and accomplishment would then gradually inspire other blacks to higher levels of aspiration and achievement.

In 1905 Du Bois convened a group called the Niagara Movement, which sought to address the escalating instances of blacks being lynched by white mobs across the country. That movement resulted in Du Bois being one of the nine founding members of the National Association for the Advancement of Colored People (NAACP) in 1909. He retired from teaching to work for the NAACP and to become the editor of its journal, *Crisis*. He served in that role from 1910 to 1934.

Du Bois is most famous for two observations he made in *The Souls of Black Folk* about race relations in the United States and around the world. In "Of Our Spiritual Strivings," Du Bois observed, "It is a peculiar sensation, this double-consciousness, this sense of always looking at one's self through the eyes of others, of measuring one's soul by the tape of a world that looks on in amused contempt and pity. One ever feels his two-ness,—an American, a Negro; two souls, two thoughts, two unreconciled strivings; two warring ideals in one dark body, whose dogged strength alone keeps it from being torn asunder." In "Of the Dawn of Freedom," Du Bois makes his other profound and prophetic observation: "The problem of the twentieth century is the problem of the color-line,— the relation of the darker to the lighter races of men in Asia and Africa, in America and the islands of the sea."

Although he was primarily a social scientist, Du Bois made several keen observations concerning the black church. "Of the Faith of the Fathers" is a valuable discussion of the components of black church life at the turn of the twentieth century and on the unique leadership role of the preacher within the black community. Du Bois referred to the preacher as

"the most unique personality developed by the Negro on American soil" and describes the preacher this way: "He early appeared on the plantation and found his function as the healer of the sick, the interpreter of the Unknown, the comforter of the sorrowing, the supernatural avenger of wrong, and the one who rudely but picturesquely expressed the longing, disappointment, and resentment of a stolen and oppressed people. Thus as bard, physician, judge, and priest, within the narrow limits allowed by the slave system, rose the Negro preacher, and under him the first Afro-American institution, the Negro church."

Du Bois was not above criticizing black preachers. In the 1898 commencement address at Fisk he said, "What we need is not more but fewer ministers, but in that lesser number we certainly need earnest, broad and cultured men; men who do a good deal more than they say." He continued: "The severest charge that can be brought against the Christian education of the Negro in the South during the last thirty years is the reckless way in which sap-headed young fellows, without ability, and in some cases without character have been urged into the ministry. It is time now to halt. It is time to say to young men like you: qualifications that would be of no service elsewhere are not needed in the church."

Among the more than twenty books written or edited by Du Bois is a collection of prayers written between 1909 and 1910, *Prayers of Darker People*. That book was released in 1961 after Du Bois took up official residence in Accra, Ghana, becoming a citizen of that country. That was a fitting act for a man who helped to develop the concept of Pan-Africanism. In that year he officially joined the Communist Party. Du Bois died on August 27, 1963, the same date as the March on Washington when **Martin Luther King Jr.** delivered his "I Have a Dream" speech. The death of Du Bois was announced only moments before the march got under way.

W. E. B. Du Bois, *The Souls of Black Folk;* Philip Foner, ed., *W. E. B. Du Bois Speaks;* Robert Michael Franklin, *Liberating Visions;* David Levering Lewis, *W. E. B. Du Bois;* Elliott Rudwick, "W. E. B. Du Bois," in *Black Leaders of the Twentieth Century,* ed. John Hope Franklin and August Meier.

◉ Dyson, Michael Eric

(1958–) Born October 23, 1958, this self-described "ghetto kid from the inner city of Detroit, Michigan," has become one of the leading black intellectuals in the world. Along with Henry Louis Gates, Stephen Carter, **Cornel West,** bell hooks, and Robin Kelly, Dyson bears the unique title of being a public intellectual. Simply stated, that means that his teaching is by no means limited to his books and classroom lectures. Instead, his insights and reflections are regularly presented on the college and university lecture circuit, on radio and television, and on the pages of newspapers and magazines across the country.

Dyson is an ordained Baptist minister who served several churches in the vicinity of Knoxville, Tennessee, in the 1980s.

His ministry met with some early disappointments when he was locked out of his church when he attempted to add women to the board of deacons at his church, a position that had previously been viewed as for men only. He also began his studies at Knoxville College after attending the prestigious Cranbrook School on a scholarship. He transferred to and graduated from Carson-Newman College in Tennessee. He then earned his master of arts and doctor of philosophy degrees from Princeton University. His life has been a blend of his convictions as a Baptist preacher and the oratorical style that is a part of that world and the rigorous intellectual scrutiny he brings to the issues about which he is speaking or writing.

Dyson's teaching has taken him to many of the most prestigious colleges and universities in the country. He has taught at Chicago Theological Seminary, Brown University, the University of North Carolina at Chapel Hill, Columbia University, and DePaul University in Chicago, Illinois. He presently serves as the Avalon Foundation Professor of Humanies and professor of religious studies and Afro-American studies at the University of Pennsylvania.

Dyson's writings as a cultural critic have appeared in such newspapers as the *New York Times,* the *Los Angeles Times, USA Today,* the *Chicago Tribune,* and the *Washington Post.* As a demonstration of the breadth of his interests and of his audience, his writings have also appeared in magazines that are as diverse in their content as they are in their audience. They include *The New Yorker, VIBE* (a magazine for the largely black and urban hip-hop generation), and

Rolling Stone (a standard periodical looking at the cultural scene in America).

As a result of these writings and his regular appearances on such television shows as *Nightline, The Charlie Rose Show, Oprah, Good Morning, America,* and many others, Dyson has become one of the most visible and in some respects one of the most controversial people in America. He is sometimes called "the hip-hop intellectual" or "the street fighter in suit and tie." *Time* has said, "In his prose one hears the fervor of a Sunday sermon; in his ideas one sees the analytical scrupulousness of a man who knows a thing or two about tenure committees." *The Village Voice* says, "Dyson possesses an irresistible preacher's cadence and a cast iron memory. He effortlessly fills academic speak with urban hip-isms." *The Chronicle of Higher Education* adds, "He can rivet classroom and chapel alike with his oratory!"

Dyson's ideas continue to flow from the steady stream of critically acclaimed books he has written. They include *Reflecting Black African-American Cultural Criticism* (1993), *Making Malcolm: The Myth and Meaning of Malcolm X* (1994), *Beyond God and Gangsta Rap: Bearing Witness to Black Culture* (1996), and *Race Rules: Navigating the Color Line* (1996). Perhaps his most controversial book is *I May Not Get There with You: The True Martin Luther King Jr.* That book was nominated for a National Association for the Advancement of Colored People (NAACP) Image Award in the nonfiction category in 2001. Dyson's most recent book, *Holler If You Hear Me: Searching for Tupac Shakur,* is a national bestseller, nominated by the American

Library Association as one of the best books for young adults.

Africana.com; www.chfestival.org/november/ events/SpeakerDetail.cfm; http://events.ucsc.edu/ mlk99/keynote.html; http//mlk.emich.edu/mlk/ dyson.htm; Michael Eric Dyson, *Beyond God and Gangsta Rap.*

◉ Felder, Cain Hope

(1945–) Largely as a result of the power and effect of his first book, *Troubling Biblical Waters* (1989), which is now in its thirteenth printing, Cain Hope Felder has become the leader of a steadily growing community of black biblical scholars who are redefining the relationship between **African Americans and the Bible.** He further strengthened his leadership role in that effort by collaborating with ten other black biblical scholars and editing a collection of their essays under the title *Stony the Road We Trod: African American Biblical Interpretation* (1991).

Felder has devoted his considerable training and talent to the study of the Bible after being the beneficiary of an extraordinary education. Born in 1945, this native of Aiken, South Carolina, grew up in Boston, Massachusetts. After graduating from the prestigious Boston Latin School in 1962, he earned a B.A. from Howard University in classics in 1966. His theological training included a diploma of theology from Oxford University in England in 1968, an M.Div. from Union Theological Seminary in New York City in 1969, a master of philosophy from Columbia in 1978, and a Ph.D. in biblical languages from Columbia University/ Union Theological Seminary in 1982.

From 1977 to 1981, Felder taught Bible at Princeton Theological Seminary. In 1981 he moved on to Howard University Divinity School in Washington, D.C., where he continues to serve as professor of New Testament language and literature. He also serves as editor of the *Journal of Religious Thought,* the official organ of that divinity school.

Prior to his emergence as a biblical scholar, Cain Hope Felder served in various capacities within the United Methodist Church. From 1975 to 1977, while pursuing his doctoral studies, he served as pastor of Grace United Methodist Church in New York City. From 1969 to 1972, he served as the first national director of the United Methodist Black Caucus. In addition to his work at Howard, Felder also

serves as the founder of the Biblical Institute for Social Change, which he organized in 1990. Through this agency, which now has affiliates in several major cities across the country, Felder has been able to extend interest in his research areas beyond the life of the academic community and into local churches and community-based groups.

Several questions have been brought to the forefront of biblical and theological studies as a result of the work done by Felder and his colleagues. One of the foremost questions involves the black presence in the Bible, ranging from the Queen of Sheba in 1 Kings 10 to the Ethiopian eunuch in Acts 8 and the African leaders of the church at Antioch in Acts 13.

Another of Felder's concerns involves reestablishing the central role that Egypt and Ethiopia played both in biblical and in Christian history, noting that most white biblical scholars have either ignored or denigrated that issue. Finally, Felder has discussed the various ways in which biblical materials are interpreted and applied within the black church, especially in the content of preaching and in the lyrics of the Negro spirituals. In his book *Africentric Christianity,* **J. Deotis Roberts** devotes considerable attention to the work of Cain Hope Felder in the fascinating area of canon formation, a matter that Felder himself discusses in *Troubling Biblical Waters.* Felder argues that even the decision of which books would be included in the Bible was influenced by what he calls "historical relativism and cultural subjectivity."

The influence and insights of Cain Hope Felder have not been limited to the classroom, the lecture circuit, or the printed page. He has had a substantial impact through the reach and power of television. He has been a frequent guest on national television talk shows. Of even greater importance, however, was his role as a consultant for two made-for-TV movies: *The Second Coming* and *Solomon and Sheba.* In both instances, his task was to make sure that the films were historically realistic through the selection of people of color to appear in the title roles or as other lead characters. He is also featured along with the well-known evangelical Tony Campolo in a video entitled *Lift Every Voice: The Bible in an Age of Diversity.*

In addition to the two books dealing with African American biblical interpretation, Felder was the editor of *The Original African Heritage Study Bible* (1993). This unique Bible serves as a walking tour of the black presence in the Bible and of the role of Africa in the Old and New Testament books. This is accomplished through maps of the biblical world that include both Egypt and Ethiopia. The study Bible also includes photographs that suggest how many biblical characters may have looked; a listing of proper names that are of African lineage; and highlighted biblical passages that make reference to an African presence in that particular portion of Scripture.

The Heritage Bible was followed by *The African Heritage Jubilee Bible,* which is targeted for a younger audience of readers and students. Felder is also the author of *The Season of Lent: Proclamation Commentary 5* (1995), *The International Catholic Bible Commentary on the Epistle of James* (1998) and *The Mercy of God in Luke–Acts* (1998).

Cain Hope Felder is married to Dr. Jewell Richardson Felder, a native of Mobile, Alabama, and they have one surviving child, Akidah.

Cain Hope Felder, *Troubling Biblical Waters and Stony the Road We Trod;* J. Deotis Roberts, *Africentric Christianity.*

☉ Frazier, E. Franklin

(1894–1962) Frazier was one of the most distinguished sociologists of the twentieth century and is most famous for *The Black Bourgeoisie* (1957), which was a scathing attack on the ways in which the emerging black middle class was cut off from and unhelpful to the struggling black underclass in America. He carried that sociological approach into the study of black religion in *The Negro Church in America* (1964). That book grew out of the Frazer Lecture, which he delivered at the University of Liverpool, England, in 1953.

Frazier was born in Baltimore, Maryland, on September 24, 1894. He earned a bachelor of arts degree from Howard University in 1916 and a doctor of philosophy degree from the University of Chicago in 1931. He spent twenty-five years in the sociology department at Howard. In 1948 he was chosen by his peers across the country to be president of the American Sociological Society. He was awarded Guggenheim Fellowships in 1940 and 1941, using them to study in Brazil and the West Indies. Among his other writings were *The Negro Family in the United States, E. Franklin Frazier on Race Relations* (posthumous), and *The Negro in the United States.*

In *The Negro Church in America* Frazier coined two terms that have served to distinguish the various types of black religious experience. One term is the **"invisible institution,"** which describes the religious practices of slaves in the South when they gathered away from the oversight of their masters and overseers. The other term is the "institutional church," which refers to the black denominations that emerged in the nineteenth century, including the **African Methodist Episcopal (AME), African Methodist Episcopal Zion (AME Zion), and Colored (Christian) Methodist Episcopal (CME).**

Frazier also claims that as a result of slavery, blacks in the United States had lost all sense of their African history and heritage and were assimilated into the religious life of the white majority. That assimilation was less a matter of faith and more a matter of social control. He doubts that any of the religious practices that may have been performed in Africa had survived intact after Middle Passage, the auction block, and the breaking-in period of chattel slavery. This is a point with which he and **W. E. B. Du Bois** were in disagreement. Anthropologist Melville Herskovits also argued against this view, believing that authentic African religious practices were still being preserved in places where a substantial black majority could be found.

Frazier discusses the developments that occurred when black people migrated from the South in massive numbers and settled in the urban centers of the North. He sees the same loss of cultural memory occurring as happened when blacks were brought from Africa to slavery in America. He describes the rise of cultic groups like the black Jews under Prophet Cherry and black Islamic groups under **Noble Drew Ali.** However, as dangerous as the possibility of Southern blacks converting to one of those **cults** was the concern that blacks from the South would become assimilated into the secular culture of the urban North. Frazier predicted that as racial segregation comes to an end, so too will end the strong leadership role the church had played for so long within the black communities of America.

Frazier died in May 1962. In 1973 **C. Eric Lincoln** published *The Negro Church Since Frazier* as a way of seeing whether the things that Frazier had envisioned in 1953 had occurred.

E. Franklin Frazier, *The Black Bourgeoisie and The Negro Church in America;* C. Eric Lincoln, *The Negro Church Since Frazier.*

☺ Johnson, Mordecai Wyatt

(1890–1976) One of the most prestigious positions available to a black person for most of the twentieth century was that of president of one of the historically black colleges and universities. **Benjamin Elijah Mays, Samuel Dewitt Proctor,** and Johnetta Coleman contributed mightily to the luster of that position. However, no one was more responsible for making that position as respected and influential as it was than Rev. Mordecai Wyatt Johnson.

Johnson, the only child of a Baptist preacher and his wife, was born in Paris, Tennessee, on January 12, 1890. He graduated from Morehouse College in 1911. He then earned a bachelor of arts degree from the University of Chicago in 1913, a bachelor of divinity degree from Rochester Theological Seminary in 1916, and a master of sacred theology from Harvard in 1922. He would be awarded a doctor of divinity degree from Gammon Theological Seminary in Atlanta in 1928.

Johnson began his career as a teacher of economics and history at Morehouse College. He then went on to a successful pastorate in Charleston, West Virginia. However, history was made in 1926, when he was named the first black president of Howard University in Washington, D.C. For the next thirty-four years he not only redesigned the role of a black college president but also changed the quality of education offered by Howard.

When Johnson began, Howard received an annual appropriation from the federal government of $218,000. When he retired in 1960, that amount had been increased to $6 million annually. With that added revenue Johnson tripled the size of the faculty and doubled faculty salaries. As a result of building programs, in 1960 the buildings and grounds were valued at $34 million.

Part of Johnson's success was his ability to attract top scholars to come to Howard during his tenure. He hired **Benjamin E. Mays** to be dean of the School of Religion. Charles Hamilton Houston became dean of the law school. **E. Franklin Frazier** became the chair of the department of sociology. The Freedmen's Hospital was also responsible for training half of the black doctors and

dentists being graduated each year. Howard University became one of the great intellectual centers of the nation. In 1929 Johnson was honored by the National Association for the Advancement of Colored People (NAACP) when it conferred on him the Spingarn Medal for outstanding service to the nation.

As a clergyman, Johnson felt a particular obligation to provide the best possible training for those seeking careers in ministry. In his inaugural address at Howard on June 10, 1927, he said, "There are forty-seven thousand Negro churches in the United States and there are in the whole country today less than sixty college graduates getting ready to fill these pulpits." At the same time, he acknowledged the importance of the work of those black churches: "There is no organization and no combination of organizations now at work in the black community which can, at this stage in the history of the Negro race, begin to compare with the fundamental importance of the Negro church." For that reason Johnson made certain that Howard would be a place where leaders for the black church could be trained.

Johnson's career was the example of excellence that he sought to pass on to students for the ministry. In *Ebony* (1954) he was listed as one of the nation's top ten black preachers.

Johnson died in 1976.

Russell L. Adams, ed., *Great Negroes Past and Present;* Robert H. Brisbane, *The Black Vanguard;* W. Augustus Low and Virgil A. Clift, eds., *The Encyclopedia of Black America;* Harry A. Ploski and Ernest Kaiser, eds. and comps., *The Negro Almanac;* Henry J. Young, *Major Black Religious Leaders Since 1940.*

☉ Jones, Lawrence N.

(1921–) Few people have had a more direct impact on the theological and personal development of young people pursuing church-related careers than Lawrence N. Jones. Known affectionately as "the Dean," Jones served as dean of the chapel at Fisk University in Nashville, Tennessee, from 1960 until 1964. He was dean of students and later dean of the faculty at Union Theological Seminary in New York City from 1965 until 1975. Finally, he was the dean of the Howard University Divinity School in Washington, D.C., from 1975 until his retirement in 1991. While he was an insightful and demanding professor, Jones was more than a teacher to his students. He was a friend and a confidante, a father figure for many, and a marriage counselor for many others.

Lawrence N. Jones was born in Moundsville, West Virginia, on April 24, 1921. He graduated from West Virginia State University in 1942 and earned an M.A. from the University of Chicago in 1948. He served in various capacities in the United States Army from 1943 until 1946, and, continuing on active duty until 1953, he taught Military Science at Virginia State College. From 1951 to 1953, he served in Germany.

Finally acknowledging a call to ministry that had first wrestled for his attention during his collegiate years, Jones enrolled at Oberlin Graduate School of Theology (Ohio) in 1953, earning a bachelor of divinity degree in 1956. While completing requirements for that degree, Jones was also beginning work on a Ph.D. at Yale University with an eye toward becoming a university chaplain. His academic work at Yale was interrupted by a two-year assignment on the staff of the Middle Atlantic region of the Student Christian Movement. There he served the needs of campus ministries in Maryland, Pennsylvania, Delaware, West Virginia, and the District of Columbia. Then it was back to Yale where he eventually earned his doctoral degree in 1960.

While working on his dissertation, Jones was invited to become dean of the chapel at Fisk University, effective September of 1960. That brought him into the heart of the emerging student-led phase of the **civil rights movement**. It was at Fisk that many of the students who participated in the sit-ins were enrolled. **James Lawson, John Lewis, Kelly Miller Smith,** and many other notables were in Nashville at that exciting time in American history. As dean of the chapel at Fisk, one of the most prominent historically black universities in the country, Jones played a crucial role in support of the students, their anxious families, and the continuing mission of the university.

In 1965, at the request of Union president John Bennett, Jones left Fisk to accept the position of dean of students at Union Theological Seminary in New York City. He was the first black member of that distinguished theological faculty, which would later be augmented by such other notable black scholars as **James Cone, C. Eric Lincoln, James Forbes,** and **Cornel West.** By 1970, Jones had become a full professor, occupied an endowed chair, and was appointed The William E. Dodge Professor of Applied Christianity. For a brief time in 1970, Jones served as interim president of Union Theological Seminary, and from 1971 until 1973 he served as the dean of the faculty. While in New York City, he was also active with the **Congress of National Black Churches (CNBC)** and the famous Schomburg Collection of the New York Public Library.

In 1975 Jones went to become dean of the faculty of the then-beleaguered Howard University School of Religion. During his tenure in that position, he increased enrollment, upgraded the quality of the faculty, led in the move of the school into a new facility in 1985, oversaw an expansion of the holdings of the library, and saw the designation of the school changed in 1982 to the Howard University Divinity School. Jones was also active with the Association for Theological Schools, the accrediting agency for most seminaries in North America, and was a founding member of the Society for the Study of Black Religion.

While Jones was raised in the **African Methodist Episcopal (AME) Church,** he was ordained in 1956 in the Evangelical and Reformed Church, which later became part of the United Church of Christ (UCC). Jones was active within his denomination, serving as pastor of a church in West Salem, Ohio, during his student years at Oberlin. He also served on three occasions as an interim pastor of congregations in New York City and Washington, D.C. In addition he served on the United Church of Christ Board for World Ministries. He coedited *Outreach and Diversity* (2000), which is volume five of a seven-volume series called *Living Theological Heritage of the UCC.* He has been a frequent speaker and workshop leader in UCC churches across the country for more than thirty years.

While most noted as an administrator, Jones made another valuable contribution as a scholar in his many journal articles. One of the most noteworthy is "They Sought a City: The Black Church and Churchmen in the Nineteenth Century." It first appeared in the *Union Seminary Quarterly Review* in the spring of 1971. It later became the first article in *The Black Experience in Religion* (1974), edited by C. Eric Lincoln. Equally seminal is his article, "The Black Churches: A New Agenda," in *Christian Century* in April 1979. That article was reprinted in the second edition of *African American Religious History: A Documentary Witness.* Jones also served on the National Advisory Board for *Eyes on the Prize: The Television History of the Civil Rights Years: 1954–1965.*

Married in 1945, Lawrence Jones and his wife, Mary Ellen (Cooley), have two children, Mary Lynn and Rodney. Jones retired from Howard University Divinity School in 1991, and he and his wife continue to live in Silver Spring, Maryland.

Michael A. Battle, *Voices of Experience: Twentieth Century Prophets Speak;* Lawrence N. Jones, "They Sought a City: The Black Church and Churchman in the Nineteenth Century," in *The Black Church Experience,* ed. C. Eric Lincoln; Lawrence N. Jones, "The Black Churches: A New Agenda," in *African American Religious History: A Documentary Witness,* 2d ed., ed. Milton C. Sernett.

Lincoln, Charles Eric

(1924–2000) Born in 1924 in Athens, Alabama, Lincoln wrote twenty-two books that deal with various aspects of the black experience in the United States; special attention is given to the religious life of black Americans. His two most notable books are *The Black Muslims in America* (1961) and *The Black Church in the African-American Experience,* coauthored by Lawrence W. Mamiya (1990). *The Black Church Since Frazier* was an attempt to discuss how the black church has evolved since the classic study, *The Negro Church in America,* done by **E. Franklin Frazier** in 1957.

Lincoln graduated from LeMoyne College in Memphis, Tennessee, in 1947. He completed a master of arts degree at Fisk University (1954), a bachelor of divinity degree at the University of Chicago (1956), and a doctor of philosophy degree in the sociology of religion at Boston University (1960). His teaching career includes work at Fisk University, Union Theological Seminary of New York City, and Duke University, from which he retired in 1993.

Lincoln coined the phrase "Black Muslims" in his 1961 book, which was the first scholarly study of the origins and inner workings of the **Nation of Islam** and its founder, **Elijah Muhammad.** That book reflected work done as part of his doctoral dissertation. A study of an Islamic group was natural for Lincoln, because while he was a United Methodist, his academic interest included all of the religious expressions present within the black community in the twentieth century.

Lincoln's other great contribution to the study of black religion came in his role as general editor of the C. Eric Lincoln Series on Black Religion. That series included *Dark Salvation* by Harry V. Richardson, *Is God a White Racist?* by William R. Jones, *Soul-Force* by Leonard Garrett, *Black Religion and Black Radicalism* by Gayraud S. Wilmore, *Black Sects and Cults* by Joseph R. Washington Jr., *Black Preaching* by Henry Mitchell, *In the Name of Elijah Muhammad: Louis Farrakhan and the Nation of Islam* by Mattias Gardell, and *A Black Theology of Liberation* by James H. Cone.

Lincoln died in 2000.

W. Augustus Low and Virgil A. Clift, eds., *Encyclopedia of Black America;* Henry J. Young, *Major Black Religious Leaders Since 1940.*

Mays, Benjamin Elijah

(1894–1984) Born to former slaves on August 1, 1894, in Ninety-Six, South Carolina, Mays's early life was defined by the return of rigid segregation as a result of the *Plessy v. Ferguson* decision of the U.S. Supreme Court (1896). That decision was followed by the disenfranchisement of blacks, the rise of Ku Klux Klan violence, and the suppression of the dreams and aspirations of black people. Mays was reared on a sharecropper's plantation in Greenwood County, South Carolina, where he planted and picked cotton most of his youth.

Mays devoted his life to achievement in the face of those harsh realities. He eventually earned a bachelor of arts degree from Bates College in Lewiston, Maine, and was elected to Phi Beta Kappa. He also earned his master of arts (1925) and doctor of philosophy (1935) degrees from the University of Chicago.

In 1921 Mays was hired to teach mathematics at Morehouse College in Atlanta, Georgia, where he remained for three years. He taught English for one year at South Carolina State College at Orangeburg in 1925. From 1926 to 1928 he worked for the National Urban League in Tampa, Florida. He spent six years working for the national Young Men's Christian Association (YMCA) headquartered in Atlanta.

During that period, Mays co-authored with Joseph W. Nicholson *The Negro's Church.* This proved to be the most comprehensive study of the black church yet written. It was based on information from 609 urban churches in twelve cities, northern and southern, and 185 rural churches in four southern counties. That study concluded that five factors gave rise to black churches and three characteristics defined their appeal to black people. The five factors that contributed to their emergence were growing racial consciousness, individual initiative, divisions and withdrawals, migration, and missions of other churches. The three

traits that marked the appeal of black churches were pride of ownership, democratic fellowship, and the spirit of freedom that blacks enjoyed within them.

From 1934 to 1940 Mays served as dean of the Howard University School of Religion in Washington, D.C., at the invitation of its president, **Mordecai Wyatt Johnson.** He was part of a remarkable faculty that included **Howard Thurman** in the School of Religion and the chapel, **E. Franklin Frazier** in sociology, and Charles Hamilton Houston at the Howard University law school.

Between 1938 and 1946 Mays met with Mohandas K. Gandhi in India on three separate occasions. He became convinced of the wisdom and power of the nonviolent philosophy. By the time **Martin Luther King Jr.** settled upon Gandhian principles to guide his nonviolent movement, Mays was positioned to

provide strong support and encouragement. When Gandhi was assassinated in 1948, Mays delivered a tribute to him, "Gandhi and Nonviolence," in the Morehouse chapel. Sitting in the front row of the chapel on that day was King, then a senior at the college.

From 1941 to 1967 Mays served as president of Morehouse College, where he mentored a generation of black men, including King. Mays preached the eulogy at the funeral service for King in the chapel at Morehouse College on April 9, 1968.

More than anyone else, Mays was responsible for creating the mystique of "the Morehouse man." Hugh Gloster, a 1931 graduate of Morehouse and Mays's successor as president, spoke about this mystique: "He was a motivator, a challenger. That was his great strength. He could take a group of ordinary high school graduates and inspire them to be somebody—to try to do everything possible to eliminate segregation, to try to establish close ties with people in other countries, especially Africa. His addresses were sermons, you see. He really felt that his mission was to build men."

Mays was instrumental in the creation of the **Interdenominational Theological Center (ITC)** in Atlanta, Georgia. He was one of four Americans sent as a formal delegation to the funeral of Pope John XXIII in 1963. President John F. Kennedy sought to appoint Mays to several high-ranking positions in his administration, but those efforts were blocked by the white U.S. senators from Georgia, who objected to Mays's outspoken views on civil rights.

In 1970 Mays was elected the first black president of the board of education in Atlanta, on which he served for twelve years. Mays was awarded forty-five honorary degrees, including one from Harvard in 1967 marking his retirement from Morehouse.

Mays's first wife, Ellen Harvin, died in 1923. He was married to Sadie Gray Mays from 1926 to 1969.

In addition to *The Negro's Church,* Mays wrote *Concerned about Man* and his autobiography, *Born to Rebel.* When he died in 1984, inscribed on his tomb were the words he often repeated in the chapel at Morehouse College and to audiences across the country:

It must be borne in mind that the tragedy in life doesn't lie in not reaching your goal. The tragedy lies in having no goal to reach. It isn't a calamity to die with dreams unfulfilled, but it is a calamity not to dream. It is not a disaster to be unable to capture your ideal, but it is a disaster to have no ideal to capture. It is not a disgrace not to reach the stars, but it is a disgrace to have no stars to reach for. Not failure, but low aim is the sin.

Samuel DuBois Cook, "The Eulogy of Benjamin Elijah Mays," *The African American Pulpit* (winter 2000–2001); Benjamin E. Mays, *Born to Rebel;* Benjamin E. Mays and Joseph W. Nicholson, *The Negro's Church;* Dick Russell, *Black Genius;* Henry J. Young, *Major Black Religious Leaders Since 1940.*

☯ McNeil, Jessie Jai

(1913-1965) As a teacher, author, and scholar in Christian education, McNeil was without peer. He was born in North Little Rock, Arkansas, on February 24, 1913. He attended Shurtleff College, and while still a college student, he was called to pastor the Tabernacle Baptist Church in East Alton, Illinois. From there his academic career took off in spectacular fashion. He earned his bachelor of divinity degree from Virginia Union University and his bachelor of science, master of arts, and doctor of philosophy degrees in education from Columbia University in New York City. McNeil had accomplished all of this by 1943.

From 1944 to 1947 McNeil was dean of the School of Religion at Bishop College in Marshall, Texas. From 1947 to 1961 he was the pastor of the Tabernacle Baptist Church of Detroit, Michigan. In 1961 he was appointed professor of Christian education at California Baptist Theological Seminary, now known as the American Baptist Seminary of the West. With this appointment, he joined an elite company of black men, including **Howard Thurman** and George Kelsey, who were given high academic rank at a predominantly white educational institution.

McNeil was a prodigious writer, authoring such works as *As Thy Days, So Thy Strength* (1960), *The Minister's Service Book for Pulpit and Parish* (1961), *The Preacher-Prophet in Mass Society* (1961), *Moments in His Presence* (1962), and *Mission in Metropolis* (1965). He also wrote *Men in the Local Church,* which was published by the Sunday School Board of the **National Baptist Convention, USA, Inc. (NBCUSA).**

Central to the thinking of McNeil is the value and importance of Christian education. Writing in *God's Bad Boys,* Charles Emerson Boddie described the educational philosophy of McNeil this way. "Black Baptist churches are pulpit centered; McNeil was desirous that they

become classroom-oriented and study-conscious. Black churches soberly call their pastors, but they merely look around for some willing man, regardless of his training, to man the Christian education leadership barracks. McNeil would make the Christian educator a part of a team associated with the pastor."

McNeil was an international church statesman, preaching before various ecumenical bodies in Switzerland (1944), Norway (1947), and Sweden and England (1949). At the height of his academic prowess, McNeil died at the age of fifty-two on July 9, 1965. He left an enormous void as preacher, professor, author, and ecumenist. He preached his last sermon on May 16, 1965, at the Second Baptist Church of Los Angeles. It was entitled "The New People of God." It was to that ministry of transforming the church into the new people of God that McNeil had devoted his brief but productive life and ministry.

Charles Emerson Boddie, *God's Bad Boys;* Thomas Kilgore Jr. and Jini Kilgore Ross, *A Servant's Journey;* Larry Murphy, J. Gordon Melton, and Gary Ward, eds., *Encyclopedia of African American Religions.*

☉ Mitchell, Henry Heywood

(1919–) One of the great oddities of the black preaching tradition, despite the power it has demonstrated over the last one hundred years, is that it has gone largely unnoticed and unexamined by whites in the academic circles of homiletics and within the larger white Christian world. Even today, a look at lists of major conference speakers and professional journal contributors illustrates the virtual absence of black preachers. No one has done more to bridge that gap than has Henry Mitchell. For the last thirty years, since the release of his landmark book, *Black Preaching* (1970), Mitchell has labored mightily to bring the sounds and substance of black preaching to the attention of the whole world.

Mitchell was born on September 10, 1919, in Columbus, Ohio. He received his bachelor of arts degree at Lincoln University in Pennsylvania (1941) and his bachelor of divinity degree from Union Theological Seminary in New York City (1944). He received a master of arts degree from California State University in Fresno (1966) and a doctor of theology degree from Claremont School of Theology (1973).

Most of Mitchell's early ministry was in California, including his service as an executive with American Baptist Churches from 1945 to 1959, serving as pastor of Second Baptist Church of Fresno from 1959 to 1966, and later as pastor of the Calvary Baptist Church of Santa Monica from 1966 to 1969. During these years as a pastor and preacher, Mitchell learned the lessons of black preaching. Beginning in 1970 he devoted himself to the task of attempting to share with others what he had learned.

Mitchell served in a series of distinguished academic positions, beginning with his appointment in 1969 to become the Martin Luther King Jr. Professor of Black Church Studies at the Colgate Rochester Divinity School. He also taught at Claremont School of Theology, Fuller Theological Seminary, and the American Baptist Seminary of the West. He served as dean of Virginia Union University School of Theology in Richmond from 1982 to 1986, and he continued to teach in the field of homiletics. He later taught preaching at the **Interdenominational Theological Center (ITC)** in Atlanta, Georgia.

While at Colgate Rochester Mitchell instituted a doctor of ministry program called The Martin Luther King Jr. Fellows. Not only did this program attract and graduate some of the leading black pastors of the 1970s, but also it served to begin the creation of a body of theological literature drawn from the dissertation projects of some of those graduates. Among the landmark books that emerged from that program were *"Somebody's Calling My Name"* by **Wyatt Tee Walker**, *God and the Ghetto* by **William A. Jones Jr.,** *Church Administration in the*

African American Perspective by Floyd Massey and Samuel McKinney, and *Images of the Black Preacher* by H. Beecher Hicks Jr.

Mitchell has been a prolific scholar. In addition to *Black Preaching,* he has written *Black Belief: Folk Beliefs of Blacks in America and West Africa* (1975), *The Recovery of Preaching* (1977), *Soul Theology: The Heart of American Black Culture* (1986), *Celebration and Experience in Preaching* (1990), and *Black Preaching: The Recovery of a Powerful Art* (1990). Scores of his printed sermons and articles have been featured in professional journals, including *Interpretation, Preaching, The Living Pulpit,* and *The African American Pulpit.* In recognition of his contributions to the field of preaching and homiletics, Mitchell was selected to deliver the Lyman Beecher Lectures on Preaching at Yale Divinity School in 1974.

Mitchell has always worked to recognize the equally impressive genius of his wife, **Ella Pearson Mitchell,** whom he married in 1944. They have been one of the great clergy teams of the twentieth century. They served together as leaders in the Academy of Homiletics, and both were honored in a collection of scholarly essays in *Born to Preach: Essays in Honor of the Ministry of Henry and Ella Mitchell* (2000). They have also co-authored a book about their life and ministry, *Together for Good: Lessons from Fifty-five Years of Marriage* (1999).

The Mitchells continue to make their home in Atlanta, but their ministry goes forth to the ends of the earth.

"An Interview with Henry Mitchell," *The African American Pulpit* (winter 1997–1998); Henry Mitchell and Ella Mitchell, *Together for Good.*

☯ Proctor, Samuel Dewitt

(1921–1997) Born amid the restrictions and limitations of the segregated South, Samuel Dewitt Proctor went on to become one of the most celebrated teachers and one of the most sought-after preachers in America. He moved with equal ease among working-class members of the black community, and among the power elite in Washington, D.C. He was as visible in black church pulpits as he was in the chapel of Ivy League universities. For forty years he traveled throughout the country and crisscrossed the globe preaching the gospel of faith, hope, and perseverance.

Proctor was born in Norfolk, Virginia, in 1921, one of six children of Herbert and Velma Proctor. He graduated from Virginia Union University with a bachelor of arts degree in 1942, Crozer Theological Seminary with a master of divinity degree in 1945, and Boston University with a doctor of theology degree in 1950. He began his doctorate at Yale Divinity School but transferred to Boston in 1948. He married Bessie Tate in 1944, and they had four sons.

In 1950 Proctor met **Martin Luther King Jr.,** who was then a student at Crozer. Proctor was an early intellectual mentor for King, and the two maintained a friendship that proved to be a mutual blessing. Proctor was a frequent guest in King's home and church in Montgomery, Alabama, during the famous bus boycott in 1955 and 1956. While working on his doctorate Proctor also served as pastor of Pond Street Baptist Church in Providence, Rhode Island. He then joined the faculty of Virginia Union University in Richmond in 1949, becoming academic dean and then president (1954). In 1960 he accepted the presidency of North Carolina A&T College in Greensboro. This move brought Proctor into the eye of the storm of the sit-in movement among Southern black college students. It also brought him into contact with the student body president at A&T, **Jesse Jackson.**

Following the election of John F. Kennedy as president of the United States, Proctor began serving in a series of positions in the federal government. They included director of the Peace Corps in Nigeria, director of the Office of Economic Opportunity in Washington, D.C., and New York, and the Institute for Services to Education. The last was a program designed to strengthen the quality of the faculty at historically black colleges and universities. He also served as a speechwriter for Lyndon B. Johnson and Hubert H. Humphrey when they appeared before black college or church crowds.

Proctor's government service was interrupted by his return to the presidency of North Carolina A&T in 1963 and a short stint in 1964 as associate general secretary of the National Council of Churches in New York City. He was continually called upon to serve in the federal government, usually at the invitation of Sargent Shriver or Bill Moyers. He repeatedly answered the nation's call, not leaving Washington until the election of Richard M. Nixon in 1968.

Proctor returned to academia in 1968 when he went to the University of Wisconsin to lead an effort to train more black people for careers in teaching at the college level. In 1969 he was appointed the Martin Luther King Memorial Professor of Education at Rutgers University in New Jersey. From that position, Proctor was responsible for recruiting, training, and graduating scores of black doctoral students who now serve the nation at the secondary, college, and graduate level.

In 1972, while continuing to serve at Rutgers, Proctor succeeded **Adam Clayton Powell Jr.** as pastor of Abyssinian Baptist Church in New York City. From that position he continued to mentor young men and women for careers in the ministry by training them as members of his staff at Abyssinian and then sending them out to churches across the country. This pattern of mentoring the next generation of preachers and teachers was Proctor's magnificent obsession. Proctor maintained that bivocational ministry until he retired from Abyssinian in 1989.

In 1985 Proctor was named one of the top fifteen black preachers in America by *Ebony*. In 1990 he delivered the Lyman Beecher Lectures on Preaching at Yale Divinity School. He continued his lifelong passion for teaching by serving on the faculty at Vanderbilt University, Duke University, and United Theological Seminary in Dayton, Ohio. At United he mentored a group of students who were enrolled in the doctor of ministry program as Proctor Fellows.

Proctor wrote or coauthored eight books: *The Young Negro in America, My Moral Odyssey, Sermons from the Black Pulpit* with William D. Watley, *We Have This Ministry* with Gardner C. Taylor, *The Certain Sound of the Trumpet, The Substance of Things Hoped For, Preaching on Social Crises,* and *How Shall They Hear* (the Beecher Lectures). He was the recipient of more than forty honorary doctoral degrees and was named by *Time* as one of the most popular baccalaureate and commencement speakers in the United States.

Proctor died in 1997. At his funeral it was announced that Virginia Union School of Theology would be renamed the Samuel Dewitt Proctor School of Theology. **Gardner C. Taylor,** who delivered the funeral eulogy, said, "With his equals he was an astute companion, and to those who had not reached his level he was gracious and concerned. One would speak about his superiors, but there were none.... Here was a man who by the very gifts of nature looked like a prince and talked like a poet ... and the word for him was 'Be thou faithful.'"

Samuel Dewitt Proctor, *My Moral Odyssey* and *The Substance of Things Hoped For;* Gardner C. Taylor, "The Eulogy for Samuel D. Proctor," *The African American Pulpit* (winter 2000–2001).

Roberts, J. Deotis

(1927–) One of the most distinguished academic careers ever to be enjoyed by an African American theologian belongs to J. Deotis Roberts. Laboring in traditionally black academic settings but also making a distinguished contribution on predominantly white campuses, few theologians have produced a larger volume of substantive scholarly material. Although Roberts is undoubtedly a man of the academy, his writings have been

invaluable to the everyday life of the black church.

Roberts was born on July 12, 1927, in Spindale, North Carolina. He earned a bachelor of arts degree from Johnson C. Smith University (1947) and a bachelor of divinity degree from Shaw University (1950), both in North Carolina. He later earned a master of sacred theology degree from Hartford Theological Seminary in Connecticut (1952) and a doctor of philosophy degree from Edinburgh University (1957). During his student years he supported himself by working in several pastoral roles, including one in Glasgow, Scotland. However, his life's work would be teaching and writing. He began as an instructor at Howard University Divinity School in 1957 and became a full professor in 1970.

In 1971 Roberts wrote his first book, *Liberation and Reconciliation,* which was seen by many as the first serious critique by a black scholar of the black theology argument being made by **James H. Cone.** From 1973 to 1974 Roberts left Howard to be dean of the Virginia Union University School of Theology in Richmond. He returned to Howard after that, only to leave again in 1981 to become president of the **Interdenominational Theological Center (ITC)** in Atlanta, Georgia.

In 1984 Roberts left the environs of a black academic setting when he joined the faculty of Eastern Baptist Theological Seminary near Philadelphia. From 1986 to 1988 he was a commonwealth professor at George Mason University in Fairfax, Virginia. He then returned to Eastern as a distinguished professor before moving on to serve as professor of theology at Duke Divinity School in Durham, North Carolina.

Roberts is widely noted for the rich body of theological material he produced over more than twenty years. His books include *A Black Political Theology* (1974), *Roots of a Black Future* (1980), *Black Theology Today* (1983), *A Philosophical Introduction to Theology* (1991), *The Prophethood of Black Believers* (1994), and *Africentric Christianity* (2000). He also produced a vast number of scholarly articles that were published in various journals and books. He served on the Theological Commission of the **National Conference of Black Churchmen (NCBC).**

Much of Roberts's theology is captured in two quotes. In *The Prophethood of Black Believers* he writes, "The priority for black religionists has been the prophetic and succoring message of the Book.... The prophetic word of social justice and the healing, comforting word of the psalmist have a special place for the black believer's faith. People that suffer from racism, a systematic form of evil with institutional expression, need a message of deliverance."

Never one to be limited to issues of personal salvation or individual success, Roberts writes in *A Black Political Theology,* "We seek the deliverance of a people as well as personal liberation. We will have the dignity of sons and daughters of God here and now."

J. Deotis Roberts, *Liberation and Reconciliation* and *A Black Political Theology;* J. Deotis Roberts, "Black Consciousness in Theological Perspective," in *The Black Experience in Religion,* ed. C. Eric Lincoln; Henry J. Young, *Major Black Religious Leaders Since 1940.*

☻ Thurman, Howard

(1900-1981) Thurman was born into the rigid segregation of the American South but rose from humble beginnings to become one of the most sought-after and highly honored preachers and lecturers in the world. Not only was he an advocate for multiculturalism in the United States, but also he was committed to the cause of justice worldwide. He was inspired by and proved to be an inspiration to no less a person than Mohandas Gandhi, with whom he met in India in 1935.

Thurman was born on November 18, 1900, in Daytona Beach, Florida. He graduated from Morehouse College in 1923. Along with his classmate James Nabrit, he read every book in the Morehouse College library. Thurman was greatly influenced by Mary McLeod Bethune, **Benjamin Elijah Mays,** and John Hope, who was his college president at Morehouse. He acknowledged his call to ministry and sought to enroll at Newton Theological Seminary in Massachusetts. He was denied admission because of racial prejudice. He then enrolled at Rochester (New York) Theological Seminary, from which he received his bachelor of divinity degree in 1926. In his senior year at Rochester he was called to be the pastor of Mt. Zion Baptist Church of Oberlin, Ohio. He did further study at the Oberlin School of Religion. During 1929 Thurman studied with Rufus Jones, a Quaker mystic, at Haverford College in Pennsylvania, and that experience marked the beginning of a lifelong commitment to an inward spiritual journey that marked Thurman as a writer, preacher, and teacher. He went to teach at Morehouse College in 1930, and in 1932 he become dean of the chapel at Howard University. Only three American universities appointed someone to be dean of the chapel with an appointment to the School of Religion: Princeton, Chicago, and Howard. In 1944 Thurman became the founding pastor of the interracial Church for the Fellowship of All Peoples in San Francisco. That congregation not only experimented with the issue of an interracial fellowship but also was a leader in interfaith affairs and in new forms of worship.

Thurman became dean of the chapel at Boston University in 1953, the first black man in American history to be appointed to an administrative position in a major research university. He also taught in the School of Theology. He accepted that position because he believed that his presence at Boston University would provide "the maximum possibility of contagion." In 1953 Thurman was listed in *Life* as one of the

twelve great preachers of the twentieth century. In 1954 he was listed in *Ebony* as one of the ten most outstanding black preachers in America. He had become a frequent speaker on college campuses and in leading churches and synagogues throughout the United States. He also traveled widely, including Europe, India, and West Africa on his itineraries.

Upon his retirement from Boston in 1965, Thurman served as a visiting professor at the Presbyterian Seminary in Louisville, Kentucky, and in the School of Religion at Earlham College in Indiana. However, he devoted himself primarily to the development of the Howard Thurman Educational Trust, a fund dedicated to the education of black college students, especially those attending schools in the Deep South. The fund was also to be used to establish Howard Thurman Listening Rooms, where his tapes and recorded sermons and lectures could be heard and where his numerous writings could be made available. There are now listening rooms across the United States and in seventeen countries around the world.

As noted for his writings as for the dramatic pauses that punctuated his preaching, Thurman wrote more than twenty books. His first book was a series of meditations on Negro spirituals entitled *Deep River* (1945). In 1947 he became the first black person ever invited to deliver the Ingersoll Lectures at Harvard Divinity School. He used that to continue his reflections on the meaning of immortality as found in the spirituals. The book that followed was *The Negro Spirituals Speak of Life and Death*.

Martin Luther King Jr. carried one of Thurman's books, *Jesus and the Disin-herited* (1949), in his briefcase at all times. That book was Thurman's attempt to answer a question from a law professor in Ceylon he had met during a pilgrimage to India in 1935. The man challenged him about why he as a black man could be a Christian, since white Christians had captured, transported, and enslaved Africans in America. Thurman argued that a poor Jew living and thinking from the margins of the Roman Empire had much to say to black people living on the margins of American society.

In preparing for the Ingersoll Lectures, Thurman debated whether he should focus on Negro spirituals. In his autobiography, *With Head and Heart*, he speaks of his concerns about discussing that topic before the Harvard community: "I was sensitive to the pervasive notion that black scholars were incapable of reflective creativity on any matters other than those that bore directly on their own struggle for survival in American society. In my view, this attitude had an inhibiting effect on otherwise creative, thoughtful minds, and I deeply resented it. I chose to examine Negro spirituals in spite of this prevailing opinion and not because of it."

After the death of his first wife due to complications after childbearing, he married Sue E. Bailey in 1932. She became his partner in life for nearly fifty years. Thurman died in San Francisco on April 10, 1981. That year an obelisk was erected in his honor on the campus of Morehouse College.

Dick Russell, *Black Genius;* Howard Thurman, *Jesus and the Disinherited* and *With Head and Heart;* Henry J. Young, *Major Black Religious Leaders Since 1940.*

☻ West, Cornel

(1953-) There are probably few professors at Harvard University who can say that among the great influences of their lives are the music of jazz saxophonist John Coltrane, the oratorical rhythms of the black Baptist pulpit, and the revolutionary spirit of the Black Panther Party of the 1960s. Couple these with a passion for Anton Chekhov and Karl Marx and a mastery of every phase of European philosophy, and you have entered into the company of Cornel West.

West was born in Tulsa, Oklahoma, on June 2, 1953. His religious values were shaped at an early age under the leadership of his grandfather, Rev. C. L. West of the Metropolitan Baptist Church of Tulsa. His family left Tulsa when he was very young, migrating to Topeka, Kansas, and finally settling in Sacramento, California. While a straight-A student in high school, West worked closely with the Black Panthers, whose home base was in California.

West graduated magna cum laude in three years from Harvard University. He earned his master of arts and doctor of philosophy degrees from Princeton University and began his teaching career at Union Theological Seminary in New York City in 1977. He also taught courses at Williams College in Massachusetts. In *Black Genius*, West tells the story of a white state trooper who arrested him on suspicion of being a drug dealer simply because that officer saw him regularly traveling the highways between New York City and Massachusetts. He had been falsely arrested on a rape charge during his sophomore year at Harvard and held even though the victim insisted that he was not the guilty party; for him the evils of racial profiling not only became apparent but also were in force long before current interest in the topic.

After a short tenure on the faculty at Yale Divinity School, West went to Princeton University to teach philosophy and to be the head of a newly formed African American studies program. Toni Morrison, a Nobel Prize–winning novelist, was already a member of that department. In 1994 he accepted an offer from Henry Louis Gates to join the African American studies department at Harvard University. He was appointed the Alphonse Fletcher Jr. University Professor at Harvard. This appointment established him as one of the leading scholars in the country, indeed in the world. Yet when asked to describe himself as a scholar in a

Booknotes interview with Brian Lamb, he says, "I'm just a brother off the block trying to make sense."

A short review of his scholarly output will reveal how much sense West has been making since the release of his first book, *Prophesy Deliverance* in 1982. Such books as *Prophetic Fragments* (1988), *Race Matters* (1993), and *Keeping the Faith* (1994) have immeasurably enriched the discussion in such fields as philosophy, race relations, cultural and literary criticism, and politics. He has collaborated with Henry Louis Gates in *The Future of the Race* (1996) and *The African American Century* (2000). He also collaborated with bell hooks on *Breaking Bread: Insurgent Black Intellectual Life* (1991) and with Michael Lerner in *Jews and Blacks: Let the Healing Begin* (1995).

J. Alfred Smith Sr., pastor of Allen Temple Baptist Church in Oakland, knows the intellectual discipline of West. He asked West how he had the time to write so many books. In response West said, "I read more than I write." West recalls that even during his college years, he would party late into the night on weekends, but only after having read a book or two earlier that evening.

While neither a teacher of theology nor an ordained minister of any denomination, West has written and spoken insightfully about the black religious tradition. He has repeatedly referenced the black preaching tradition, along with music and athletics, as among the three leading forms of cultural expression within the black community. In making that point, West not only links the preaching excellence of **Gardner C.**

Taylor to the level of the musical excellence of John Coltrane and the athletic excellence of Michael Jordan or Willie Mays; he also observes that black intellectuals, in order to achieve that level of mastery and fame, will need the kind of institutional context that has long been available to those who have long since demonstrated mastery of the fields of music, preaching, and athletics.

That is a challenge not so much to the intellectuals who already exist as to society to provide those black intellectuals with access to the journals, faculties, and academic societies that are necessary for high-level intellectual life. West is an example of the mastery of the field that can take place when black intellectual excellence becomes as valued by blacks and whites in society as excellence in the other three fields.

West has not limited himself to the classroom. He was an active and visible member of the inner circle of the Bill Bradley for President campaign in 2000. He is the honorary chairman of the Democratic Socialists of America, a reflection of his appreciation of the leadership role of Eugene V. Debs. This combination of academic and political involvement helps in understanding West's working definition of an intellectual. He says, "I understand the vocation of the intellectual as trying to turn easy answers into critical questions, and ask those critical questions to those with power."

"An Interview with J. Alfred Smith Sr.," *The African American Pulpit* (winter 1998–1999); Brian Lamb, "An Interview with Cornel West," *Booknotes* online service; Dick Russell, *Black Genius;* Cornel West, *The Cornel West Reader, Keeping the Faith,* and *Race Matters.*

◔ Woodson, Carter G.

(1875–1950) Woodson is popularly known as the father of Negro history, and he is credited with the establishment of Black History Month in the United States. However, Woodson must also be recognized for the enormous contribution he made to the scholarly study of the African American church in his landmark 1921 book, *History of the Negro Church.*

Woodson was born on December 19, 1875, in New Canton, Virginia. He received his education at Berea College in Kentucky (bachelor of arts) and the University of Chicago (master of arts). In 1912 he became the second African American to receive a doctor of philosophy degree in history from Harvard University. **W. E. B. Du Bois** was the first in 1895. Woodson also studied at the Sorbonne in Paris.

In 1916 Woodson organized the Association for the Study of Negro Life and History. So that materials by and about black Americans could be published, in 1921 he organized The Associated Publishers, which published his *History of the Negro Church.* At that time, few other publishing firms would accept such material. In 1933 he published his second seminal book, *The Miseducation of the Negro.* His other books included *The Education of the Negro Prior to 1861* (1915), *A Century of Negro Migration* (1918), *The Negro in Our History* (1922), and *The Rural Negro (1930).*

In 1926 Woodson established Negro History Week, an observance that later (1976) was expanded to cover the month of February. He also established the *Journal of Negro History,* and he served as dean of liberal arts at Howard University in Washington, D.C. However, his inclusion in this volume is due to his study of the black church, a study that considers the rise of that venerable institution from the era of colonial America in the seventeenth and eighteenth centuries to the rise of the Northern urban churches of the 1930s. Many subsequent studies of the history of the black church are deeply indebted to the initial research done by Woodson in *History of the Negro Church.* Woodson died in 1950.

Tom Cowan and Jack McGuire, *Timelines of African American History;* Harry A. Ploski and Ernest Kaiser, eds. and comps., *The Negro Almanac;* Carter G. Woodson, *History of the Negro Church.* ▣

SECTION 4

Politicians

⊙ Cain, Richard Harvey

(1825–1887) During the era of Reconstruction (1865–1877), many black people served in the United States Congress. Reverend **Hiram R. Revels** of Mississippi was the first to serve in the U.S. Senate (1869–1871). Reverend Richard Cain from South Carolina was among the first group of blacks to serve in the House of Representatives (1873–1875 and 1877–1879).

Cain was born of free parents on April 12, 1825, in Green Briar County, Virginia. By the age of nineteen he had entered the Methodist Episcopal ministry and affiliated with the **African Methodist Episcopal (AME) Church.** He attended Wilberforce University and then served churches in Iowa, New York, and throughout South Carolina. In 1868 he was appointed to the constitutional convention that was required in order for South Carolina to be readmitted to the Union after the Civil War. In that position he worked tirelessly to provide land grants to former slaves, which were secured by breaking up former slaveholding plantations throughout the state. He also incorporated language in the new state constitution that provided an opportunity for freedmen to secure land. South Carolina was the only state to include such provisions in its state constitution.

Cain served two terms in the state senate, representing the region of Charleston (1868–1872). During that time he also served as president of the Enterprise Railroad Company, a black-owned, horse-drawn freight company that operated in Charleston. That operation lasted less than a year and was taken over by white ownership in 1871. He also edited a magazine, *The Missionary Record* (1868–1872). In 1873 Cain was elected to the first of two separate terms in the U.S. Congress.

In 1879 Cain returned full time to his work with the AME Church, and in 1880 he was elected bishop for the region covering Louisiana and Texas. During that time he helped to organize Paul Quinn College in honor of AME bishop William Paul Quinn in Waco, Texas (1881). Cain served for a short time as president of that college. He died in 1887.

Eric Foner, *A Short History of Reconstruction;* Howard N. Rabinowitz, ed., *Southern Black Leaders of the Reconstruction Era;* Carter G. Woodson, *The History of the Negro Church.*

☉ Fauntroy, Walter Edward

(1933–) The political status of the residents of Washington, D.C., has been a matter of much contention for more than one hundred years. Nowhere in the United States does the phrase "taxation without representation" carry more meaning than in that city. No person has been a stronger and more consistent advocate for the full and equal political status of the residents of the nation's capitol than has Walter Fauntroy. Not only was he born (1933) and reared in Washington, D.C., but also from 1971 to 1991 he was the first person elected to represent that city in the U.S. Congress in more than a hundred years.

Fauntroy graduated with a bachelor of arts degree from Virginia Union University in 1955. He earned a bachelor of divinity degree from Yale Divinity School in 1958. The next year he became pastor of New Bethel Baptist Church in Washington, D.C., the church in which he had grown up. Fauntroy continues to serve that congregation, and he is an active member of the **Progressive National Baptist Convention (PNBC)**.

In 1960 Fauntroy was appointed by **Martin Luther King Jr.** to be the director of the Washington bureau of the **Southern Christian Leadership Conference (SCLC)**. He was the Washington, D.C., coordinator of the historic March on Washington on August 28, 1963. He also served as the main coordinator of the Selma to Montgomery march in the spring of 1965 and the James Meredith Mississippi Freedom March in 1966. In 1968 Fauntroy served as the national coordinator of the Poor People's Campaign, the SCLC antipoverty demonstra-

tion held in the weeks following the assassination of King.

In 1970 Congress passed the District of Columbia Act, which provided for Washington's representation in the House of Representatives. Fauntroy won the Democratic primary for that seat in January 1971 and was elected by an overwhelming margin of victory in March of that year. He spent a total of ten terms (twenty years) as a member of the U.S. Congress, and all the while he continued his duties as pastor of New Bethel Baptist Church.

Among Fauntroy's first actions after being elected was steering to enactment the District of Columbia Self-Government and Government Reorganization Act in 1973. That law granted limited self-rule for the district, permitting the citizens to elect a mayor and city council. However, his appeals for statehood so that the district could also have representation by two members in the U.S. Senate have not yet been acted upon. It has long been believed that Congress is withholding statehood because both senators from the District of Columbia would almost certainly be black.

Between 1981 and 1983, Fauntroy was the chairman of the Congressional Black Caucus. He served on the Banking and Urban Affairs Committee and was actively involved with the House Select Committee on Narcotics. He led a group of African American political and civil rights leaders in a dramatic protest in front of the South African Embassy in Washington, D.C. Their willingness to picket, protest, and be arrested day after day helped end American support for the apartheid regime in South Africa and helped to speed the release from prison of Nelson Mandela.

Fauntroy chose not to seek another term in Congress and unsuccessfully ran for the office of mayor of Washington, D.C. He has remained active outside of political life. He is the chairman of the National Black Leadership Roundtable, a consortium of civil rights groups from across the country. In January 2001 he worked with **Alfred Sharpton** to arrange a series of demonstrations and a shadow inaugural. That was done in order to protest the election and inauguration of President George W. Bush, who lost the popular vote and gained the White House through a controversial decision by the U.S. Supreme Court.

In addition to being an outstanding preacher and orator, Fauntroy is a gifted singer. He is as likely to end a speech or sermon with a rendition of a hymn or pop song as he is to quote from the Bible or a literary source.

Taylor Branch, *Parting the Waters: America in the King Years, 1954–63;* Adam Fairclough, *To Redeem the Soul of America: The Southern Christian Leadership Conference and Martin Luther King, Jr.;* www.dcmilitary.com/navy/ journal/ 6_3/local_new; www.usbol.com/ctjournal/ Wfauntroybio.

☯ Flake, Floyd H.

(1945–) In a career that has moved him from corporate America to the college campus to the halls of the U.S. Congress to the pulpit of a ten-thousand-member congregation, Flake has made an indelible impression on the American political and religious landscape. His life has taken him from one end of the country to the other, but he is the head of a church with a nonprofit arm that has become the third largest private employer in the borough of Queens in New York City. Only the Long Island Railroad and John F. Kennedy International Airport employ more people than the combined ministries and nonprofit corporations of the church headed by Flake.

Flake was born in Los Angeles, California, on January 30, 1945. He was one of thirteen children born to parents who eventually moved their family to Houston, Texas. Flake graduated from Wilberforce University and attended Payne Theological Seminary (Ohio) and Northeastern University (Boston, Massachusetts). He began his career in the private sector with Xerox and Reynolds Tobacco

Co. He then went into campus work, serving from 1970 to 1973 as an assistant dean of students and campus life at Lincoln University in Pennsylvania. From there he became dean of the chapel and director of the Martin Luther King Jr. Afro-American Center at Boston University (1973–1976).

In 1976 Flake became the pastor of Allen Temple African Methodist Episcopal (AME) Church in Jamaica, Queens, New York. In the intervening twenty-five years, he has overseen the growth of that congregation into ten thousand members. Of equal interest is the fact that Allen Temple has led the way among black congregations in America in developing nonprofit corporations that have brought massive economic revival to the inner city. The church has a $27 million operating budget, expansive commercial and residential developments, a five-hundred-student private school, and a workforce of 825 persons.

Flake was elected to the U.S. Congress on his second bid for public office in the fall of 1986, having lost earlier that year in a special election for the seat from the sixth congressional district following the death of Joseph Addabbo. He served five terms in Congress and was a member of the banking committee. The skills and contacts he garnered on that committee helped Flake develop the enormous economic development programs of Allen Temple. Flake never stopped serving his church while he was a member of Congress; he returned to New York City almost every night after his work in Washington, D.C., was completed. During his time in Congress, Flake also earned a doctor of ministry degree from

United Theological Seminary in Dayton, Ohio (1994).

Flake chose not to be run for reelection in the fall of 1997. Instead, he has devoted himself to the ministries and the eleven nonprofit corporations of the Allen Temple AME Church. However, his former colleagues in Washington did not forget him. In June 2000 the U.S. Congress voted to name the federal building in Jamaica, Queens, New York, the Floyd H. Flake Federal Building. Democrats and Republicans, liberals and conservatives spoke in favor of that action and expressed their deep appreciation for the bipartisan relationships that Flake had developed in a Congress that so often worked only along party lines.

Since leaving Congress, Flake has become an outspoken advocate of school vouchers and of giving parents as many alternatives as possible to the public school system. He has also written *The Way of the Bootstrapper: Nine Action Steps for Achieving Your Dreams.* Flake is a senior fellow at the Manhattan Institute for Social and Economic Policy, a columnist for the *New York Post,* and a member of the Fannie Mae Foundation board of directors. He is also on the board of the Export-Import Bank and the Brookings Institute Center on Urban and Metropolitan Policy.

His wife, Elaine, is his copastor at Allen Temple AME Church, and they have four children.

Russ Baker, "The Ecumenist," *The American Prospect,* January 2000; www.allentempleame.org; www.lexingtoninstitute.org; www.manhattan-institute.org; www.govnews.org.

☻ Gray, William H., III

(1941-) For thirteen years, between 1978 and 1991, one of the brightest political stars in America belonged to Reverend William H. Gray III of Philadelphia, Pennsylvania. He was elected to the U.S. Congress in 1978 on his second attempt, having run and lost to Congressman Robert Nix in 1976. When he defeated Nix in 1978, Gray became the first black person ever elected to Congress who had defeated an incumbent black member of that body. He served on the prestigious and influential foreign affairs, budget, and appropriations committees, and he became chairman of the budget committee in 1985.

Gray was born in Baton Rouge, Louisiana, on August 20, 1941. His family moved to Philadelphia when his father was called to be the pastor of Bright

Hope Baptist Church of that city in 1949. In 1963 he graduated from Franklin and Marshall College in Lancaster, Pennsylvania. Deciding to follow his father and grandfather into the ministry, he graduated from Drew University School of Religion in Madison, New Jersey, in 1966.

That same year Gray was installed as pastor of Union Baptist Church of Montclair, New Jersey. In 1972 he succeeded his father as pastor of Bright Hope in Philadelphia. With that church as his political base, Gray ventured into a successful political career while continuing to serve as a pastor.

Gray was an outspoken advocate for Africa who decried the apartheid system in South Africa and was present for the independence ceremonies for the new nation of Zimbabwe, formerly Rhodesia. And he was the author of the African Development Fund, a bill that directed U.S. foreign aid to various towns and

projects in Africa. He also helped organize Project Understanding, which sent black and Jewish high school students on cultural enrichment trips to Israel and Senegal. Many cities and school districts have replicated that learning program.

In 1988 Gray became the first black to be elected chair of the Democratic Caucus, and later that same year he became the first black appointed majority whip of the U.S. House of Representatives, the third-ranking leadership position. He was talked about as part of a national political ticket for the Democratic Party and was in line to become a future Speaker of the House. However, in 1991, he resigned from the Congress to become president of the United Negro College Fund (UNCF). He continues to serve in that position, where he has raised more than $1.2 billion in his ten-year tenure. Although many saw Gray's move from Congress to the UNCF as a surprise, a close look at his personal history explains his decision. His father was president of two black colleges; his mother was dean of a black college; his sister is a professor at a black college; and Gray himself served as a faculty member at five colleges prior to being elected to Congress.

W. Augustus Low and Virgil A. Clift, eds., *Encyclopedia of Black America;* Larry G. Murphy, J. Gordon Melton, and Gary L. Ward, eds., *Encyclopedia of African American Religions.*

☻ Lewis, John

(1940–) The life of John Lewis offers an important angle from which the role of the African American church and its clergy can be considered. Although Lewis

initially planned to pursue the ministry and was licensed to preach in 1956, his exposure to a wide array of activist black preachers resulted in his decision to make civil rights and politics his chief vocations. Unlike **Walter Edward Fauntroy, William H. Gray III, Adam Clayton Powell Jr.,** and **Floyd H. Flake,** who continued to serve as pastors while they served in Congress, Lewis gave up a pastoral career early on, because "I had lost any desire to be a preacher." However, under the influence of the church, he still found a ministry in the streets, on the buses, and at the lunch counters of the South.

Lewis was born on February 21, 1940, in Pike County, Alabama. He grew up within the tightly defined limitations of segregation in the Deep South. However, he early on fell under the influence of the black church. In *Walking with the Wind*, he offers an excellent description of the important role played by the church from the days of slavery into the 1940s: "For people whose lives were circumscribed by the rhythms and routines of hard, hard work, with relatively little time or opportunity for contact with others beyond their immediate neighbors, church was literally a time of congregation, a social event much like going into town, a chance to see and spend time with friends you might not see at all the rest of the month."

Lewis was called Preacher as a boy, largely because he dreamed of becoming a preacher. In preparation for that career, he used to preach to the chickens in the henhouse on his family farm, and he even preached eulogies for them when they died. However, his interest in preaching took on a more serious dimension when he began hearing about the preacher who was leading the bus boycott in Montgomery, Alabama.

It is safe to say that the impact that **Martin Luther King Jr.** had on the life of Lewis was incalculable. However, other activist clergy would also greatly influence his thinking and the course of his life; among them were **Kelly Miller Smith,** James Bevel, **James Lawson,** C. T. Vivian, **Andrew J. Young,** and **Fred Shuttlesworth.** When Lewis went to Nashville, Tennessee, in 1956 to study at American Baptist Theological Seminary, he also began a course that would allow him to encounter nonclergy black leaders such as **W. E. B. Du Bois,** James Farmer, James Forman, Stokely Carmichael, Julian Bond, and Marion Barry.

By 1960 it was clear that Lewis would not be entering the ministry. But it was just as clear that his church-based sense of social justice and prophetic consciousness were leading him into a courageous and costly role in the front ranks of the **civil rights movement.** He was arrested and beaten during the sit-ins that occurred in Nashville in the spring of 1960. He was arrested and beaten several times during his involvement in the Freedom Rides of 1961. He was beaten again on March 7, 1965, when he and A. D. King attempted to lead a group of marchers over the Edmund Pettus Bridge in Selma, Alabama, to dramatize the issue of voting rights for blacks throughout the South. That event has gone down in history as **Bloody Sunday.**

Although he is best known for his roles in those bloody encounters, it must not be overlooked that Lewis was a member of the Big Six civil rights leaders who planned the 1963 March on Washington. He was then serving as chairman of the Student Nonviolent Coordinating Committee (SNCC). Lewis was one of the speakers on that historic occasion, even though many of the other leaders insisted that he tone down some of the remarks he was set to deliver that day. He finally yielded, but only due to the revered status of A. Philip Randolph, who personally appealed to Lewis to make the changes.

In 1967 Lewis earned a degree in philosophy from Fisk University. His thesis discussed the central role played by the black church in becoming the host and heart of the civil rights movement. In 1976 he was termed one of the Living Saints of the World by *Time.* In 1977 he ran unsuccessfully for the seat in the U.S. Congress from the fifth district of Georgia, made vacant by the resignation of Andrew Young to become United Nations ambassador under President Jimmy Carter. **Ralph David Abernathy** also ran, but both men lost to Wyche Fowler.

In 1981 Lewis was elected to the first of two terms that he served on the city council of Atlanta, Georgia. In 1986, when Fowler ran for a seat in the U.S. Senate, Lewis once again ran for a seat in the Congress. This time he was in the race against his longtime friend and civil rights colleague Julian Bond. In a hotly contested and somewhat divisive campaign, Lewis prevailed over Bond, 52 percent to 48 percent. The election was finally decided by Lewis's ability to attract most of the white vote. He has been repeatedly returned to Congress, where he serves with great distinction.

Taylor Branch, *Parting the Waters;* John Lewis with Michael D'Orso, *Walking with the Wind;* Aldon D. Morris, *Origins of the Civil Rights Movement.*

☻ Powell, Adam Clayton, Jr.

(1908–1972) Adam Clayton Powell Jr. was born November 29, 1908, in New Haven, Connecticut, but moved to New York City that year when his father, **Adam Clayton Powell Sr.,** was called to be the pastor of Abyssinian Baptist Church. He graduated from Colgate University in 1930, where, for a time, he passed as white. When his campus roommates discovered that he was black, they petitioned the university to have him removed from the dormitory, and their request was granted.

While Powell was at Colgate, he experienced his call to ministry. He had

intended to study medicine, but following his experience of hearing a "still small voice" in February 1930, he acknowledged his call and made plans to follow his father into the ministry. He later attended Union Theological Seminary in New York City and graduated from Columbia University in 1931. He served as the assistant pastor of Abyssinian from 1931 to1937 and was installed as pastor in September 1937.

Powell's involvement with civil rights began in 1930, prior to his pastoral ministry. Powell organized and led street demonstrations that protested job discrimination against black people in New York City in the 1930s. First he protested the dismissal of five black physicians from the staff of Harlem Hospital. Then he led demonstrations to protest the stores along 125th Street in Harlem that would not employ black workers.

It is important to note that Adam Clayton Powell Jr. was leading street demonstrations in pursuit of civil rights and economic justice in 1930, the year after **Martin Luther King Jr.** was born. His activities led to the Coordinating Committee for Employment in 1937. This led to the formation of the Fair Employment Practices Commission of the federal government during his years as a member of Congress.

In 1941 Powell was the first black person ever elected to serve in the city council of New York. In 1945 he was sworn in for the first of eleven terms in the U.S. House of Representatives. He created the Powell Amendment, which he attached to any bills proposing federal funding for school construction. This amendment called for a withholding of

federal funds from any state or local agency that continued to practice discrimination against African Americans. Powell spoke about the effect of this amendment when he first applied it to a program that supported school lunch programs in 1946: "With the support of my colleagues, the first civil rights amendment, attached to the school lunch program was passed. It is Public Law 396, enacted by the 79th Congress, June 4, 1946. From then on I was to use this important weapon with success, to bring about opportunities for the good of man and to stop those efforts that would harm democracy's forward progress. Sometimes I used it only as a deterrent against the undemocratic practices that would have resulted if that amendment had not been offered."

Another way in which the Powell Amendment would be used was in withholding federal funds from schools that continued to practice segregation after the landmark *Brown v. Board of Education* ruling (1954).

Always a political independent, Powell crossed party lines in 1956 and supported the reelection campaign of Republican Dwight D. Eisenhower because white Southern Democrats refused to support that civil rights bill. Powell's crossing party lines resulted in Eisenhower's signing of the 1957 Civil Rights Act. In 1955, when the government decided not to send a representative to the Bandung Conference, a gathering of the heads of newly independent nations from Africa and Asia, Powell attended the conference at his own expense. His presence as a black member of the U.S. Congress prevented the Soviet Union from using the absence of an American delegation as an indication of U.S. nonsupport for the aspirations of former colonized nations. In 1961 he became the chairman of the Education and Labor Committee. During his six-year term as chairman, that committee passed into law more than sixty pieces of progressive legislation, with the active support of Presidents Kennedy and Johnson. Among the areas of social advancement for which his committee was responsible were such things as Head Start programs, the Job Corps, minimum wage increases, workplace safety regulations, hot lunch programs for poor children, federal aid to education, antipoverty programs, and many more.

President Lyndon B. Johnson commended Powell for the effectiveness of his leadership in Congress. Johnson wrote on March 18, 1966: "I congratulate you for your brilliant record of accomplishment and the successful reporting to the Congress of 49 bedrock pieces of legislation. Only with progressive leadership could so much have been accomplished by one committee in so short a time. I speak for millions of Americans who benefit from these laws when I say that I am truly grateful."

However, later in 1966 Powell was removed from his chairmanship and denied a seat in the Congress on the grounds of ethics violations. He was re-elected to the Congress, after a two-year absence, by a 7-1 margin. The U.S. Supreme Court ruled that his earlier removal was unconstitutional because it denied congressional representation to the thousands of voters in his district in New York.

Along with King and Thurgood Marshall, the work of Adam Clayton Powell Jr. was essential in achieving the civil rights advances of the 1950s and 1960s. It was his influential presence in Congress that helped to steer the 1964 Civil Rights Bill and the 1965 Voting Rights Act into law. Powell had come full circle, beginning as a street activist for civil rights in Harlem in the 1930s and ending up as a powerful member of Congress twisting the arms of white politicians, including that of the president of the United States. He was able to persuade them to vote on legislation that was not widely supported by their constituents.

Along with Stokely Carmichael, Powell helped to popularize the term "black power." First using it in a commencement address at Howard in 1966, Powell displayed a militancy that distanced him from many other ministers who were involved in the nonviolent civil rights struggle. His power was tied to this pastoral role with the eighteen thousand members of Abyssinian Baptist Church and his tenure as a member of the Congress. He was free to do things that others were afraid to try. **Samuel Dewitt Proctor** spoke about the key to Powell's independence in his funeral eulogy delivered at Abyssinian in April of 1972: "Adam Powell, Jr. was the first black leader in America whose financial support came from the people he served. His money was indigenous. Homegrown. Right here. And he was therefore free to speak his mind, and this did not make him friends among those in power."

That freedom may also have bred recklessness. Powell was as noted for the flair of his private life as he was for the productivity of his public career. He was married four times; his first two wives were in the entertainment industry: Isabella Washington was a Broadway actress, and Hazel Scott was a cabaret singer. His somewhat flamboyant lifestyle and the legal wranglings that followed his indictment for libel against Esther James, whom he called a "bag woman for the Mafia," have obscured Powell's political genius and his many accomplishments. The sociologist of religion Peter Paris puts Powell's political skill in perspective in *Black Leaders in Conflict* and *Black Religious Leaders*. Powell wrote an insightful book about the history of blacks in America, *Marching Blacks*. He also wrote his autobiography, *Adam by Adam*.

Powell died on April 4, 1972.

V. P. Franklin, "Adam Clayton Powell Jr.: The Need for Independent Black Leadership," in *Living Our Stories/Telling Our Truths*; Charles V. Hamilton,

Adam Clayton Powell Jr.; Will Haygood, *King of the Cats;* Peter Paris, *Black Leaders in Conflict* and *Black Religious Leaders;* Adam Clayton Powell Jr., *Adam by Adam* and *Marching Blacks;* Samuel D. Proctor, "The Eulogy of Adam Clayton Powell Jr.," *The African American Pulpit* (winter 2000–2001).

☻ Revels, Hiram R.

(1822–1901) Born free in Fayetteville, North Carolina, in 1822, Revels was educated at Knox College in Illinois. He entered the ministry at the age of twenty-five and served several African Methodist Episcopal (AME) parishes in Indiana, Missouri, Maryland, Kentucky, and Kansas. He also served as principal of a school for black children in Baltimore, Maryland.

During the Civil War, Revels became a recruiter who raised the first all-black regiments from Missouri and Maryland. President Abraham Lincoln appointed

him to be a military chaplain, and he served the units he had helped to recruit, as well as a unit from Mississippi.

Following the war, Revels migrated to Mississippi, became active in Republican politics, and continued his active involvement in the ministry of the AME church in that state. In 1867 he was appointed to the Mississippi State Legislature, and in 1869 he was appointed to the U.S. Senate from Mississippi by the state legislature. After three days of contentious debate he was sworn in on February 25, 1870, and became the first black person ever to serve in that body. At this writing, only three other black people have ever served in the U.S. Senate: Blanche K. Bruce of Mississippi (appointed), Edward Brooke of Massachusetts, and Carol Mosley Braun of Illinois.

Revels served in the Senate for only fourteen months, filling the unexpired term of Jefferson Davis, who had resigned from that seat to become president of the Confederate States of America. This transition from white secessionist to black abolitionist as one of the senators from Mississippi is one of the great ironies of American political history. The career of Revels, and of Bruce, another black man who served in the U.S. Senate from Mississippi, makes that state's hostility to black voter registration in the 1950s and 1960s all the more notable.

Following his short tenure in politics, Revels went on to become president of the all-black Alcorn A&M University in Mississippi, the oldest land-grant college for blacks in the United States (1871–1882). In 1876 he became editor of the religious journal *Southwestern Christian Advocate.* Revels died in 1901.

Marvin A. McMickle, *From Pulpit to Politics;* Harry A. Ploski and Ernest Kaiser, eds. and comps., *The Negro Almanac;* Howard N. Rabinowitz, *Southern Black Leaders of the Reconstruction Era;* Bernard Weisberger, "A Quartet to Remember," *American Heritage,* April 1999; Carter G. Woodson, *The History of the Negro Church.*

☯ Young, Andrew J.

(1932–) It is difficult to know how best to categorize the life of Andrew Young, because his contributions have been made in so many different fields of endeavor. He has been a lifelong churchman. He was a major figure in the **civil rights movement**, especially during the 1960s. But his career as an elected and appointed public official may best reflect the breadth and depth of his life and work.

Young was born on March 12, 1932, in New Orleans, Louisiana. He was the son of a middle-class family, his father being a dentist and his mother a schoolteacher. His early participation in such groups as Jack and Jill, a networking program for the children of affluent black families, placed him within such groups as the black bourgeois and the talented tenth. He and his family attended Central Congregational Church.

Young graduated from Howard University with a bachelor of arts degree in 1951 and Hartford Theological Seminary with a bachelor of divinity degree in 1955. Acknowledging his call to the ministry, he was ordained in 1955 and assumed the pastorate of Bethany Congregational Church in Thomasville, Georgia. He also served the Evergreen Congregational Church in nearby Beach-

ton, Georgia. While in Thomasville, Young organized a voter registration campaign in 1956 that attracted the admiration of the black community and the anger of the Ku Klux Klan.

In 1957 Young met **Martin Luther King Jr.** at a fraternal event on the campus of Talladega College in Alabama. Their lives would soon become entwined through the **Southern Christian Leadership Conference (SCLC)**, which King founded in 1957 and which Young would join in 1961. Before that time, however, Young left the South and took a position with the Youth Division of the National Council of Churches in New York City. This position allowed him to establish relationships with church leaders across the country and with future political leaders in nations around the world.

Those contacts proved invaluable for the rest of his life.

Inspired by the work of the Student Nonviolent Coordinating Committee (SNCC), which had launched a series of sit-ins at lunch counters throughout the South, Young felt compelled to return to the South to help in that struggle. He had first intended to work with Myles Horton at the Highlander Folk School in Tennessee. When that school was forcibly closed in 1961, Young took a position with SCLC that was funded by the United Church of Christ (formerly the Congregational Church). He worked in the Leadership Training Program and helped organize communities across the South and aided in voter registration and education efforts.

However, because Young was working out of the offices of SCLC in Atlanta, he invariably was drawn into more direct involvement with the various civil rights campaigns that SCLC was spearheading. He played a leading role in the campaign that occurred in Albany, Georgia; Birmingham, Alabama; St. Augustine, Florida; the 1963 March on Washington; the 1965 march from Selma to Montgomery, Alabama; Chicago, Illinois; and the sanitation workers' strike in Memphis, Tennessee, when King was assassinated.

By 1964 Young had become the executive director of SCLC, third in rank behind King and **Ralph David Abernathy.** Young was on the balcony of the Lorraine Motel in Memphis on April 4, 1968, when King was killed. There is a gripping photograph of him, taken by a South African journalist: he is trying to point the police in the direction from which the fatal shot was fired. There is an even more touching scene in the documentary *From Montgomery to Memphis,* which shows Young weeping at King's funeral.

In 1970 Young resigned from SCLC and made an unsuccessful bid for election to Congress from the fifth congressional district of Georgia. He lost that election by a wide margin, largely because he was unable to win much white support. However, during that campaign he did meet Jimmy Carter, who was then running for governor of Georgia. That friendship would blossom, and Young's career would take yet another turn when Carter was elected president of the United States in 1976. In 1972, due in part to a redrawing of the district lines, in accordance with the 1965 Voting Rights Act, Young was elected to the U.S. Congress from Georgia. He became the first black person elected to the Congress from Georgia since 1871. He was reelected in 1974 and 1976.

In 1977, with the election of Jimmy Carter as president, Young was appointed the ambassador to the United Nations. He established valuable relations with the leaders of delegations from around the world but with a strong emphasis on African nations. He served a term as president of the Security Council in 1977. However, after a secret meeting with a representative from the Palestine Liberation Organization (PLO), which was a violation of existing U.S. policy, and at the urging of the Israeli delegation to the United Nations, Young was forced to resign as ambassador in August 1979.

Young returned to Atlanta and became chairman of the city's Community Relations Committee. In 1981 he was elected to the first of two terms as mayor of Atlanta. During those years the city experienced unprecedented growth as a regional economic center and as headquarters to many Fortune 500 companies. He made an unsuccessful bid for governor of Georgia in 1990. He was successful, however, in using all of his international contacts to bring the Olympic Games to Atlanta in 1996. He was the chairman of the host committee. Once again Young was playing on an international stage.

In 1999 Young returned to the National Council of Churches, this time as president. He was installed at the organization's fiftieth anniversary meeting in Cleveland, Ohio.

Young married Jean Childs in 1954, and they had four children.

C. Eric Lincoln and Lawrence W. Mamiya, *The Black Church in the African American Experience;* W. Augustus Low and Virgil A. Clift, eds., *Encyclopedia of Black America;* Andrew Young, *Andrew Young.* 回

Prophets

◑-◑-◑

◑ Abernathy, Ralph David

(1926–1990) When charismatic leaders die there is often scrambling and dissension about who should be the successor. The men who surrounded **Martin Luther King Jr.** all had a high profile. A highly competitive spirit often existed among them, in terms of presence in the media and access to King. It is therefore remarkable to note that when King was suddenly removed from the scene by an assassin's bullet, there was never a question about who would succeed him as president of the **Southern Christian Leadership Conference (SCLC)**. King had repeatedly made it clear that he wanted his successor to be Abernathy.

It is little wonder that Abernathy was the choice, since no other person in the **civil rights movement** had known King longer or been more intimately involved with him. Their friendship and partnership dated back to Montgomery, Alabama, before the bus boycott. They were both pastors in that city, King at Dexter Avenue Baptist Church and Abernathy at First Baptist Church. When Rosa Parks was arrested on December 1, 1955, Abernathy suggested the boycott, even though King became the leader of the movement.

Abernathy was born on March 11, 1926, in Linden, Alabama. He served in the army during World War II and then attended Alabama State College in Montgomery. He graduated with a bachelor of science degree in mathematics in 1950. Having been ordained into the ministry in 1948, he continued his education with a master of arts degree in sociology from Atlanta University in 1951. He was called to First Baptist Church in Montgomery that year, three years before King arrived in that city. However, once the two men were brought together in the intense drama of the bus boycott (1955–1956), they remained virtually inseparable from that moment until King's death thirteen years later.

When King left Montgomery to organize the SCLC in 1957, Abernathy was appointed the secretary/treasurer of the group. In 1961 Abernathy resigned from his church in Montgomery and became pastor of West Hunter Street Baptist Church in Atlanta so he could be closer to King and to the daily workings of SCLC. At every major civil rights campaign, and usually on the platform for every major address given by King, Abernathy was by King's side. Even when it came to going to jail, Abernathy was with King on seventeen separate occasions. He and King were dramatically arrested together on Easter Sunday 1963 in Birmingham, Alabama. Abernathy was with King in that jail when King wrote the now-famous "Letter from a Birmingham Jail." The two men were together for an unprecedented twenty-five-minute private audience with Pope Paul VI in Rome. Abernathy was part of the entourage that went to Oslo, Norway, when King was awarded the Nobel Prize for peace in 1964.

Abernathy cradled King's body on the balcony of the Lorraine Motel in Memphis, Tennessee, on April 4, 1968, when King was shot. King had asked Abernathy to give the speech the night before in Mason Temple. However, it was clear to Abernathy that the crowd would not be satisfied unless King made an appearance. It was in that speech that King observed, "I've been to the mountaintop." Following the death of King, Abernathy ascended to the presidency of SCLC without dispute.

Abernathy worked tirelessly to keep the organization focused on the Poor People's Campaign, which was held in Washington, D.C., in the late spring of 1968. He helped to build the shantytown on the Capitol Mall that came to be known as Resurrection City. When it was torn down by the police, Abernathy sought to block their efforts, and he was jailed for twenty days. He also continued King's anti-Vietnam war focus.

In 1962 Abernathy became the leader of a new initiative by SCLC called Operation Breadbasket. Based upon the selective buying program created by **Leon Howard Sullivan** in Philadelphia,

Operation Breadbasket was intended to have black ministers work with corporations and small businesses to increase opportunities for black employment and the use of black-owned service companies. He eventually appointed **Jesse Jackson** as leader of that initiative, and that was the beginning of Jackson's civil rights leadership role.

Over time, tensions emerged between Jackson and Abernathy, largely as a result of Jackson's enormous popularity. After having stood in the shadows during King's lifetime, Abernathy, it now seemed, was again being pushed into the shadows by the media that seemed far more drawn to the young and charismatic Jackson. The relations between the two men hit rock bottom in 1971, when Jackson resigned from Operation Breadbasket

and SCLC and formed a new group that he called People United to Save Humanity (PUSH).

That move by Jackson had disastrous effects on the staffing and funding of SCLC. Within two years the income for SCLC had dropped from $2 million to less than $500,000. By 1973 Abernathy had announced his decision to resign from SCLC due to those funding shortfalls and staff dissension, but the board of the organization refused to accept the resignation. He then served in that position until 1977, when he was succeeded by Joseph Lowery.

In 1977 Abernathy ran for the U.S. Congress, trying to fill the seat left vacant when **Andrew J. Young** resigned in order to become the United Nations ambassador for President Jimmy Carter. In a surprise move, Abernathy and Hosea Williams, both residents of Atlanta, Georgia (Carter's home state), refused to endorse Carter's reelection effort. Instead, they endorsed Ronald Reagan, hoping for the same relationship with him that Young enjoyed with Jimmy Carter. Abernathy, however, was defeated.

The tension with Jackson was not the only instance of Abernathy being unable to get along with other leaders in the movement. Despite the close friendship between Abernathy and King, others in the movement were less enamored with Abernathy. They saw him as jealous of the attention that was always being given to King. There was a famous incident in a hotel in Stockholm where Abernathy and his wife, Juanita, insisted that they be given rooms and perquisites to match whatever the hotel management had offered the Kings. **Wyatt Tee Walker**

once stated that Abernathy's role in SCLC was "tangential." However, he was an invaluable companion for King, and as such he remained close at hand.

Because of the friendship between the two men and an assumption of confidentiality, many people were shocked by revelations about King's extramarital activities in Abernathy's 1989 autobiography, *And the Walls Came Tumbling Down*. Those revelations, coming from King's closest and most trusted friend, were met with harsh criticism of Abernathy. He justified his decision to write about those allegations by saying that all of those issues had been discussed in public over the years. Nevertheless, it seemed to many observers to have been a strange decision given the history between the two men.

Less than one year after his book was released, Abernathy died on April 17, 1990, at the age of sixty-four.

Ralph Abernathy, *And the Walls Came Tumbling Down;* Adam Fairclough, *To Redeem the Soul of America: The Southern Christian Leadership Conference and Martin Luther King, Jr.;* David Garrow, *Bearing the Cross: Martin Luther King, Jr. and the Southern Christian Leadership Conference.*

☯ Brown, Oliver

(1919–1961) This African Methodist Episcopal (AME) minister was the plaintiff in the *Brown v. Board of Education of Topeka, Kansas,* desegregation case. He filed suit against the local school board in 1950 when it refused to allow him to enroll his daughter, Linda, in an all-white school in that city. His suit became the lead case of the five school desegregation cases grouped together by the National Association for the Advancement of Colored People (NAACP) that resulted in the decision by the U. S. Supreme Court that segregation in public education is unconstitutional. That ruling was handed down on May 17, 1954.

Brown was born in Topeka, Kansas, in 1919. As a lifelong resident of the community, he was an ideal person to challenge segregation in public education. He was a veteran of World War II. He worked as a welder for the Santa Fe Railroad. He was the assistant pastor of the St. John AME Church of Topeka. He had no prior history of civil rights militancy. He was a taxpaying resident who wanted his children to receive the best education available, and that meant enrolling them in the schools that were at that time all white.

Brown was encouraged by the local and national NAACP to seek to enroll his daughter in an all-white school, because he could not be dismissed by whites in the community as "an outside agitator." That was a title that was regularly given to any black person from outside any Southern community who attempted to alter the social or political status quo. The other advantage of Brown being the plaintiff was that his job with the Santa Fe Railroad was unionized; therefore he could not be fired as a reprisal for his political activism. The threat of being fired and losing one's economic livelihood had long discouraged many black people from challenging the laws and customs that supported racial segregation.

Brown died in 1961.

Richard Kluger, *Simple Justice;* Aldon D. Morris, *The Origins of the Civil Rights Movement;* Mark Whitman, *Removing a Badge of Slavery.*

☮ Cornish, Samuel

(1795–1859) One of the most important voices in the historic struggle for black liberation, though it has often been overlooked and undervalued, has been that of black newspapers and the editors and writers for those journals. Cornish was a part of the first wave of black people who waged the struggle for freedom as much with ink and paper as with any other method.

Cornish was born to free parents in Delaware in 1795 and was educated in the Free African Schools of Philadelphia and New York City. Following the completion of his education, he began a career as a Presbyterian minister, organizing the first black Presbyterian church in New York City.

However, Cornish is most noted not for his work as a minister but for being

the cofounder and coeditor, with John Russworm, of a weekly newspaper called *Freedom's Journal.* When the paper appeared in New York City on March 16, 1827, it was the first newspaper in America to be owned and operated by black people. It was also one of the few papers that reported positively on life in the black community. Among its contributing writers were such notable black people as James Forten, David Walker, and **Richard Allen.**

Freedom's Journal began as an abolitionist newspaper, clearly predating William Lloyd Garrison's *The Liberator* or Frederick Douglass's *The North Star.* The inaugural issue of *Freedom's Journal* set forth its mission: "We wish to plead our own cause. Too long have others spoken for us. Too long has the publick been deceived by misrepresentations, in thinking which concerns us dearly, though in the estimation of some mere trifles; for though there are many in society who exercise towards us benevolent feelings; still (with sorrow we confess it) there are others who make it their business to enlarge upon the least trifle…. It shall never be our object to court controversy, though we must at all times consider ourselves as champions in defense of oppressed humanity."

By September 1827 Cornish left *Freedom's Journal* to devote his time and attention to developing free African schools such as he had attended. Russworm took editorial control of the newspaper and shifted its focus from the abolitionist movement to the nationalist movement and the back-to-Africa message. This shift resulted in a loss of advertising and subscriptions. In 1829 Russworm resigned from the paper, the name of which had been changed to *Rights of All,* expatriated to Liberia, West Africa, and founded the *Liberian Herald.*

Cornish returned to the paper, tried to save it financially, and tried to return its focus to its abolitionist message. However, the damage had been done, and the enterprise went bankrupt. This proved to be one of the earliest conflicts within the black community of the early nineteenth century between abolition and expatriation, or between free blacks claiming and attaining status as Americans or renouncing America and establishing new lives in Africa. Cornish and Russworm represented both sides of that argument.

In 1837 Cornish was appointed editor of another abolitionist newspaper, *Colored American.* Joining the two words *Colored* and *American* was done intentionally to suggest that the black people who produced that paper were committed to an abolitionist message and to claiming full citizenship rights for black people in America. The *Colored American* was one of the few newspapers in the country that reported on the slave revolt led by Joseph Cinque on board the *Amistad* in 1839.

Cornish not only advocated for an end to slavery through the pages of his newspapers but also worked for that goal as a founding member of the American Antislavery Society, which was organized in 1833. He died in 1859.

Lerone Bennett Jr., *Pioneers in Protest;* W. Augustus Low and Virgil A. Clift, eds., *Encyclopedia of Black America;* Benjamin Quarles, *Black Abolitionists;* Carl Senna, *The Black Press and the Struggle for Civil Rights.*

☻ Garnet, Henry Highland

(1815–1882) Born into slavery in Maryland on December 23, 1815, Garnet was the descendant of an African king from the Mandingo tribe. His grandfather had been captured in Africa and brought to the United States. His father escaped with him and the rest of his family to Wilmington, Delaware, and then to New York City, where they arrived in 1825. Thus resistance to slavery was the earliest and the longest-lasting impression made upon Garnet's mind.

Garnet would continue to oppose slavery first through his association with the New York Manumission Society and the American Antislavery Society and by allowing the predominantly white Presbyterian church he pastored in Troy, New York, to serve as a station for the Underground Railroad. He later became the founding pastor of the Liberty Street Negro Presbyterian Church of Troy.

Garnet was a part of a circle of remarkably talented black men who migrated to New York City at the same time. The group included the Shakespearean actor Ira Aldridge; **Samuel Cornish,** who would soon begin publishing *Freedom Journal,* the first black newspaper published in the United States; and **Alexander Crummell,** who like Garnet would enter the ministry and be active in emigration efforts.

Garnet and Crummell were also class mates during their formative educational years. In 1835 they were enrolled at Noyes Academy in Canaan, New Hampshire. That school was forcibly closed by its neighbors, who objected to the idea of having a school in their vicinity that offered education to blacks. The building was destroyed when teams of horses or oxen tore it from its foundation and dragged it into a nearby lake. Both men then enrolled in Oneida Institute in Troy, New York, graduating in 1840.

Garnet may be best known for a single speech he delivered before the Colored National Convention in Buffalo, New York, in 1843. In his "Address to the Slaves of the United States," he called upon slaves throughout the South to throw off their chains, not solely by engaging in full-scale rebellion but rather by first refusing to work without compensation. The most famous lines of the speech were, "Rather die freemen than live to be slaves," and "Let your motto be Resistance! Resistance! Resistance!" His language became even more volatile as the speech went along. He went on to

say: "To such degradation it is sinful in the extreme for you to make voluntary submission.... Neither God, nor angels, or just men, command you to suffer for a single moment. Therefore, it is your solemn and imperative duty to use every means, both moral, intellectual, and physical, that promises success."

Garnet's speech met with immediate opposition from Frederick Douglass, a peer within the **abolitionist movement,** and many others who favored the use of moral suasion over direct physical attack or work stoppages. Nevertheless, Garnet's views continued to be printed in Douglass's abolitionist newspaper, *The North Star.* The tension with Douglass increased in 1849, when Garnet emigrated to England, an act that Douglass thought removed him too far from the struggle for abolition of slavery. Garnet had another idea, which was to urge England directly to cease purchasing goods made by slave labor, thus affecting the economy of slavery. He left England to do missionary work in Jamaica in 1852, and due to illness he returned to the United States in 1856. He assumed the pastorate of the Shiloh Presbyterian Church of New York City.

In 1858 Garnet founded the African Civilization Society. This society was created to aid free blacks who desired to emigrate from America to Liberia and Sierra Leone. Once there, they would work to introduce Christianity and other aspects of Western civilization to the people of West Africa. That being done, it was Garnet's hope that those free blacks and native Africans could create an agricultural economy that produced cotton at a price substantially lower than the price of cotton grown in slave-holding states. If European nations would purchase cotton from West Africa and not from the United States, slavery could be dealt a deathblow.

Garnet was the first African American clergyman to preach a sermon before a session of the U.S. Congress, delivering his memorial discourse before the House of Representatives on February 12, 1865. In 1881 he was appointed the United States minister resident and consul general to Liberia. He died in Liberia in February 1882.

Howard Brotz, ed., *Negro Social and Political Thought 1850–1920;* Henry Highland Garnet, "An Address to the Slaves of the United States of America"; "Henry Highland Garnet," in *Black Leaders of the Nineteenth Century,* ed. Leon Litwack and August Meier; Wilson Jeremiah Moses, *The Golden Age of Black Nationalism, 1850–1925;* Deirdre Mullane, ed., *Crossing the Danger Water;* Earl Ofari, *"Let Your Motto Be Resistance": The Life and Thought of Henry Highland Garnet;* Henry J. Young, *Major Black Religious Leaders, 1755–1940.*

☾ Hood, James Walker

(1831-1918) It was difficult if not impossible for the black Methodist denominations to evangelize in the South prior to the end of the Civil War. That was because Southern states, in response to the **Nat Turner** rebellion in 1831, had put tight restrictions on the movement of free blacks and especially black preachers. Also in response to the Turner rebellion, slave owners rarely allowed their slaves to hear black preachers except within the plantation setting. One of the first black Methodist preachers to evangelize within

the South, even before the Civil War had ended, was James Walker Hood.

Hood was born in Pennsylvania on May 30, 1831. He worked alongside his father as a tenant farmer, and though he had sensed his call when he was twenty-one, he did not begin his ministry until a few years later. He joined the **African Methodist Episcopal Zion (AME Zion) Church** in 1857, and in 1858 he was sent by the New England annual conference to Halifax, Nova Scotia, as a missionary to the fugitive slaves who had fled there from various locations in the United States. He served another AME Zion church in Connecticut in 1860. Then he was sent to North Carolina to work behind the Union army lines as a missionary to the newly freed slaves. He was literally preaching to the freedmen while buildings that had been torched by the advancing Union army were still burning. His min-

istry gives new meaning to the old song "I am on the battlefield for my Lord."

With the end of the war, Hood became active in Republican Party politics. In 1867 he was a delegate to the North Carolina constitutional convention. In 1868 he was named assistant superintendent for public instruction for the state of North Carolina. By 1870 more than forty-nine thousand black children were enrolled in school in that state because of his initiatives. In 1872 he was a delegate to the Republican National Convention, and in 1876 he was appointed chairman of the Republican State Convention of North Carolina. He was also nominated to run as a Republican for secretary of state of North Carolina on several occasions, but he declined the honor.

However, Hood served in all of those political offices while maintaining his role as pastor of a steadily growing congregation in Charlotte. He was elected a bishop of the AME Zion Church in 1872, and he served in that position for more than forty years. In 1879 he led the way in the founding of Livingstone College in Salisbury, North Carolina. Over time the religion department of that college evolved into Hood Theological Seminary, named in his honor. In 1881 he was a preacher at the Ecumenical Methodist Conference in London, England. In 1884 Hood became the first black preacher to publish a volume of sermons, *The Negro in the Christian Pulpit*.

In 1891 Hood challenged his fellow AME Zion bishops to ordain women as delegates to their respective general conference meetings. He took the lead in that area on May 20, 1894, when he presided at the ordination of Julia Foote. She became the first woman to be ordained an elder in any of the black or white Methodist bodies in the United States. The **African Methodist Episcopal (AME) Church** did not ordain a woman until 1948, and the **Colored (Christian) Methodist Episcopal Church** (CME) did not follow suit until 1954.

Along with Booker T. Washington, Hood was one of the African American leaders who regularly consulted with President Theodore Roosevelt. Hood retired as bishop in 1916, after forty-four years in the episcopacy. He died in 1918. He had made a great contribution to the state of North Carolina as a pastor, government official, preacher, educator, and bishop.

C. Eric Lincoln and Lawrence W. Mamiya, *The Black Church in the African American Experience;* Larry Murphy, J, Gordon Melton, and Gary Ward, eds., *Encyclopedia of African American Religions;* Harry V. Richardson, *Dark Salvation;* Carter G. Woodson, *The History of the Negro Church.*

Hooks, Benjamin Lawson

(1925–) As a lawyer, judge, federal official, civil rights activist, and Baptist pastor, few people in American history have made more contributions to the cause of justice and from more positions of influence than has Benjamin Hooks. He was a major player in the fight for social equality and equal opportunity for all people in twentieth-century American history.

Hooks was born in Memphis, Tennessee, on January 31, 1925. He began his education at LeMoyne College in Memphis, but his studies were interrupted by military service. After the war he

completed his college work at Howard University, graduating with a bachelor of arts degree in 1944. He earned a law degree from DePaul University in Chicago in 1948. At that time, no law school in Tennessee would admit a black student. He then began the practice of law in Memphis and throughout Shelby County, Tennessee, running for various public offices from time to time. He never won, but he was steadily building up a political base in the white and black electorate.

In 1956 Hooks was ordained to the ministry and installed as pastor of the Middle Baptist Church in Memphis. He quickly became active in the **civil rights movement** in the South, and in 1958 he became a member of the board of the **Southern Christian Leadership Conference** (SCLC) organized by **Martin Luther King Jr.** Hooks became active in the **Progressive National Baptist Convention (PNBC)** and in the local and regional work of the National Association for the Advancement of Colored People (NAACP). In his role on the board of the SCLC, Hooks opposed King's decision to speak out against the war in Vietnam, saying, "I question whether it is wise for us to go too far in the international arena." However, that disagreement had no effect on the friendship between the two men. King had dinner at the home of Hooks in Memphis on April 3, 1968, the night before King was assassinated.

In 1964 Hooks added a second pastoral role to his workload when he was called to the Greater New Mount Moriah Baptist Church in Detroit, Michigan. For the next several years he shuttled between the two churches, preaching at each one on alternate Sundays. In 1962 he became an assistant county prosecutor, and his political aspirations paid off in 1965, when he was tapped to fill an unexpired term as a criminal court judge in Shelby County. In 1966 he ran for and was elected to a full term. However, he resigned from the bench in 1968 to pursue his ministerial career and several private ventures.

Among those private ventures was Hooks's role as producer and host of a television program in Memphis. That involvement in television set the stage for President Richard M. Nixon to appoint Hooks in 1972 to become the first black member of the Federal Communications Commission (FCC), a body that oversees all radio and television operations in the country. Hooks was a tireless crusader for increased minority ownership of electronic media outlets in the United States.

In 1977 Hooks made the move that most defines his contribution to the cause of justice when he succeeded Roy Wilkins as executive secretary of the national office of the NAACP. He served in that role until his retirement in 1992. During that time, Hooks was a constant advocate for increased political and economic power for black Americans. For his service to the NAACP and to the nation, Hooks was awarded the Spingarn Medal by the NAACP in 1986.

Lucius J. Barker and Mack H. Jones, *African Americans and the American Political System*, 3d ed.; *Encyclopedia Britannica 2001* deluxe ed. CD; David Garrow, *Bearing the Cross*.

☻ Jackson, Jesse Louis

(1941-) Comparable only to Booker T. Washington in terms of the length of his career and the breadth of his influence, this country preacher was born in Greenville, South Carolina, on October 8, 1941. He was born to Helen Burns, an unwed teenage mother; his father was Noah Robinson, a prominent black man in the community who lived next door to Helen Burns. He acknowledged that Jesse was his son, but he accepted no responsibility for rearing him. The name Jackson came when his mother married Charles Jackson in 1957 and Jesse was formally adopted.

Jackson was a star athlete at Sterling High School in Greenville. He was offered a contract to play professional baseball by the New York (now San Francisco) Giants but rejected the contract when he was offered $6,000 while a white player was offered $95,000. Instead, he accepted an athletic scholarship to the University of Illinois, hoping to become the first black person to play quarterback for a Big Ten school.

When he was told that he would not be allowed to play that position, Jackson transferred to North Carolina Agricultural and Technical College in Greensboro, North Carolina, in 1961. There he was able to fulfill his athletic ambitions and to emerge as the campus leader. He also fell under the influence of the college's president, **Samuel Dewitt Proctor,** who was the kind of mentor and confidant to Jackson that **Benjamin Elijah Mays** had been to **Martin Luther King Jr.**

More importantly, it was in Greensboro that Jackson's civil rights activities began. He became a leader of the student sit-in movement in that city and was arrested for his leadership of a demonstration in downtown Greensboro on June 6, 1963. A civil rights leader had been born.

Jackson worked as the field director of the Congress of Racial Equality (CORE) for the southeastern region. He sensed a call to ministry and attended Chicago Theological Seminary. However, he went to participate in the Selma to Montgomery march in Alabama in 1965, and he never returned to finish his degree. He became closely involved with King, who appointed him the Chicago director of Operation Breadbasket, the economic development arm of the **Southern Christian Leadership Conference (SCLC),** in 1966. He was named the national director in 1967.

Jackson was standing on the balcony of the Lorraine Motel in Memphis, Tennessee, when King was assassinated. From that moment, it seemed to him that he was destined to be the heir to the fallen leader. After a series of disputes with **Ralph David Abernathy** and the board of SCLC, Jackson broke away and formed Operation PUSH (People United to Save Humanity) in 1971. Through his weekly meetings, his frequent radio and television appearances, and his constant travel schedule across the country, Jackson had become the most visible and influential black person in America by the age of thirty. He had already appeared on the cover of *Time* at the age of twenty-seven.

Jackson's early career focus was in the area of the economic empowerment of black businesses. He would work with white corporations, often through the threat of economic boycotts, to persuade them to grant franchises to black investors, to do business with black service providers, and to hire blacks at every level of their corporate structure. He also began a program called Black EXPO, which highlighted the skills and abilities of black-owned businesses.

Jackson's prominence on the national scene was increased in 1983, when he secured the release of an American naval pilot, Lt. Robert Goodman, whose plane had been shot down over Syria. This was an accomplishment that the government had not been able to achieve. In 1991 in Iraq, and again in 1999 in Serbia, Jackson was able to secure the release of persons who were being held as hostages by foreign governments.

In 1984 Jackson sought the Democratic nomination for president of the United States. His campaign was hurt when he referred to New York City as Hymietown, thus alienating Jewish voters, who make up a sizeable portion of the Democratic Party nationally. His association with **Louis Farrakhan,** who had recently referred to Judaism as "a gutter religion," made matters worse between Jackson and Jewish voters.

Despite his loss, Jackson redefined American politics forever. More black people registered to vote that year than at any time in the past. More blacks also began running for public office in response to his courageous campaign. The **Nation of Islam,** historically apolitical, was encouraged by Farrakhan to break with history and register to vote, and then members of the Nation were encouraged to vote for Jackson.

In 1986 Jackson formed a new organization, the Rainbow Coalition. His vision was one of people of all races, religions, and regions of the country working together to reshape social and political life. He moved from Chicago to Washington, D.C., to oversee that work. In 1988 he again ran for president. This time he won several state primaries and one-third of the delegates present at the nominating convention. Although he did not gain the nomination, his speech to the delegates is believed to be the finest political speech of the twentieth century. It seems that Jackson has been the unofficial president of black America since the 1988 campaign.

Jackson is the eulogist or wedding celebrant for many of the nation's most visible black entertainers, athletes, and business leaders. He remains visible in local civil rights cases across the country, usually invited by local leaders who hope to benefit from the media attention his presence will create. His career has often been marked by the charge that he has sought out those events where he can gain media attention.

While living in Washington, D.C., Jackson served as "shadow" senator for the District of Columbia, advocating for statehood for its residents. However, he refused to seek the office of mayor of Washington, D.C., when that post became available in 1989, perhaps viewing such a job as being too confining and leaving him unable to respond to issues that could erupt across the country or around the world.

In 1998 Jackson organized The Wall Street Project, an effort to increase black participation in the nation's financial markets and to further the economic development of black people through savings, investments, home ownership, and debt reduction. He helped coin the phrase "economic literacy," which means that blacks and others learn how to work within the wealth creation systems in the United States.

Famous for turning phrases that excite the crowds he addresses, Jackson's most famous phrases may be "I am somebody," "Keep hope alive," and "It's nation time." For nearly thirty-five years, Jackson has been one of the most powerful and provocative speakers in American history. *Ebony* listed him as one of the fifteen greatest black preachers in the country in 1984 and 1993.

After his long career of being interviewed by members of the news media, CNN gave Jackson the opportunity to change places and become an interviewer. He hosts a weekly television show, "Both Sides with Jesse Jackson," which airs weekly and is viewed nationally. His guests are a who's who in American politics, business, the arts, and religion.

Jackson and his wife, Jacqueline, were married in 1962 while both were students in Greensboro. They have five children. His oldest child, Jesse Jackson Jr., is a member of the United States Congress representing a portion of Chicago's south side. Jackson and his wife continue to live in Chicago, but his mission and ministry are truly global. He has weathered a revelation of having fathered a child out of wedlock and has undergone constant scrutiny by government agencies over the financial records of his various organizations. Despite that, he remains a powerful player on the world stage.

Adam Fairclough, *To Redeem the Soul of the Nation;* David Garrow, *Bearing the Cross;* Jesse Jackson, *Straight from the Heart;* Barbara Reynolds, *Jesse Jackson: The Man, the Myth, the Movement.*

☙ Jemison, Theodore Judson

(1918-) The bus boycott that occurred in Montgomery, Alabama (1955–1956), may have been the most famous bus boycott in civil rights history, but it was not the first. What happened in Montgomery was strengthened and aided by many of the lessons learned in the bus boycott in Baton Rouge, Louisiana, in 1953. The leader of that boycott was Rev. Theodore J. Jemison.

Jemison was born on August 1, 1918, in Selma, Alabama. His father was David Jemison, who not only was a leading pastor in that city but also served as president of the **National Baptist Convention, USA, Inc. (NBCUSA)** from 1940 to 1952. Theodore Jemison later followed his father in that office, serving from 1982–1994.

Jemison earned a bachelor of arts degree from Alabama State University in 1940 and a bachelor of divinity degree from Virginia Union University School of Theology in 1945. He was called to Mt. Zion First Baptist Church in Baton Rouge in 1949; there he served for the remainder of his ministry. In 1953, when his father stepped down as convention president, Theodore Jemison was elected to be the general secretary of the convention. He served alongside the new president of NBCUSA, **Joseph Harrison Jackson.** The two men served in those offices for the next twenty-nine years, until Jemison challenged Jackson and succeeded him into the presidency.

Because of Jemison's stature as an officer of the convention and as the son of a beloved former president of the convention, his role in Baton Rouge took on larger implications. He was not simply a single courageous pastor working outside of the national spotlight. He was the second-highest ranking officer of the largest black organization in the world. Whatever he said or did would have immediate national implications. Before **Martin Luther King Jr.** and the Montgomery bus boycott, and before the National Association for the Advancement of Colored People (NAACP) and *Brown v. Board of Education* (1954), the first shot of the civil rights revolution was fired by Jemison and the black citizens of Baton Rouge, Louisiana.

As was the case in cities all across the South, black bus passengers had to pay at the front, get off the bus, and reenter through the back door. They also were restricted to seats in the back of the bus, and they had to abandon those seats when seating reserved for whites in the front of the bus was filled. In March 1953 the Baton Rouge city council had passed a resolution that effectively ended segregation in seating and allowed black and white passengers to sit wherever a seat was available on a first-come, first-served basis. The only restriction was that blacks would agree to sit from the rear to the front and whites would sit from the front to the rear. The company's bus drivers refused to drive under those conditions, preferring the old segregated model. They went on strike and did not return until the Louisiana attorney general overturned the new city ordinance on the grounds that it was a violation of the state law that mandated segregation in seating on public buses. It must be remembered that segregation in all of its forms throughout the South was based upon

Plessy v. Ferguson, the U.S. Supreme Court case (1896) that created the separate but equal principle that supported racial segregation. That court ruling was based upon a law mandating segregation in public transportation in Louisiana. That is what led to the decision for black passengers to boycott the busses.

The boycott began on June 18, 1953, and was 100 percent effective by the end of the first day. Black riders stayed off of the buses, thus costing the bus company more than $1,600 a day in lost fares. There was a parallel loss in retail spending, since black customers were not riding the bus to various stores. Those who needed rides to work and for other essential purposes would be transported through a sophisticated network of private cars that served as taxis during the boycott. That would be an important model for the boycott that later took place in Montgomery. The boycott in Baton Rouge ended in eight days, when Jemison recommended a compromise solution to the problem. It was agreed, over some dissent within the community, that the front seats on both sides of the aisle would be reserved for whites. The long seat at the very back of the bus would be reserved for blacks. All other seats would be filled on a nonsegregated basis.

With differing results, the boycott in Baton Rouge set off a flurry of similar events. King led the boycott in Montgomery in 1955. C. K. Steele led a bus boycott in Tallahassee, Florida, in 1956. A. L. Davis led one in New Orleans in 1957. It is not by coincidence that all of these ministers came together to serve as founding members of the **Southern Christian Leadership Conference (SCLC)** in 1957. Jemison became the first general secretary of SCLC.

C. Eric Lincoln and Lawrence W. Mamiya, *The Black Church in the African American Experience;* Aldon D. Morris, *The Origins of the Civil Rights Movement;* Juan Williams, *Eyes on the Prize.*

☉ Johns, Vernon

(1892-1963) Johns was born in 1892 in Farmville, Prince Edward County, Virginia. The son of a Baptist preacher-farmer, Johns plowed the ground in the pulpit and in the fields. He was as noted for his willingness to sell fruits and vegetables outside the church as he was for the power of his preaching inside the sanctuary.

Johns is most noted for having been the pastor of the Dexter Avenue Baptist Church of Montgomery, Alabama, from 1947 to 1952. His agitation for an end to segregation and his incendiary sermons on issues of justice created a climate of acceptance for the work that would be done in that city by his successor at Dexter, **Martin Luther King Jr.** King wrote glowingly about Vernon Johns in *Stride Toward Freedom* (1958), noting that several years before Rosa Parks refused to give up her seat in the black section of a bus in Montgomery, Johns had taken a seat in the white section. He refused to move from that seat and finally did so after his fare had been refunded. He encouraged other blacks to get off the bus in protest, but none did so at that time. Thus Johns challenged segregation in public transportation in a way that even Parks had not done, but not with the same results that followed her arrest in 1955.

At the same time, Johns helped organize Farm and City Cooperative, a black-owned business that grew and sold food items within Montgomery's black community. This link to the land and to farming remained a part of John's self-understanding, celebrating the virtue of manual labor and the lessons of being self-sufficient. He was something of an eccentric in this regard, often going to preach directly after plowing a field, standing in the pulpit in dirty overalls and muddy shoes.

Johns's tenure at Dexter was marked by constant friction with the membership and board of deacons. Johns submitted his resignation on five separate occasions, and it was, much to his surprise, accepted the fifth time he did so. Having no place to go, his wife took a teaching job in Virginia, and he remained in the parsonage of the Dexter Avenue Baptist Church, against the will of the leaders, for another year. He did not leave until the gas and electricity were turned off.

Johns and King remained friends after their paths crossed at Dexter. The day before King was scheduled to deliver his trial sermon at Dexter, he provided a ride from Atlanta to Montgomery to Johns, who was scheduled to preach that next morning at First Baptist Church of Montgomery, where **Ralph David Abernathy** was the pastor. Johns would return occasionally to Montgomery to encourage and support King during the long Montgomery bus boycott (1955–1956).

When he left Montgomery, Johns returned to his native Prince Edward County, Virginia. There he played an active role in the integration of the public schools, in accordance with the 1954

Brown v. Board of Education ruling of the U.S. Supreme Court. His involvement is documented in *They Closed the Schools* by Robert Smith. Johns then went to work for the Maryland Baptist Center in Baltimore, Maryland. However, his efforts at racial reconciliation among blacks and whites were dashed by the same blunt speaking that had marked his ministry at Dexter. He was forced to resign from that position as well.

Johns's sermons focused as much on the apathy of blacks in the face of oppression as on the involvement of whites in perpetuating that oppression. He was a prophet to both communities, challenging them to "do justice," albeit from opposite ends of the spectrum. One of his colleagues wrote, "Vernon Johns has been endowed to do nothing but traverse the country irritating the Negro."

The sermons that Johns preached at Dexter Avenue Baptist Church frequently chastised his congregation so severely that it made for a tenuous pastor/people relationship. The hope of the congregation was that the next pastor would not be as outspoken on issues of race relations. How wrong they were about Johns's successor. This dual focus in the preaching of Johns is attested to in an HBO film on his life with James Earl Jones in the title role. That film also has several comments from Johns's contemporaries, who speak to the power and "withering assaults on injustice" that were the hallmark of his sermons.

Johns was a graduate of Oberlin College in Ohio and the Divinity School at the University of Chicago. He had prepared at least one manuscript for publication, *Human Possibilities*. However,

it, along with many other documents, was destroyed in a fire. One of his sermons, "Transfigured Moments," was published in the 1926 edition of *Best Sermons*. He was the first black preacher to appear in that notable book that presents what are affirmed by the editors to be the best sermons preached in the United States each year.

Johns collapsed, dead, after delivering a lecture on "The Romance of Death" at Howard University in 1963.

Charles Emerson Boddie, *God's Bad Boys;* Taylor Branch, *Parting the Waters;* Martin Luther King Jr., *Stride Toward Freedom;* Maelinda Turner, *Vernon Johns: Farmer, Preacher, Civil-Rights Pioneer.*

☯ King, Martin Luther, Jr.

(1929–1968) "I have a dream..." Those words were spoken before an audience of more than 250,000 persons in Washington, D.C., at the end of the largest civil rights demonstration in American history. They were spoken by Martin Luther King Jr., arguably the most influential and effective advocate for human and civil rights in all of American history.

King was born on January 15, 1929, in Atlanta, Georgia. He was a third-generation Baptist preacher. His maternal grandfather, A. D. Williams, founded Ebenezer Baptist Church in Atlanta. His father, Martin Luther King Sr., succeeded Williams as pastor of that congregation. An eloquent speaker from his childhood, King won an oratorical contest sponsored by the Elks. During the bus ride home from the contest in 1944, he was

ordered to give up his seat to a white passenger and ride the ninety miles from Valdosta, Georgia, to Atlanta standing in the aisle. That event made a lasting impression upon the young King.

King entered Morehouse College in Atlanta at the age of fifteen and was greatly influenced by its president, **Benjamin Elijah Mays.** King went on to earn a bachelor of divinity degree at Crozer Theological Seminary in Chester, Pennsylvania, in 1951, and a doctor of philosophy degree in systematic theology from Boston University in 1955.

While enrolled at Boston University he met and married Coretta Scott, and the couple moved to Montgomery, Alabama, where King had accepted the call to be the pastor of Dexter Avenue Baptist Church. On December 1, 1955, Rosa Parks was arrested for refusing to surrender her seat in the black section of a bus to a white passenger. That set in motion a series of events that propelled King into the forefront of the **civil rights movement.** He became the president of the Montgomery Improvement Association, which led a successful 381-day boycott by black citizens of the busses of Montgomery until the laws governing segregation in public transportation had been eliminated.

In 1957 King helped to organize the Southern Leadership Conference on Transportation and Nonviolent Integration; it was a precursor to the **Southern Christian Leadership Conference (SCLC),** of which King was elected the first president. He left Dexter and moved to Atlanta in 1958 to devote himself to the work of SCLC while serving as copastor of Ebenezer with his father. In 1960 he was also instrumental in the founding of the Student Nonviolent Coordinating Committee (SNCC) at Shaw University in Raleigh, North Carolina.

King's emergence as a national leader can be traced to his leadership in the May 17, 1957, Prayer Pilgrimage that was held on the steps of the Lincoln Memorial. He later returned to that site to deliver his "I Have a Dream" speech, the finale of the August 27, 1963, March on Washington.

King's commitment to nonviolence was the defining ideology of his life. That philosophy was initially shaped by his reading of the life and work of Mohandas K. Gandhi, who led a nonviolent struggle for independence in India that culminated in Britain's withdrawal from India in 1948. His commitment to nonviolence was further informed and influenced by a 1957 visit to Ghana, which had undergone a nonviolent independence struggle, and a 1959 visit to India, where he learned more about the struggle led there by Gandhi.

King's commitment to nonviolence was in marked contrast to the violence that regularly surrounded his life. His home in Montgomery was bombed. He was stabbed in the chest by a black woman while signing copies of his first book, *Stride Toward Freedom*, in New York City. He was the frequent victim of physical assaults, rock throwing, and numerous arrests.

Two imprisonments were especially notable. In 1960, in response to a violation of the terms of his probation for an earlier arrest, King was sentenced to four to twelve months of hard labor at Reids-ville State Prison in Georgia. The direct involvement of John F. Kennedy and Robert F. Kennedy led to his release from prison. The news of that intervention spread throughout black communities across the country and contributed to Kennedy's election as president of the United States the next month.

While confined in the city jail in Birmingham, Alabama, in 1963, King wrote his impassioned "Letter from a Birmingham Jail," perhaps the greatest protest document of the twentieth century. King was in Birmingham to lead a demonstration to end segregation in all of the public accommodations of that city. While his efforts in Birmingham met with success, he was less successful when he led a similar demonstration in Albany, Georgia, in 1962. In that city the sheriff, Laurie Pritchett, used restraint in his handling of the protesters. By not using force he was able to diminish the sense of drama that usually accompanied a nonviolent demonstration.

King's leadership of the nonviolent campaign in Birmingham in the spring of 1963 and his leadership role in the March on Washington contributed to his being awarded the Nobel Prize for peace on December 10, 1964. His leadership also directly contributed to the passage of the 1964 Civil Rights Bill. In 1965 he led the historic march from Selma to Montgomery, Alabama, that sought to secure voting rights for black people in that state. That march contributed to the passage of the 1965 Voting Rights Act.

Beginning in 1966, King began to widen his focus from issues of civil rights to include the issues of economic justice and poverty. He led a demonstration in

Chicago, Illinois, in the summer of 1966, documenting the abject poverty in which many in that Northern city were forced to live, as well as to demonstrate that racism and segregation were as prevalent in the North as they were in the South.

King's boldest move may have been his decision on April 4, 1967, to deliver a speech at Riverside Church in New York City to condemn the Vietnam War. That not only resulted in a loss of support from other civil rights leaders, among them Roy Wilkins and Whitney Young, but also placed him at odds with President Lyndon B. Johnson, who had been supportive of King's civil rights agenda. However, King believed that his commitment to nonviolence demanded that he speak out. His stature as a peace prize recipient gave his words international reach. And he believed that Johnson's announced War on Poverty and the Vietnam War could not be funded by the federal government at the same time.

King's leadership on issues of civil rights, economic justice, and the antiwar movement led many to urge him to consider accepting a third-party nomination and run to become president of the United States in the 1968 election. He decided against such a move. However, King's expanding influence beyond issues of civil rights caused J. Edgar Hoover of the Federal Bureau of Investigation (FBI) to label King "the most dangerous Negro in America." The FBI regularly wire-tapped his telephone conversations, believing or contending that he had some ties to the Communist Party through a friend named Stanley Levinson.

In 1968 King was planning a Poor People's Campaign in Washington, D.C., to address the issue of poverty in America. He took time out from that planning process to lend support to striking sanitation workers in Memphis, Tennessee, in March and April 1968. While he was in Memphis, he was assassinated on April 4, 1968, at the age of thirty-nine. He is survived by his wife and their four children: Yolanda, Martin III, Dexter, and Bernice.

King wrote several books, including *Stride Toward Freedom, Why We Can't Wait, Where Do We Go from Here?* and *Strength to Love.* In 1985 President Ronald Reagan signed a bill establishing King's birthday, January 15, as a federal holiday. He is the third American to receive such recognition.

Lerone Bennett Jr., *What Manner of Man;* Taylor Branch, *Parting the Waters;* Leon Litwack and August Meier, eds., *Black Leaders of the Twentieth Century;* James H. Cone, *Martin and Malcolm and America;* David Garrow, *Bearing the Cross* and *The FBI and Martin Luther King Jr.;* David L. Lewis, *King;* Aldon D. Morris, *The Origins of the Civil Rights Movement.*

☯ Lawson, James

(1928–) Born September 22, 1928, and reared in Massillon, Ohio, Lawson was the principal theoretician of the philosophy of nonviolence and passive resistance during the **civil rights movement** of the 1950s and 1960s. The great-grandson of a runaway slave and the son of a Methodist minister, Lawson went on to pastor several United Methodist churches during an activist career that spanned more than forty years.

Lawson graduated from Baldwin Wallace College in Berea, Ohio. He served a one-year sentence in federal prison in 1951 when he refused induction into the armed forces during the Korean conflict on the grounds of conscientious objection. He was released from prison on early parole due to the intervention of several Methodist ministers, who then sent him as a missionary to India for three years. His time in India was supported by the American Friends Service Committee, a pacifist group. During those years in India, he studied the philosophy of nonviolence and passive resistance with followers of Mohandas K. Gandhi.

Upon his return to the United States, Lawson pursued ministerial training at Oberlin School of Theology in Ohio. While Lawson was a student there, **Martin Luther King Jr.** visited that campus, and a friendship and collaboration began that would span the following turbulent decade. Lawson withdrew from Oberlin, went to work for the Fellowship of Reconciliation (FOR), a pacifist group founded in 1941, and began teaching the principles of pacifism to college students throughout the South.

While serving the FOR in Nashville, Lawson trained the black students who participated in the first wave of sit-ins in that city in the spring of 1960. His involvement in the sit-ins caused him to be expelled from Vanderbilt Divinity School, where he had been enrolled for a short time. Ten members of the Vanderbilt faculty resigned to protest his expulsion.

Lawson went on to play a leadership role in the Freedom Rides through Mississippi and Alabama in 1961, always practicing and being a proponent of passive resistance. Lawson collaborated with King in every major civil rights campaign of the 1960s. He trained people in the philosophy of nonviolence in Albany, Georgia (1962), Birmingham (1963) and Selma (1965), Alabama, and Chicago, Illinois (1966).

Lawson became the pastor of the Centenary Methodist Church in Memphis, Tennessee. In 1968 he helped to organize the sanitation workers who were protesting their wages and working conditions. Lawson's invitation brought King to Memphis to support those striking workers. The nonviolence that Lawson was urging upon the marchers in Memphis broke down, and looting erupted, forcing King to be taken from the scene for his own safety.

King decided to remain involved in the events in Memphis, primarily to demonstrate that a nonviolent demonstration was still possible. If he could not do that in Memphis, the Poor People's Campaign he was planning later that summer in Washington, D.C., might have to be cancelled. On April 4, 1968, while still in Memphis, King was assassinated.

Lawson ended his career by serving as pastor of the Holman Avenue Methodist Church in Los Angeles and as president of the Los Angeles chapter of the **Southern Christian Leadership Conference (SCLC).** In 2000 Lawson was featured in a PBS television special, *A Force More Powerful,* which examined nonviolent movements in the United States, India, and South Africa.

Taylor Branch, *Parting the Waters;* Karen Long, "The Power of Passive Resistance," *The Plain Dealer* (Cleveland, Ohio), September 16, 2000; Aldon D. Morris, *The Origins of the Civil Rights Movement;* Juan Williams, *Eyes on the Prize.*

☻ Murray, Anna Pauline (Pauli)

(1910–1985) "Renaissance woman" may be the best way to describe Murray. She made an important contribution to American life in four different professional areas. She was a poet and author who was a protégé of Langston Hughes during the Harlem Renaissance. She was a practicing attorney who wrote the amendment to Title VII of the 1964 Civil Rights Bill that outlawed discrimination in hiring on the basis of gender. She was an academician who taught law at Brandeis University and served as a vice president of Benedict College in South Carolina. She also served as a senior lecturer in law at the Ghana School of Law in Accra. In 1977 she became the first African American woman to be ordained to the priesthood of the Protestant Episcopal Church.

Murray was born in Baltimore, Maryland, in 1910. She was orphaned at an early age and was reared by members of her extended family in Durham, North Carolina. She received a bachelor of arts degree from Hunter College in New York City in 1933 with a major in English literature. In 1934 Hughes assisted her in having her first poem published: "The Song of the Highway."

Murray was denied admission to Harvard Law School due to gender bias, so she received her law degree from Howard University in 1944, where she was the valedictorian and the only woman in the class. She later sued Harvard over the issue of gender bias and discrimination. Murray earned an L.L.M degree from Berkeley in California in 1945 and was the first woman to receive a law degree from Yale in 1965. Her experience with that form of discrimination made a deep impression on her. Murray, with Betty Friedan, was a cofounder of the National Organization of Women (NOW), one of the earliest feminist organizations in the country.

Murray was involved in civil rights issues in the 1940s, being arrested for challenging segregation in seating on interstate buses that traveled through the South. She also became an outspoken critic of the gender bias exhibited by black male leaders of the American **civil rights movement.** She discovered over and over again that people who oppose discrimination based upon race are fully capable of practicing discrimination based upon gender. Her crusading work against gender bias places Murray in this listing of religious leaders who fulfilled a prophetic role in American society.

Murray knocked down the greatest wall of her career when in 1977 she became the first African American woman and the second woman ordained to the priesthood of the Episcopal Church. She served as a priest at The Church of the Atonement in Washington, D.C., for only five years, because that church has a mandatory retirement age of seventy-two. However, during that brief ministry career Murray became a force within the life of that church body.

Murray wrote three books. *Proud Shoes: The Story of an American Family —The Fitzgeralds of North Carolina* (1956) dealt with her extended family. Her second book, *Dark Testament and Other Poems,* was a collection of poems written in the 1930s but not published until 1970. *Pauli Murray: The Autobiography of a Black Activist* was released posthumously in 1989. Murray died in 1985.

Bettye Collier-Thomas, *Daughters of Thunder;* Sonia Pressman Fuentes, "Pauli Murray," in *The Legendary Feminists;* William Andrews, Frances Smith Foster, and Trudie Harris, eds., *The Oxford Companion to African American Literature.*

☉ Pennington, James W. C.

(1809-1871) A fugitive slave from Maryland and a leading voice in the **abolitionist movement** in the United States and throughout Europe, Pennington was one of the most highly regarded Presbyterian ministers of the nineteenth century. He was born in slavery in 1809 and was trained to be a blacksmith. However, he ran away from his owner and settled eventually in Hartford, Connecticut. He showed great skill with foreign languages and also trained for the ministry. He served several black Presbyterian congregations, including the prestigious Shiloh Presbyterian Church in New York City. In 1853 he was elected moderator of the presbytery of New York City.

By 1841 Pennington was actively involved in the abolitionist movement. He traveled to London in 1843 and again in 1851 as a delegate from the Connecticut Antislavery Society to the World Antislavery Society. He also attended the World Peace Conference when that body met in Paris, Brussels, and London. During one of his European trips the doctor of divinity degree was conferred upon him by the University of Heidelberg in Germany.

Pennington was an outspoken critic of the American Colonization Society (ACS), which sought to settle free blacks in newly established colonies in West Africa. He insisted that blacks should seek full citizenship within American society. He argued that the fate of America and the fate of black people were inseparably bound together. On that issue he wrote, "Our destiny is bound up with that of America; her ship is ours, her pilot is ours, her storms are ours, her calms are ours. If she breaks upon any rock, we break with her. We love America and hate slavery the more; and thus, loving the one and hating the other, we are resolved that they shall NOT LONG DWELL TOGETHER."

However, Pennington was supportive of the Union Missionary Society, founded in Hartford in 1841 to spread the Christian gospel among the people living on the African continent. This focus on the Christianization of Africa was common among black clergy in the nineteenth century, whether or not they supported colonization.

Pennington's greatest contribution to the church came in his relentless efforts to prove that the Bible did not support slavery, as many pro-slavery preachers in America were suggesting. Using various New Testament passages he demonstrated that those biblical texts spoke against slavery, not in defense of it. He firmly believed that slavery was incompatible with biblical teachings. He went so far as to say that he would reject the Bible if it did

support the idea of slavery: "Is the word of God silent on this subject? I, for one, desire to know. My repentance, my faith, my hope, my love, and my perseverance all, all, I conceal it not, I repeat it, all turn upon this point. If I am deceived here—if the word of God does sanction slavery, I want another book, another repentance, another faith, and another hope."

In his abolitionist efforts, Pennington worked closely with other persons in that movement, including William Lloyd Garrison and Frederick Douglass. Pennington presided at the marriage ceremony of Douglass and his first wife, Anna Murray, on September 15, 1838. In 1853 Pennington was elected president of the National Council of Colored People by the 140 delegates who had gathered at the first annual session of that convention in Rochester, New York. That city had long been a center of abolitionist activity and had been a base of operation for **Sojourner Truth** and Douglass.

In 1855 Pennington was forcibly removed and seriously injured when he was thrown from a horse-drawn trolley that carried passengers through New York City. The driver was attempting to prohibit him from riding on the basis of laws that denied blacks access to the trolleys. Pennington sued the company for his injury and for refusal to provide him with equal access to public transportation. He won that case and opened the trolleys in New York City to all passengers without regard to race.

Like Douglass, Pennington wrote a slave narrative that recounted his life in slavery and his subsequent escape to the North. His narrative, *The Fugitive Blacksmith: or Events in the History of James*

W. C. Pennington, was released in 1844. He also wrote *A Textbook on the Origins and History of the Colored People* (1841) and *The Past and Present Condition, and the Destiny of the Colored Race* (1848). Pennington frequently contributed articles to various abolitionist journals and newspapers. On November 5, 1859, the *Weekly Anglo-American* ran one of his articles, "Pray for John Brown." It was a call for support of Brown after his arrest and trial following the raid at Harper's Ferry, Virginia.

Pennington died in 1871.

Cleophus LaRue, *The Heart of Black Preaching;* Carter G. Woodson, *History of the Negro Church;* Henry J. Young, *Major Black Religious Leaders, 1755–1940.*

☻ Sharpton, Alfred

(1954–) Born in Brooklyn, New York, on October 3, 1954, Sharpton began preaching in public at the age of four under the inspiration and oversight of his pastor, Bishop F. D. Washington, a prominent pastor in **The Church of God in Christ (COGIC).** He was ordained into the ministry of that Pentecostal group at the age of ten. Later he attended Brooklyn College for a short time. He was also influenced at an early age by the work of **Marcus Garvey, Adam Clayton Powell Jr.,** and **Martin Luther King Jr.** He especially admired Powell's combining preaching and politics. It helped establish the model for his ministry.

In the late 1960s Sharpton became active in Operation Breadbasket, the economic arm of the **Southern Christian Leadership Conference (SCLC).** His relationship with **Jesse Jackson** dates to that time. He formed the National Youth Movement (NYM) in 1971; it sought to gain economic concessions from major corporations in hiring and promoting blacks and other minorities. James Brown, the soul singer, was a principal supporter of the NYM. Sharpton's pompadour hairstyle is modeled after Brown's. From 1973 to 1980, Sharpton traveled with Brown as his tour manager.

Although he spent some time working with music and fight promoters in the 1980s, Sharpton is most identified with a series of civil rights cases in the New York City area. Among them is the case of Bernard Goetz, the white man who was exonerated of having intentionally shot four blacks who he said were attempting to rob him on the subway. He also worked to get a black person appointed to the all-white Metropolitan Transit Authority board in 1986.

Sharpton was the chief advocate for Tawana Brawley, a young black woman who claimed to have been covered with dog feces and racist graffiti and left inside a plastic bag by a group of white police officers. His advocacy in that case resulted in his becoming a target in several criminal prosecutions involving fraud and tax evasion. He was acquitted of all charges.

Sharpton also played a leading role in calling public attention to other cases of civil rights violations, among them Yusef Hawkins, who was murdered in Brooklyn in 1989 by a white mob. He played a leading role in protesting the death of Amadou Diallo, a native of Guinea, West Africa, who was shot nineteen times by four police officers in the Bronx in 1999. He also led demonstrations calling for justice for Abner Louima, a Haitian immigrant who was brutally sodomized by several New York City police officers in 1997.

Sharpton survived a stabbing attack in 1991 while leading a demonstration through the Bensonhurst section of Brooklyn. Also in 1991 he organized the National Action Network, a civil rights organization that worked on issues of economic justice and political empowerment.

In 1992 and 1994 Sharpton unsuccessfully sought the Democratic Party nomination for the U.S. Senate from New York. However, he garnered more than 18 percent of the statewide vote, 21 percent of the vote in New York City, and more than 70 percent of the African American vote. He had also been the first African American to run for a seat in the New York state senate in 1978. In 1997 he garnered 32 percent of the vote in an unsuccessful bid for the Democratic Party nomination for mayor of New York City.

In 2000 Sharpton joined with Martin Luther King III in a reenactment of the 1963 March on Washington, an act that seemed to suggest that the two men were positioning themselves as successors to that legacy of civil rights leadership. Sharpton also organized a daylong demonstration in Washington, D.C., to protest the 2000 presidential election that resulted in the controversial U.S. Supreme Court ruling that gave the election to George W. Bush.

In 2001 Sharpton announced that he was considering running in the 2004 Democratic Party primary for president of the United States. He restated his commitment to do so following his arrest on the island of Vieques, Puerto Rico, where he was found guilty of trespassing on federal property. Sharpton was participating in a protest against the use of that island as a training ground for U.S. military forces to test bombs, rockets, and other weapons on land that also has a large human population.

Sharpton, his wife, Kathy, and their children still live in Brooklyn. Never an active pastor, Sharpton has always blended his religious passions with a keen social conscience that has resulted in a ministry that has seen him as willing to spend as much time in the streets as he has in the sanctuary. Tom Wolfe seems to offer a caricature of Sharpton in the character Reverend Bacon in his novel, which also became a film, *Bonfire of the Vanities*.

"Holding Up the Stones: The Social Ministry of Reverend Al Sharpton," *Gospel Today*, January 1999; Al Sharpton and Anthony Walton, *Go and Tell Pharaoh*; "Sharpton, Alfred, Jr.," www.Africana.com.

◉ Shuttlesworth, Fred Lee

(1922-) Born in 1922 in rural Muggler, Alabama, this fearless and tenacious advocate for justice was the founder of the Alabama Christian Movement for Human Rights (ACMHR) in Birmingham in 1956. This organization sought to parallel the activities to challenge segregation then underway with the Montgomery Improvement Association headed by **Martin Luther King Jr.** The ACMHR became an affiliate of the **Southern Christian Leadership Conference (SCLC)** when that group was founded in 1958, and Shuttlesworth became one of King's inner circle of advisors and confidants.

Shuttlesworth began his career working odd jobs. In 1941 he was arrested for operating a still. He worked as a truck driver and as a cement worker. It was during these hard years that he sensed his call to ministry. He would preach as many as five times per Sunday in order to support himself and his family and provide for his tuition. He was educated at Selma University and Alabama State Teachers' College. He began his pastoral ministry in Selma before moving on to a history-making ministry in Birmingham. His home was a place of refuge for Freedom Riders who in 1961 had been attacked by Klansmen when their buses arrived in Birmingham. In 1963 he convinced SCLC to join his ongoing struggle to end segregation in public accommodations in Birmingham.

Shuttlesworth was one of the victims of the water hoses that were turned on marchers to break up the demonstrations. He was lifted off the ground and hurled against the wall of a building. He was taken away by ambulance, having suffered severe bruises, but he returned to action the next day. During the time that he led the civil rights efforts in Birmingham, his church was bombed several times. On one occasion fifteen sticks of dynamite were placed near his home while he was in bed. He was thrown from the bed and ended up in the basement because the blast had blown a gaping hole in the floor. When he was warned by the police that he should leave town before another bomb killed him, he said that he would never run away.

Shuttlesworth was one of the speakers at the Prayer Pilgrimage held at the Lincoln Memorial on May 17, 1957, the third anniversary of the *Brown v. Board of Education* decision (1954). He also gave

the eulogy for Carole Robertson, one of the four girls killed in a bomb attack on the Sixteenth Street Baptist Church in Birmingham on September 15, 1963. He relocated to Cincinnati in 1964 to serve as pastor of Revelation Baptist Church and continues to reside there.

Shuttlesworth was one of five or six ministers who worked alongside King for a decade or more, but he never received the attention or adulation that fell upon King. That list would include **Ralph David Abernathy**, **Wyatt Tee Walker**, James Bevel, C. T. Vivian, Bernard Lee, and **Andrew J. Young.** Gayraud S. Wilmore wrote movingly of that group: "King … and a hundred other Black preachers, most of them undistinguished and unsung, were there only as the instruments—sometimes the reluctant instruments—upon which the theme of freedom, rising like a great crescendo from the depths of Black religion, were played out."

Taylor Branch, *Parting the Waters;* Vincent Harding, *Hope and History;* Martin Luther King Jr., *Why We Can't Wait;* Aldon D. Morris, *Origins of the Civil Rights Movement;* Gayraud S. Wilmore, *Black Religion and Black Radicalism.*

☯ Sullivan, Leon Howard

(1922–2001) No other person in the twentieth century played a larger role in improving the employment and economic opportunities of black people in the United States of America and the Union of South Africa than did Sullivan. He was the architect of Opportunities Industrialization Center (OIC) and the Sullivan Principles for foreign companies doing

business in South Africa, and hundreds of thousands of persons were made better off because of his efforts.

Sullivan was born in Charleston, West Virginia, on October 16, 1922. He went to West Virginia State University on an athletic scholarship and graduated with a bachelor of arts degree in 1943. Having been called to the ministry, he was hired by **Adam Clayton Powell Jr.** to be the assistant pastor at Abyssinian Baptist Church in New York City in the fall of 1943. He was also enrolled at Union Theological Seminary of New York City. He graduated from Union with a bachelor of divinity degree in 1945, and he then became pastor of the First Baptist Church of South Orange, New Jersey. He also earned a master of arts degree in sociology from Columbia University in 1947.

In 1950 Sullivan was called to the Zion Baptist Church of Philadelphia, Pennsylvania, where he remained until his retirement in 1988. Over those thirty-eight years he saw that congregation grow from six hundred to five thousand members. But his greatest contribution was not as a local pastor; it was as an advocate and agitator for economic empowerment for the poor and powerless of the world. By 1960 he was leading boycotts in Philadelphia against companies that would not hire black people, even though blacks made up a substantial amount of their customer base. Sullivan helped to popularize the phrase "Don't buy where you cannot work!"

Sullivan was successful in getting many of Philadelphia's largest employers to hire black workers. However, he then discovered that many people lacked the job skills and the work ethic to get or retain a job. To that end, in 1964 he organized the Opportunities Industrialization Center (OIC) in Philadelphia, which was a job-training program that prepared people for the workforce. That program eventually spread across the country and around the world. Within twenty years of its founding, OIC was operating out of 142 centers worldwide and has trained more than 1.5 million persons for jobs in various industries.

Sullivan's success with OIC caught the attention of General Motors Corporation, and in 1971 he became the first black person ever appointed to the board of directors of what was then the largest corporation in the world. Sullivan described his role on the General Motors board as "a voice from the outside sitting on the inside." The secretary of that board, Rod Gilleum, described Sullivan's role: "Sullivan represented the conscience of the board." By 1976, as a result of that conscience working inside the boardroom, General Motors was buying $50 million in parts from black suppliers and was spending heavily from its advertising budget in publications owned by blacks. The number of black executives also steadily increased.

However, it may be that Sullivan is most widely known for the Sullivan Principles, six rules that he offered as guidelines for American and other foreign-owned companies doing business in South Africa during the apartheid era. Apartheid was the principle established in South African law and daily life that kept political and economic power in the hands of a white population minority. At the same time, apartheid required that the black majority work only in the

lowest-paying jobs and live in the most desolate and undeveloped regions of the country. It was because of their opposition to apartheid that persons like Nelson Mandela were imprisoned.

The Sullivan Principles were introduced on April 1, 1977, and the first twelve corporations to become signatories to those principles were IBM, Ford, Mobil, CalTex, Citibank, 3M, Otis Elevator, International Harvester, American Cyanamid, Union Carbide, Burroughs, and General Motors. Those American companies agreed to treat their black South African employees in exactly the same way they treated their white South African employees. That action was the beginning of the end for the racial separation system known as apartheid.

The six principles involved integration in all work and eating areas. They required equal and fair hiring practices for all positions, as well as equal pay for equal or comparable work. They included training programs that would allow for promotion on the job, increasing the number of black South Africans in supervisory and management positions. Most importantly, they urged companies to improve the quality of life for their employees outside of the workplace in such areas as housing and health. As a follow-up to the Sullivan Principles, Sullivan organized annual summits between African and African American leaders to improve communication and enhance business partnerships. The first summit was held in 1991. He was planning the sixth annual summit in Nigeria when he died.

Sullivan is noted for another initiative, Zion Investment Associates, Inc. This was a self-help economic development program that began when 650 members of his church invested $10 per week for thirty-six weeks. The proceeds were then used to build moderate-income housing, the first black-owned and black-operated shopping center in America, and many other commercial enterprises. In recognition of this initiative, the University of Wisconsin School of Social Welfare has established a Leon Howard Sullivan endowed chair.

Sullivan was the recipient of the 1971 Spingarn Medal, the highest award given by the National Association for the Advancement of Colored People (NAACP). In 1992 President George Bush awarded him the Presidential Medal of Freedom, the highest civilian honor given to an American citizen. Sullivan wrote several books, including *Build, Brother, Build* and *Moving Mountains: The Prin-*

ciples and Purposes of Leon Sullivan. He died on April 25, 2001.

"Leon Sullivan Dies, Helped to End Apartheid," obituary of Leon Sullivan, *The Plain Dealer* (Cleveland, Ohio), April 26, 2001; Leon Sullivan, *Build, Brother, Build: From Poverty to Economic Power* and *Moving Mountains: The Principles and Purposes of Leon Sullivan.*

☻ Truth, Sojourner

(1797–1883) Sojourner Truth was born into slavery in Ulster County, New York, in 1797, and her slave name was Isabella. After she ran away in 1827, she was taken in by a group of Quakers who eventually purchased her freedom from her former master. She took the last name of that Quaker family and became known as Isabella Van Wagener. However, in response to a vision she received from God in 1843, she took a name to match her mission. She would be known as Sojourner Truth, because she had to "sojourn" the land and speak God's truth.

In the introduction to *Narrative of Sojourner Truth,* edited by Margaret Washington, this description is found: "Sojourner Truth was the most notable and highly regarded African American woman in the nineteenth century. She was devoted to the antislavery movement and was a fiery advocate of women's rights. Sojourner Truth was an omnipresent, quintessential figure among the progressive forces that refashioned nineteenth century America."

There were three distinct phases in the life of Sojourner Truth. The first phase was from 1797 to 1827, when she lived under the brutality of slavery. She was first owned by a Dutch family, sold on more than one occasion, and regularly and cruelly beaten beginning when she was only nine years old. Slavery officially ended in New York State in 1827, but her owner had promised to free her one year ahead of that time and provide her with a log cabin in which to live with her children. When he refused to honor that promise, she ran away, even though she would have been legally freed only three months later. In retaliation, her owner sold one of her sons into slavery in Alabama, where the practice was still legal. She sued him on the grounds that New York law prohibited a slave from being sold out of state. She won that case, and her son was restored to her.

After Sojourner Truth escaped slavery, she entered the second phase of her life (1827–1843), when she lived with a Quaker family and then migrated to various locations before settling in New York City. She was briefly affiliated with various cultic groups in that city led by Elijah Pierson, who called himself the Tishbite, and Robert Matthews, whose group was called Zion Hill. She eventually broke away from those groups and became a member of the Mother African Methodist Episcopal Zion Church in New York City (the first church founded in the AME Zion denomination), an affiliation she maintained for the rest of her life.

In 1843 the third phase of her life began when she literally walked away from New York City and began her career as an itinerant preacher by the name of Sojourner Truth. She left New York City in June of that year, and by November she had made her way to Northampton, Massachusetts. There she joined a communal group known as the Northampton Association of Education and Industry. It was her first experience in a community where race was not the dominant factor. It was also there that she first encountered William Lloyd Garrison, whose brother-in-law, George Benson, was the leader of the commune. Garrison introduced Sojourner Truth to Frederick Douglass, and she became one of the leading voices in the country for the abolition of slavery.

In 1850 she published her life story, *Narrative of Sojourner Truth.* It was written by Olive Gilbert, because Sojourner Truth remained illiterate. She had to have someone read a Bible story over and over until she was grabbed by some point that would become the basis of one of her sermons. It was also in 1850 that she became active in the women's rights movement. While delivering a

women's rights speech in Akron, Ohio, in 1851, she first used the phrase "And ain't I a woman?" She used that phrase to challenge the idea that women were too delicate and weak to make any good use of rights and freedoms.

Sojourner Truth remains famous for two other comments she made during her long career. When she was accused of being a man, perhaps because she stood over six feet tall and spoke with a heavy, Dutch-accented voice, she opened her blouse and revealed her breasts while on stage. She told the crowd that she had suckled many a white baby over the years. Then she turned to her accusers and asked, "Do you also wish to suck?" In 1852 Frederick Douglass spoke in Salem, Ohio, despairing that slavery would end. Sojourner Truth, who was seated in the audience, rose to her feet and shouted, "Frederick, is God dead?"

Harriet Beecher Stowe wrote an article about Sojourner Truth, "Libyan Sybil," which appeared in the April 1863 issue of *Atlantic Monthly.* Truth was allowed a private audience with President Abraham Lincoln in the White House on October 29, 1864. He gave her an autographed Bible that had been given to him by the leaders of the black community of Baltimore, Maryland. She actively supported the Union cause during the Civil War, helping to recruit soldiers for the all-black regiments from Massachusetts and Michigan. In 1865 she successfully challenged segregation in the streetcars of Washington, D.C. She was thrown from a streetcar by a conductor and badly injured, because she would not obey the segregation policy. But her valor resulted in that practice being suspended. That

was ninety years before Rosa Parks's act of resistance in Montgomery, Alabama.

After the war Sojourner Truth worked with disabled black veterans in Freedmen's Hospital in Washington, D.C., and with the Freedmen's Bureau. She advocated that freed blacks should be awarded a "Negro state" on public lands in the western part of the country as compensation for slavery. She presented a petition to that effect to President Ulysses S. Grant in 1870. Her plan was never adopted, but it might have been the incentive for the Exoduster movement that saw thousands of blacks leave the South later in the 1870s and settle in Kansas and Nebraska.

As early as the 1850s, Sojourner Truth had made her home in Battle Creek, Michigan, where she died on November 26, 1883, at the age of eighty-six. Her eulogy was delivered by Douglass. In 1972 Congresswoman Shirley Chisholm kicked off her campaign for the presidency of the United States while standing by the grave of Sojourner Truth.

Lerone Bennett Jr., *Pioneers in Protest;* Nancy A. Hewitt, *Women's Activism and Social Change;* Margaret Washington, ed., *Narrative of Sojourner Truth;* Dick Russell, *Black Genius.*

☾ Turner, Nat

(1800–1831) In the early morning hours of August 22, 1831, the bloodiest slave uprising in American history took place. Nearly seventy slaves managed to kill fifty-three white people over a twenty-mile radius in less than twenty-four hours in Southampton County, Virginia. The leader of that slave uprising was a slave preacher named Nat Turner.

Turner was born in Southampton County on October 2, 1800, the year in which a planned slave uprising led by Gabriel Prosser was uncovered and prevented. Nat Turner's mother tried to kill him at birth, because she did not want to see another slave born into the world. His father eventually ran away from slavery. That hatred of slavery present in his parents had a profound impact upon Turner's life. As he grew older he gradually came to believe that God was going to use him in some way to strike a blow against slavery.

Turner learned how to read and write, and he showed early signs of being called to some form of preaching ministry. His owner, Benjamin Turner, encouraged Nat in all three of those areas, as did his two subsequent owners, Thomas Moore and Joseph Travis. By 1825 he was traveling throughout the area to preach on various plantations, and his face became familiar to whites who passed him on the roads. However, as Nat studied the Bible he came to see that the Bible did not support the enslavement or brutalization of blacks, as so many whites, including white preachers, had been saying. This only strengthened his resolve to find a way to oppose slavery.

In the *Confessions of Nat Turner,* he claims to have seen a vision of drops of blood on stalks of corn in the middle of a field, which he understood to be the blood of Christ. He had further visions of black and white spirits engaged in battle. He took these as signs of the battle that he was meant to fight. On one occasion he ran away from his owner, as his father had done. He managed to stay away for thirty days and probably could have

remained a free man forever. However, he believed that it was not God's will for him to enjoy freedom while other blacks continued in slavery. To the shock of everyone on the plantation, black and white, Turner returned to slavery. His plan was not to remain content in that status but to await a sign that would tell him that the hour had come to begin his work of rebellion.

On May 12, 1828, Turner heard a voice telling him that the sign would be some unusual event in the heavens, and when he saw it, he said that "I should arise and prepare myself, and slay my enemies with their own sword." That sign came for Turner in February 1831, when he observed a total eclipse of the sun. He began making his plans and recruiting four others to go along with him: Henry, Hank, Nelson, and Sam. They were going to begin their uprising on July 4, 1831. First they would kill their owner, Joseph Travis, along with all the

members of his family. Then they would spread out and go from one plantation to the next, killing all the whites, freeing all the slaves, seizing all the weapons they could find, and eventually capturing the county seat of Jerusalem, Virginia.

When the day for the uprising came, Turner took ill, and everything had to be postponed. Another sign came on August 3, 1831, in the form of an unusual color that seemed to cover the sun. Turner believed that the sign was an indicator that God still wanted the rebellion to take place, so it was set for the early morning of August 22. He and his men met at a place called Cabin Pond. That place carried special significance, because on that spot a slave had been burned alive after having whipped his master to death. That spirit of rebellion and retribution fueled Turner and his men that night.

First they shared a meal of pork and brandy, and then they began their killing spree. At first, the only weapons they had were a hatchet and an ax. However, as they moved from one house to the next, they also gathered swords, rifles, and handguns. Not only did they kill white males; women and the youngest babies were not spared. Their plan went perfectly until they were encountered about twenty hours later by a group of armed white militiamen who were quickly reinforced by soldiers from nearby Fort Monroe. After one initial battle, Turner's men scattered, and the rebellion was put down. In the days following the uprising, more than three thousand white soldiers and militiamen joined in the search for Turner and his comrades. Those men also visited cruel punishment on any and all blacks they encountered,

whether or not they were involved in the insurrection. More than one hundred uninvolved slaves were shot or lynched as a result of the sheer rage of whites who could not believe that blacks had killed so many whites in that uprising.

After hiding in the nearby woods for nearly two months, being fed and sheltered by friendly blacks who knew where he was, Turner was captured by whites on October 30. While he was in the county jail awaiting trial, he dictated his now famous *Confessions of Nat Turner* to Thomas Gray. One of the most gripping parts involves Gray's description of Nat Turner: "He is a complete fanatic, or plays the part most admirably. The calm, deliberative composure with which he spoke of his late deeds and intentions, the expression of his fiend-like face when excited by enthusiasm, still bearing the stains of the blood of helpless innocents about him; clothed with rags and covered with chains; yet daring to raise his manacled hands to heaven, with a spirit soaring above the attributes of man; I looked on him and my blood curdled in my veins."

Fifty-three blacks were put on trial over a period of five days beginning on November 5. Twenty-one were acquitted, twelve were banished from the state, and twenty were hanged. Turner was among those convicted and condemned. He was hanged on November 11, 1831. Rumor has it that after his death, his skin was peeled off and turned into grease. That gruesome act, coupled with other acts of retribution that angry whites visited on innocent blacks, was meant to send the message that any further attempts to rebel would be dealt with in the most ruthless and brutal means possible.

The effects of the rebellion were twofold. First, state legislatures throughout the South quickly passed new and restrictive laws called black codes that greatly increased white control over every movement of black people. Blacks could no longer travel off the plantation without written permission. No more than three black people could gather without a white person being present. It became illegal for slaves to learn how to read and write, under penalty of whipping for the learner and the teacher. And the movements of black preachers were limited and in many cases banned.

However, the Turner uprising was the first blow of the **abolitionist movement.** By 1833 the American Antislavery Society was organized, and state societies followed all over the North. Nonslaveholding whites throughout the South began calling for the abolition of slavery, fearing that future slave uprisings could claim their lives even though they had never owned slaves. Within thirty years the Civil War erupted, and slavery was one of the contributing factors to that conflict. Turner's rebellion did not end with the success he had hoped for, but it did plant the seeds that eventually gave birth to emancipation for the nation's four million slaves.

Molefi K. Asante and Mark T. Mattson, *Historical and Cultural Atlas of African Americans;* Lerone Bennett Jr., *Pioneers in Protest;* Leon Litwack and August Meier, eds., *Black Leaders of the Nineteenth Century;* Herbert S. Klein, ed., *Slavery in the Americas;* William Andrews, Frances Smith Foster, and Trudie Harris, eds., *Oxford Companion to African American Literature;* Eric J. Sundquist, *To Wake the Nations;* Gayraud S. Wilmore, *Black Religion and Black Radicalism.*

☮ Walker, Wyatt Tee

(1929–) During the most critical period of the civil rights era, from 1960 to 1964, few people played a more crucial role than did Walker. As executive director of the **Southern Christian Leadership Conference (SCLC),** Walker helped to shape the events that most in America only watched on television or read about in newspapers. And his role as a prophetic voice did not begin with the 1960s. Before he joined SCLC, Walker was already fighting the good fight for freedom.

Walker was born on August 15, 1929, in Brockton, Massachusetts. He graduated from Virginia Union University with a bachelor of science degree in 1950 and a bachelor of divinity degree in 1953. From 1953 to 1960 he was the pastor of the Gillfield Baptist Church in Petersburg, Virginia. It was then that his involvement in civil rights began. He served as president of the local branch of the National Association for the Advancement of Colored People (NAACP) and as the Virginia chairman of the Congress of Racial Equality (CORE). In that role he organized a two-thousand-person pilgrimage to Richmond in 1959 to lobby the Virginia legislature to integrate the public schools in compliance with the U.S. Supreme Court ruling in *Brown v. Board of Education* (1954).

Modeling a program after what had happened in Baton Rouge, Louisiana, and Montgomery, Alabama, Walker organized the Petersburg Improvement Association. That became the agency through which other initiatives were launched to attack segregation in public accommodations in Virginia. After the formation of

SCLC in 1957, Walker not only served on the national board but also founded the Virginia Christian Leadership Conference, the first state affiliate for SCLC. That association between Walker and **Martin Luther King Jr.** resulted in Walker being hired in 1960 to manage the day-to-day affairs of King's organization and to oversee the staff of SCLC.

Walker was at the center of the action for some of the most dramatic moments in the history of the **civil rights movement.** He worked closely with the Freedom Rides in 1960, the sit-ins in 1961, the failed Albany, Georgia, campaign in 1962, the Birmingham, Alabama, campaign in the spring of 1963, the March on Washington later in 1963, and the St. Augustine, Florida, demonstrations in 1964. Walker typed King's handwritten draft of his famous "I Have a Dream" speech and also transcribed King's "Letter from a Birmingham Jail," which King had written on the edges of newspaper and on other available scraps of paper. Walker met privately with representatives of Billy Graham to maintain open channels of communication between Graham and King, a fact that was unknown to most of the public. He also traveled with King and many other SCLC stalwarts to Oslo, Norway, in 1964 when King was awarded the Nobel Prize for peace.

Although Walker was never noted for being one of the leading voices of the movement, he was clearly in charge when it came to providing the organization, discipline, and daily administration that SCLC and the whole movement so badly needed. Walker's directive, top-down style of leadership irritated many in the movement, and in 1964 he left his role with SCLC and returned to the North.

Between 1964 and 1968 Walker served in various capacities. He became the assistant pastor of Abyssinian Baptist Church in New York City. He served there only for a year, and then he went to work for a publishing company that produced The Negro Heritage Library. He became special assistant for urban affairs to New York Governor Nelson Rockefeller. In 1968 he became the pastor of Canaan Baptist Church in Harlem. His old friend, King, preached the installation sermon. Walker continues to serve at Canaan.

In 1975 Walker received a doctor of ministry degree as one the Martin Luther

King Jr. Fellows at Colgate Rochester Divinity School. His dissertation became the basis for his first and most important book, *"Somebody's Calling My Name": Black Sacred Music and Social Change.* Walker has written at least seven other books, including *Spirits That Dwell in Deep Woods, The Soul of Black Worship, Common Thieves,* and *The Road to Damascus.* This last book is an eyewitness account of the 1983 negotiations between **Jesse Jackson** and the Syrian government that resulted in the release of Lt. Robert Goodman, a captured American pilot.

Walker served as chairman of the board of Freedom National Bank in New York City, a minority-owned and minority-controlled bank in Harlem. He also led Canaan in the construction of several senior citizens' apartment complexes and in the formation of a ministry for people attempting to recover from addiction. Always possessed of a global perspective, Walker served as chairman of the Religious Action Network of the American Committee on Africa. That was one of the groups most instrumental in maintaining pressure in Washington, D.C., and in South Africa until the apartheid system was dismantled.

Walker has been a major figure on the national stage in religion, civil rights, and business for more than forty years. His appearances as a preacher at the Hampton Ministers' Conference for many years were the occasions when he spelled out his expertise on the tithing principle. It is reported that of the eighteen hundred members of Canaan Baptist Church, more than twelve hundred tithe on a regular basis. Walker has also been an active leader within the **Progressive National Baptist Convention (PNBC)**. In 1994 Walker was listed in *Ebony* as one of the top fifteen black preachers in America.

Taylor Branch, *Parting the Waters;* Adam Fairclough, *To Redeem the Soul of America;* David Garrow, *Bearing the Cross;* Wyatt Tee Walker, *Common Thieves, The Road to Damascus, "Somebody's Calling My Name,"* and *The Soul of Black Worship.*   回

SECTION 6

Nationalists

◉–◉–◉

◉ Cleage, Albert Buford

(1911–2000) When one thinks about **black theology**, the name of **James H. Cone** comes to mind. When one thinks about twentieth-century black nationalism, the name of **Marcus Garvey** is mentioned. Albert Cleage was the bridge between these two ideological positions. He was a devoted Christian clergyman, but he was convinced that traditional Christianity as taught and practiced, even in black churches, had become so Europeanized that it was incapable of addressing the needs of black people in America. For Cleage the only solution was the development of a theology based upon faith in a black Messiah.

Cleage was born in Indianapolis, Indiana, in 1911. He graduated with a bachelor of arts degree from Wayne State University in Detroit, Michigan, in 1937. He spent two years working as a social worker in Detroit, then enrolled in Oberlin School of Religion in Ohio, where he earned a bachelor of divinity degree. From 1942 to 1952 he served in a series of pastoral roles in Kentucky, Massachusetts, California, and Michigan. In California he served as copastor of the interracial Fellowship Church in San Francisco, which had been organized by **Howard Thurman** in 1944.

In 1952 Cleage began a church he called The Shrine of the Black Madonna in Detroit. He did so in order to develop a theology and a faith community that took seriously the reality of white racism and the inability and unwillingness of most people attached to mainline Christianity to address that and related issues. Cleage was concerned that many black people were turning away from the church, even though he acknowledged that it has "served as the heart and center of black communities everywhere." However, he continued, it has done so "without a consciousness of its responsibility and potential power to give a lost people a sense of earthly purpose and direction." Through The Shrine of the Black Madonna, Cleage sought to mold a biblical faith and a theological system that spoke directly to the reality of being black in America and to expose white Christianity of being incapable and unwilling to do the same.

The other motivation for Cleage's development of a black Messiah was to retain within the Christian faith black believers who had come under the influence of the growing anger of the civil rights and black power movements. Many of them could no longer embrace a white Jesus, a white God, or a white theology, none of which seemed to have anything to say about the black condition either in the rural South or in the urban North. Many of them were leaving Christianity and embracing Islam, especially as **Elijah Muhammad** and **Malcolm X** continued to attack Christianity as "the white man's religion." Others could not embrace Islam because they were aware that Arab slave traders had played a leading role in the trans-Atlantic slave trade and therefore were as guilty as white Europeans. The Shrine of the Black Madonna could become their spiritual home, a Christian faith in a black Messiah.

Cleage acknowledged that in the 1920s Garvey had attempted a similar move when he and George Alexander McGuire organized the African Orthodox Church. That movement did not take off, however, due to Garvey's arrest and subsequent deportation from the country. Cleage wanted to resurrect the ideas of Garvey, who in the 1920s proudly displayed a picture of a black Jesus in all of his meetings and rallies.

Cone, principal proponent of black theology, acknowledges his indebtedness to Cleage in *A Black Theology of Liberation* (1970). Cone writes, "Black Theology must show that the Reverend Albert Cleage's description of Jesus as the Black Messiah is not the product of minds distorted by their own oppressed condition, but is rather the only meaningful Christological statement in our time. Any other statement about Christ is at best irrelevant and at worst blasphemous."

Cleage spelled out his views in a book of sermons, *The Black Messiah* (1968).

He wrote a second book, *Black Christian Nationalism* (1972). He was also an active participant with the **National Conference of Black Churchmen** in the 1970s.

Cleage died in 2000.

Albert Cleage, *The Black Messiah and Black Christian Nationalism*; James H. Cone, *A Black Theology of Liberation*; Gayraud S. Wilmore and James H. Cone, eds., *Black Theology: A Documentary History, 1966–1979*.

☯ Crummell, Alexander

(1819-1898) Alexander Crummell, an early proponent of black nationalism and the expatriation of free blacks in America to the nation of Liberia, was born in New York City to free parents on March 3, 1819. A man of keen African features and extremely dark skin, he held a lifelong resentment toward mulattoes (lightskinned blacks), who he thought exhibited a sense of superiority over their darker-skinned kinsmen.

Crummell was educated at the African Free School in New York City. He, along with **Henry Highland Garnet**, attended Hayes Academy in Canaan, New Hampshire. However, that school was subsequently destroyed by a mob of whites who opposed the idea of blacks being enrolled in a school in that state. The school was literally pulled off of its foundations by teams of horses or oxen and dragged into a nearby lake. He then transferred to and furthered his education at the Oneida Institute in Whitesboro, New York. He pursued a ministry in the Episcopal Church while still at Oneida. He was denied admission to the Episcopal General Theological Seminary in New York City because of his race, so he studied independently with a priest in Providence, Rhode Island.

Crummell became a priest in the Protestant Episcopal Church under the influence of **Peter Williams Jr.,** the rector of his home church, St. Philip's Episcopal Church of New York. However, the Episcopal bishop of New York would not support his efforts, so he was ordained in 1844 under the authority of the bishop of New England by a congregation in Delaware.

Crummell was active in such causes as abolition, suffrage, the improvement of education for blacks, and the Negro convention movement. He was not especially successful as a local priest, because his sermons were considered too erudite and scholarly for the working-class people he served. In 1847 he sailed for England to raise the funds he needed to work on black self-help programs that he would establish in the United States.

Crummell did not return to America for the next twenty-six years. He stayed in England for six years, being awarded a bachelor of arts degree from Queens College at Cambridge in 1853. He then went as a missionary to Liberia, West Africa, where he remained for the next twenty years. Having initially opposed black emigration and the efforts of the American Colonization Society (ACS), he changed his view and was supported in Liberia by the ACS. He returned twice to the United States during those years to encourage increased black emigration to Liberia.

Crummell was a strong proponent of the Christianization and Westernization of the indigenous African tribes by those blacks who were emigrating from Amer-

ica. However, he discovered that the indigenous people viewed the newly arrived black Americans with suspicion and hostility. He also believed, spoke, and wrote frequently that blacks would never achieve full equality in America and that emigration to Africa was their best chance of reaching their full potential.

Like his lifelong friend, Garnet, Crummell believed that creating a cotton-growing industry in Liberia would both provide an economy for the young African nation and undercut the economy of the slave-holding South. However, Crummell grew increasingly disenchanted with the progress being made in Liberia. In 1866 he resigned from Liberia College in a dispute with its president. In 1870 he encouraged the United States government to assume control of the country and make it a U.S. protectorate. He left Liberia in 1873, frustrated by what he saw as the racism displayed toward the indigenous people and the dark-skinned former Americans by the mulatto ruling elite and by white missionaries.

Upon Crummell's return to the United States, the Episcopal bishop of Maryland appointed him a minister at large to the black population of Washington, D.C. By 1880 he had organized the St. Luke's Episcopal Church in that city, the center of much of the intellectual and racial uplift activities in that center of black life in the nineteenth century. In 1883 he helped to organize a national organization of black Episcopal priests to combat racism in that denomination. He remained active at St. Luke's until his retirement in 1894.

In 1897 Crummell helped to organize the American Negro Academy, a group of black scholars and intellectuals that became the precursor of **W. E. B. Du Bois's** idea of the talented tenth. Among the purposes of the Academy were protesting violent attacks against blacks, publication of scholarly works, fostering higher education among blacks, and increasing interest among blacks in literature, science, and the arts.

Although he was initially critical of the focus on industrial arts education as advocated by Booker T. Washington, Crummell eventually came to advocate for industrial education as one of the stepping stones to success for blacks in America at the end of the nineteenth century. He had spent his life arguing that black progress would come as a result of black people, under the leadership of an enlightened black elite, reaching a measure of civilization that had already been attained by western Europeans. However, he also urged that blacks should seek to be self-governing, whether in national life as in Liberia or over their institutions in the United States. Crummell died in 1898.

Alfred Moss, "Alexander Crummell: Black Nationalist and Apostle of Western Civilization," in *Black Leaders of the Nineteenth Century,* ed. Leon Litwack and August Meier; Wilson Jeremiah Moses, *The Golden Age of Black Nationalism, 1850–1925;* Harry A. Ploski and Ernest Kaiser, eds. and comps., *The Negro Almanac;* Benjamin Quarles, *Black Abolitionists;* Henry J. Young, *Major Black Religious Leaders, 1755–1940.*

☮ Farrakhan, Louis

(1933–) One of the most powerful and compelling orators on the American scene, Farrakhan has been called "the

most feared man in America." Born Louis Eugene Walcott in Boston, Massachusetts in 1933, the son of West Indian parents, he was reared in St. Cyprian's Episcopal Church. He studied the violin from his youth and was greatly influenced by the style of Jascha Heifetz. He graduated from the prestigious Boston Latin School.

In 1950, unable to attend Julliard School of Music due to a lack of financial resources, Farrakhan attended Winston-Salem State University in North Carolina on an athletic scholarship. That experience in the South was his first encounter with the kind of racism and segregation he had not experienced in Boston in his largely West Indian community in the 1930s and 1940s.

Farrakhan dropped out of college and began a career as a calypso singer, calling himself The Charmer. Exposure to racism resulted in a growing disillusionment with Christianity. An invitation to hear **Elijah Muhammad,** founder of the **Nation of Islam,** in 1955 resulted in his joining that organization. His calypso music talents produced a song that became popular within the Nation of Islam, "A White Man's Heaven Is a Black Man's Hell."

Farrakhan wrote and starred in a play, *The Trial,* in which he played a lawyer who accuses white America of a series of heinous crimes against black people around the world. Portions of that play were also featured in the 1959 documentary on the Nation of Islam done by Mike Wallace, *The Hate That Hate Produced.* Parts of that play can also be heard during the opening scenes of the Spike Lee film *Malcolm X.*

Adopting the name Louis X, Farrakhan became the minister of Muhammad's Mosque in Boston. He was later given the name Louis Farrakhan by Elijah Muhammad. Following the death of Malcolm X in 1965, Farrakhan succeeded him as minister of Muhammad's Mosque in Harlem and as Elijah Muhammad's national representative. It has been widely speculated that Farrakhan's comments about Malcolm X printed in the Nation's newspaper, *Muhammad Speaks,* may have resulted in the assassination of Malcolm X. In a 1998 appearance on *60 Minutes* with Mike Wallace and one of the children of Malcolm X, Farrakhan expressed regret for any role his words may have played in causing the death of Malcolm X.

Following the death of Elijah Muhammad in 1975, Farrakhan broke away from the leadership of Muhammad's son Waruthuddin Muhammad, whom he viewed as distorting the teachings of his father and moving the Nation toward orthodox Islam. In 1977 he reconstituted the Nation of Islam according to the original doctrines of Elijah Muhammad and began a new newspaper, *The Final Call.*

Farrakhan emerged as a controversial national figure in 1984 as a result of comments he made alleging that "Hitler was a wickedly great man" and that Judaism was "a gutter religion." Both comments may have been taken out of context, but they nonetheless resulted in constant turmoil between him and the American Jewish community. The Nation of Islam also published a book, *The Secret Relationship Between Blacks and Jews.* It alleged that 75 percent of the Jews in America during the slave era were involved as slave owners. It also sets forth a conspiracy theory about a secret Jewish cabal that controls major sectors of the nation's economy.

Also in 1984 Farrakhan urged members of the Nation of Islam to register and vote for the first time in the organization's history, in order to support **Jesse Jackson**'s bid for the Democratic Party nomination for president of the United States. He also supported Jackson in the 1988 election. That perceived partnership between the two Chicago-based leaders caused a stir of enthusiasm in black America but added to Jackson's campaign troubles in the various state primaries.

Farrakhan is best known for having organized the Million Man March, which took place in Washington, D.C., in October 1995. It was billed as "A Day of Atonement," and African American men from across the country gathered in the nation's capitol. The absence of an immediate public-policy focus may have dissipated the effect such a gathering could have had. However, that event continues to be a moment of great importance for those who were present. Spike Lee's *Get on the Bus* was a dramatization of that historic gathering.

In January and February of 1996, Farrakhan undertook a five-week "World Friendship Tour" that took him to twenty-five countries in Africa and the Middle East. During that time he met with a wide variety of religious and political leaders. This was reminiscent of a tour taken by Malcolm X in 1964 as part of his pilgrimage to Mecca. Unfortunately, that tour greatly undermined much of the prestige that the Million Man March had conferred upon him, largely because of several inflammatory statements he made and because of some of the people with whom he visited.

He met with Libyan leader Muammar Khaddafi, who pledged to Farrakhan $1 billion to be used to influence the 1996 presidential election and to influence American foreign policy in the Middle East and North Africa. In Teheran, Iran, he declared, "god will destroy America by the hands of the Muslims." He then went to Iraq where he met with Saddam Hussein and called the United Nations sanctions against Iraq "a crime against humanity."

Farrakhan's continued presence on the national stage keeps alive the tension between black nationalism (separatism) and integration, a tension that is as old as **Richard Allen** and **Absalom Jones** at the end of the eighteenth century. He continues to call for increased black self-help programs, economic cooperation, family

stability, and an end to the use of drugs that has plagued black communities across the country.

Farrakhan lives in Chicago, Illinois, with his wife and family. Despite an acknowledged battle with cancer and rumors that he had died from the disease, Farrakhan continues to serve as leader of the Nation of Islam.

In the foreword to *Prophet of Rage*, Julian Bond writes: "Louis Farrakhan's present prominence ought to make the nation question itself. An understanding of who he is and where he comes from and from what sources his thinking arises and his views were formed is important to our understanding of ourselves."

Michael Eric Dyson, *Race Rules;* Minister Louis Farrakhan, *A Torchlight for America;* Matthias Gardell, *In the Name of Elijah Muhammad;* Henry Louis Gates Jr., "The Charmer," *The New Yorker,* April 29 and May 6, 1996; Arthur J. Magida, *Prophet of Rage: A Life of Louis Farrakhan and His Nation.*

Garvey, Marcus Mosiah

(1887-1940) Lawrence W. Levine introduces an essay about the remarkable life of Marcus Garvey by saying, "In 1916, Marcus Garvey, a West Indian black without funds, influence, or substantial contacts, arrived in the United States for the first time. By the early 1920s he had built the largest and most influential Afro-American mass movement in American history."

Garvey was born in Jamaica in 1887. He was one of eleven children, nine of whom died during childhood. Only he and his older sister, Indiana, survived into

adulthood. It is important in understanding Garvey to note that in 1887, Jamaica was part of the British West Indies; thus Garvey grew up under colonial rule. Unlike black people in America, who endured racial discrimination from a white majority, Garvey's experience with racism came as part of a black majority that was governed by a tiny white minority that was separated from blacks by a colored middle class.

Three aspects of his early life would remain important in the development of Garvey's character. First, he was apprenticed at the age of fourteen in the printing industry, first in his godfather's shop and later with an uncle in Kingston who published a newspaper. Through the publication and distribution of newspapers and magazines, Garvey eventually was able to communicate his ideas to millions of black people around the world.

Second, Garvey was also an avid churchgoer, but he was not seeking salvation. Instead, he went to study the oratorical styles of various preachers in an attempt to refine his oratorical skills. By all accounts, his ability to speak powerfully and picturesquely was the key to his ability to become a grassroots leader.

The third formative experience for Garvey involved his travel outside of Jamaica between 1910 and 1914. He spent two years working various jobs throughout Central and South America between 1910 and 1912 and another two years living and working in London, England, between 1912 and 1914. In every place where he traveled, he noticed that black people were at the bottom of the social order, and he wondered why that was. While living in London, Garvey read *Up from Slavery*, the autobiography of Booker T. Washington. That book and his travels made it clear to Garvey that he was destined to become a "race leader." Garvey raised a question as a result of that experience: "Where is the black man's Government? Where is his king and his kingdom? Where is his president, his country, and his ambassador, his army, his navy, his men of big affairs? I could not find them, I will help to raise them up."

Garvey returned to Jamaica in 1915 and organized the Universal Negro Improvement and Conservation Association and African Communities League, later the Universal Negro Improvement Association (UNIA). The mission of that group was twofold: to uplift the status of black people in Jamaica and to "establish a universal confraternity among the race, to promote the spirit of race pride and love, and to establish Commissionaries or Agencies in the principal countries of the world for the protection of all Negroes irrespective of nationality... and to strengthen the imperialism of independent African states."

Behind the motto of One God! One Aim! One Destiny! Garvey was setting in motion a pan-African movement that he hoped would affect the living conditions of the black people he had encountered during his four years of travel. He did not meet with much success in Jamaica, largely because the colored middle class objected to leadership coming from a member of the black majority. Thus in 1915 he wrote to Booker T. Washington and inquired about coming to the United States to establish his movement there. Washington agreed to receive him, but he died before Garvey could make plans to travel. Nevertheless, Garvey arrived in New York City in March 1916. There he encountered a large number of black people who had either migrated from the South or immigrated from throughout the West Indies. That proved to be fertile soil for the UNIA, which had been made operational in New York by 1917.

Garvey was challenging black people to throw off their second-class status by no longer looking at or thinking about themselves as being second-class people. He reminded them of the glories of the African past. Through the use of religious symbols, including a black madonna and child, black angels and biblical saints, and the use of biblical passages that referred to Africa (especially Psalm 68:31), he built racial pride and

solidarity. His most notable phrase was "Up, you mighty race!" He said, "The Negro was not at the bottom because he was held in contempt by whites, he was held in contempt by whites because he was at the bottom." Through the UNIA he sought to encourage blacks to lift themselves, much as he had read in *Up from Slavery.*

By 1919 Garvey claimed two million followers, and by 1923 he announced that he had six million members of UNIA. In a speech he delivered at Royal Albert Hall in London, on June 6, 1928, he claimed eleven million members residing in Africa, the United States, South and Central America, Canada, and the West Indies. He had established Liberty Halls, the name of UNIA meeting places, in cities across the country. He began circulation of the movement's magazine, *The Negro World,* in 1918, and by 1922 it had a circulation of more than two hundred thousand. He even published the magazine in Spanish and French for West Indian immigrants who had not yet learned English.

James Weldon Johnson, who was present at many of Garvey's weekly meetings in New York City, observed that the events mirrored almost exactly a normal black worship service with hymns, prayers, a sermon by Garvey or another speaker, and an offering. Many followers of Garvey were also active pastors of various churches, as with Earl Little, the father of **Malcolm X.** Another such person was George Alexander McGuire, an Episcopal priest who eventually founded the African Orthodox Church in 1924. Although McGuire was not an affiliate of UNIA, McGuire and Garvey agreed on one thing: "No constructive program for the Negro can be effective which underestimates the hold his religious institutions have upon him."

Garvey may be most famous as an entrepreneur. He established the Negro Factories Corporation in 1919, selling shares to raise capital to open black-owned factories throughout the Americas and Africa. He also opened a string of restaurants, clothing stores, steam laundries, and print shops that employed more than one thousand persons by 1922. His most ambitious project, also begun in 1919, was the formation of the Black Star Line, a steamship company that would transport black people to Africa, where they could begin to build up that continent. It would also provide jobs for ship workers and investment dividends for those who provided the initial capital. Within three months of announcing the venture, Garvey had raised $610,000 and purchased three ships.

This venture failed on two counts. First, Garvey was unsuccessful in negotiating with the government of Liberia in providing land where his passengers could resettle. He had ships and ticket holders but no destination to which he could deliver them. Second, he was indicted on mail fraud in 1922 for improperly using the mail to solicit and receive funds for the Black Star Line. He was convicted and sentenced to five years in prison. After many months of appeals, he served in the Atlanta penitentiary from February 2, 1925, to November 18, 1927. His sentence was commuted by President Calvin Coolidge with two years remaining, on the condition that Garvey agree to be deported to Jamaica.

Garvey remained active with UNIA even after he moved permanently to London. He was never allowed to reenter the United States, though he did hold two UNIA conventions in Toronto, Canada, in 1936 and 1938. He died in London on June 10, 1940.

Edmund David Cronon, *Black Moses;* Amy Jacques Garvey, ed., *Philosophy and Opinions of Marcus Garvey;* Marcus Garvey, speech presenting the case of the Negro for International Racial Adjustment, in minutes of proceedings of the meeting held at The Royal Albert Hall on June 6, 1928; Lawrence W. Levine, "Marcus Garvey and the Politics of Revitalization," in *Black Leaders of the Twentieth Century,* ed. John Hope Franklin and August Meier.

☮ Muhammad, Elijah

(1897-1975) Born Elijah Poole on a tenant farm in Sandersville, Georgia, in October of 1897, this son of a former slave became the leader of the most important and controversial black nationalist movement in American history.

In 1923 Poole migrated to Detroit, Michigan, where he worked for several years in the auto industry. In Detroit he encountered **W. D. Fard,** who claimed to have come from the holy city of Mecca in Saudi Arabia to bring truth and freedom to black people in North America. Fard organized the **Nation of Islam** in Detroit in 1930 and also gave Elijah Poole the new name of Elijah Muhammad. Fard was probably a follower of an earlier cultic leader, **Noble Drew Ali,** who had organized a series of congregations under the banner of The Moorish Science Temple. Some followers of Ali claimed that

Fard was the reincarnation of their leader, who had died violently in Chicago in the late 1920s.

When Fard suddenly disappeared in 1934, a power struggle ensued for leadership in the Nation. Elijah Muhammad relocated to Chicago, established Temple of Islam #2, and from that base soon emerged as the national leader of the movement that eventually had temples and followers all across the country. He elevated Fard to the status of divinity, declaring him to be the incarnation of Allah, much as Christians believe that Jesus of Nazareth was the incarnation of God. Muhammad then said that Fard had designated him to be known by the title Messenger of Allah. That was the name by which Elijah Muhammad was known by his followers until his death in 1975.

Part of Muhammad's authority within the Nation was tied to his twice having been arrested and once imprisoned rather than compromise on his religious convictions. He was arrested and given six months' probation in Detroit in 1933, when he refused to enroll his children in the public schools. He preferred to enroll them in the University of Islam, a parochial school established by Fard. Between 1942 and 1946 Muhammad was in a federal prison for having urged his followers not to bear arms or submit to the draft during World War II. More than one hundred male members of the Nation of Islam were imprisoned during those years as a result of heeding his call.

Following his release from prison in 1946, Muhammad quickly began increasing the size of his following, focusing his recruitment efforts (fishing) on persons at the lowest level of urban society. His ability to transform the lives of former drug addicts, criminals, prostitutes, and pimps, and especially prison inmates, was impressive. As a result of this kind of fishing, **Malcolm X** was brought into the Nation of Islam in 1952. In *The Fire Next Time,* James Baldwin states,

"Elijah Muhammad has been able to do what generations of welfare workers and committees and resolutions and reports and housing projects and playgrounds have failed to do: to heal and redeem drunkards and junkies, to convert people who have come out of prison and to keep them out, to make men chaste and women virtuous, and to invest both the male and the female with a pride and a serenity that hang about them like an unfailing light. He has done all these things, which our Christian church has spectacularly failed to do."

Not only was Elijah Muhammad successful in redeeming the lives of thousands of persons who might otherwise have been considered hopelessly beyond the reach of society, but also he established a thriving network of black-owned businesses in which many of those persons could find employment. Those businesses included restaurants, bakeries, barbershops, dry cleaners, and thousand-acre farms in Michigan and Georgia. At the height of his influence in the 1950s and 1960s, Elijah Muhammad and the Nation of Islam were the embodiment of **Marcus Garvey**'s emphasis on black separatism and Booker T. Washington's focus on black economic self-sufficiency.

One aspect of the structure of the Nation of Islam that was remarkable and intimidating was the creation by Fard of a paramilitary unit called the Fruit of Islam. These men served as his personal bodyguards and provided security at all events sponsored by the Nation. In uniforms that gave them a regimented appearance and with their training in martial arts, they were greatly admired by black people, Muslim and Christian alike, and were of great concern to many whites.

Muhammad and the Nation lived in relative obscurity within and beyond the black communities of the nation until the late 1950s. That is when four events moved the man and the movement into the headlines. First was the emergence of Malcolm X as the national spokesman. Next was the 1959 documentary by Mike Wallace, *The Hate That Hate Produced.* Then came the 1961 study of the Nation of Islam, *The Black Muslims in America,* by **C. Eric Lincoln**. Most significant of all

was the 1964 announcement that heavyweight boxing champion Cassius Clay had converted to the Nation of Islam and announced that his new name was Muhammad Ali.

One can only wonder how much larger the Nation would have grown had it not been for some of its bizarre religious claims, including the idea that the creation of the white and black races were the work of a mad scientist named Yakub, who had rebelled against Allah. Yakub had made the white race and had made the "blue-eyed white devil" incapable of living peacefully with nonwhite people. The only answer was the complete separation of the races.

This led Muhammad to demand that five states in the Deep South be given to black people as reparations for slavery. Failing that, Muhammad challenged the government to provide land, at its expense, somewhere else in the world where blacks from America could migrate and form a nation. He also challenged the government to support that new nation for a period of twenty to twenty-five years, until it became self-sufficient.

This demand for a separate nation was one of ten demands set forth by Elijah Muhammad in *Message to the Blackman* and in every edition of *Muhammad Speaks,* the weekly newspaper of the Nation of Islam. That paper was sold on street corners across the country by clean-cut and unfailingly polite members of the movement. It was a rite of passage for recent converts to the Nation and a means of fundraising. That paper is still sold, and largely by the same method, under its new name, *The Final Call.*

Claims about marital infidelity involving several younger female members of the movement damaged Muhammad's credibility, given how much emphasis he had placed upon sexual purity and marital fidelity. This was the issue that may have caused the initial rift between Muhammad and Malcolm X. Those claims were supported by Federal Bureau of Investigation (FBI) wiretaps, but they did not have the desired effect of causing the Nation of Islam to repudiate Muhammad's leadership.

Following Muhammad's death in 1975, the movement eventually divided into two factions. Muhammad's son, Wallace D. Muhammad, was named his successor. He changed his name to **Warithuddin Muhammad** and eventually moved .the Nation away from the racial and religious extremes taught by his father, choosing instead to adhere to the path of traditional, orthodox Islam. He changed the name of the group to·The American Muslim Movement in the West. That group has now largely dissolved, and Warithuddin Muhammad has urged his followers to worship at any local Sunni Muslim mosque. The other faction was and is headed by **Louis Farrakhan,** and it retains the original name that dates back to Fard in Detroit in 1930, the Nation of Islam.

John Bracey, August Meier, and Elliott Rudwick, *Black Nationalism in America;* Bernard Cushmeer, *This Is the One;* E. U. Essien-Udom, *Black Nationalism;* Arthur Huff Fauset, *Black Gods of the Metropolis;* Mattias Gardell, *In the Name of Elijah Muhammad;* C. Eric Lincoln, *The Black Muslims in America;* Malcolm X with Alex Haley, *The Autobiography of Malcolm X.*

☉ Turner, Henry McNeal

(1834-1915) Born a free man in South Carolina on February 1, 1834, Henry McNeal Turner was the grandson of David Greer, who had been manumitted when he proved to a colonial court that he was the son of an African tribal prince. Such persons were typically exempted from slavery, usually to minimize their leadership potential among the slaves. Turner nevertheless found himself forced to work alongside slaves in the cotton fields.

Turner began his ministry as an itinerant preacher for the Methodist Episcopal Church in 1853, and in 1858 he switched to the **African Methodist Episcopal (AME) Church.** He served parishes in Baltimore, Maryland, and Washington, D.C. He was befriended by Charles Sumner and Thaddeus Stevens, powerful members of Congress and the leading white abolitionists in that city. He made history when President Abraham Lincoln appointed him to be the first black military chaplain in the nation's history.

After the Civil War, Turner was assigned by Bishop **Daniel A. Payne** to lead the efforts to organize the AME Church in Georgia. That denomination had been banned throughout the South since the failed uprising planned by Denmark Vesey in 1822, largely because it was believed that the AME Church had known about and assisted in the planning. At the same time, Turner became an organizer for the Republican Party among the black population of that state. In 1867 he was elected to serve on the Georgia Constitutional Reconstruction Committee that resulted in Georgia being readmitted to the Union.

In 1868 Turner was elected to the Georgia state legislature. While there he became increasingly outspoken about the abuses that blacks, now free, continued to experience throughout the South. He began to advocate for state subsidies for black higher education. He called for the creation of a black militia in accordance with the Second Amendment to the U.S. Constitution to allow for protection against Klan violence. He vigorously opposed the sharecropping system that he saw as a path to the reenslavement of hundreds of thousands of blacks throughout the South. To correct that abuse he called for an eight-hour workday and the end to the convict lease system.

So outspoken had Turner and the other thirty-one black legislators become that the conservative white majority in the Georgia state legislature voted in 1869 to expel all black members from that body. This resulted in one of Turner's famous "Speech on the Eligibility of Colored Members to Seats in the Georgia Legislature," in which he said, "I am here to demand my rights, and to hurl thunderbolts at the men who would dare to cross the threshold of my manhood." Under the protection of the fixed bayonets of the Union army still stationed in Georgia, the black members were reinstated in 1870.

This refusal to allow a duly elected black man to sit in the state legislature set in motion Turner's later belief that expatriation to Africa was the only course of action that black people in America could take. He came to believe that a black man could earn a living in this country, "but he [could] never be a man—full, symmetrical and undwarfed." Much of the thought of

black nationalism is traceable to Turner. Believing that black people would only find justice and opportunity when they lived in a country of their own, he wrote, "I am taking the ground that we will never get justice here, that God is, and will continue to withhold political rights from us, for the purpose of turning our attention to our fatherland."

Turner's passion for black emigration was fueled not only by his being denied a seat in the legislature in 1869 but also by the 1883 civil rights ruling by the U.S. Supreme Court that declared unconstitutional most of the social and political gains made by blacks during the Reconstruction. Like **Henry Highland Garnet,** he saw emigration not only as the only hope for the full liberation of black people in the United States but also as a way to Christianize and Westernize the African continent.

Turner is the father of **black theology,** espousing as early as the 1880s that "God is a Negro." He made this observation because he wanted to use theology to improve the self-image of blacks. If they are made in the image of God (black), then the historic claims about black inferiority made by whites must be false. **James H. Cone** states that Turner's theology served in exactly that way: "Throughout black history Scripture was used for a definition of God and Jesus that was consistent with the black struggle for liberation."

Like many black leaders of the Reconstruction period, Turner was also an aggressive supporter of women's suffrage. And unlike many of his peers, he was an advocate for the role of women in ministry. While in the Georgia legislature he introduced a bill to give women the right to vote. In 1888 he ordained a woman to the office of deacon in the AME Church.

Turner was elected a bishop of the AME Church in 1880 and served in that role for thirty-five years. During those years, he led the way in establishing AME churches in Liberia, Sierra Leone, and South Africa. He visited those regions in 1891, 1893, and 1895. A monthly newsletter, *The Voice of Missions*, was established, as were additional schools for the training of persons for ministry in the AME Church. During this period his call for emigration to Africa by blacks in America was strongest. In 1893 he convened eight hundred delegates at a conference in Cincinnati, Ohio, where he stated, "the Negro cannot remain here in this present condition and be a man ... for at the present rate his extermination is only a question of time."

Turner was a contemporary of Frederick Douglass and Booker T. Washington, both of whom openly opposed the idea or practicality of emigration. The fact that Turner persisted with his call for black emigration may have prevented him from reaching their level of prominence. The idea never took root in the nineteenth century. Many groups did travel to Africa with the intention of emigration but soon returned as a result of disease, malnutrition, and hardship due to the absence of any physical infrastructure in Liberia or Sierra Leone. However, Turner's views were a precursor to the rise of **Marcus Garvey**'s back-to-Africa movement.

Turner strongly opposed the Spanish-American War of 1898 and the invasion of the Philippines in 1900, viewing them as acts of American imperialism. He also soundly condemned those black men who volunteered to serve on those excursions. He died in Ontario, Canada, on April 8, 1915, at the age of eighty-one. Turner Theological Seminary in Atlanta, Georgia, now part of the **Interdenominational Theological Center (ITC),** is named in his honor.

James H. Cone, *God of the Oppressed;* John Dittmer, "The Education of Henry McNeal Turner," in *Black Leaders of the Nineteenth Century,* ed. Leon Litwack and August Meier; C. Eric Lincoln and Lawrence W. Mamiya, *The Black Church in the African American Experience;* August Meier, *Negro Thought in America: 1880–1915;* Wilson Jeremiah Moses, *The Golden Age of Black Nationalism, 1850–1925;* Henry J. Young, *Major Black Religious Leaders, 1755–1940.*

☾ X, Malcolm

(1925-1965) If **Martin Luther King Jr.** was the voice of reason appealing to white America for racial justice, Malcolm X was the leading voice of rage. Both men sought to interpret public events during the turbulent 1950s and 1960s. Both men had careers that lasted thirteen years. Both men died at the age of thirty-nine. Both men were assassinated. Both men are probably more widely acclaimed in death than they were in life by black and white Americans alike.

Malcom X was born Malcolm Little on May 19, 1925, in Omaha, Nebraska. He was one of eight children born to Earl Little. Malcolm's mother, Louise Little, was Earl's second wife. Earl Little was an itinerant Baptist preacher and a follower of **Marcus Garvey** and an organizer for

Garvey's United Negro Improvement Association (UNIA), a black nationalist movement that focused on a back-to-Africa message.

Malcolm's father was killed in 1931 by a white hate group called the Black Legion in Lansing, Michigan, where the family had moved after threats had been received from the Ku Klux Klan, which had firebombed their home in Omaha. In *The Autobiography of Malcolm X*, Malcom speculates that his father was targeted and finally killed as a result of his black nationalist rhetoric and his independent lifestyle. The death of his father resulted in the breakup of the Little family. The children became wards of the state, and in 1937 his mother was confined to a mental institution, where she remained for twenty-six years.

Malcolm Little finished the eighth grade and then went to live with his stepsister, Ella, in Boston, Massachusetts. Young Malcom quickly was drawn into the nightlife, street life, and criminal life of the Roxbury section of Boston. A job on the railroad brought him to New York City, where he became even more deeply involved in prostitution, drugs, gambling, robbery, and other criminal activities. That life came to an abrupt end in 1946, when, upon his return to Boston, he was arrested and sentenced to ten years in prison on multiple robbery charges.

At the age of twenty, Malcolm Little entered the Charlestown State Prison. It was while he was in prison that members of his family began writing to him about their decision to join the **Nation of Islam** under the leadership of **Elijah Muhammad.** Eventually Malcolm corresponded with Muhammad and received a letter in response with a gift of $5 enclosed. Muhammad told Malcolm that prison was one of the ways that white society sought to eliminate black men: "The black prisoner symbolized white society's crime of keeping black men oppressed and deprived and ignorant, and unable to get decent jobs, turning them into criminals."

Sitting in a prison cell at the age of twenty-three, when that letter came from Elijah Muhammad, triggered something of a conversion experience in Malcolm Little. Following his parole from prison in 1952, Malcolm went to Detroit, Michigan, to live with his brother Wilfred and to affiliate with Temple #1 of the Nation of Islam. In Detroit he finally met Muhammad, who gave him the name Malcom X. The X represented the black man's unknown African name and replaced the slave name given to black people when they came to this country. In 1953 Malcolm's ministry within the nation of Islam formally began.

Malcolm organized temples in Philadelphia, Boston, and Los Angeles and was eventually assigned to Temple #7 in New York City. The Nation of Islam and Malcolm X went largely unnoticed in America until two separate events brought them to the attention of the nation. The first was a television documentary by Mike Wallace, *The Hate That Hate Produced.* This program featured speeches by Malcolm X and Elijah Muhammad and showed members of the Nation cheering as the sins of white society were recounted.

The other major event that brought the Nation of Islam to national attention was the 1961 release of *Black Muslims in America* by the black sociologist of religion **C. Eric Lincoln.** That book became required reading in college classrooms across the country. Eventually Malcolm X became not only the national spokesman for the Nation of Islam but also one of the most frequent faces seen and most controversial voices heard on American television and on college campus. *The New York Times* reported in 1963 that Malcolm X was the second most popular speaker on college campuses, following only Barry Goldwater, who was running for president at that time. In each day's mail Malcolm often received more than twenty invitations to speak.

That popularity increased the nation's awareness of Muhammad and the Nation of Islam, but it may also have begun to fracture the once close, almost father-

and-son relationship that Malcolm X had enjoyed with Muhammad. The relationship was furthered weakened when Malcolm was able to confirm several rumors about paternity suits brought against Muhammad by young women in the Nation. The final break seemed to come when Malcolm X was officially silenced by Muhammad in 1963 following comments made by Malcolm concerning the assassination of President John F. Kennedy. Malcolm called it a case of "chickens coming home to roost," implying that the violence that American society had unleashed against black people had now come back to claim one of its own. Malcolm made his comments even though Muhammad had ordered all of his ministers to offer no comments on the death of President Kennedy.

By 1964 Malcolm had left the Nation of Islam, although death threats followed him. One threat in particular was linked to Malcolm's former protégé, Louis X of Boston, now known as **Louis Farrakhan.** In a much-publicized interview on *60 Minutes,* Farrakhan apologized to one of Malcolm's daughters for any role he or his words may have played in creating the climate that resulted in Malcolm's assassination in 1965.

Malcolm organized a new organization called The Muslim Mosque, Inc. He then set out on the hajj, the pilgrimage to the holy city of Mecca in Saudi Arabia that is required of all observant Muslims. During the hajj Malcolm X can be said to have experienced a second conversion. Despite the racial views he had held and espoused as a member of the Nation of Islam, which viewed all white people as "the blue-eyed devil," his time in

Mecca began to change his mind. In a letter to his wife, Betty, he wrote, "During the past eleven days here in the Muslim world, I have eaten from the same plate, drunk from the same glass, and slept in the same bed (or on the same rug)—while praying to the same God—with fellow Muslims whose eyes were the bluest of blue, whose hair was the blondest of blond, and whose skin was the whitest of white."

Following the hajj, Malcolm X took on yet another name, el-Hajj Malik el-Shabazz. As spiritually important as were the events in Mecca, the real change in Malcolm's social and political agenda occurred during stops he made in various African nations on his way home from Mecca. In meetings with leaders from Ghana, Nigeria, Algeria, and Egypt, Malcolm began to think about race relations not only as an American problem but also as a global issue. He dropped the use of the term *Negro* and began to speak about Afro-Americans, suggesting a more global and interconnected relationship with people of African origin scattered around the world.

Malcolm made the jump from civil rights to human rights. He returned to the United States determined to work through one of the African ambassadors to the United Nations to file charges of human rights violations against the government of the United States. That decision, as much as any rift between himself and the Nation of Islam, put Malcolm's life on a collision course with a premature death. Here is yet another link between Malcolm X and King. Both of them were probably killed not as a result of any racial views

and comments they may have held or made but because of their entry into the more delicate world of U.S. foreign policy. King spoke out about the Vietnam War, and Malcolm X began decrying America's role in global oppression and exploitation.

In early 1965 Malcolm organized yet another group, calling it the Organization for Afro-American Unity (OAAU). He insisted that whites could not join this organization, but he did indicate a willingness to work with many groups and persons he had earlier attacked and condemned when he operated under the ideology of the Nation of Islam. While giving a speech at a weekly gathering of that group in New York City, Malcolm X was shot and killed on February 21, 1965.

His friend and admirer Ossie Davis captured the meaning of the life of Malcom X when he said at the funeral service, "Malcolm was our manhood, our living, black manhood! This was his meaning to his people. And in honoring him, we honor the best in ourselves.... And we will know him then for what he was and is—a Prince—our own black shining Prince!—who didn't hesitate to die, because he loved us so."

Malcolm and his wife, Betty Shabazz, whom he married in 1956, had four daughters: Attilah, Qubilah, Ilasah, and Amilah.

C. Eric Lincoln, *The Black Muslims in America;* V. P. Franklin, "Malcolm X and the Resurrection of the Dead," in *Living Our Stories and Telling Our Truths;* "Malcolm X," in *The African American Century,* ed. by Henry Louis Gates Jr. and Cornel West; Malcolm X with Alex Haley, *The Autobiography of Malcolm X;* Henry J. Young, *Major Black Religious Leaders Since 1940.*

SECTION 7

Cult Leaders

Ali, Noble Drew

(1886–1929) For most of the twentieth century there were groups that advocated that black people living in the United States would not be truly free until they radically changed their self-identity. This involved changing their religious faith from Christianity to Islam and changing their group name from Negro, black, colored, or similar designations to some name associated with the African continent. The first person to make this argument was the Noble Prophet Drew Ali, also known as Noble Drew Ali.

He was born in North Carolina in 1886 under the given name of Timothy Drew. Nothing is known of his earlier life until he appeared in Newark, New Jersey, in 1913 and began preaching from street corners to those who passed by. Within a few years he had established temples in Pittsburgh, Pennsylvania, Detroit, Michigan, and Chicago, Illinois, where his greatest following was located. He contended that black people in America needed to begin referring to themselves as Moors or Moorish Americans. He borrowed the name from the people from North Africa who migrated into Spain and Portugal during the Crusades of the thirteenth century and who spread Islamic culture as they journeyed. He stated that their true homeland was Morocco.

A contemporary of and something of a rival to **Marcus Garvey**, Ali did not advocate a back-to-Africa movement. Rather, he wanted to use the term *Moorish* and the adoption of the Islamic religion as a basis for allowing black Americans to separate themselves from the legacy of slavery and second-class citizenship that he saw as a biblical legacy tied to the curse of Canaan. He adopted the star and crescent symbol of Islam and then said that the followers of Islam are Asiatic people, part of a glorious culture and a worldwide community. Ali believed that if black Americans could come to view themselves as part of that group of Asiatics, they could throw off the inherited sense of inferiority that American society had imposed upon them.

In adopting Islam, Ali offered a rationale for repudiating Christianity. He stated that if the white people who had been oppressing and exploiting black people for so long were members of the Christian faith, then surely it made no sense for the oppressed and exploited to share in that religious tradition. Thus Ali urged his followers to literally reinvent themselves. He did not encourage them to take on new names, but he did urge them to incorporate into their name the terms *el* or *bey* in order to have a more Islamic or Asiatic sound. He gave them new identification cards and birth certificates to announce their new identity and status. The cards carried this message: "This is your Nationality and Identification Card for the Moorish Science Temple of America, and Birthrights for the Moorish Americans. We honor all the Divine prophets; Jesus, Mohammed, Buddha and Confucius. May the blessings of the God of our Father Allah be upon you that carry this card. I do hereby declare that you are a Moslem under the Divine Laws of the Holy Koran of Mecca, Love, Truth, Peace, Freedom and Justice."

Many of the followers of Noble Drew Ali would accost white people on the street, waving the membership card in their faces and saying that their new prophet had set them free from the domination of whites. That zeal only increased racial tensions in the cities where Ali had a following. At the peak of his popularity, Noble Drew Ali and the Moorish Science Temple had upwards of twenty thousand members. The importance of the group is not related to its size, however, but to its central claim that Christianity is the religion for white people (Europeans) and that blacks living in America will not be free until they embrace a new identity rooted in Islamic, not Western, identity.

That idea resurfaced in the 1930s with **W. D. Fard,** who had been a follower of Noble Drew Ali, and **Elijah Muhammad** and the **Nation of Islam.** However, it was Noble Drew Ali who planted the seed twenty years earlier. For the rest of the twentieth century, the black church has had to respond to the charge first raised by Ali that Christianity is "the white man's religion."

The movement began to weaken when the elders Ali had appointed began using their position to sell herbs, charms, and potions. They kept the proceeds from those sales for themselves. When Ali tried to end those abuses, he suddenly and mysteriously died. It has been suggested that he was killed in 1929 by those followers who objected to his attempt to restore orthodoxy to the group. However, during his lifetime the Moorish Science Temple offered an alternative view of the world to black people, many of them recently arrived in the North and looking for some kind of identity and stability that traditional Christianity seemed not to offer to them.

Arthur Huff Fauset, *Black Gods of the Metropolis;* Gayraud S. Wilmore, *Black Religion and Black Radicalism;* Arthur J. Magida, *Prophet of Rage: A Life of Louis Farrakhan and His Nation.*

☽ Divine, Father (Major J.)

(1877-1965) He was born George Baker Jr. sometime between 1877 and 1883. Various biographers fix the place of his birth as either coastal South Carolina or Rockville, Maryland. It is commonly agreed that he made his way to Baltimore in 1899 and became involved with several religious groups in that city. The most notable contacts he established involved Samuel Morris, a black preacher who believed that he was God incarnate. This was based upon his reading of 1 Corinthians 3:16, "You are the temple of God, and the spirit of God dwells in you." If Morris was God, then George Baker became God's associate and took on the title of the Messenger of God.

A second follower of Morris, John (Reverend St. John Divine Bishop) Hickerson, objected to Morris's limiting the claim of divinity and insisted that he too was divine. This exposure to two men who perceived themselves to be God on earth made an early and deep impression on George Baker. It was the decisive issue that set him on his path to become a cultic leader. The three men parted company, with Morris remaining in Baltimore. Hickerson went to New York and established The Church of the Living God. Baker began preaching throughout the South, being arrested and jailed in Valdosta, Georgia, on the charge of being "a troublemaker," because he now was called John Doe alias God.

By 1915 The Messenger had made his way to New York City, and eventually he purchased a home in Sayville, Long Island. The name that appeared on the deed was Major J. Devine. As his ministry took root in and around New York City, he changed the spelling of his name to Divine and took on the title *Father,* which had been affectionately bestowed upon him by his growing band of followers.

Father Divine's early followers were the domestic workers who lived at homes where they served as cooks, gardeners, chauffeurs, and housecleaners. He also drew people from New York City who began traveling to Sayville to share in his growing movement. In order to ease the strain of their commute, Divine helped

such persons find work in the big houses on Long Island.

Thus Father Divine was appealing to people at several levels: employment, fellowship, and food. They would meet at his home in Sayville for an event that he called the banquet. It was a time of fellowship, an elaborate meal, and a time when he would preach and teach. His was not by any means a traditional Christian message based upon biblical teachings. Baker avoided using the Bible and continued to argue that he was God and had come to offer help to people whose plight was being ignored by traditional black churches and black preachers.

Central to his teaching was the doctrine of communitarianism. New members would divest themselves of their

worldly possessions, including homes, and turn over their funds to Father Divine. Members would be able to draw from that pool of money as they had need. Moreover, that became the means by which Father Divine was able to pay for the meals he served to a steadily increasing number of persons who would gather weekly at his Sayville home. It also allowed him eventually to live a luxurious lifestyle.

Central to his teaching was the idea of living frugally so that money would be available to members and others during times of hardship. By the time of the Great Depression in 1929, Father Divine was in a position to offer enormous assistance especially to black migrants from the South who could find neither employment, housing, nor food. Providing those three resources was the centerpiece of his work for the next decade.

In 1933 Father Divine's white neighbors in Sayville, who had initially welcomed him to the community, worked to have him arrested because of the large numbers of people moving in and out of that eight-room house at all hours. He was convicted of being "a public nuisance," much the same charge as he had faced in Baltimore twenty years earlier. He was fined $500 and sentenced to one year in jail. His aura of divinity greatly increased when the judge who sentenced him suddenly died of a heart attack, though he was known to have been in perfect health. When he was told what had happened to the judge, Father Divine responded, "I hated to do it."

After his early release from jail, Father Divine's fame and popularity skyrocketed, with black newspapers like *The Amsterdam News* in New York heralding him as a victim of harassment and as a model of black self-sufficiency. Divine shifted his headquarters to the Harlem community of New York City. There he opened the first of his Peace Mission Centers, the buildings in which his various benevolent programs were housed. Initially his clientele largely consisted of Southern migrants who could not find work or housing in the North.

As his movement spread beyond New York City, Father Divine began to draw large numbers of black and white followers from the higher strata of society. At the peak of his influence during the Great Depression he had an estimated 150 Peace Missions scattered across the country, in Canada, western Europe, and Australia. He also had an estimated 2.5 million followers he called angels.

Father Divine's missions never lost their focus in terms of benevolence underwritten by the communal property principle, and they also became centers of racial diversity where Father Divine's message of integration became a key element. He spread his teachings not only through his sermons and appearances at the various centers but also through two magazines that became the official organs of the movement. *The Spoken Word* was produced in Los Angeles and served the centers west of the Mississippi. The *New Day* was printed in New York and served the East Coast and Midwest regions.

Father Divine never had much of a presence in the South. This was largely because of his focus on interracial communities. It is also doubtful that the racial policies in the South at that time would have allowed for so influential a black leader as Father Divine to emerge, especially given his penchant for surrounding himself with white female secretaries and assistants.

In 1936 Father Divine purchased a farm, "The Promised Land," in Ulster County, New York, and invited many of his followers to live and work there. It was an ideal setting for many of his followers, who had been farmers in the South for most of their lives. He also invested in other real estate throughout Harlem, including apartments, stores, and other properties. Part of the wealth he amassed was the result of these real estate ventures, in addition to the property followers had turned over to him for use as he determined.

Also in 1936 Father Divine set up a political movement called The Righteous Government Platform, which sought to influence local elections in New York City. His expanding influence, economically and politically, earned him the contempt of the more traditional black clergy in New York City. His most ardent critic was **Adam Clayton Powell Jr.** of the Abyssinian Baptist Church. However, in 1941, when Powell was preparing to run for city council in New York, he forgot his earlier condemnations of Father Divine and eagerly sought his endorsement in that race. Divine also forgot Powell's earlier attacks and gave him that endorsement.

Father Divine ordered his followers not to marry, and those who were married when they joined the movement had to live separately thereafter. He also ordered them to cut off all relationships with family and friends who were not members of the cult. He had two relationships that challenged that model. The first was with a woman named Penninah (Sister Penny), who became known as Mother Divine after they were united in 1919. Though he never claimed to be married, he and Mother Divine were understood to be husband and wife. In 1946 he openly married a twenty-one-year-old white Canadian woman named Edna Rose Ritching, who had been known as Sweet Rose and later replaced Penninah as Mother Divine. It was never explained why Penninah had lost her position.

Following some legal battles over misuse of funds, Father Divine moved his headquarters from New York City to Philadelphia, Pennsylvania. There he continued to preside over his movement, but with the end of the Depression and a gradual change in the economic status of black people, his movement began to lose its appeal. Most notably, fewer and fewer people were willing to become angels by divesting themselves of their property and money. By that time, however, Father Divine had amassed a huge fortune, largely through real estate holdings, including seventy-five homes across the country that he called his heavens. Each of those homes was run and occupied by his followers.

Failing health caused him to cut back his public appearances, and Father Divine died in 1965.

Arthur Huff Fauset, *Black Gods of the Metropolis;* C. Eric Lincoln, *The Black Church Since Frazier;* Joseph R. Washington Jr., *Black Sects and Cults;* Jill Watts, *God, Harlem USA;* Robert Weisbrot, *Father Divine.*

☾ Fard, Wallace D. (W. D.)

(1877?–1934?) On July 4, 1930, there appeared in the black community of Detroit, Michigan, a man who claimed that he had come from the holy city of Mecca in Arabia. He said he had been born there in 1877 and was a descendant of the Prophet Muhammad.

Arthur J. Magida reports that Fard was actually born of interracial parents. His mother was black, and his father was either a Syrian or Palestinian Muslim. The location of his birth is variously reported as being Jamaica, New Zealand, or Portland, Oregon. A 1943 FBI file reveals that Fard was imprisoned in San Quentin Prison in California between 1926 and 1929 for selling narcotics in Los Angeles. Upon his release from prison his life took a decidedly different direction.

He went door to door peddling silk and other exotic products "of the East." He also spread the message that he was God, who had come to save black people of America whom he called "the lost Tribe of Shabazz." Nothing more is known of the origins of this man, but it is widely thought that he was a follower of **Noble Drew Ali,** who had organized the Moorish Science Temple in 1913. Some even claimed that he was the reincarnation of Noble Drew Ali.

Among the people in Detroit who responded to his message was Elijah Poole, who said about Fard, "He opened my blinded eyes, and unstopped my ears, and loosened the knot in my tongue." Fard organized the Lost-Found Nation of Islam on July 4, 1930. He changed Poole's name to **Elijah Muhammad,** and together they set out to attract others to the new movement. During Fard's lifetime his followers numbered approximately eight thousand persons. When Muhammad asked Fard who he was, Fard answered, "I am the one the world has been expecting for the past 2,000 years. I am God, and I came to guide you into the right path that you my be successful and see the hereafter."

Among the things that Fard came to teach were that black people were the original people on the earth. Whites were a genetic accident created by a doctor Yakub. White domination of the earth would last for 6,070 years, ending in 1984. Buddhism and Christianity would be swept away from the earth once the teachings of Fard took root. Orthodox Islam will recognize that the **Nation of Islam** is the truest expression of the will of Allah. These and other teachings were set down in two books, *The Secret Ritual of the Nation of Islam* and *Teaching for the Lost-Found Nation of Islam in a Mathematical Way*.

Muhammad repeatedly said that God came to earth in the person of Fard, whom Muhammad often called the Mahdi. Fard is credited with starting the paramilitary group called the Fruit of Islam. He began the practice of having his followers abandon their last (slave) names and use the title X for unknown until he assigned them a new name. He also organized the University of Islam, an upper elementary and secondary school where the children of the Nation of Islam could be educated in the ways of Islam and in the truth of their history. These schools were not accredited. When Fard insisted that the children of his followers attend that school, he was arrested in 1932 for breaking the state law that required that all children be involved in compulsory education in the public school system or some other accredited school through age eighteen.

Upon release from jail, Fard relocated to Chicago, where he soon suffered a similar fate for the same reasons. In June 1934 Fard disappeared as suddenly and as mysteriously as he had arrived. He was succeeded in the leadership of the Nation of Islam by Muhammad. Every year since 1934 the Nation of Islam honors the memory of Fard on February 26 with a holiday and celebration called Savior's Day. Orthodox Islam not only refuses to acknowledge the legitimacy of

the Nation of Islam as an Islamic community but also vigorously rejects the idea that God (Allah) came to earth in the form of a human being. It is interesting to note that **Warithuddin Muhammad** (Wallace D.), the son of Elijah Muhammad who was named after Fard, succeeded his father as head of the Nation of Islam in 1975. He repeatedly argued that Fard was still alive and that he could speak with him by telephone any time he chose to do so. However, there were no further sightings of or contact from Fard after 1934.

Bernard Cushmeer, *This Is the One;* E. U. Essien-Udom, *Black Nationalism;* C. Eric Lincoln, *The Black Muslims in America;* Arthur J. Magida, *Prophet of Rage: A Life of Louis Farrakhan and His Nation;* Elijah Muhammad, *Message to the Blackman;* Malcolm X with Alex Haley, *The Autobiography of Malcolm X.*

☯ Grace, Charles (Daddy Grace)

(1881-1961) Grace was born Marcelino Manoel de Graca in Cape Verde, West Africa, on January 25, 1881. He migrated to the United States in 1900, settling in New Bedford, Massachusetts. He worked on a variety of odd jobs until he made the claim in 1920 that he had just returned from a tour of the Holy Land during which he had demonstrated the power to heal persons of a wide variety of ailments. That was the beginning of his ministry, which began in nearby Wareham, Massachusetts, and then expanded to New Bedford.

Within two years Grace had established a large following along the Atlantic seaboard as far south as North Carolina.

In 1925 he formally organized his followers into branches of The United
House of Prayer for All People. That
movement eventually grew into 111 mission centers located in more than ninety
cities and towns across the country. The
name "Daddy Grace" came into use after
1925 and was the affectionate title given
to him by his followers. His formal name
became Bishop Charles Emanuel Grace.

Drawing upon the Pentecostal-holiness
traditions that were prevalent in urban
black communities in the 1920s, Grace's
movement was substantially different in
that he was the central object of veneration. It has been contested that he ever
claimed to be God. However, it is not contested that on more than one occasion he
said, "If you get in trouble with God,
Grace can save you. But if you get in trouble with Grace, God cannot save you."

Grace also taught his followers that
every use of the word *grace* in the Bible
was a direct reference to himself. Thus he
was the incarnation of the Spirit of God
that was being discussed in the Scriptures.
He may never have said that he was God,
but it is clear that many of his followers
related to him as if he were God.

Worship services in Grace's churches
were marked by extreme manifestations
of ecstatic dancing that resulted in trances
in which persons fell prostrate to the
floor. The floor was conveniently covered
with sawdust to cushion their fall to the
ground. However, according to Arthur
Huff Fauset, who observed several of the
services in progress, the center of the service seemed to be the frequent offerings
that were taken up from the congregation with the proceeds going directly to
Daddy Grace.

In addition to the worship service,
members were expected to visit the place
in each of the churches where a variety
of Daddy Grace products were sold.
These included household cleaning
products, cosmetics and toiletries for
men and women, and drinks and snacks.
Members were assured that if they
washed with Daddy Grace Soap they
would lose weight. If they used Daddy
Grace Writing Tablets they would write
better letters. If they placed a copy of
Grace Magazine, which sold for ten
cents, upon their chest, it could cure
them of everything from the common
cold to tuberculosis. All proceeds from
the sales went directly to Daddy Grace.

Grace lived a lavish lifestyle; he owned more than seventeen residences across the country. He was a flamboyant personality, with hair that touched upon his neck and shoulders, flashy jewelry, and three-inch fingernails that were painted red, white, and blue. He was driven about in chauffeur-driven limousines.

There is no indication that Grace urged his followers to support any social or civil rights issues. He opposed war, urged marital fidelity and condemned adultery, and urged his members to obey the law. It is reported that his followers seldom if ever ended up in trouble with the law. He, however, was often charged with either sexual or financial misconduct. He was regularly investigated by the Internal Revenue Service, which wanted an accounting of the cash contributions that were handed over to him from his churches across the country. By the end of his life, his personal estate was valued at more than $4 million.

Along with **Father Divine** and Prophet Cherry, Daddy Grace was one of the major black cult leaders of the twentieth century. As if to demonstrate that he was greater than Cherry or Divine, Daddy Grace eventually bought buildings that had formerly been used by the other two leaders. He outlasted both of them in that United House of Prayer churches continue to exist into the twenty-first century. Twenty new buildings were erected in cities across the country with funds provided by the sale of commercial real estate purchased over the years in the name of the church.

Grace died suddenly on January 21, 1960, during a trip to visit his churches on the West Coast. His funeral cortege stopped in cities across the country to allow his followers to pay their respects. Those memorial services inevitably resulted in enormous outbursts of grief. He was eventually buried in New Bedford.

Arthur Huff Fauset, *Black Gods of the Metropolis;* E. Franklin Frazier, *The Negro Church in America;* Joseph R. Washington Jr., *Black Sects and Cults;* Gayraud S. Wilmore, *Black Religion and Black Radicalism.*

☻ Matthew, Wentworth Arthur

(1892–1973) Islam has never been the only alternative religion among the major faith traditions chosen by blacks who wanted to separate themselves from Christianity. For most of the twentieth century, many black Americans, especially in the urban centers of the North, turned to various leaders who made the claim that American blacks are the lost tribe of Israel or the descendants of some major figure from the Old Testament. The largest such group, though not the first, was the Commandment Keepers, also known as the Black Jews of Harlem. Their leader was Rabbi Wentworth A. Matthew.

Matthew was born in Lagos, Nigeria, on June 23, 1892. He migrated first to the West Indies and then to New York City in 1913, during the Great Migration. He affiliated with **Marcus Garvey** and the Universal Negro Improvement Association (UNIA) and with a West Indian man named Arnold Ford, who told him that all black people were originally Jewish in heritage and that slavery and other events had caused them to lose the knowledge of their true selves. This was the same claim made by those who argued on behalf of Islam at that time.

The idea of Jewish heritage took hold of Matthew, and he began to build a group around that idea. He claimed that he was a rabbi who had been credentialed by the Falashas, an orthodox Jewish community then living in Ethiopia. He established a congregation in New York City that he called the Commandment Keepers. The central authority of the community was the Torah, the first five books of the Old Testament, which contains many of the laws of Judaism. Among the commandments that Matthew stressed were Sabbath worship from sundown Friday to sundown Saturday, a kosher diet, the observance of Passover and other Jewish holy days, the reading from the Torah in Hebrew, and the study of the Talmud and the Mishnah (commentaries and reflections by rabbis over hundreds of years on the interpretation and application of Jewish ritual law). There is no evidence that he urged circumcision.

Christianity was not only rejected by the Commandment Keepers but also was attacked as the religion of those who stole the Jewish religion from blacks through slavery and then used Christianity as a method of pacifying them in their oppressed state. The truth about black people, according to Matthew, is that they are the offspring of Jacob and the offspring of the union between King Solomon and the Queen of Sheba. The existence of the Falashas in Ethiopia is proof of the historic link between black people and Judaism.

Matthew's claim to be an orthodox Jewish rabbi was never fully embraced by the European Jews who lived in New York when he was establishing the Commandment Keepers. However, Israel has recognized the Jews of Ethiopia as an authentic, orthodox Jewish community that has maintained Jewish ritual law, including circumcision, dietary codes, and the study of Torah. Thousands of Ethiopian Jews were rescued from political oppression in that country in the 1980s and 1990s and brought to Israel.

At the peak of prominence, the Commandment Keepers may have numbered in excess of three thousand adherents in New York City. There were other black Jewish communities in the Northeast, including The Church of God organized by Prophet Cherry and the Church of God and Saints of Christ under Bishop Crowdy. The attraction of Judaism has never matched the appeal that Islam has had in America's black communities. However, there is a group of black Jews living in Debir, in the desert south of Jerusalem. They cling to the claim that they are Jews not by conversion but by heritage. Their leader is called Yahweh ben Yahweh. They have been appealing to Israel to be recognized as citizens of the Jewish state on the basis of their genealogical claim. So far, their request has not been granted.

Wentworth Matthew died in 1973. His grandson, David M. Dore, received a rabbinical degree from Yeshiva University in 1977.

Howard Brotz, *The Black Jews of Harlem;* Arthur Huff Fauset, *Black Gods of the Metropolis;* C. Eric Lincoln, ed., *The Black Experience in Religion;* Larry G. Murphy, J. Gordon Melton, and Gary L. Ward, eds., *The Encyclopedia of African American Religions.*

☯ Robinson, Ida

(1891–1946) Born in Florida in 1891 and reared in Georgia, Robinson migrated to Philadelphia, Pennsylvania, and in 1924 founded the Mt. Sinai Holy Church of America. This Pentecostal-holiness group was unique among black urban religious communities for its predominantly female leadership and membership. The group eventually spread throughout the rapidly expanding black communities of the urban North during the Great Depression.

The church was typical of most Pentecostal-holiness movements of that era. Membership required some manifestation of sanctification, typically speaking in tongues. There was a long list of forbidden practices that were believed to be in conflict with holiness. They included sexual promiscuity, attending sporting events, and the use of cosmetic products. Divorce was strictly forbidden, and marriage outside of the community was grounds for dismissal.

The primary rituals of the community included faith healing, communion, and foot washing. Worship services often led participants into a state of frenzy in which they danced and shouted until they fell from exhaustion.

Little is known about Bishop Ida Robinson except that she was a keen student of the Bible, a good organizer, and a cult leader for many people who were in search of community when they moved to the North during the Great Migration. She died in 1946. Nothing more is known about the Mt. Sinai Holy Church of America, and it is no longer in existence today.

Arthur Huff Fauset, *Black Gods of the Metropolis;* E. Franklin Frazier, *The Negro Church in America;* Joseph R. Washington Jr., *Black Sects and Cults;* Gayraud S. Wilmore, *Black Religion and Black Radicalism.* ▣

Singers and Songwriters

Caesar, Shirley

(1938-) For more than forty years, vocalist and evangelist Shirley Caesar has been at the forefront of **gospel music,** defining what some have called the rock-gospel style. She was born in Durham, North Carolina, on October 13, 1938. She began singing at the age of seven in the choir of the Mt. Calvary Holy Church of Durham. Her father died when she was only twelve, and as a result she began to sing professionally to support her family.

In 1958 Caesar began to sing with **Albertina Walker** and The Caravans, one of the top touring gospel groups of that era. She remained with The Caravans, becoming the lead singer, until 1996, when she left to form The Shirley Caesar Singers. She also acknowledged a call to the preaching ministry, and on many of her songs, beginning with a classic recording, *Hold My Mule,* she integrates preaching and evangelization with her singing.

Over the course of her career Caesar has won six Grammy Awards, more than any other female artist in the history of gospel music. That includes one for her best-known song, "Put Your Hand in the Hand of the Man from Galilee." She has also won a Dove Award and the Image Award from the National Association for the Advancement of Colored People (NAACP). Her 1989 album *Live in Chicago* was listed as the number-one gospel album for that year in *Billboard.* The same magazine named her the outstanding artist for 1989. *Ebony* has named her the outstanding gospel singer in America on three occasions.

In addition to singing in concerts around the world, Caesar was elected to the city council of her native city. She serves as copastor with her husband, Bishop Harold Ivory Williams, of the Mt. Calvary Holy Church of Winston-Salem, North Carolina. She also oversees the Shirley Caesar Outreach Ministries, which distributes food and clothing to needy persons. As an evangelist, she preaches what she calls the ABCs of faith:

• admit that you need the Lord
• believe that God is God, and that God gave us his Son
• commit your ways unto the Lord

Like most top gospel singers, Caesar was regularly approached by secular recording companies to record either rhythm and blues or rock 'n roll. She eventually stopped them from pursuing her when she told them that "the only way I'd sing Rock 'n Roll is if they let me rock for Jesus and roll for God." Caesar has never performed or recorded outside of the genre of gospel music.

Shirley Caesar was featured in a video entitled *Shirley Caesar Live*. It was taped at a 1996 performance she gave at the Greater Bibleway Miracle Temple in Atlanta, Georgia. That concert and video resulted in Shirley Caesar winning a Grammy Award as Best Traditional Gospel Singer for 1996.

Bobby Jones, *Touched by God;* Jessie Carney Smith, ed., *Notable Black American Women;* Eileen Southern, *The Music of Black Americans.*

☺ Campbell, Lucie E. (Williams)

(1885–1963) Standing as the bridge between the era of **Charles Albert Tindley** and the emergence of **Thomas A. Dorsey** was the life and work of Lucie E. Campbell. In a musical career that spanned six decades, she was the first black woman to make a major impact on American **gospel music.** Many of her songs remain standards into the twenty-first century and helped to launch the careers of many other gospel performers.

Campbell was born on April 30, 1885, in Duck Hill, Mississippi, and her parents had been slaves. She finished high school in Memphis, Tennessee, in 1899 at the age of fourteen. She then began what would be her lifelong career as a public school teacher in Memphis. When she began teaching she was earning $40 per month. However, it would be in her role as a composer and publisher of gospel music that Campbell would make her mark on history. A self-taught musician, she had been appointed director of music for the Sunday School and Baptist Training Union (BTU) Congress of the **National Baptist Convention, USA, Inc. (NBCUSA)** in 1916. She continued in that role every year until 1962.

Campbell earned national acclaim in 1919 when she composed "Something Within Me," which opens with a tribute to two of the most respected members of the black community at that time, "preachers and teachers." The song was premiered at the National Baptist Convention in Atlantic City, New Jersey, and it quickly spread across the country to give her recognition as the leading black female gospel songwriter in the country. That song continues to be popular, and the pop group Take Six has recorded it. Her other major songs were "Just to Behold His Face" (1923), "He Understands;

He'll Say, 'Well Done'" (1933), and "In the Upper Room" (1947), which was made internationally popular by **Mahalia Jackson.** She also composed "Jesus Gave Me Water" (1946), which was recorded and popularized by the Soul Stirrers.

Campbell played other leadership roles in the popularization of gospel music, working primarily through her position within the NBCUSA. In 1921 she was on the editorial board for the hymnal *Gospel Pearls.* She introduced Dorsey to the National Baptist Convention, and she forged a lifelong partnership with Dr. J. Robert Bradley, who often sang her newest songs each year at the convention. As a world-renowned concert singer, Bradley also made Campbell's songs a part of his concert repertoire. He even sang several of them in a command performance for the British royal family in 1955. Campbell was in attendance, and Bradley presented her to that audience.

Campbell became more than a composer. She also became a protégé of **Nannie Helen Burroughs** and Mary McLeod Bethune. As such, she was frequently called upon to address women's groups within the life of the black church and beyond. However, she remained committed to one goal, which was to introduce one new song every year at the annual session of the NBCUSA. She did exactly that between 1930 and 1962.

Campbell married Rev. C. R. Williams in 1960, when she was seventy-five years old. She died in Nashville, Tennessee, on January 3, 1963. At her death she was still serving as music director of Sunday School and BTU Congress of the NBCUSA.

Bernice Johnson Reagon, ed., *We'll Understand It Better By and By;* Eileen Southern, *The Music of Black Americans.*

☻ Cleveland, James

(1931–1991) Any list of the most influential male singers, composers, accompanists, and choir leaders of gospel music would have to include the name of James Cleveland. He is the bridge that links the first generation of gospel musicians—**Thomas A. Dorsey,** Sallie Martin, and **Mahalia Jackson**—with the contemporary performers of this musical genre—Walter Hawkins, **Andraé Crouch,** the **Richard Smallwood** Singers, and the Winans.

Cleveland was born in Chicago on December 5, 1931. He seemed destined to be a part of the gospel music hierarchy. He was reared in Pilgrim Baptist Church in Chicago, where Dorsey had been the minister of music. He began playing the piano and singing before the age of ten, and soon he was singing with and composing songs for The **Roberta Martin** Singers.

In 1959 Cleveland formed his first group, The Gospel Chimes. In 1960 he recorded his first national hit, "The Love of God," with the Voices of Tabernacle Choir from Detroit, Michigan. His greatest hit, "Peace, Be Still," was recorded with the three-hundred-voice Angelic Choir of Nutley, New Jersey, in 1963. That recording remains the biggest seller in the history of the Savoy record label. It established Cleveland as the king of **gospel music.** Cleveland released forty-six albums, eight of which were gold records, meaning that one million copies were sold. He also received a Grammy Award for excellence in recording gospel music.

In 1962 Cleveland was ordained a Baptist minister. He moved from Chicago to Los Angeles to become the pastor of New Greater Harvest Baptist Church. He later organized the Cornerstone Institutional Baptist Church in Los Angeles. However, he continued his musical career, organizing the Southern California Community Choir. That group is most noted for accompanying **Aretha Franklin** on her gospel music album *Amazing Grace* in 1972. Cleveland was one of her musical influences, having trained the choir at the church in Detroit where her father, **Clarence LaVaughn (C. L.) Franklin,** served as pastor.

Cleveland composed more than three hundred songs. In 1968 he organized James Cleveland's Gospel Music Workshop, which attracted thousands of delegates every year to study the art of writing, arranging, and performing gospel music. He also wanted to train them in the art of transmitting the emotion that is so much a part of gospel music. Bernice Johnson Reagon wrote about the emotion that gospel musicians like Cleveland can evoke: "They are able to take the anxieties, joys, and aspirations of the poor, rejected, and often uneducated African American population and express them in lyrics that not only captured the very essence of the Christian movement, but also spoke for each Christian as if he or she were making a personal statement."

There was tremendous pressure on gospel musicians of that era to take their material into secular settings like nightclubs and theaters and present them for sheer entertainment. Gospel singers Clara Ward, Rosetta Tharpe, Sam Cooke, and Della Reese acknowledge that they did precisely that, singing to entertain and not to inspire. Reese went so far as to say, "We don't perform in night clubs to save souls." Cleveland resisted that pressure and continued to present to church groups and with an eye toward sharing his faith with the audience. In explaining his decision to avoid nightclubs, Cleveland said, "I don't feel I can do much good in a club. I don't feel that the atmosphere is conducive, and I don't feel that the reason for bringing me there is the reason for which I am singing."

C. Eric Lincoln speaks about the effectiveness of gospel musicians like Cleveland who refuse to become entertainers

and choose instead to be evangelists: "They use the medium of Gospel music as a homiletical instrument.... They literally preach their compositions to their concert hall." Despite his refusal to be viewed as an entertainer, Cleveland was the first gospel singer to be included in the Hollywood Walk of Fame. He died on February 9, 1991.

"James Cleveland: King of Gospel," *Ebony,* November 1968; Bernice Johnson Reagon, ed., *We'll Understand It Better By and By;* Eileen Southern, *The Music of Black Americans.*

☺ Crouch, Andraé

(1947–) Born on July 1, 1947, in Los Angeles, California, Crouch is the son of a **Church of God in Christ (COGIC)** preacher whose musical career began in his father's church when he was eleven years of age. He began playing the piano without any formal musical training. By his middle teens he had organized a COGIC youth choir that included the future pop recording artist Billy Preston.

From there he organized a group called Andraé Crouch and the Disciples; that group toured in Europe, Africa, Asia, and throughout the Americas.

Crouch ventured into a solo career, and out of hundreds of songs, many of his **gospel music** compositions have become standards in the church and on the performing circuit. Among his biggest hits are "My Tribute (To God Be the Glory)," "Through It All," and "The Blood Will Never Lose Its Power." Over the years he has recorded twenty-five albums and won nine Grammy Awards and five Dove Awards. His songs have been translated and performed in twenty-six different languages. His music has also served as an inspiration for successive generations of gospel singers. CeCe Winans says, "Andraé's music has had by far the most impact on me and my family... that impact has probably grown over the years because his music is still the greatest." Billy Graham says, "Andraé Crouch is without doubt one of the most prolific songwriters of the age."

This is all the more remarkable when it is remembered that from 1984 to 1994 Crouch stepped away from gospel music to try his hand at songwriting for motion pictures and for pop artists. He received Oscar nominations for his musical score contributions to *The Lion King* and *The Color Purple,* of which Quincy Jones was the executive producer. He also collaborated with such diverse artists as Elvis Presley, Michael Jackson, Quincy Jones, and Madonna. Jones persuaded Crouch to return to gospel music, and he produced Crouch's 1994 comeback album, *Mercy,* on the Qwest label. *Mercy* was followed by several more new releases, such as the Grammy-nominated albums *Pray* and *The Gift of Christmas*. The Christmas album featured Kirk Whalum, Chaka Khan, Patty Austin, and Yolanda Adams.

Within a span of two years (1992–1994), Crouch suffered the death of both of his parents and his brother. As a result, he was divinely lead to continue the family ministry and become pastor of New Christ Memorial Church of God in Christ in Los Angeles. His twin sister, Sandra Crouch, is his copastor. Crouch himself continues in the dual role of pastor and songwriter/performer.

Eileen Southern notes that Crouch introduced changes to gospel music equal to the impact that **Thomas A. Dorsey** had on black church music. "He combined elements of popular music, rock, country music, and soul with traditional Gospel; his accompanying forces consisted of both acoustical and electronic instruments, including synthesizers." In 2001 Andraé Crouch began work on creating his own record company.

Bernice Johnson Reagon, *We'll Understand It Better By and By;* Eileen Southern, *The Music of Black Americans;* www.jamsline.com–crouch; www.Gospel-city.com.

☉ Dorsey, Thomas A.

(1899–1993) Known as the father of **gospel music** and as the composer of many of the most beloved songs within the African American church, Dorsey was responsible for bridging the gap that existed between the music of the church and the blues and jazz rhythms that were popular at the same time. He embodied the struggle within the black community between sacred and secular music, a struggle that would be reflected in the lives of other musicians, including W. C. Handy, Nat "King" Cole, Sam Cooke, and **Aretha Franklin.**

Dorsey was born on July 1, 1899, in Villa Rica, Georgia. He was the son of a Baptist preacher who was also a sharecropper. By living in that home, Dorsey learned the lessons of faith and hope and the hardships and sufferings that engulfed many black people that he encountered every day. There was an organ in their home, and under the tutelage of his mother, he began playing by ear at an early age. One of his uncles was a blues guitar player, so Dorsey was exposed to the spirituals and the blues from his youth, and he would continue an almost thirty-year struggle over which of those musical genres would claim his time and talent.

By the age of twelve, Dorsey was playing the blues in nightclubs, brothels, and gambling houses in Atlanta, where his family had moved in 1903 to escape the rigors of sharecropping. He gravitated to a vaudeville theater called The Eighty-One, where such blues singers as Bessie Smith and Ma Rainey performed regularly. Soon he was accompanying both of them on the piano, and he became known by two stage names, Georgia Tom and Barrelhouse Tom. He never took sustained, formal musical training. For a short while, he took lessons from a Mrs. Graves who was affiliated with Morehouse College. However, he was not interested in the classical sounds she was interested in having him create. He was far more intrigued with playing by ear the music he heard in the clubs and theaters. Thus ended his formal musical training, though he would continue to study music theory on his own.

In 1916 Dorsey followed millions of other black Southerners and headed north as part of the Great Migration. He intended to go to Philadelphia and find work in the naval shipyard, but he went by way of Chicago and never left that city. Between 1916 and 1919, he spent his summers in Chicago and his winters in Georgia; he permanently settled in Chicago in 1919. Living and performing in Chicago at that time were such great jazz and blues artists as King Oliver, W. C. Handy, and Louis Armstrong. Dorsey was becoming more involved with that style of music. However, between the rigors of his performance schedule and his frequent trips back and forth to Georgia, he suffered a nervous breakdown in 1920.

The next year Dorsey happened to be invited by a friend to a session of the National Baptist Convention that was meeting in Chicago. That event proved to be a turning point in his life. He heard Rev. W. M. Nix sing "I Do, Don't You?" The power and style with which Nix sang that song resulted in something of a conversion experience for Dorsey. He said, "My inner being was thrilled. My soul was a deluge of divine rapture; my emotions were aroused; my heart was inspired to become a great singer and worker in the Kingdom of the Lord— and impress people just as this great singer did that Sunday morning."

Dorsey began to realize that God wanted him to direct more of his time to writing and performing gospel music. He composed his first gospel song in 1921. It was "If I Don't Get There with You."

Dorsey found his music being influenced from two different directions. He was greatly influenced by the lyricism and deep spirituality of **Charles Albert Tindley** of Philadelphia. However, he could not escape the rhythms and delivery he had heard from Bessie Smith and Ma Rainey. As Michael Harris has argued, Dorsey was the founder of gospel blues. **Wyatt Tee Walker** makes a similar case when he seeks to distinguish the gospel music of Dorsey from the gospel songs popularized by Dwight L. Moody and Ira D. Sankey in their crusades.

For most of the 1920s Dorsey performed gospel music and the blues; between 1925 and 1926 he wrote and copyrighted more than twelve blues songs. In 1924 he was at the peak of his popularity as a blues musician when he appeared with Ma Rainey in a triumphant concert at the Grand Theatre in Chicago. At the same time he was the director of music at New Hope Baptist Church in Chicago. He continued to be a man of two worlds.

Dorsey's gospel blues was not immediately accepted in the sophisticated black churches of the North. Between 1926 and 1928, he could barely find a church that would allow him to perform. That all changed in 1930, after one of his gospel songs, "If You See My Savior, Tell Him You Saw Me," was performed at the National Baptist Convention meeting in Chicago. As a result of that rendition by Willie Mae Fisher, four thousand copies of that song were sold, and Dorsey could see that his future course was clear. That song would eventually be translated into fifty languages.

By 1932 Dorsey and Sallie Martin had founded the National Convention of Gospel Choirs and Choruses, which was headquartered in Chicago. He had finally come back home to the church. He became the director of music at the prestigious Pilgrim Baptist Church of Chicago, whose pastor was the nationally renowned **Junius Caesar (J. C.) Austin.** It was Austin who continually brought Dorsey before the annual gatherings of the National Baptist Convention. That was the primary mechanism by which his music gained national acceptance and ultimately gained great popularity.

In 1928 Dorsey met a young gospel singer named **Mahalia Jackson,** and their collaboration would continue for years to come. She possessed exactly the right combination of piety and power to interpret the songs he was writing, although at many points he tried but failed to persuade her to contain some of her power. Their most popular collaboration was

with Dorsey's "Precious Lord, Take My Hand." He wrote that song in 1932 after hearing of the deaths of his wife, Nettie, in childbirth, and of their newborn son, who died the next day. That song would become his most popular tune, though he acknowledges that he made use of the melody of another song, "Must Jesus Bear the Cross Alone?"

Other gospel songs by Dorsey include "Peace in the Valley," "I Am on the Battlefield for My Lord," "My Desire," "'Tis the Old Ship of Zion," "The Lord Will Make a Way Somehow," and "Then My Lord Will Carry Me Home." His songs continue to be sung and played in black churches to this day. In 1983 a documentary, *Say Amen, Somebody,* was released that focused on Dorsey's life and work.

Dorsey died at the age of ninety-three in 1993 in his adopted hometown of Chicago.

Louis Gianetti, *Understanding Movies;* Michael Harris, "Conflict and Resolution in the Life of Thomas Andrew Dorsey," in *African American Religion,* ed. Timothy E. Fulop and Albert J. Raboteau; Michael Harris, *Thomas A. Dorsey and the Rise of Urban Gospel Blues;* C. Eric Lincoln and Lawrence W. Mamiya, *The Church in the African American Community;* Wyatt Tee Walker, *"Somebody's Calling My Name."*

☺ Ellington, Edward Kennedy (Duke)

(1899–1974) For the first forty years of his prolific musical career, Duke Ellington was best known for his contribution to the world of jazz. However, beginning in 1965 he made substantial contributions to the world of sacred music as well.

Ellington was born on April 29, 1899, in Washington, D.C. His father was a White House butler, a highly coveted position among that city's black community, and throughout his life he was devoted to his parents. Ellington is perhaps best known for such classic jazz compositions as "Mood Indigo," "In a Sentimental Mood," "Sophisticated Lady," and "Solitude." It is estimated that he composed more than two thousand musical arrangements over a career that stretched more than forty-five years. The song most often associated with Ellington and his orchestra, "Take the 'A' Train," was written by his long-time collaborator Billy Strayhorn.

In 1965, after a career in which he constantly sought new forms of expression, Ellington moved into the realm of sacred music. The Grace Episcopal Cathedral of San Francisco, then in the final stages of new construction, commissioned Ellington to write a liturgical work that was to be performed as part of the building's yearlong consecration celebration. It premiered on September 16, 1965, as *Concert of Sacred Music*. This composition drew upon many songs that Ellington had written twenty years earlier for full-length productions entitled *Black, Brown, and Beige* and *My People*. The recording of that concert earned him a Grammy Award in 1966. One critic said of that concert: "It is a remarkable religious synthesis ... of Western Christianity, with African roots and Pantheism, gospel singing, the chronicles of the Bible, the aspirations of the New Testament and, not least, the extra problems faced by mankind in our modern society."

In 1967 the *Concert of Sacred Music* aired over the National Education Television network and won an Emmy Award. The concert was repeated numerous times in churches throughout the United States and Britain. The most popular movement from *Concert of Sacred Music* was a haunting song entitled "Come Sunday" that was originally written for *Black, Brown, and Beige* in 1943.

Ellington wrote another body of sacred music that he called *The Second Sacred Concert*. It premiered at the Cathedral of St. John the Divine in New York City on January 19, 1968. It was a 155-minute program that involved a one-hundred-voice choir and full orchestra. More than six thousand persons crowded that Episcopal cathedral for the concert.

Ellington said, "I regard this concert as the most important thing I have ever done." Unlike the first sacred concert, which used materials he had written as much as twenty-two years earlier, the second concert involved all new compositions.

At the end of his musical career, Ellington composed a *Third Concert of Sacred Music,* which was premiered in Westminster Abbey in London on United Nations Day, October 24, 1973. That was his last major composition.

Ellington died on May 24, 1974. Ten thousand people attended his funeral, which was held at the church in New York where his *Second Concert of Sacred Music* had premiered six years earlier. A famous credo of this great composer was that "every man prays in his own language, and there is no language that God does not understand."

James Haskins, *Black Music in America;* John Edward Hasse, *Beyond Category;* Eileen Southern, *The Music of Black Americans.*

☺ Franklin, Aretha

(1942–) Aretha Franklin is unquestionably the Queen of Soul and the undisputed diva of rhythm and blues, but she has long been one of the greatest gospel singers of all time. She was born in Memphis, Tennessee, on March 25, 1942. Her father, **Clarence LaVaughn (C. L.) Franklin,** was a phenomenal evangelistic preacher and a successful gospel recording artist in his own right. He toured with the Clara Ward Singers during the 1940s and 1950s and also cut more than fifty records of his singing and preaching. Since her mother abandoned the family when Aretha was

only six years old, Aretha frequently traveled with her father. Thus she was exposed to **gospel music** and being part of a touring musical group before she reached the age of ten.

By the age of twelve Aretha was a regular performer in the evangelistic services and at her father's church in Detroit, Michigan. **James Cleveland,** who for a time lived with the Franklin family in Detroit, taught Aretha how to play the piano, and he also coached her to develop the incredible vocal range for which she is noted. Under his guidance she recorded her first gospel album when she was fourteen years old. C. L. Franklin and Cleveland remained her

best supporters, even when she crossed over from gospel music to rhythm and blues in 1960 at the age of eighteen.

It took her a while to establish herself in that new musical world, but when Aretha released "Respect" in 1967, a star was born. It seemed that she had turned her back on her musical roots, preferring nightclubs and concert halls to sanctuaries and crusade meetings. But in 1972, once again with the help of her father and Cleveland, she recorded a live gospel concert with the Southern California Choir. The result was her Grammy-winning album *Amazing Grace*. She won another Grammy for a gospel recording in 1985 for the song "One Lord, One Faith, One Baptism."

Because of her father's close connection to **Martin Luther King Jr.**, Aretha frequently performed at fundraising events for the **Southern Christian Leadership Conference** (SCLC) and on other occasions when King made the request. She also returned to New Bethel Baptist Church in Detroit to help raise funds for special projects being sponsored by the church. When asked to bring comments during the intermission of the *Amazing Grace* concert, C. L. Franklin spoke glowingly about his daughter and then said, "If you want to know the truth about it, Aretha has never left the church."

Phil Garland quotes an unnamed female contemporary who says of the artist, "Aretha is still singing the same thing that she used to sing in church, except that now instead of saying 'My Lord,' she says 'My man.'"

"Aretha Franklin, 'Queen of Soul.'" in *Notable Black American Women*, ed. Jessye Carney Smith; Hettie Jones, *Big Star, Fallin' Mama*.

☺ Franklin, Kirk

(1971-) It is a long journey from being a gang member and thug in the streets of Fort Worth, Texas, to being among the elite recording artists in the world, but that is the road that gospel superstar Kirk Franklin has traveled. He was born in Fort Worth in 1971. His life was troubled from the start, when his teenage mother abandoned him at the age of three. Kirk never knew his father. This orphaned boy was taken in by a great-aunt, Gertrude Franklin, when he was four years old. She introduced him to the church and encouraged his early interest in music. He was a musical prodigy who was offered a recording contract by a local producer when he was only seven. His aunt would not allow him to get involved in recording at that time, but it was an early sign of things to come.

By the age of eleven Franklin had been appointed the minister of music at Mount Rose Baptist Church in Dallas, Texas. His biggest challenge was giving musical instruction and direction to persons who were six times his age. Another opportunity to record came when he was nineteen. The Savoy Record Company invited him to work with a new group called the Dallas–Fort Worth Mass Choir in its debut album. Following that the producer invited Franklin to write some music for the group. Franklin recruited seventeen singers to work with him, and he called them The Family. In 1990 that group was offered a contract from Savoy, and Kirk Franklin and the Family was born.

Franklin later changed labels and began recording for the newly formed

Gospo-Centric record label. His first album, *Kirk Franklin and the Family* (1992), went to the top of the *Billboard* chart for contemporary gospel music and sold more than one million copies. The second album, *Kirk Franklin and the Family Christmas* (1994), sold more than five hundred thousand copies in the first fourteen weeks. That album featured the hugely popular song "Now Behold the Lamb." In 1996 the third album, *Whatcha Lookin' 4,* also sold more than one million copies, and Franklin earned his first Grammy Award for Best Contemporary Soul Gospel. He won a second Grammy for his fourth album, *The Nu Nation Project.* Another album, *God's Property,* was shipped gold and debuted at number 1 on the *Billboard* contemporary gospel chart.

Franklin's musical style has revolutionized **gospel music,** setting the lyrics to an urban, hip-hop rhythm and stage presence that has won over a new generation of gospel music fans. Franklin suggests that his style is the key to his success: "Generation X doesn't want to hear from the reverend behind the pulpit, or go to any Bible conferences. So we need to go about getting the message to them in another way. That doesn't mean my way isn't godly just because I'm not using the same tools they're using. The bottom line is to reach the kids too."

Franklin may be able to communicate with Generation X effectively because during his early teen years he was so deeply involved in the gangster life that is celebrated in much secular music in urban communities. It was not until a friend was accidentally killed by a handgun in 1985 that Kirk turned away from the life of the streets and embraced his music ministry in the church. Since that time, however, Franklin has extended gospel music to young people around the world like no other performer in the history of gospel music.

Franklin's music has not been limited to albums and CDs. He has also produced sound tracks for three motion pictures. The song "Joy" was heard in *The Preacher's Wife,* and "My Life Is In Your Hands" was performed in *Get on the Bus.* Most recently Franklin produced the sound track for *Kingdom Come,* which stars Whoopi Goldberg, L.L. Cool J, and many other top Hollywood performers. As *Gospel Today* puts it, Franklin is walking the road "From Hip-Hop to Hollywood."

Franklin and his wife, Tammy, live in Arlington, Texas, with their three children.

Theresa E. Hairston, "From Hip-Hop to Hollywood: Is Gospel Too Commercial?" *Gospel Today,* May/June 2001; Bobby Jones, *Touched by God*; www.nunation.com/html.

⊙ Jackson, Mahalia

(1911–1972) When **E. Franklin Frazier** wrote about the influence of "the Gospel Singer," the first name he mentioned was that of Mahalia Jackson. For more than forty years, she was the most popular and the most prolific gospel singer in the world. She not only took the music of the rural South to the black churches of cities like Chicago, Cleveland, and Detroit but also introduced that music to white audiences in concert halls ranging from Carnegie Hall in New York City to such European countries as England, France, and Denmark.

Jackson was born in New Orleans on October 26, 1911, and was heavily influenced by the sounds of ragtime, jazz, blues, and the **spirituals** that could be heard everywhere in that city. However, through the insistence of her family, she devoted herself to the music of the black church. She was once offered the chance to record with her fellow New Orleans native, Louis Armstrong, and on another occasion to earn $10,000 weekly by singing jazz in a nightclub, but her talent was dedicated to "singing for the Lord."

Jackson began to sing at the age of five in the choir at Mount Moriah Baptist Church of New Orleans, where her father, Rev. John Andrew Jackson, served as pastor. She was reared by an aunt after her mother died when Mahalia was five. Mahalia went only through the eighth grade in school, because to support her

family she had to work as a laundress in the homes of wealthy white families in New Orleans.

However, Jackson dreamed of becoming a nurse after reading in the *Chicago Defender* about the nurses' training program at Provident Hospital in Chicago. Along with millions of other black people from the South, Jackson moved to the North as part of the Great Migration. She settled on the south side of Chicago in 1928. Her dreams of becoming a nurse were never realized, however, because the family members she was living with needed her to bring in money to help pay the rent when the Great Depression hit in 1929. She had moved from the South to the North, and she had ended where she started: doing laundry and cleaning for white families.

However, Jackson's singing career began to take off in Chicago. First she sang with a group called the Johnson Singers, consisting of three brothers and herself, all of them members of Greater Salem Baptist Church of Chicago. They did not simply sing for inspirational purposes. The effects of the Great Depression were so hard on black churches that many times the Johnson Singers were hired by churches to help raise money to pay the mortgage and utilities. Those concerts also helped Jackson make ends meet. She called herself a "fish and bread singer," meaning that she sang for her supper.

Jackson became a well-known gospel singer in Chicago, in part because her style of singing was so similar to the kind of music black people in Chicago remembered from their earlier years in the South. Her singing was considered by many to be a link to the worship style of the rural churches of the South. She referred to her singing style as "letters from home," meaning that when black people in the North heard her sing it reminded them of their Southern roots and heritage.

Not everyone liked Jackson's style of singing or approved of **gospel music.** Many black people in Chicago wanted to leave their Southern roots in the past, and that meant that they did not want to continue Southern ways of singing, preaching, and worshiping. In 1932 Jackson took one music lesson from a Professor Du Bois, a black operatic tenor in Chicago, who told her that she was not singing, she was only hollering. She rejected his advice and remained true not only to the songs she sang but also to the manner in which she sang them: full of passion and bodily movement.

In 1934 Jackson's recording career began when she recorded "God Gonna Separate the Wheat from the Tares" for Decca Records in Chicago. It was not a commercial success, but it did confirm her decision to reject the advice she had been given by Du Bois. It also coincided with her first meeting with **Thomas A. Dorsey,** a well-known gospel music composer then living in Chicago. His composition "Precious Lord, Take My Hand" would become one of Jackson's trademark concert selections.

Jackson married Isaac Hockenhull in 1935. He was a Fisk and Tuskegee graduate in chemistry who could find a job in Chicago only as a mail carrier. The marriage ended in divorce a few years later. She then devoted herself to her music and to two business ventures. One was Mahalia's Beauty Salon, where her fame

as a gospel singer attracted clients. The other was Mahalia's Florist Shop. Many people who came to her shop to buy flowers for the funeral of a loved one would also invite her to sing at the funeral. That opened up another lucrative career as a professional funeral singer in Chicago. She made a cameo appearance in that role in the 1941 film *Imitation of Life.*

Jackson remained largely unknown outside of Chicago until she recorded "I'm Gonna Move On Up a Little Higher" in 1946 for Decca Records. That song sold more than two million copies, and she became a national phenomenon, singing at black church conventions across the country. However, while she was nationally known in African American church circles, she was still unknown in the larger white society.

In 1950 Marshall Stearns, a music professor at The New School for Social Research in New York City, invited Jackson to a music symposium near Tanglewood, Massachusetts. Musicians and music instructors from across the country heard her sing and talk about gospel music. She said that after that one event, "the dam opened," and her career took off. She performed to a capacity crowd at Carnegie Hall in 1954. She appeared on *The Ed Sullivan Show*. She was offered a contract to record with Columbia Records. She went on several European tours with her pianist, Mildred Falls. Her recording of "Silent Night" sold fifty thousand copies after she sang that carol in Denmark in 1955.

The capstone of Jackson's career as a celebrity artist came in 1961 when she was invited to sing at the inaugural gala for President John F. Kennedy in Washington, D.C. The laundress from New Orleans had become an international celebrity, and she had done so by keeping her pledge to sing only for the Lord.

Upon her return to the United States, Jackson began singing to raise money for the **civil rights movement.** She went to Montgomery, Alabama, to sing for the people involved in the bus boycott. She subsequently sang for people involved in protests and boycotts across the country. She sang "Precious Lord" at the Prayer Pilgrimage in 1957 and the March on Washington in 1963. She sang that song at the funeral of **Martin Luther King Jr.** in April 1968. Along with Harry Bela-

fonte, Jackson was one of the great financial and moral supporters of the civil rights movement.

In 1971 President Richard M. Nixon invited Jackson to sing for American soldiers in Japan and for service personnel in Germany. While performing in Germany on Thanksgiving Day, 1971, she collapsed on stage from heart failure. She was returned to Chicago for treatment, but she died in January 1972. Most appropriately, **Aretha Franklin** sang "Precious Lord" at the funeral service at the Arie Crown Theatre in Chicago. Jackson never performed in a theater while she was alive, but the largest theater in Chicago was the only place large enough to accommodate the crowds that attended her funeral.

Hettie Jones, *Big Star, Fallin' Mama*; Bernice Johnson Reagon, ed., *We'll Understand It Better By and By*; Evelyn Witter, *Mahalia Jackson*.

☽ Martin, Roberta

(1907-1969) Few gospel musicians can claim to have performed with **Thomas A. Dorsey** in the 1930s and with **James Cleveland** in the 1960s. Even fewer persons' singing ability can be mentioned in the same breath with the legendary **Mahalia Jackson.** Roberta Martin was such a person.

Martin was born in Helena, Arkansas, on February 12, 1907. When she was six her family moved to Cairo, Illinois, and then to Chicago. She began playing the piano for the Young People's Choir at Ebenezer Baptist Church of Chicago, where Dorsey was the minister of music. In 1933 she formed her own choral group, The Roberta Martin Singers, which became one of the preeminent groups in the history of gospel music. It began with six men: Eugene Smith, Norsalus McKissick, Robert Anderson, James Lawrence, Willie Webb, and Romance Watson.

In 1940 two women, Bessie Folk and Deloris Barrett, were added to the group. Many other persons would perform with the group over a thirty-year period. The group toured throughout the United States and Europe. However, like many other gospel performers, Martin resisted the temptation to perform in nightclubs and before entirely secular audiences.

Over her thirty-year career Martin wrote more than one hundred songs, and she earned six gold records. Her most popular compositions included "He Knows Just How Much You Can Bear" (1939), "Try Jesus, He Satisfies" (1943), and "God Is Still on the Throne" (1959). From 1956 to 1968 she was the minister of music at Mt. Pisgah Baptist Church of Chicago. She married James Austin in 1947. They had one son, Sonny. Her husband worked full-time managing the Roberta Martin Music Studio, which handled the steady requests for her personal appearances, the sale of sheet music and albums, and planning gospel music workshops across the country.

The repertoire of The Roberta Martin Singers points out the importance of her contribution to this musical genre. They include songs that she wrote and arranged as well as songs written by **Charles Albert Tindley,** Dorsey, Cleveland, and Alex Bradford. As Bernice Johnson Reagon states, "This is very impressive because Tindley influenced Dorsey, Dorsey influenced Martin, Martin influenced Cleveland, and the genealogy goes on and on." In fact, The Roberta Martin Singers served as a kind of university for emerging singers. In addition to Cleveland, who sang with and arranged for that group, other notable singers such as Dinah Washington and Della Reese got their start as members of The Roberta Martin Singers.

Leona Price, the business manager of The Roberta Martin Singers for thirty years, offered an appropriate memorial for Martin's life and legacy: "My Marty, as I so affectionately called her, expired at six o'clock Monday morning, January 13, 1969, in the manner of the song, 'Ride on, King Jesus, I want to go to Heaven in the morning.' A gospel giant closed the book of life; … her songwriting's ended, but the melodies linger on."

On July 15, 1998, Martin and three other gospel singers—Jackson, Clara Ward, and Rosetta Tharpe—were honored by the issuance of four U.S. postal stamps that bore their images.

Bernice Johnson Reagon, ed., *We'll Understand It Better By and By;* multiple web pages dealing with The Roberta Martin Singers.

Smallwood, Richard

(1948–) While much of **gospel music** is defined by the power and personality of solo performers, others in this musical genre are best known for their contribution to gospel music as a choral form. Richard Smallwood may be the leading contemporary composer, arranger, and accompanist of the choral aspect of gospel music. From the formation of his first gospel group at the age of eleven to the appearance of The Richard Smallwood Singers at such places as the Kennedy Performing Arts Center, the Smithsonian Institution, and the White House, he has been redefining the sound of the gospel choir.

Smallwood was born in Atlanta, Georgia, on November 30, 1948. He began playing the piano by ear at the age of five. He started formal training in piano at the age of seven. His formal training culminated with his graduation from Howard University with degrees in vocal performance and piano. While at Howard he organized The Celestials, the first gospel choir to exist on that campus. That group would later appear at the Montreux Jazz Festival in Switzerland, bringing gospel music to a new audience.

Smallwood organized The Richard Smallwood Singers in the late 1970s. Their first album remained on the *Billboard* charts of the top songs in the country for eighty-seven weeks. The group received Grammy nominations for the album *Psalms and Textures*. Smallwood won a Grammy Award and a Dove Award for producing Quincy Jones's gospel project entitled *Handel's Soulful Messiah*. The Richard Smallwood Singers toured the country with Jennifer Holiday in the Broadway hit musical, *Sing Mahalia Sing*, about the career of **Mahalia Jackson**. They also appeared on an episode of the ABC-TV program *Ryan's Hope.*

Smallwood wrote "I Love the Lord," which was sung by Whitney Houston in *The Preacher's Wife.* He wrote "The Center of My Joy" with the help of Bill and Gloria Gaither. Many other songs written by Smallwood, such as "Total Praise," "I Will Sing Praises," and "We've Come to Praise Him," have become standards in churches all over the world. Bill Gaither spoke about the spiritual focus of Smallwood's music, despite his popularity in secular settings: "I love Richard Smallwood because he is church. His songs speak to the heart of people."

Smallwood is candid about his dependence upon God as the source of his musical inspiration and his desire to serve God through music: "People need to know Someone can heal their hurts. I take no credit for the work we do. I owe it all to God and I feel blessed that for some reason He has chosen me to make a difference in people's lives.... I have learned to depend more on God than ever before, and I've acquired a hunger for His word like never before."

This world-class composer, pianist, and arranger has been inducted into the Gospel Music Hall of Fame. Smallwood is changing the face of gospel music in the United States and around the world. Audiences seldom hear his voice, but the whole world is listening to and singing along with his music.

www.richardsmallwood.com/bio

☻ Tindley, Charles Albert

(1851?–1933) Born into a slave family in Berlin, Maryland, between 1851 and 1856, Tindley was hired out to work in Maryland and Delaware. He was given no formal education. Despite the challenges of his beginnings, Tindley became one of the most popular preachers and prolific hymn writers of his generation.

Tindley moved to Philadelphia, Pennsylvania, and studied for the ministry by reading the books in the library of the John Wesley Methodist Episcopal Church, where he worked as the sexton. He was ordained in 1885 and subsequently became pastor of that congregation in 1900, though by that time the church had changed its name and become a largely black congregation. Nevertheless, Tindley was the pastor in the same building in which he had been the janitor. The membership swelled to more than five thousand during his years as pastor.

Tindley's ministry in Philadelphia overlapped the Great Migration that saw millions of black people leave the southern states to seek better opportunities in the cities of the North. Many of them came to Philadelphia. His church provided food, housing, medical care, and spiritual direction.

Despite his popularity in Philadelphia among blacks and whites, Tindley was defeated three times in his attempt to become a bishop in the Methodist Episcopal Church, largely due to racial bias at the general conferences and probably due to his lack of formal theological training. Tindley subsequently threw himself into plans to build a cathedral, which he did with the help of John Wanamaker, the department store magnate in Philadelphia. The new church was initially funded by members who mortgaged their homes to provide for construction costs. The sanctuary, which opened in 1925, seated thirty-five hundred persons, and it was filled twice each Sunday. In honor of their pastor, the members of the church eventually voted to change the name of the church building to Tindley Temple.

However, today Tindley is best remembered for the forty-five hymns he wrote, usually in reaction to some trauma or crisis in his life. His hymns include "I'll Overcome Some Day" (1901), "We'll Understand It Better By and By" (1905), "Nothing Between" (1901), "The Storm Is Passing Over" (1905), "Beams of Heaven" (1905), "Leave Them There" (1916), and "Stand by Me" (1905). One of the traumas in Tindley's life was the sudden death of his wife in 1925, the same year his new church opened. He also wrote songs that could be used in the context of his preaching to help him make his point. He was known to break out in song in the middle of his sermons and then return to his message. One observer of this practice said, "He didn't write gospel music just to write gospel music.

His music came out of experience, in most instances, some type of personal experience or some scriptural experience led to his seeking to put to music—for those who would perhaps not get it in the sermon—the gospel message."

Tindley is unique among black composers in that his songs appear in hymnals of nearly every nonblack denomination, and most whites who sing his songs have no idea that he was black. His songs have been sung and translated into foreign languages from Japanese to Afrikaaner in South Africa. He was also the first to encourage the use of small groups for the singing of gospel music. Seven male members of his church formed the Tindley Gospel Singers in 1922. By 1929 they were singing in revivals across the East and the Midwest. The major portion of their repertoire consisted of Tindley songs.

Tindley died on July 26, 1933, of complications from gangrene.

Ralph H. Jones, *Charles Albert Tindley;* Birdie Wilson Johnson, *Succeed, My People;* Bernice Johnson Reagon, ed., *We'll Understand It Better By and By;* Wyatt Tee Walker, *"Somebody's Calling My Name."*

☮ Walker, Albertina

(1930–) Many names could be associated with the royalty of **gospel music,** but only a few are unquestionably entitled to that designation. Albertina Walker, whose career spanned more than four decades, is among that elite group of gospel singers. She recorded more than sixty albums, won a Grammy as Best Traditional Gospel Singer, and was nominated for a Grammy on twelve other

occasions. She was a protégé of **Mahalia Jackson,** and she helped to launch the careers of **James Cleveland** and **Shirley Caesar.** Walker was a major force in the history of gospel music.

Walker was born in Chicago in 1930, and her entire career centered around the musical life of that city. As a member of West Point Baptist Church, she sat in the audience when such legendary singers as **Thomas A. Dorsey, Roberta Martin,** and Jackson came to perform. Jackson first recognized Walker's talents and urged her to continue to sing gospel music. Both Jackson and Walker employed a style of singing that was characterized by Bernice Johnson Reagon as being "percussive and shouting" in its approach, in contrast to the "lyrical and semi-classical style of such other Gospel performers as Roberta Martin and Inez Andrews."

Walker began her career with The Robert Anderson Singers in Chicago. However, between 1952 and 1966 she emerged onto the national scene as the founder and lead singer of The Caravans. That group became the most popular female group in the history of gospel music. They recorded and performed such standard songs as "Oh, Mary, Don't You Weep," "Soldiers in the Army," "The Solid Rock," and "The Blood Will Never Lose Its Power." Walker and The Caravans were an integral part of what **Wyatt Tee Walker** calls "the golden era of gospel music," which he sees as stretching from 1945 to 1960.

The Caravans launched the career of Caesar, who eventually replaced Walker as the lead singer. In fact, Caesar's departure to pursue a solo career led to the group disbanding in 1966. The Caravans also launched the career of Cleveland, who was its arranger and accompanist as well as an occasional singer. Other notable gospel singers such as Dorothy Norwood and Inez Andrews also got their start with The Caravans. No other group in gospel music can claim to have launched as many stellar careers as The Caravans, and no other gospel musician, with the exception of Dorsey, can claim to have had as large an impact on how gospel music is performed as did Walker.

After The Caravans disbanded, Walker continued with a solo career of concerts and recordings. She refused to follow many of her gospel music friends into nightclubs, where gospel music was performed simply for its entertainment value. She understood why so many of her colleagues would make that move, since she was aware of how gospel music promoters would often cheat those who performed the music. She once said, "Gospel music was big business. It was a good money-making business for everybody except the singer." The thousands of dollars offered to such singers as Clara Ward and others to perform in nightclubs was probably all the more attractive in the light of this history of exploitation of the performers within the black church circuit. Still, Walker never sang for the money.

However, Walker did take her career to an all-time high of popularity when she appeared as a gospel singer in Steve

Martin's *Leap of Faith* (1992), which was a parody of white Pentecostal itinerant evangelists. Her singing in that film brought the only touch of spiritual authenticity to an otherwise comic venture. The film revived her career, and she finally won a Grammy in 1995, after being nominated twelve times.

Walker and her husband live in Chicago.

Bobby Jones, *Touched by God;* Bernice Johnson Reagon, ed., *We'll Understand It Better By and By;* Wyatt Tee Walker, *"Somebody's Calling My Name."*

Movements, Terms, and Events

◉ Abolitionist Movement

Between the Revolutionary War and the Civil War there was a movement in the United States and in England, first to end the trans-Atlantic portion of the slave trade and later to end the practice of holding persons in slavery anywhere in the Americas and the Caribbean. This was called the abolitionist movement, and many black preachers and black churches were active supporters of this effort.

The practice of importing and enslaving blacks from Africa had gone on in

North America since the first black indentured servants were unloaded at Jamestown, Virginia, in 1619. While white indentured servants were freed after a seven-year period of labor, by 1630 the children of black indentured servants were relegated to the status of lifelong servitude. Prior to the Revolutionary War, slavery was practiced in every state of colonial America. The legal importation of slaves into the United States from Africa and from the Caribbean ended in 1808. This was accomplished by Article I, Section 9 of the U.S. Constitution, which outlawed the importation of persons after that year. That policy was the result of the advocacy of the abolitionist movement.

Attention was then turned to the second phase of the abolitionist movement, which was ending the practice of slavery among those black people who were born in the United States before and after 1808. That form of slavery did not end until after the end of the Civil War, when the Union Army swept through the

An abolitionist publication promoting antislavery principles

South, freeing slaves as they went. However, slavery was officially abolished when the Thirteenth Amendment to the U.S. Constitution was ratified on December 6, 1865. It is estimated that at the time slavery was finally abolished, more than four million black people were living as slaves in the United States.

In addition to antislavery societies in many Northern states, the abolitionist movement was greatly aided by the formation of the American Antislavery Society in 1833. In addition to whites like William Lloyd Garrison, many notable black religious leaders, such as **James Pennington, Sojourner Truth, Samuel Cornish,** Samuel Ringgold Ward, **Alexander Crummell, Peter Williams Jr.** and **Henry Highland Garnet,** were also active in that abolitionist organization.

Many publications written and distributed by black religious leaders were also intended to advance the abolitionist cause. *The North Star* by Frederick Douglass and *Freedom's Journal* by John Russworm and Cornish fit into this category. Peter Williams Jr. gave a famous antislavery speech on July 4, 1830, that was widely circulated. The most famous abolitionist statements of all were "David Walker's Appeal" in 1829 and "An Address to the Slaves of the United States of America" by Garnet in 1843, and another Fourth of July speech by Frederick Douglass in 1852.

On October 16, 1859, in Harper's Ferry, Virginia, John Brown of Kansas engaged in the most radical action of the abolitionist movement. Leading a group of twenty-one men, Brown raided the federal arsenal in that town. He intended to arm fugitive slaves and other white abolitionists and lead a slave insurrection throughout the state of Virginia. His plan was short-lived, primarily because a regiment of the state militia led by Colonel Robert E. Lee heard of the capture of the arsenal. The building was surrounded and stormed. Ten of the men inside were killed, and Brown was captured, tried, and convicted, and on December 2, 1859, he was hanged. Brown became a martyr for the abolitionist cause, and his raid was one of the events that ignited the Civil War.

Although the abolitionist movement agitated against slavery, it did not end that institution in American society, any more than did the Emancipation Proclamation (1863), which affected only slaves living in the border states of Missouri, West Virginia, Maryland, Delaware, and Kentucky, and slaves in parts of Louisiana. Slavery was ended by the advances of the Union army and by the ratification of the Thirteenth Amendment to the U.S. Constitution in 1865.

John Bracey, August Meier, and Elliot Rudwick, *Blacks in the Abolitionist Movement;* William Loren Katz, ed., *An Address to the Slaves of the United States of America by Henry Highland Garnet* and "Walker's Appeal"; Benjamin Quarles, *Black Abolitionists.*

☾ African Americans and the Bible

It is safe to say that the stories and characters of the Bible have had an enormous impact on African American religious life and thought. Going back to the days of antebellum slavery, the Bible was used by slave owners to justify that slavery. At the same time, parts of the Bible were used by the slaves themselves to make the point that God, who had led Israel out of slavery

in Egypt, was desirous of their liberation from slavery as well.

The content of sermons, prayers, and **spirituals** employed in the black church are drenched in the language and imagery of the Bible. A literal rendering of certain biblical passages has resulted in much of the church polity and social policy by which many black churches are organized. The most notable of these involves the status of women in leadership positions in the church, based largely on the reading of certain passages by Paul, in 1 Corinthians 14:34 and 1 Timothy 2:12. One of the ongoing struggles within the black church is how to incorporate the lessons of biblical criticism in the interpretation and application of Scripture.

During the twentieth century, the scholarly study of the Bible took on several distinct and informative perspectives

beyond the simple issue of the authority of Scripture in the life of the black church. The first to emerge was an interest in documenting and further examining the presence of black (African) people throughout the Old and New Testaments. The second was the use of the Bible, notably the exodus story, as the basis for the formulation of a **black theology** by **James H. Cone** and **J. Deotis Roberts.** The third approach was the development by black biblical scholars of certain principles of interpretation that make the message of the Bible even more relevant to the lives and conditions of black people living in America.

Beginning with the work of black biblical scholars like Charles B. Copher, the Bible was studied not simply for what it said but more precisely for "who many of these people actually were." Who were the Cushites, the Egyptians, the Naba-teans, and other African nations mentioned in the Bible? Where were Cyrene, Niger, Sheba, and other locations that are mentioned? Africa and African people played a large role in the telling of the biblical story. How is it possible that traditional European-dominated biblical studies managed to overlook or ignore these issues? Copher's thoughts are most carefully captured in his *Black Biblical Studies: Biblical and Theological Issues on the Black Presence in the Bible* (1993).

Other books have also been published that pursue the issue of the black presence in the Bible. Among them are *The Black Presence in the Bible,* volumes 1 and 2 (1990) by Walter Arthur McCray. One can also consider *The Black Man in the Old Testament* (1974) by Bishop

Alfred Dunston and *Beyond Roots: In Search of Blacks in the Bible* (1990) by William Dwight McKissic Sr.

The second intersect between black people and the Bible has been the use of the exodus motif by black theology as it has sought to use that story as its point of departure in terms of God's perspective on the issue of black oppression. Thus the work of Cone and Roberts is of special importance at this point.

Most recently the issue of black people and the Bible has moved into the field of hermeneutics, or the principles of interpretation that are employed when the Bible as an ancient document is read and its teachings are applied in any contemporary setting. That is where the work of black biblical scholars such as **Cain Hope Felder** becomes especially significant. He served as editor and contributor to the signature study in this new field of study, *Stony the Road We Trod: African American Biblical Interpretation* (1991).

This book seeks to address several questions and uses the work of eleven black biblical scholars in the process. The first question is how black biblical scholars can break away from the Eurocentric approach to biblical studies that has so long dominated the universities and seminaries where that study is centered. The second issue is how to tap into sources other than those that come from Eurocentric approaches to better understand how the Bible can be applied to the lives of black people in America. The third section of the book revisits and expands upon the issue of the black presence in the Bible, focusing especially on how a racist approach to the study of Scripture

may have contributed to the continuation of black oppression. The fourth section of the book offers examples of what happens when biblical texts are studied from the perspective of a black or African American hermeneutic.

The work of black biblical scholars has been somewhat frustrated, as Felder acknowledges, by the difficulty of earning a doctor of philosophy or a doctor of theology degree in the biblical field. There are far fewer black scholars in that field than in any other of the theological disciplines. *Stony the Road We Trod* serves two purposes. First, it allows black biblical scholars to speak with one voice in one book, as opposed to having their scholarship possibly dissipated by being found in a wide variety of journals and books. Second, the difficulty of the road to earning a doctoral degree in biblical studies is described by the title of the book. Those words are taken from the opening lines of the second verse of "Lift Every Voice and Sing," the so-called black national anthem by James Weldon Johnson and J. Rosamond Johnson.

Despite their relatively small numbers, black biblical scholars are beginning to make the same impact in their field that Cone and Roberts made a generation earlier. As a result of the work of the scholars listed in this entry, the issues of black people and the Bible are regularly found within seminary curricula, as topics of doctoral dissertations, and in papers and discussions within the Society of Biblical Literature (SBL).

Marvin McMickle, *Living Water for Thirsty Souls: Unleashing the Power of Exegetical Preaching;* J. Deotis Roberts, *Africentric Christianity;* Renita Weems, *Just a Sister Away.*

☻ African Methodist Episcopal (AME) Church

This denomination was formed in Philadelphia, Pennsylvania, at the Bethel Church of **Richard Allen** in April 1816, when sixteen delegates from five black Methodist congregations from the mid-Atlantic region convened to unify their witness. The five congregations had all withdrawn from predominantly white Methodist Episcopal churches in Pennsylvania, Maryland, and Delaware. In every case they left as a result of not being allowed equal treatment in seating in the church or equal access to leadership roles within the congregation. They also wanted to organize under one banner so that they could incorporate the buildings and properties they had built or acquired but the ownership of which was being contested by the white Methodist Episcopal churches as a matter of connectional church polity.

Allen became the first bishop of the AME Church after **Daniel Coker** declined the office. The church was organized to resemble in almost every respect the Methodist Episcopal (United Methodist) Church. *The Book of Discipline* says,

"The mission and purpose of the African Methodist Episcopal Church is to minister to the spiritual, intellectual, physical and emotional needs of all people by spreading Christ's liberating gospel by word and deed. Each local African Methodist Episcopal Church shall engage in carrying out the spirit of the original Free African Society out of which the AME Church evolved, that is to seek and save the lost and serve the needy through a continuing program

of (1) preaching the gospel, (2) feeding the hungry, (3) clothing the naked, (4) housing the homeless, (5) cheering the fallen, (6) providing jobs for the jobless, (7) administering to the needs of those in prisons, hospitals, nursing homes, asylums and mental institutions, senior citizens' homes, caring for the sick, the shut-in, the mentally and socially disturbed, and (8) encouraging thrift and economic advancement."

The AME Church took an early interest in establishing churches in Africa and the Caribbean. It also supports five colleges, two seminaries, and two Job Corps centers. It has more than three million members, with more than one million of them belonging to AME churches operating outside of the United States. It is the largest of the black Methodist bodies and made history in 2000 when it elected **Vashti Murphy McKenzie** to become the first female bishop in the history of any black Methodist body.

Richard Allen, *The Life Experience and Gospel Labors of the Rt. Rev. Richard Allen;* Carol V. R. George, *Segregated Sabbaths: Richard Allen and the Rise of Independent Black Churches, 1760–1840;* C. Eric Lincoln and Lawrence H. Mamiya, *The Black Church in the African American Experience;* Daniel A. Payne, *Recollections of Seventy Years;* Harry V. Richardson, *Dark Salvation: The Story of Methodism As It Developed among Blacks in America.*

☻ African Methodist Episcopal Zion (AME Zion) Church

In 1796 a group of black Methodists walked out of the John Street Methodist Episcopal Church in New York City. Led by Peter Williams Sr. and **James Varick,** they were objecting to that white church's refusal to allow black clergy equal access to ordination and to status as itinerant preachers. Bishop Francis Asbury granted them permission to meet separately as a Methodist body; by 1801 a building had been secured, and the black group took the name of the African Methodist Episcopal Church of the City of New York. That first church building was named the Zion Church.

In 1821 several black Methodist congregations in New York, Pennsylvania, Connecticut, and New Jersey met in New York City to formalize a relationship among themselves and to become an independent Methodist conference. The black Methodists in New York decided not to affiliate with the **African Methodist Episcopal (AME) Church,** the denomination that had already been organized by **Richard Allen.** Their principal objection was the fact that Allen had been actively attempting to work through a former member of the Zion Church to recruit members into his body based in Philadelphia. The black Methodists in New York viewed that action as an encroachment on their territory for evangelism and as a sign of the kind of dominating oversight they could expect from Allen.

In 1822 the black Methodists in New York elected Varick the first bishop of the new denomination, and he served in that role until the group held its first general conference in 1828. It was not until 1848 that the word *Zion* was officially added to the name of the church body to distinguish it from the Allen churches. Like the AME Church, the AME Zion Church also adopted most of its governance procedures from the *Book of Discipline* of the Methodist Episcopal (United Methodist) Church.

The AME Zion Church came to be known as the freedom church, largely because it numbered among its members such notable black leaders in the freedom struggle as Harriet Tubman, Frederick Douglass, **Sojourner Truth,** and Paul Robeson. However, the AME Zion Church has never grown to the size of the AME Church. Today its membership numbers approximately 1.5 million persons in sixty-five hundred congregations scattered throughout the United States, the Caribbean, South and Central America, and various locations in West Africa.

Outside of New York City, the church's strongest region has always been North Carolina, where it operates Livingstone College and Hood Theological Seminary in Salisbury, North Carolina. The office of the general secretary and the Zion Publishing House are located in Charlotte, North Carolina. Although the AME Zion Church has not yet elected a woman to the office of bishop, it did lead the way among black Methodists with the ordination of women when Julia Foote was ordained a deacon in 1884 and a full elder in 1895. At that time, the AME Church refused to ordain women, which resulted in Foote's decision to move into the Zion Church.

Richard Allen, *The Life Experience and Gospel Labors of the Rt. Rev. Richard Allen;* Carol V. R. George, *Segregated Sabbaths: Richard Allen and the Rise of Independent Black Churches, 1760–1840;* C. Eric Lincoln and Lawrence H. Mamiya, *The Black Church in the African American Experience;* Daniel A. Payne, *Recollections of*

Seventy Years; Harry V. Richardson, *Dark Salvation: The Story of Methodism As It Developed among Blacks in America.*

☉ Afrocentricity

When black persons have been reared within the values, cultural norms, literary traditions, and political assumptions of the United States and other Western societies, it is possible for them to lose all sense of themselves as being in any way tied to an African past. It is also possible, perhaps highly likely, that they will not be conditioned to view anything with origins in Africa as being of equal worth as things that were developed in the West. Afrocentricity describes the mental transformation that reverses that process of assimilation into a Western worldview and attempts to understand the self and the world through the history and heritage of Africa.

Afrocentricty is not a matter of occasionally wearing clothing or accessories made of Kente cloth or other vibrantly colored fabrics associated with life in some African countries. Rather, as Molefi Kete Asante of Temple University observes in *The Afrocentric Idea,* "Afrocentricity is the practice of placing African ideals at the center of any analysis that involves African culture and behavior." For Asante, that means that the behavior and culture of black people cannot be completely grasped without understanding that these are African people, whether they are located in Africa, the West Indies, Central and South America, or communities throughout the United States.

African American religious groups have engaged the issue of Afrocentricity at many levels. When **black theology** argues that the Christian faith must be read and interpreted in ways that make it relevant to the experience of being black in the United States and around the world, it is engaging in a form of Afrocentricity. When worship services in black churches seek to honor and retain such customs as call and response, in which there is a verbal interaction between worship leaders and the congregation,

whether in song or sermon, that is a form of Afrocentricity.

Afrocentricity has taken another form where religion is concerned, and that is the adoption of religions that are rooted in the African continent and have been influenced by some exposure to Roman Catholicism. Such religious traditions as Candomble (Brazil), **santeria** (the Dominican Republic and Cuba), and **vodun** or voodoo (Haiti) are essentially African religions that continue to be practiced by people living outside of the African continent and as an alternative to or in addition to some form of Christianity.

Afrocentricity is not practiced simply by making occasional use of African songs, dances, or modes of dress in worship and other public gatherings. Such things as jumping the broom at a wedding are not Afrocentric. As Asante notes, to be Afrocentric is to think about life by way of three fundamental issues: human relations, humans' relationship to the supernatural, and humans' relationship to their own being. The most radical way to understand Afrocentricity is to see it as a way to decolonize the mind so that one's African past and Africa's continuing cultural heritage can be seen and affirmed.

J. Deotis Roberts provides several useful links between Asante's concept of Afrocentricity and various aspects of Christian life and thought in his book *Africentric Christianity* (2000). Roberts emphasizes the variant of *Africentric* over Afrocentric because of the former's stronger etymological connection to the word *Africa*. He seeks to push the Africentric concept beyond the superficial level of clothing and ceremonies. Instead, he explores the more substantive areas of biblical interpretation, congregational worship, family life, and the social witness of black Christians who are acting out of an Africentric perspective.

There is an obvious challenge to the practice of Afrocentricity, and that is the fact that Africa is a continent and not a country. Little can be said about life in North Africa (Libya, Sudan, Egypt, and Ethiopia) that translates perfectly into life in South Africa (the Republic of South Africa, Zimbabwe, Mozambique, and Lesotho). Afrocentricity needs to find a way to acknowledge the colonial and tribal issues that still divide people and nations in Africa. The conflicts between the Zulus and the African National Congress (ANC) in South Africa are real. So too are the feuds between tribal groups such as Hutus and Tutsis in Rwanda, Burundi, and Uganda. Africa is more than the Nile Valley, and Afrocentricity is more than arguing whether Egypt is considered part of Africa or of Eurasia. These two themes seem to occupy most of the attention of those who most vocally address the issue of Afrocentricity.

As a result of nineteenth-century and twentieth-century imperialist policies by European nations, Africa is divided between French-speaking and English-speaking nations. Beneath that are layers of tribal languages that can either facilitate or frustrate communication between groups in the same nation. Hence Afrocentricity can be a false claim either because it is never linked to culture and behavior among a specific group of people in Africa or because it adopts the culture and behavior of a certain group that does not reflect the behavior or worldview of many other groups on the continent.

As practiced in the United States, Afrocentricity is probably best understood as a way to reconnect with one's African past. The question is whether one should fully give up one's identification with American life and values. It was this struggle that **W. E. B. Du Bois** expressed in "Of Our Spiritual Strivings" in *The Souls of Black Folk* (1903). He speaks about a feeling of "two-ness" and "double consciousness." He also says, "The history of the American Negro is the history of this strife…. He would not Africanize America for America has much to teach the world and Africa. He would not bleach his Negro soul in a flood of white Americanism, for he knows that Negro blood has a message for the world."

The issue of Afrocentricity remains outside the mainstream for most black Americans. As long as assimilation into the mainstream remains the primary goal for black people in this country, it is doubtful if Afrocentricity will ever become anything more than an occasional display of African garb, drummers, or other ceremonial practices.

Molefe Kete Asante, *Afrocentricity* and *The Afrocentric Idea;* W. E. B. Du Bois, *The Souls of Black Folk;* J. Deotis Roberts, *Africentric Christianity.*

Apostolic Pentecostalism

Apostolic Pentecostalism refers to a movement within **holiness** and **Pentecostal** churches that rejects the doctrine of the Trinity (Father, Son, and Holy Ghost) as being tritheistic, or affirming faith in three different gods. Instead, the term *apostolic* is used to speak of the fol-

lowers of a monotheistic faith who understand God only through the person of Jesus. Also known as the "Jesus Only" movement, followers of this tradition are most noted for performing baptism only in the name of Jesus. They base their views on a narrow reading of such biblical passages as Acts 8:16 and Acts 19:5.

The apostolic movement seems to have emerged from the **Azusa Street revival** in 1907, and the first group to form was the Pentecostal Assemblies of the World. Rather than teaching that God is understood as three in one, they taught that the name of the Father-Son-Holy Ghost was Jesus, just one person. The leading black member of the early oneness or Jesus Only movement was Garfield Thomas Haywood.

C. Eric Lincoln and Larry H. Mamiya, *The Black Church in the African American Experience;* Iain MacRoberts, "The Black Roots of Pentecostalism," in *African American Religion,* ed. Timothy E. Fulop and Albert J. Raboteau; Larry Murphy, J. Gordon Melton, and Gary Ward, *Encyclopedia of African American Religions.*

Azusa Street Revival

In April 1906 a black preacher named **William Joseph Seymour** began a revival in Los Angeles, California, with a great emphasis on the Pentecostal experience of being baptized in the Holy Spirit and then speaking in tongues (glossolalia). The revival began in a private home, but as the crowds grew the revival was moved to a building on Azusa Street that had formerly been the home of the First African Methodist Episcopal Church.

From the start, Seymour preached to

a racially integrated crowd, and this revival was one of the best opportunities given to America in the twentieth century to overcome the racial divide that was strictly enforced during that period. Regrettably, white Pentecostals separated themselves from their black brothers and sisters by 1914, when they formed the Assemblies of God denomination.

The Azusa Street revival lasted from 1906 to 1908. In 1907 Seymour had organized the Azusa Street Apostolic Faith Mission of Los Angeles. It was also in 1907 that **Charles Harrison (C. H.) Mason,** who had been a founder of **The Church of God in Christ (COGIC)** along with **Charles Price (C. P.) Jones,** visited the Azusa Street mission. Mason underwent the Pentecostal experience, and upon his return to Memphis he began to incorporate that doctrine into the life of The Church of God in Christ. Jones, who did not attend the Azusa Street revival, objected to this doctrine, and that became the basis of the rupture in their friendship and denominational partnership. After a court battle in 1909, Jones withdrew from COGIC and formed The Church of Christ (Holiness), USA.

The Pentecostal movement is the fastest-growing Christian movement among African Americans. The growth is occurring primarily in The Church of God in Christ and the Full Gospel Baptist Church under Bishop **Paul Morton Sr.** Both movements trace their roots to the Azusa Street revival and Seymour.

Ithiel C. Clemmons, *Bishop C. H. Mason and the Roots of the Church of God in Christ;* Iain Mac-Roberts, "The Black Roots of Pentecostalism," in *African American Religion,* ed. Timothy E. Fulop and Albert J. Raboteau; Elsie W. Mason, "Bishop C. H. Mason, Church of God in Christ," in *African American Religious History,* ed. Milton C. Sernett.

☮ Black Preaching

Like the diversity of forms and structures that make up the black church in the United States, black preaching encompasses a wide variety of forms and styles. No single approach to preaching can be called authentic black preaching to the exclusion of all other forms and styles. There may be some common traits that cut across that diversity of oral styles that can be heard in black churches and from black preachers. Yet the preaching style of **Gardner C. Taylor** or **Otis Moss Jr.** is not like the preaching style of **T. D. Jakes** or Tony Evans, but all of them are great black preachers. **Ella Pearson Mitchell** does not preach in the same manner as does Carolyn Knight, nor does **Prathia Hall** immediately remind one of the preaching style of **Leontine T. C. Kelly** or **Barbara Harris.** Yet all of them are outstanding black preachers.

Black preaching, like all preaching, is a matter of oral technique. Whether one intends to describe the musicality and intonation that is so often associated with black preaching or the use of rhythm and repetition that is equally descriptive of this preaching tradition, the oral components of black preaching are the intentional and often the inspirational employment of four devices: pitch, pace, pause, and volume. These four elements define all forms of human speech, whether from behind the pulpit, on a platform, in a classroom, or on a theatrical stage. Human speech is made possible by these four variables:

pitch, pace, pause, and volume.

Black preachers may vary widely in their theological perspectives. Some are as biblically conservative as the most conservative white person in the so-called Religious Right. Others are as biblically and theologically liberal as can be imagined. Some are committed to preaching that focuses on cultural and contemporary issues. Others are strictly expositional preachers who make no attempt to engage and interpret the issues of the day. While their use of Scripture makes their preaching content quite different, they are all bound by the use of the same four vocal variables of pitch, pace, pause, and volume.

The "whooping" approach to sermon conclusions that is so often associated with black preachers like **Clarence LaVaughn (C. L.) Franklin**, Jasper Williams, and **Caesar Clark** is an authentic form of black preaching that can be traced to the slave preachers of the eighteenth and nineteenth centuries in Amer-

Carolyn Ann Knight

ica. However, that approach to black preaching is not the same as the melodic tone often known as "the hum" that is heard in the preaching of **William A. Jones Jr.** or **Manuel Lee Scott Sr.** By the same token, great black preachers like **Jeremiah A. Wright Jr., Sandy F. Ray, James Alexander Forbes Jr.**, or **Vashti McKenzie** have made no regular use of any of the above-mentioned devices. Yet they too have predecessors in the eighteenth and nineteenth centuries. There may be differences among these preachers in terms of style, but those differences are easily definable in relation to their use of the same four vocal variables of pitch, pace, pause, and volume.

No one would argue that **Samuel Dewitt Proctor** and **Charles G. Adams** were or are among the greatest preachers of the modern era. Both make use of scholarly materials. They engage social and political issues, and they have a left-of-center biblical and theological perspective. Both were or are manuscript preachers who read every word of their sermons. But the difference is in the reading, or in the use of pitch, pace, pause, and volume in the context of reading their sermons. Both represent authentic traditions within the history of black preaching, but they were not the same style in terms of delivery.

Black preaching, as an oral technique, is the increased mastery of the shifting pace of how rapidly or slowly one speaks. Added to that are shifts in volume within the body of the sermon and even more so as the sermon builds to a conclusion. It includes, to varying degrees, the use of tonality, which is the willingness and ability to make changes in the use of pitch at various points in the sermon, and especially as the sermon celebration or application unfolds. Black preaching also includes deliberate pauses between words or phrases that allow for congregational response to what has just been said. Preachers who use repetition, recitation, alliteration, or what is classically called peroration are making use of pauses as part of their delivery. Add all of these devices together, color them with the natural talents and intellectual habits of the preacher, and you have the oral components of black preaching.

Black preaching cannot be fully defined by limiting the discussion to what is being said by the preacher. One must account for the call and response, the verbal interaction between the pulpit and the pew, between the preacher and the congregation. This is the part of black preaching that is the most exciting to observe and the most exhilarating to experience. It does not occur in every black church setting, and it does not happen in every sermon even where the practice is common. However, it is so common within the black churches of America, and it is so much associated with the essence of black preaching, that one cannot help but acknowledge its importance.

The interaction begins, like the sermon, as understated and encouraging: "All right now," "Let's see," "Lord, help." It builds as the sermon builds, with the congregation returning as much energy to the preacher as the preacher is directing toward them. One can hear the volume of the response increasing, as well as the numbers of persons who are making responses. They are saying, "Yes, Lord," "Preach!" "I hear you," and "Come on,

now." Finally, as the sermon builds to its conclusion, a genuine call and response pattern can be detected, with the congregation repeating the words or the lyrics or the biblical verses that are being used by the preacher. It is not uncommon for the congregation to continue to respond to the message even after the preacher has finished and taken a seat. This kind of conclusion to the sermon is variously referred to as "the gravy," "pulling it," or "coming on through." It is this verbal exchange that most people point to as the essence of black preaching.

Again, not every sermon preached will create this response, and not every sermon is meant to do so. There is an inherent danger in this area, and one that has often been exploited. Namely, it is possible for certain preachers to focus less on what they are saying to the congregation and concentrate instead on how they are able to manipulate this aspect of black preaching. Two warnings are appropriate at this point. The first is, "If you cook your meat well, it will produce its own gravy." Good handling of the text and the application of that text to the lives of the congregation will give people something to shout about. The other comes from Gardner C. Taylor's Lyman Beecher Lectures in 1976, when he said, "If you do not focus first on the *matter* (what to say), you cannot expect the *manner* (how you say it) to save you."

However, black preaching is ill served if it is discussed only in terms of oral techniques. The classic definition of preaching used by Phillips Brooks in the nineteenth century (truth through personality), applies especially well to black preaching. It is also necessary to define black preaching in relation to the context in which preaching occurs and the content of the message that is being communicated. Black preaching is that wrestling with and delivery of the Word of God that has been filtered through the experience of being black in America on the part of the preacher. Black preaching is also the process of receiving and responding to the Word of God by hearers, most of whom have been shaped by that same experience of living as black people in America. That is the setting in which the truth emerges. Black preaching, like **black theology,** is an effort to make the claims and comforts of the gospel applicable to people whose history in this country has been one of oppression, discrimination, and what novelist Ralph Ellison calls "invisibility."

Black preaching at its best is not just the manipulation of oral techniques or the verbal exchange between pulpit and pew. It is the use of those oral techniques coupled with an emotional and experiential identification with that history of oppression and invisibility. Add to these two a determination to speak to that experience and its victims through the gospel of Jesus Christ in order to empower the hearers of that message to face their future with faith, and that constitutes the fullest and richest understanding of black preaching.

Black preaching is not simply a black person preaching to other black people. Black preaching is Jeremiah 37:17 at work within the life of a community of believers struggling to make sense of their lives in a racist and hostile environment: "Is there any word from the Lord?" (NJKV). In truth, Jeremiah 37:17 can and

should be the basis of preaching in all racial and cultural settings. The difference is the manner in which that word from the Lord is interpreted and applied to speak to the unique experiences of being black in America.

Several scholars have sought to analyze black preaching. They include **Henry Mitchell,** *Black Preaching;* Cleophus LaRue, *The Heart of Black Preaching;* Evans E. Crawford with Thomas Troeger, *The Hum;* Marvin A. McMickle, *Living Water for Thirsty Souls;* and Warren Stewart, *Interpreting God's Word in Black Preaching.* **W. E. B. Du Bois** offers a haunting description of black preaching in "The Faith of the Fathers" in *The Souls of Black Folk.* **Wyatt Tee Walker** also talks about the role of black preaching in *The Soul of Black Worship.*

Collections of great black preaching are to be found in several sermon collections published by Judson Press, including *Those Preaching Women,* volumes 1–3, edited by Ella Pearson Mitchell; *Outstanding Black Sermons,* volumes 1–4, edited respectively by **J. Alfred Smith Sr.,** Walter B. Hoard, Milton E. Owens Jr., and Walter S. Thomas; and *Best Black Sermons,* edited by William M. Philpot.

☻ Black Theology

The concept of a black theology has roots in the nineteenth century through the ministry of **Henry McNeil Turner** and in the mid-twentieth century with the writings of **Albert Buford Cleage** and his understanding of Jesus as the black Messiah. However, the term "black theology" is most closely associated with the work of **James H. Cone** and **J. Deotis Roberts.** Cone coined the phrase in *Black Theology and Black Power* (1970). Roberts offered something of a rebuttal to Cone's views in *Liberation and Reconciliation* (1971). The two men disagreed over the influence that the black power movement should have on black Christian theologians.

Cone speaks of black theology by saying, "Black Theology is that theology which arises out of the need to articulate the significance of black presence in a hostile white world. It is black people reflecting religiously on the black experience, attempting to redefine the relevance of the Christian Gospel for their lives." Roberts responds by saying, "Black Theology is a theology of liberation…. Reconciliation is also crucial."

Cone argues that "the purpose of Black Theology is to place the actions of black people toward liberation in the Christian perspective, showing that Christ himself is participating in the black struggle for freedom." Roberts counters by saying, "Christ is the Liberator. But the liberating Christ is also the reconciling Christ."

Despite this apparent difference over liberation versus reconciliation, both men agree that the central biblical paradigm for black theology is the exodus and the deliverance of the people of Israel from bondage. Black theology employs that motif in order to say that God is identified in history with the plight of the oppressed. As a result, for Cone and Roberts, all of the people of God must also identify with the elimination of whatever things contribute to the oppression of black people.

The most unique thing about black theology is what Cone calls "the sources," or the influences that shape and inform a black theologian. The six sources are the black experience, black history, black culture, revelation, Scripture, and theological tradition. Traditional European theology had made no use of the first three sources mentioned by Cone.

From a historical perspective, black theology not only offered a new way to view Scripture and to interpret the message of the gospel; it also offered a new way for black Christians to embrace their faith at a time when it was being widely dismissed by others in the African American community as "the white man's religion." This point is convincingly made by Dwight N. Hopkins in his book *Black Faith and Public Talk,* which is a critical analysis of James Cone's *Black Theology and Black Power.* In his book, Hopkins writes:

> For many at that time, it was not possible to be black and a Christian. Black power advocates in the larger American society derided Christianity as "the white man's religion"; therefore, to be black was to be a non-Christian, and to be Christian was, for black power activists, to be an Uncle Tom…. Cone concluded a whole new way of viewing the black freedom struggle and for interpreting the good news of Jesus Christ.

As a result of black theology, many other groups have revisited the biblical record to see how it can address their particular form of oppression. It can be argued that liberation theology as framed by Latin American and African scholars, feminist theology as defined primarily by white female theologians, and **womanist theology** as conceived by black women working in Bible and theology have all emerged as a result of the initial work done by Cone and Roberts in black theology.

James H. Cone, "Black Consciousness and the Black Church: A Historical-Theological Interpretation," *The Annals of the American Academy of Political and Social Science* (January 1970).

☙ Bloody Sunday

Sunday, March 7, 1965, was when a group of six hundred marchers, led by Hosea Williams of the **Southern Christian Leadership Conference (SCLC)** and **John Lewis** of the Student Nonviolent Coordinating Committee (SNCC), attempted to walk across the Edmund Pettus Bridge in Selma, Alabama. Their objective was to march to Montgomery, Alabama, the state capitol, and appeal to Governor George Wallace to call for an end to the violence that had been occurring against blacks and to uphold the right of black

A sherrif's deputy pushes back peaceful protestors during the Bloody Sunday march.

people to register and vote. It was also meant to dramatize the Voting Rights Bill that was bottled up in Congressional committees in Washington, D.C. By this time, voting rights had clearly surpassed issues of public accommodations as the chief concern of the **civil rights movement.**

In Alabama in 1963, only 13 percent of the eligible black voters were registered. In order to change that, SNCC began a voter registration drive in that state in February 1963. Little progress was made, largely because of intimidation directed toward those blacks who attempted to register and violence directed toward anyone, black or white, who sought to assist blacks in registering. On October 7, 1963, SNCC held a Freedom Day at the Dallas County Courthouse in Selma. That effort at registration was blocked through the brutal tactics of county sheriff James G. Clark and his deputies.

Throughout 1964 SNCC continued its efforts at voter registration but met with little success for the same reasons: intimidation and violence. In January 1965, **Martin Luther King Jr.** and SCLC entered the conflict, thus bringing national media and political attention to Selma. On January 2, 1965, King preached at Brown Memorial Christian Methodist Episcopal Church in Selma. The marches and demonstrations for voting rights began on January 18. King was arrested during one of the marches on February 1. On February 4, by invitation of SNCC, **Malcolm X** came to Selma to further dramatize the events occurring in that city.

It was believed that in order to keep national attention focused on Selma and on the issue of voting rights, some use of excessive violence by the police would have to be provoked. That was the lesson learned in Birmingham in 1963, when officials in that city used fire hoses and police dogs to break up peaceful marches. A great deal of violence had already occurred, including the shooting death of Jimmie Lee Jackson and the beating of Rev. C. T. Vivian by Clark on the steps of the county courthouse. The march across the Edmund Pettus Bridge was meant not only to begin the walk to Montgomery but also to provoke a response from Clark that could be captured on national television. Clark did not disappoint.

The march commenced outside the Brown Chapel and proceeded to the top of the bridge, where the marchers were met by lines of sheriff's deputies and state police sent by Wallace, who did not want the march to take place. Many of the police were on horseback, and all were outfitted with billy clubs, gas masks, and tear gas canisters. They also held cattle prods that sent electric shocks into those they touched. The marchers were told, "It would be detrimental to your safety to continue this march. You are ordered to disperse, go home or to your church. This march will not continue. You have two minutes."

When the marchers refused to leave the bridge, they were beaten, trampled by the horses, gassed, and pursued not only off the bridge but also back into the vicinity of the church. Williams and Lewis were badly beaten, and the scene was captured by reporters and photographers from national newspapers and by the radio and television networks. That march on Bloody Sunday was followed by another march led two days later by King called Turnaround Tuesday. That march also went no further than the top of the Edmund Pettus Bridge, where marchers were met by a similar display of police force, and they returned to the church.

When the federal government agreed to provide protection for the marchers along the highway from Selma to Montgomery, the march did take place on March 21, when four thousand people gathered in front of Brown Chapel. The march took five days, and on March 25, 1965, more than twenty-five thousand marchers arrived in Montgomery. The Voting Rights Bill passed in the U.S. Senate on May 26, 1965. It passed in the U.S. House, after a five-week debate, on July 9, 1965. It was signed into law by President Lyndon B. Johnson on August 6, 1965. Bloody Sunday had been the decisive event in gaining national voting rights for black people.

J. L. Chestnut Jr. and Julia Cass, *Black in Selma;* Henry Hampton and Steve Fayer, *Voices of Freedom: An Oral History of the Civil Rights Movement from the 1950s through the 1980s;* Juan Williams, *Eyes on the Prize: America's Civil Rights Years, 1954–1965.*

The Church of God in Christ (COGIC)

In order to discuss the beginnings of The Church of God in Christ (COGIC), it is necessary to speak of two events, one in 1897 and the other in a span of time between 1907 and 1909. In 1897 two men, **Charles Harrison (C. H.) Mason** and **Charles Price (C. P.) Jones,** sought to establish a new church communion that emphasized not only justification by faith but also holiness as a second work of the Spirit. Both men had been Baptist preachers who sought to introduce into the Baptist church the doctrine of perfectionism, or the necessity of being sanctified by the Holy Spirit after one's initial conversion.

On June 6, 1897, Jones hosted a holy convocation at the Mt. Helm Baptist Church in Jackson, Mississippi, where he served as pastor. The meeting lasted for two weeks, and at the end of the convocation several pastors and congregations from Baptist churches in Mississippi and several surrounding states agreed to adopt the doctrine of sanctification. In an effort to distinguish themselves from those Baptists who did not adhere to the doctrine of sanctification, Mason was led to refer to this new movement as The Church of God in Christ, drawing from language found in 1 Thessalonians 2:14 and 2 Thessalonians 1:1.

In 1899 Mason, Jones, and other members of COGIC were expelled from the newly formed National Baptist Convention. The reasons were twofold: the strong disapproval of the majority of black Baptists in that region over the issue of sanctification and Mason's insistence on maintaining the extremely emotional religious practices that had marked the black church during slavery. Having been chartered in Tennessee as a **holiness movement,** the followers of Mason and Jones continued as an independent holiness community, establishing their first church in Lexington, Mississippi. Mason and Jones labored to build COGIC, and the new movement spread rapidly in Mississippi, Alabama, and Tennessee. From 1897 to 1906, COGIC was essentially a holiness movement comprised largely of former Baptists who were desirous of being sanctified by the Holy Spirit as a second act of grace.

The history and direction of COGIC was drastically altered in 1907, when Mason attended the **Azusa Street revival** in Los Angeles, California, under the direction of **William Joseph Seymour.** Mason, who was already a sanctified holiness preacher, now underwent the Pentecostal experience of the baptism of the Holy Spirit and speaking in tongues (glossolalia). After five weeks at Azusa Street, Mason became convinced that even holiness was not sufficient and that evidence of sanctification had to be given, and that evidence was the Pentecostal experience.

Upon his return to Memphis, where COGIC had established headquarters, Mason began to emphasize this new doctrine and to urge his followers to pray and tarry for this experience. He also called for another holy convocation, as had occurred with the original formation of COGIC. Meeting in September 1907, delegates to the Pentecostal Assembly of the Church of God in Christ took two major actions. First, they replaced Jones as general overseer and appointed Mason as the Chief Apostle. Second, they agreed to convene an annual holy convocation in Memphis as the unifying experience of their denomination.

This new emphasis introduced by Mason marks the second phase in the history of COGIC. It had evolved from being a holiness movement comprised of former Baptists to being a Pentecostal movement, which is its emphasis to this day. Just as many in the Baptist church resisted the doctrine of sanctification when it was brought to them by Mason and Jones, now Jones, who was the general overseer of COGIC, resisted the doctrine of the Pentecostal experience as shared with him by his dear friend Mason. After a two-year court fight over the use of the name Church of God in Christ, Jones withdrew from the church, and his followers organized The Church of Christ (Holiness), USA. From 1909 to the present, COGIC has been the fastest-growing segment of the African American religious community, with a membership that exceeded five million in 2000.

The departure of Jones and his followers was not the only schism that occurred within COGIC. After his Pentecostal experience in 1907, Mason went back to Memphis and was at that point the only Pentecostal leader in the South with the authority to ordain other persons into the ministry of the Pentecostal church. That authority rested on his having chartered COGIC in Tennessee in 1897. As a result, black and white preachers were ordained by Mason into the ministry of COGIC. Like the story of Pentecost in Acts 2, one of the great outcomes of Mason and COGIC was the interracial nature of that community of believers.

The prevailing racial views of the time began to take precedence over the great work that the Holy Spirit was doing through Mason and COGIC throughout the South. Many of the white pastors in COGIC withdrew in 1914 and reformed under the name Assemblies of God. That largely white Pentecostal group has evolved into the largest Pentecostal body in the world. However, many of its ministers traced ordination

and initial ministry experience to COGIC and the work of Mason.

The rapid growth of COGIC has resulted in an organizational structure that involves a presiding bishop, a general board, and a board of bishops that oversee more than 150 jurisdictions around the world. Mason served as presiding bishop until his death in 1961. He was followed in that role by O. T. Jones Sr. (1962–1968), James O. Patterson (1968–1989), L. H. Ford (1990–1995), Chandler David Owens (1995–2000), and Gilbert E. Patterson (2000–).

In 1970 COGIC, which initially did not emphasize having a theologically trained clergy, established the Charles Harrison Mason Theological Seminary. Today that school is one of the institutions that make up the **Interdenominational Theological Center (ITC)** in Atlanta, Georgia.

Taylor Branch, *Parting the Waters: America During the King Years, 1954–1965;* Stokely Carmichael and Charles V. Hamilton, *Black Power;* Ithiel C. Clemmons, *Bishop C. H. Mason and the Roots of the Church of God in Christ;* Henry Hampton and Steve Fayer, *Voices of Freedom: An Oral History of the Civil Rights Movement from the 1950s through the 1980s;* Elsie W. Mason, "Bishop C. H. Mason and the Church of God in Christ," in *African American Religious History,* ed. Milton C. Sernett.

☺ Civil Rights Movement

It can be argued that since the end of the Civil War, many people and groups in American history have worked to remove the vestiges of slavery and racial discrimination that had been entrenched

Martin Luther King Jr. at the March on Washington, 1963

in American society for the preceding two hundred years. However, between 1953 and 1968 there was a particularly intense effort, employing a set of methods, aimed at a set of goals, and involving a wide array of groups and charismatic leaders. That effort began with the bus boycott in Baton Rouge, Louisiana, in 1953 and seems to have ended with a series of social upheavals in 1968 that included the assassination of **Martin Luther King Jr.** and the election of Richard M. Nixon as president of the United States.

The initial focus of the movement was the removal of all forms of racial segregation that had taken root as a result of the *Plessy v. Ferguson* ruling by the U.S. Supreme Court (1896). That ruling set in place a society based upon the principle of separate but equal. The idea of separate but equal quickly came to mean separate and woefully unequal, with black people being systematically prohibited from sharing in many areas of American life and being totally segregated in those areas where they were allowed to participate. The first target of the civil rights move-

ment was public accommodations and publicly funded educational institutions.

The momentum for the civil rights movement was created by earlier groups and efforts such as the Fellowship of Reconciliation (FOR, 1941) and the National Association for the Advancement of Colored People (NAACP), especially its efforts in the 1930s and 1940s under Charles Hamilton Houston to enroll blacks in various state-supported graduate schools across the country. Other important steps forward were an executive order given by Franklin Roosevelt in 1941, which integrated war production facilities in the United States, and an executive order by Harry Truman in 1948, which ended segregation in the U.S. armed forces. All of these activities set the stage for the landmark U.S. Supreme Court decision in *Brown v. Board of Education* (1954), which essentially overturned *Plessy v. Ferguson.* It called for the end of segregation in public education "with all deliberate speed."

What made the civil rights movement different from these earlier efforts was the scale and length of grassroots, community-based, public demonstrations that took place over this time. Also important was the way in which the civil rights movement sought to make the various agencies of the federal government work on behalf of black people to uphold the Fourteenth Amendment's guarantee of "equal protection under the law." Most important for this study was the central role that was played by black churches as rallying points and by black religious leaders at the local and national levels.

Although the boycott in Baton Rouge lasted for only six days, it used a methodology for dealing with segregation in public transportation that was employed in Montgomery, Alabama, for 381 days in 1955 and 1956. That boycott ended when a federal court ruled that segregation in public transportation is unconstitutional. Then came the integration of Central High School in Little Rock, Arkansas, in 1957. The Arkansas National Guard and the 101st Airborne Division of the U.S. Army, working under the orders of President Dwight D. Eisenhower, protected black students seeking to enroll in that school in accordance with *Brown v. Board of Education.*

In 1957 the **Southern Christian Leadership Conference (SCLC)** was formed under the leadership of King. That group joined with other civil rights groups already at work, such as the NAACP, the Urban League, the Congress of Racial Equality (CORE), and the National Council of Negro Women. In 1960 a group known as the Student Nonviolent Coordinating Committee (SNCC) was created, and these six groups and their leaders, known as the Big Six, provided the frontline leadership for the movement for the next five years.

Under the supervision of one or more of these groups, the civil rights movement engaged in student-led sit-ins at lunch counters throughout the South in 1960. Then came the Freedom Rides, which resulted in massive white resistance and violent attacks on the riders in 1961. In 1962 SCLC led an unsuccessful nonviolent campaign for integration in Albany, Georgia. These groups cooperated on the 1963 March on Washington, at which each of the leaders had a place on the program. In 1964 SNCC directed what was

called Freedom Summer, during which voter registration became the new emphasis of the movement. In 1965 SNCC and SCLC collaborated on the march from Selma to Montgomery, Alabama, when once again voter registration was the focus. This phase of the civil rights movement can be said to have enjoyed considerable success. The 1964 Civil Rights Bill and the 1965 Voting Rights Act were signed into federal law largely as a result of the efforts of the leaders and organizations that made up the civil rights movement.

By 1966 the nonviolent strategy of the civil rights movement was being challenged by new voices, such as Stokely Carmichael and H. Rap Brown within SNCC and by the far more militant voices of Huey P. Newton and Bobby Seale of the Black Panther Party, headquartered in Oakland, California. At the same time, the separatist and nationalist rhetoric of **Malcolm X** was resonating even though he had been assassinated in February 1965.

In 1966 SCLC led its first Northern effort with a summer-long campaign against segregated housing patterns in Chicago. In addition to issues of racism, that campaign was also intended to identify poverty and economic opportunity as the next phase of the movement. That campaign clearly revealed that racism and segregation were not simply Southern problems. However, it also revealed that nonviolent demonstrations were no longer the most effective means for addressing issues of racism and poverty.

Beginning in 1967, largely because of King, national attention began to shift away from civil rights issues to the issue of the war in Vietnam. Riots that erupted in the Watts section of Los Angeles in

1965 were followed by even more intense urban uprisings in Cleveland, Ohio; Detroit, Michigan; Newark, New Jersey; and other Northern cities between 1965 and 1968. The term "long hot summer" became a way of describing those violent encounters. These were radical departures from the message and methodology of the nonviolent civil rights movement.

White supporters of the civil rights movement either objected to King's outspoken opposition to the war or agreed with him and shifted their money and their passion to that cause. Whites who had long opposed the gains of the civil rights movement now clamored for law and order in the face of the urban riots (black protesters) and the steadily increasing antiwar movement (white protesters). This resulted in the chaos that was the year of 1968. There was the emergence of Governor George Wallace of Alabama as a candidate for president of the United States, the street battle in Chicago at the Democratic National Convention, the election of Richard M. Nixon, and the almost simultaneous murders of King and Robert F. Kennedy.

The mood and spirit of the nation shifted, and the nonviolent civil rights movement came to an end. The work of freedom continues through the efforts of political leaders rather than grassroots street demonstrations. As Katherine Tate argues, the struggle has shifted "from protest to politics." To be sure, occasional street demonstrations still occur, and **Jesse Jackson** and **Alfred Sharpton** continue to use some of the methods of the civil rights movement as a way of addressing the somewhat more complex issues of the twenty-first century. How-

ever, nothing has happened since the summer of 1968 that begins to rival the remarkable combination of events that shook and shaped the United States between 1953 and 1968.

Aldon D. Morris, *The Origins of the Civil Rights Movement;* Juan Williams, *Eyes on the Prize.*

☻ Colonization Movement

As early as 1770, white leaders such as Thomas Jefferson, Henry Clay, and Andrew Johnson began advocating that slavery should be ended and that those blacks who were set free should be resettled either in Africa or Haiti or somewhere in the American Western frontier. The effort to resettle black people in new communities outside of the United States was called colonization. This hotly contested movement was largely opposed by black leaders, but many black religious leaders actively supported the concept, including **Lott Carey, Daniel Coker, Alexander Crummell, Henry Highland Garnet,** and **Henry McNeil Turner.**

In the first issue of *Freedom's Journal* in 1829, John Russworm offered the first compelling argument by a black leader for colonization. The essence of his argument was that there was little likelihood that America would ever be a hospitable place for black people when they were finally released from slavery. He went on to argue that in the North, free blacks were either been constantly harassed or were being prohibited from migrating into certain states. Colonization seemed to him to be the only solution.

The driving force of the colonization movement was the American Colonization Society (ACS), formed in Washington, D.C., in 1817. The issue of colonization was linked to the issue of Christianization, or the idea that those free blacks who were willing to be resettled in Sierra Leone and later in Liberia would then be in a position to share the Christian faith with the native African populations they would encounter. This appeal was especially popular among persons like Carey and Coker, who went to Africa with the expressed purpose of establishing churches among the native population.

In 1858, under the leadership of Garnet, the African Civilization Society was founded with the dual focus of "the civilization and Christianization of Africa, and of the descendants of African ancestors in any portion of the earth, wherever dispersed." Garnet's other focus was to establish a thriving economy in those new colonies, especially in the cotton industry, that could provide an alternative to the cotton being produced by slave labor. Under this approach colonization not only removed blacks from America but also had the potential of striking a blow against the slave trade in the United States.

However, most black leaders, most notably Frederick Douglass, opposed colonization because they viewed America, not Africa or Haiti, as their native land. They objected to the idea that whites could bring blacks from Africa to labor in lifelong slavery generating wealth for their owners and for American society. Then, either because slaves became free or slavery was abolished, those same whites wanted to remove black persons from the country that they had helped to build.

Richard Allen directed his opposition to the colonization idea specifically at the issue of Christianization and civilization. Given the fact that the vast majority of black people could still neither read nor write, he wondered what sense it made to expect that such persons could bring civilization or evangelization to Africa when so many of them remained in need of those very things.

President Abraham Lincoln proposed a colonization plan for the free blacks living in the United States and for the black people who would become free as a result of the Emancipation Proclamation. His plan would have resettled free blacks on the island of Vache, off the coast of Haiti. An initial group of five hundred colonists were sent in 1862, of whom two hundred died within months of arrival from tropical diseases and other hardships. That plan was abandoned. The last American political leader to propose a colonization plan for black people was the infamous Senator Theodore Bilbo of Mississippi, who introduced a bill for the colonization of all black people to Africa in 1939.

Howard Brotz, *Negro Social and Political Thought, 1850–1920;* Deirdre Mullane, "Colonization: For and Against," in *Crossing the Danger Water.*

☙ Colored (Christian) Methodist Episcopal (CME) Church

The smallest of the three major black Methodist bodies in the United States, this denomination was birthed in the South when slavery had ended and black people were free to evangelize and organize churches in areas that had previously been hostile to such activity. The CME Church was first organized in Jackson,

Tennessee, on January 16, 1870. The original name was Colored Methodist Episcopal Church but was changed from Colored to Christian in 1954.

Harry V. Richardson in *Dark Salvation* says, "The founding of the Christian Methodist Episcopal Church was in some ways quite different from the founding of the other black Methodist denominations. In the first place, the CME Church did not begin in conflict with whites or in ill-feeling. It began in the mutual recognition of a changed situation which called for a new organizational relationship." That changed situation was the end of slavery.

Most of the black Methodists who organized the CME Church had been members of the Methodist Episcopal Church of the South (MECS), a group that split away from the Methodist Episcopal Church in 1844 over the question of slavery. The founders of the CME Church also included many persons who had been enslaved prior to the end of the Civil War. When they gained freedom, they wanted to remain Methodist but under an independent status. Unlike the experience of the **African Methodist Episcopal (AME)** and **African Methodist Episcopal Zion (AME Zion)** bodies, the CME's request for independence was warmly received by the MECS. The white Methodist body not only organized and chartered the new black group but also ordained its first bishops, **William Henry Miles** and Richard Vanderhost. In another departure from the experience of black Methodists in the North, the MECS relinquished all claims to the properties in which the CME churches met and worshiped.

In the charter of the CME Church the founders speak warmly about their historical connection to the MECS and about their hope for continued good relations: "We shall ever hold in grateful remembrance what the Methodist Episcopal church, South, has done for us; we shall ever cherish the kindliest feelings toward the bishops and General Conference for giving to us all that they enjoy of religious privileges, the ordination of our deacons and elders.... We most sincerely pray, earnestly desire, and confidently believe that there will ever be the kindliest feelings cherished toward the Methodist Episcopal Church, South, and that we may ever receive their warmest sympathy and support."

Those were not the sentiments of the AMEs and AME Zions when **Richard Allen** and **James Varick** organized those two black Methodist bodies.

The Christian Methodist Episcopal Church never grew to the size of its Northern counterparts. The main reason is that at the end of the Civil War in 1865, most ex-slaves looking to join a church preferred the already established AME and AME Zion churches rather than remain within the MECS structure. By the time the CME Church was organized in 1870, many of the possible converts had already been claimed by the other black Methodist bodies. The CME Church seems to have peaked in membership at approximately nine hundred thousand persons worldwide divided among about three thousand congregations.

In 1961 bishops of the CME Church traveled to Nigeria to receive into membership the forty thousand members and the two hundred clergy of the United

African Church, a Church of England fellowship that wanted to affiliate with a black denomination. The CME Church now has more than two hundred thousand members in Ghana and Nigeria. The CME Church established headquarters in Memphis, Tennessee, in 1970. The church sponsors five colleges, a seminary that is affiliated with the **Interdenominational Theological Center (ITC)** in Atlanta, Georgia, and a publishing house.

C. Eric Lincoln and Lawrence W. Mamiya, *The Black Church in the African American Experience;* Harry V. Richardson, *Dark Salvation.*

◉ Congress of National Black Churches (CNBC)

This ecumenical agency, organized in 1978 with funding from the Lilly Foundation, comprises the seven major denominational bodies within the African American church community. The member groups are the **African Methodist Episcopal (AME) Church,** the **African Methodist Episcopal Zion (AME Zion) Church,** the **Christian Methodist Episcopal (CME) Church, The Church of God in Christ (COGIC),** the **National Baptist Convention, USA, Inc. (NBCUSA),** the **National Baptist Convention of America,** and the **Progressive National Baptist Convention (PNBC).** The recently organized National Missionary Baptist Convention has also joined the group.

Picking up where the **National Conference of Black Churchmen (NCBC)** left off, CNBC attempts to move beyond the political and social issues of the 1960s and 1970s and to begin to address the underlying economic problems that afflict America's black communities. It is also a way to use the assets, influence, and cooperative strength of the black churches to create economic opportunities. Among the early goals of CNBC was to create black-owned insurance, publishing, and banking companies that would do business in areas where white-owned businesses either had left or refused to go. Informed by the self-help philosophy that traces back to Booker T. Washington, CNBC was intended to put economic issues on the table for discussion and implementation where integration and black power had once been the main focus.

The founding president of CNBC was AME bishop **John Hurst Adams.** The current president is AME Zion bishop Cecil Bishop of North Carolina. The group publishes a periodical entitled *VISIONS.* With headquarters in Washington, D.C., CNBC also hosts forums and conferences on matters of interest to church leaders such as health care in the black community, the digital divide, and black student achievement in public schools. In 2000 CNBC hosted a major ecumenical conference involving all of its member bodies, The Black Church Leadership Conference.

C. Eric Lincoln and Larry H. Mamiya, *The Black Church in the African American Experience;* Gayraud S. Wilmore and James H. Cone, *Black Theology: A Documentary History, 1966–1979.*

◉ Cults

As discussed by Arthur Huff Fauset in *Black Gods of the Metropolis* and Joseph R. Washington Jr. in *Black Religion and Black Sects and Cults,* cults are religious groups that grow up around the charismatic personality of an individual leader who typically makes claims about his or her divinity or divine inspiration. Cultic groups such as the **Father Divine** Peace Mission Movement or **Daddy Grace**'s United House of Prayer for All People originated primarily in the urban centers of the North during the Great Migration (1895–1945). They grew be-cause they provided some social service that was needed by the recent immigrants from the South or an immediate community for persons who may still have felt uprooted and adrift in the large cities of the North.

Cults in the black communities of the North have reflected various religious traditions and have made equally various claims about the true ancestry of black people now living in the United States. Among the cults of the twentieth century have been those that adopted a Jewish identity (black Jews of Harlem under **Wentworth A. Matthew** and the Church of God under Prophet Cherry), an Islamic perspective (Moorish Science Temple under **Noble Drew Ali** and the **Nation of Islam** under **W. D. Fard**). Many other cults made use of Christian terms and rituals but were nonetheless centered around the personality of the leader and some doctrine that was not at the heart of the Christian faith. Then there were the cults that had no connection to any traditional faith community and were little more than reflections of the original teachings of the founder, such as Daddy Grace or Father Divine.

More recently, many black members were among the followers of white cult leaders such as Jim Jones, who led his fol-

lowers to their death in the jungles of Guyana, South America, and David Koresh, whose followers died with him in a fire at their compound in Waco, Texas. The appeal of the cults has outlasted the era of the Great Migration, but cults may still provide the same benefits: a sense of community and a set of beliefs that seem divinely ordered.

Arthur Huff Fauset, *Black Gods of the Metropolis;* Joseph R. Washington Jr., *Black Sects and Cults.*

 "Doc"

One of the most frequently used terms or titles used when speaking about a member of the black clergy is that of doctor, as in Rev. Doctor Johnson or Dr. Brown. In a good many cases, the use of that title is appropriate in that the person in question has earned an academic doctoral degree or has been awarded an honorary doctoral degree by an educational institution in recognition of distinguished service or lifetime achievement.

Two standard earned degrees result in a clergyperson bearing the title of doctor. The most established and the most rigorous degree awarded by any university or graduate school is the doctor of philosophy (Ph.D.). At one time, many schools offered a doctor of theology (Th.D.) degree, which was viewed as a degree on par with the Ph.D. Persons discussed in this study who earned the Ph.D. or Th.D. include **Martin Luther King Jr., C. Eric Lincoln, Samuel Dewitt Proctor, Katie Cannon, Prathia Hall, James H. Cone, J. Deotis Roberts, Cornel West, Michael Eric Dyson, E. Franklin Frazier, W. E. B. Du Bois, Benjamin Elijah Mays, Henry**

Heywood Mitchell, Carter G. Woodson, and **Jessie Jai McNeil.**

Within the last thirty years, another doctoral degree program has been offered only by seminaries and schools of theology. That degree is called the doctor of ministry (D.Min.). This doctoral degree is considered a professional degree rather than an academic degree, meaning that its focus is to further equip and train clergy for the pastoral ministry in which they are already engaged rather than training them for teaching and research at the college and graduate level. However, many persons who hold a doctor of ministry degree go on to do excellent work as teachers and writers, especially in the various fields of Christian and pastoral ministry. Some persons also hold both D.Min. and Ph.D. degrees.

Many seminaries have been especially effective at graduating African American clergy with this degree. Among them are United Theological Seminary in Dayton, Ohio; Colgate Rochester Divinity School in Rochester, New York; Howard University Divinity School in Washington, D.C.; New York Theological Seminary in New York City; and Ashland Theological Seminary in Ashland, Ohio (with campuses also in Cleveland, Columbus, and Detroit).

The people in this study who hold the D.Min. degree are **Vashti Murphy McKenzie, J. Alfred Smith Sr., Suzan D. Johnson Cook, James Alexander Forbes Jr., William A. Jones Jr., Otis Moss Jr., Jeremiah A. Wright Jr., Calvin O. Butts III,** and **Wyatt Tee Walker.**

The third method by which many black clergy can earn the title of doctor is by receiving an honorary degree from an undergraduate or graduate school. There are two honorary doctoral degrees typically awarded to members of the clergy, the doctor of divinity (D.D.) and the doctor of humane letters (L.H.D.) The words *Honoris Causae* are printed on the diploma as an indication that it is an honorary degree.

Such degrees are awarded to persons who have offered exemplary service to the granting institution or have made a distinguished contribution to society, in keeping with the values of the granting institution. Most of the clergy with entries in this study have been awarded at least one honorary degree. Many of them have earned academic or professional degrees and an honorary doctorate. Mays and Proctor probably lead the way in this category. Both earned the Ph.D. or Th.D., and each was also awarded at least twenty honorary doctoral degrees from white and historically black colleges and universities.

Other black clergy claim the title of doctor but do not fit in any of the preceding categories. In many circles within the black church, the act of ordination brings with it the right to refer to one's self as Doctor. It is most common that older clergy are referred to by this title as a sign of deference and respect for their years of service. Critics of this practice must remember that for many years, African American clergy were barred from the schools that might have allowed them to earn an academic doctoral degree. As a result, the church in general and the clergy community in particular have awarded the title even if they could not offer a diploma to go with it. There is no more cherished term employed within the ranks of black preachers than Doc.

Emigration Movement

If the colonization of free blacks was being advocated and largely funded by whites, largely through the American Colonization Society (ACS), emigration was the call from black leaders to renounce American citizenship and establish a new home for themselves in Canada, the Caribbean, or various locations in Africa. If colonization was perceived as a solution for white people on how to remove an unwanted black population, emigration was understood as a solution by black people who no longer believed that their assimilation into American society was possible or desirable.

No one was more outspoken about emigration to Africa in the nineteenth century than Edward Wilmot Blyden, who was born in St. Thomas, Virgin Islands, in 1832. He came to the United States to pursue theological education. However, he was unable to enroll at any seminary because of his race. Convinced that there was no hope for full citizenship even for free blacks in the North, Blyden emigrated to Liberia in December 1850. He urged black people not only in the United States, but also in Canada and throughout the Caribbean to emigrate to Liberia and assist in building up that infant nation. Blyden was most famous for the phrase "Liberia with outstretched arms, earnestly invites all to come."

The most famous emigration movement sponsored by blacks in the twentieth century, which was modeled after the philosophy of Edward Wilmot Blyden, was led by **Marcus Garvey** and the Universal Negro Improvement Association (UNIA). Garvey planned to sell shares in a steamship company and transport disaffected blacks from throughout the African Diaspora to Liberia and Sierra Leone in West Africa, where they could build a nation of their own. Other back-to-Africa movements have appeared from time to time; however, they have met with little success. It seems that most African Americans are more interested in working to transform the United States into a colorblind society than they are in emigrating to a separate, all-black nation somewhere else in the world.

Elijah Muhammad also offered an emigration plan that called upon black people in America to resettle in five states in the Deep South that would be set aside by the federal government as reparations for slavery. The states suggested included Mississippi, Alabama, Arkansas, Tennessee, and Louisiana. These were the states made rich by slave labor in the cotton fields, and Muhammad's desire was to see that land offered to the descendants of those who toiled there in slavery.

Another form of emigration, known as the Great Migration, took place within the United States between 1896 and 1945. That was when more than four million black people left the rural South and relocated primarily in the industrial cities of the North, such as New York City; Chicago, Illinois; Detroit, Michigan; Cleveland, Ohio; and Pittsburgh, Pennsylvania. Those persons were escaping the racial oppression that was steadily occurring throughout the South, largely under the influence of the Ku Klux Klan, the membership of which had reached almost nine million persons by 1925.

If racial hostility was pushing people from the South, the hope of greater economic opportunity was pulling them as well. The sharecropping system of the South had become a virtual replica of slavery, and black people could never advance economically. By contrast, the steel mills, meat-packing factories, car assembly lines, and other manufacturing and labor-intensive jobs in the North proved to be attractive to black people looking for a better life.

An equally important migration movement within the United States involved the movement of black people from former slave-holding states, such as Louisiana, Tennessee, and Texas, to locations on the western frontier, such as Kansas, Nebraska, and Oklahoma during the 1870s. The most famous movement in the western migration was the Exodusters, led by Benjamin Singleton, which established hundreds of new homesteads in Kansas during Reconstruction.

A third form of emigration was also taking place in the twentieth century, and that was the emigration of many black families from the Caribbean into the United States. They too were looking for improved economic opportunity. Their presence in many of the urban centers of the North, along with the millions of black people who moved from the South, resulted in the creation of a diverse, multicultural black community in cities across the country. As a result of these last two forms of emigration, it is impossible to speak of the black population in the United States in any homogenous terms. While being black is something they have

in common, their experience of being black in the urban North, the rural South, or among the black majority islands of the Caribbean is quite different.

Much of the religious diversity present within urban black communities is a result of emigration. Ranging from storefront holiness churches, to highly formal Episcopal churches with a largely West Indian membership, to the innumerable Baptist and Methodist churches that line the avenues and boulevards, one can see a reflection of the population shifts that occurred because of various emigration movements.

Thus emigration has been an ongoing movement within the African Diaspora, but it is has taken several forms. For some it is back to Africa, for others it is out of the South, and for those living in the Caribbean it is into the wider opportunities they saw in the United States. The patterns and arguments for emigration are among the most interesting lenses through which to study the complexity of black life in the United States and around the world.

Edmund David Cronon, *Black Moses: The Story of Marcus Garvey and the Universal Improvement Association;* Nell Irvin Painter, *Exodusters: Black Migration to Kansas after Reconstruction;* Milton C. Sernett, *Bound for the Promised Land;* Joe William Trotter Jr., ed., *The Great Migration in Historical Perspective;* Henry J. Young, "Edward Wilmot Blyden" and "Marcus Garvey" in *Major Black Religious Leaders.*

Gospel Music

In the city of Chicago, Illinois, beginning in the 1930s, there emerged a fusion of the lyrics and passion of the **spirituals,** the hymns, and the camp meeting songs of the nineteenth-century white Protestant church and the syncopated rhythms of the blues and jazz. The result of that fusion of musical traditions is gospel music. From its beginnings in Chicago, gospel music has become a worldwide musical genre and a legitimate contender with pop music for radio and cable television airtime, concert ticket prices, and tape and CD sales.

Bernice Johnson Reagon in *We'll Understand It Better By and By* observes that "gospel music is both a repertoire and a singing style." Gospel music is a combination of what is being sung and how it is being sung. No one was more instrumental in establishing the initial repertoire of gospel music or the manner in which the songs should be sung than **Thomas A. Dorsey**. While **Charles Albert Tindley** and **Lucie E. (Williams) Campbell** were composing and performing prior to his emergence, it was Dorsey who became known as the father of gospel music.

Dorsey was a former blues musician who performed under the name of Georgia Tom and accompanied such renowned blues singers as Ma Rainey

during the 1920s. However, after he "got religion," he decided to bring his blues style of singing and playing and to reinterpret the way in which the established songs of the church could be sung. He also became the most prolific composer of gospel music, writing more than one hundred songs, many of which continue to be used by soloists and choirs. His most popular composition is "Precious Lord, Take My Hand."

Dorsey established the National Convention of Gospel Choirs and Choruses. This annual gathering of musicians and singers was the vehicle through which he spread the repertoire he was continually producing and through which he taught the manner in which he thought his songs should be sung. This network, along with regular appearances at the annual sessions of the **National Baptist Convention, USA, Inc. (NBCUSA)** helped make gospel music a national phenomenon and helped make Dorsey a household name.

Two women were instrumental in Dorsey's career. The first was Sallie Martin, his business manager, who promoted his music at conventions and concerts.

She often sang them first and then offered the sheet music for sale at ten cents per copy. The remarkable partnership between Dorsey and Martin is captured in the 1982 video on the life and times of Thomas A. Dorsey and Willie Mae Ford Smith, *Say Amen, Somebody.*

The other woman who was instrumental in Dorsey's career was **Mahalia Jackson**, who became the principal singer and interpreter of his music and of all gospel music being produced at that time. She began working with Dorsey in 1929 in Chicago. Jackson combined the singing power of the "shout singers" who sang the blues in her hometown of New Orleans with the fervor and deep spirituality of the Baptist and holiness churches in which she regularly appeared. Although she sang gospel music all over the world, she was reluctant to sing in concert halls and refused to sing in nightclubs, because she did not want her concerts to be mistaken as mere entertainment. Her songs were songs of praise and worship. That struggle to draw the line between praise and performance is a continuing challenge for gospel singers.

Many of Jackson's contemporaries were not as reluctant to cross that line as she was. Rosetta Tharpe performed in the Apollo Theatre in New York City in 1943. The Clara Ward Singers appeared at the Newport Jazz Festival in 1957. Jackson finally made some concessions and appeared at Carnegie Hall in 1950, at Newport in 1958, and at the inaugural of President John F. Kennedy in 1961.

The next person to greatly influence the repertoire and singing style of gospel music was **James Cleveland,** also of Chicago. As a singer, accompanist, and musical arranger, he was a force in gospel music for more than forty years. He is most famous as a singer for his recording of "Peace, Be Still." He is most famous as an arranger and accompanist for his work with **Albertina Walker** and The Caravans. He was also responsible for establishing the singing style of **Aretha Franklin,** who began her singing career in gospe music at her father's church in Detroit, Michigan. Cleveland planned and produced

Franklin's historic gospel concert in 1972 that resulted in the album *Amazing Grace.*

Like Dorsey, Cleveland saw the value of establishing a network through which gospel music could be spread. He organized the Gospel Music Workshop of America. At this annual gathering, usually held in Chicago, thousands of singers and musicians come to work on the repertoire and singing style of gospel music.

A watershed event took place in the history of gospel music in 1968 with the release of "Oh Happy Day" by Edwin Hawkins. Not only did this recording break the dominance of Chicago as the gospel music capital of the world, but also it heralded the emergence of a new repertoire and singing style that came to be known as contemporary gospel. This recording created a backlash among many gospel artists who thought that Hawkins had crossed the line from praise music to pure pop music. Nevertheless, the song sold seven million copies, was sung by choirs across the country, and won for Hawkins the first of his four Grammy Awards.

Hawkins was followed by other new composers such as **Andraé Crouch** and **Richard Smallwood.** The sounds of the blues and jazz began to be replaced by more contemporary rhythms and by a much fuller orchestration. New performers also began to emerge, including several members of the Hawkins and Winans families, Vanessa Bell Armstrong, Dottie Peoples, Larnelle Harris, and Fred Hammond. More recently Donnie McClurkin and Yolanda Adams have become internationally renowned gospel artists.

Over the last twenty years, many of the new gospel singers have begun to water down the lyrics of their songs, downplaying any explicit references to Jesus, God, Bible characters, or the vocabulary of Christian faith. One wonders at what point the music ceases to be gospel music and becomes another form of pop music. That is the concern that Jackson and Cleveland expressed over the preceding sixty years.

Gospel music took another step in terms of a repertoire and a style of singing with the career of **Kirk Franklin.** He has employed not only the singing style of the hip-hop generation but much of the dress and mannerisms as well. In doing so, Franklin has undoubtedly found a way to introduce gospel music and the message of faith that his music retains to people who might never enter a church to hear the music performed.

In addition to the denominational hymnals of the various black church bodies, many of the classic gospel music standards have been preserved in two books. The first was *Gospel Pearls* (1921), and the second is *Songs of Zion* (1981). Gospel music is in its seventieth year, and it shows no signs of losing its appeal.

Bobby Jones, *Touched by God;* Bernice Johnson Reagon, ed., *We'll Understand It Better By and By;* Eileen Southern, *The Music of Black Americans;* Wyatt Tee Walker, *"Somebody's Calling My Name."*

☺ Holiness Movement

The roots of the holiness movement extend to the Wesleyan doctrine of sanctification, but the movement's origins are in the years from 1867 to 1887, when the doctrine of perfectionism emerged within the American church. There was much controversy over whether those who were pursuing perfectionism had to remain within the Methodist structure. By the mid-1890s, the holiness movement had moved beyond its original Methodist beginnings and had become an independent movement.

Within the life of the African American church, holiness was first introduced by **Charles Price (C. P.) Jones** and **Charles Harrison (C. H.) Mason,** who attempted to add the issue of perfectionism (sanctification) to their Baptist polity. They were voted out of the Baptist church for their insistence on including holiness as a second stage of Christian formation; first is justification, which is the forgiveness of sins, and then is sanctification or perfectionism, which is being baptized in the Holy Spirit and being made perfect in love. This baptism in the Holy Spirit is also called the second work of grace and results in making a person holy.

Mason and Jones formed **The Church of God in Christ (COGIC)** as a holiness movement in 1897. It was not until 1907, when Mason returned to Memphis from the **Azusa Street revival,** that the additional emphasis on a Pentecostal experience (glossolalia, or speaking in tongues) was added to COGIC polity. Jones objected to adding the Pentecostal emphasis, much as the Baptists had objected to having the holiness emphasis added to their polity. Jones left COGIC in 1909 after a two-year court battle over whether he or Mason had the right to keep the name Church of God in Christ. Mason prevailed in that legal action; Jones left to form **The Church of Christ,**

(**Holiness**), **USA.** That church continues to this day as the first of the black holiness movements.

There is some confusion over how to distinguish between holiness and Pentecostal churches. The most consistent distinction involves the role of glossolalia, or speaking in tongues. Both the holiness and the vast majority of the Pentecostal groups affirm the need for sanctification, but all Pentecostals affirm the importance of speaking in tongues, or what is known as the third gift of grace. Most holiness groups do not embrace that doctrine as a necessity for salvation.

Lincoln and Mamiya note that approximately 100,000 African Americans are affiliated with four predominantly black holiness movements. Those four movements are Church of the Living God (1889), Free Christian Zion Church of Christ (1905), C. P. Jones's Church of Christ (Holiness) USA (1909), and National Convention of the Churches of God Holiness (1914). Another significant number of African Americans are affiliated with several predominantly white holiness groups, including the Church of the Nazarene (1895) and the Church of God (Anderson, Indiana, 1881). **James Earl Massey** is a leading minister of the latter group.

Ithiel C. Clemmons, *Bishop C. H. Mason and the Roots of the Church of God in Christ;* C. Eric Lincoln and Larry H. Mamiya, *The Black Church in the African American Experience;* Elsie W. Mason, "Bishop C. H. Mason and the Church of God in Christ," in *African American Religious History: A Documentary Witness,* 2d ed., ed. Milton C. Sernett; Daniel G. Reid, et al., "Holiness Movement," in *Dictionary of Christianity in America;* H. Shelton Smith, Robert T. Handy, and Lefferts A. Loetscher,

American Christianity, Volume II, 1820–1960; Joseph R. Washington Jr., *Black Religion.*

☻ Interdenominational Theological Center (ITC)

This theological seminary located in Atlanta, Georgia, is a cooperative arrangement among six schools representing six Christian denominations. The member schools are Gammon Theological Seminary (United Methodist Church), Morehouse School of Religion (Baptist), Phillips School of Theology (Christian Methodist Episcopal), Turner Theological Seminary (African Methodist Episcopal), Johnson C. Smith Theological Seminary (Presbyterian), and the Charles H. Mason Theological Seminary (The Church of God in Christ).

The school was founded in 1958 and is part of the extensive Atlanta University Center, which also includes several undergraduate colleges and Atlanta University. ITC also has cooperative relations with Emory University in Atlanta.

www.itc.edu

☻ Invisible Institution

E. Franklin Frazier used this term to describe the religious practices of slaves during the eighteenth and nineteenth centuries. Those services occurred on the plantations, often in the presence of white overseers and frequently with a heavy focus either on life in heaven after death or on the comfort that God can give to help slaves live under oppression. The religious services were typically conducted by a slave preacher who had some limited knowledge of the Bible and had experienced a call to preach that was affirmed by whites and blacks. **John Jasper** fit into this category.

The term "invisible institution" was used by Frazier to distinguish between the religious practices of those blacks still living in slavery and those free blacks who were organizing denominations such as the **African Methodist Episcopal (AME) Church,** the **African Methodist Episcopal Zion (AME Zion) Church,** and the **Colored (Christian) Methodist Episcopal (CME) Church.** Frazier referred to those black church denominations as the institutional church. These two groups blended together after the Civil War, when the black Methodist bodies began actively to evangelize among the newly freed slaves throughout the South.

Although Frazier did not intend this usage, the term "invisible institution" also came to represent those instances when slaves would meet outside of the view of whites. In those clandestine meetings, they might worship with more fervor than they would in the presence of whites. They might also plan their escape or other acts of resistance, using the language or images of the Bible as the basis for their actions.

Yet another use of this term deals with the issue of coded language. Many of the slave songs were believed to carry a double meaning that allowed slaves to communicate with one another in the presence of whites but to keep the real meaning of their conversation from being known.

Consider the song "Way down yonder by myself and I couldn't hear nobody pray." That song was not just about a poor soul who was expressing regret because he could not hear the voice of any other person praying to God. That song was said to be a statement to slaves who had been involved in a clandestine meeting the night before. It was someone's job to listen while the meeting was going on to see if the sounds could be heard by those in the master's or the overseer's house. The song meant that nobody had heard them when they prayed together the night before. It must be remembered that after the Denmark Vesey uprising in 1822 and even more after **Nat Turner's** rebellion in 1831, it was illegal for more than five blacks to gather without a white person being present.

The songs "Steal Away to Jesus" and "Swing Low, Sweet Chariot" also had double meanings. When slaves sang those songs they were communicating among themselves about the Underground Railroad passing through for any slaves willing to risk running away from their life of bondage. A slave could sing that song in the presence of the master or the overseer, who would not have known the message that was being communicated. That too was part of the invisible institution.

Melville J. Herskovits, *The Myth of the Negro Past;* E. Franklin Frazier, *The Negro Church in America.*

☾ Islam in the African American Community

It would be a mistake for anyone to assume that the influence of Islam as a religious alternative to Christianity among African Americans is either recent or insignificant. The presence of Islam among African Americans is as old as the beginnings of the slave trade into North America, when many of the persons who were forcibly brought to this country came from nations that had been under Islamic influence for more than five hundred years. Thus Christianity was replacing Islam as the religion of choice for many Africans. This preference for Islam would remain strong for as long as direct importation of slaves from Africa into the United States continued. Only when slave owners began to breed slaves instead of import them did the influence of Islam begin to diminish.

Even into the nineteenth century, many slaves who were being introduced to Christianity through various evangelistic activities were adapting the Christian faith in ways that allowed them to continue to adhere to Islam. Charles Colcock Jones, a leader in the movement to evangelize slaves during that period, made this observation in his manual, *The Religious Instruction of Negroes in the United States* (1842): "The Mohammedan Africans remaining of the old stock of importations, although accustomed to hear the Gospel preached, have been known to accommodate Christianity to Mohammedans. God, they say, is Allah, and Jesus Christ is Mohammed—the religion is the same, but different countries have different names."

Part of the approach to population control used by slave owners in the United States was to eliminate as many aspects of life in the slaves' native land as possible. For that reason, the slaves' allegiance to Islam was repressed along with many other traditional beliefs and practices. Over time, therefore, the influence of Islam

among African Americans did become negligible. By the turn of the twentieth century, it had all but passed away.

However, when **Noble Drew Ali** appeared in Newark, New Jersey, in 1913, he was trying to resurrect the historic connection between African Americans and Islam through the Moorish Science Temple. He urged his followers to call themselves Moors and to adopt Islam, which was the religion of the Moors of North Africa. He was followed by **W. D. Fard,** who organized the **Nation of Islam** in Detroit in 1930. He too was calling African Americans back to their historic connection to Islam, a connection of which many black people at that time were unaware.

Elijah Muhammad, a disciple of Fard, extended the idea of black people converting to Islam even further during his forty years of leadership over the Nation of Islam. However, the teachings of Fard and Elijah Muhammad were widely different from the teachings of orthodox Islam. The reach of Islam became wider still as a result of the ministry of **Malcolm X** in the 1950s and 1960s. The conversion of heavyweight boxing champion Cassius Clay, who took the new name of Muhammad Ali, was probably as significant as anything done by any of the other persons mentioned.

The influence of Islam reached further still and began to encompass more of the teachings of orthodox Islam with the conversion of the basketball superstar Kareem Abdul Jabbar and many other professional athletes. In 1975, following the death of Elijah Muhammad, his son **Warithuddin (Wallace Deen) Muhammad** began to transform the

Nation of Islam into an orthodox Muslim community. Many of his followers remained in his new movement, the American Muslim Mission. Others blended into existing orthodox Muslim mosques in their communities.

In 1978 **Louis Farrakhan** split with Warithuddin Muhammad and reestablished the Nation of Islam, though even he did not reinitiate all of the original teachings of Fard and Elijah Muhammad. As a result, Islam is present within most urban black communities in one of three forms: Nation of Islam, American Muslim Mission, or an increasing number of black people who are converting to orthodox Islam.

Mattias Gardell, *In the Name of Elijah Muhammad: Louis Farrakhan and the Nation of Islam;* C. Eric Lincoln, *The Black Muslims in America;* Gayraud S. Wilmore, *Black Religion and Black Radicalism;* Malcolm X and Alex Haley, *The Autobiography of Malcolm X.*

Jackleg Preacher

The precise origin of this term is unknown, but it certainly dates back to the time of the slave preachers of the eighteenth and nineteenth centuries who, in the absence of any opportunity for religious training of any kind, simply relied on volume and emotionalism to move their listeners. Albert Raboteau in *Slave Religion* speaks about "Uncle Jack," a popular slave preacher in Virginia. Thus, the term may have begun with reference to an actual person.

The term did not become derogatory until after the end of slavery, when some black preachers continued to rely on volume and emotionalism, and sought neither formal theological training, denominational affiliation, or any other form of accountability. The term also began to carry the sense of a preacher who was unscrupulous in terms of personal conduct or professional integrity, or both. In his book, *The Black Preacher in America,* Charles V. Hamilton underscores this issue of unethical conduct, coupled with a lack of accountability, as the primary components that shape the term jackleg preacher.

Obviously, there are many black preachers who have never received formal theological training or who minister within the context of independent congregations who are in no sense to be viewed as jackleg preachers. Their ministries have been productive because their sense of call was powerful, their spiritual giftedness was apparent, and their sense of personal integrity was unchallenged. Many such preachers have earned the honorific title **"Doc."** By the same token, there have been preachers who have had the best theological training and have had good standing within denominational structures whose personal and professional conduct were inconsistent with the values they preached. Over the years, it has been the combination of unscrupulous conduct and excessive emotionalism that were being conveyed by the term *jackleg preacher.*

The Black Preacher in America by Charles V. Hamilton; *Slave Religion,* by Albert Raboteau.

Kwanzaa

Kwanzaa is not a religious festival but an African American cultural festival that was created by Maulana "Ron" Karenga, chairman of the black studies program at the University of California at Long Beach. The term *Kwanzaa* is a Swahili word that means "the first fruits of the harvest." Thus it is a symbolic reminder of the agrarian life that black people in Africa and America once knew. Kwanzaa is a seven-day ceremony, with each day devoted to one of seven principles that are designed to promote values and enhance community among African Americans.

The seven principles are *Umoja*, which means unity among black people; *Kujichagulia*, which calls for increased self-determination by individuals, families, and the community; *Ujima*, which means collective work and mutual responsibility; *Ujamaa*, which is a call for cooperative economics for the mutual advancement of the community; *Nia*, which means purpose or setting an agenda; *Kuumba*, which calls for creativity in all aspects of life and work; and *Imani*, which means faith. It is not clear in who or what that faith should be placed, whether it is God, one another, or one's self.

Kwanzaa extends from December 26 to January 1. It is observed in homes, community centers, and even in churches. This celebration has often been misunderstood as an alternative to Christmas for black people in America. Maulana Karenga may have intended Kwanzaa to be an alternative to Christmas for the followers of the Kawaida faith that he also established in his role as founder and leader of a movement called US. However, for those black people who do observe Kwanzaa it is more a cultural celebration than a faith commitment equivalent to Christianity or Islam.

The Kwanzaa ceremony involves a table that is adorned with symbols such as a candleholder, the seven candles that represent the seven principles, fruits and vegetables, ears of corn, a place mat, gifts meant to be shared, and a cup used for various purposes during the ceremony. The use of these symbols makes Kwanzaa reminiscent of the Jewish festival of Passover with the ceremonial foods and the festival of Hanukkah and the menorah that holds nine candles. However, Kwanzaa is meant to be a distinctly African American festival designed to build an increased sense of community in this country and an increased affinity with the African past.

Deirdre Mullane, "Kwanzaa," in *Crossing the Danger Water*; A. P. Porter, *Kwanzaa*.

☻ Long Meter Singing

One of the traditions that links the worship style of black churches in the slave era to worship services today is the continued use of what is known as long meter singing. This is a form of congregational singing that is call and response in nature. The song leader "lines out" a certain phrase with the proper pitch, rhythm, and tune that should be used. Then the congregation responds with that lyric, pitch, rhythm, and tune. The technique of lining out a hymn dates to the time when widespread illiteracy made written hymns and music inaccessible to many black worshipers. Through this method of singing, all one had to do was repeat exactly what one was hearing from the leader. The pace was usually very slow so that one could follow along with the congregation. Eventually a substantial number of songs could be learned through this method and sung from memory.

A sample of long meter singing would include such lyrics as:

Alas, and did my Savior bleed, and did my Sovereign die

That phrase would be repeated by the congregation. Then the leader would line out these words:

Would he devote that sacred head for such a worm as I?

That line would then be repeated. The same pattern could be used with such songs as "A charge to keep have I, a God to glorify.... A never dying soul to save and fit it for the sky," or "I love the Lord, he heard my cry and pitied every groan.... Long as I live and troubles rise I'll hasten to his throne." The number of standard hymns that can be presented through this long meter method of lining out the words is almost unlimited.

In many circles within the black church community long meter hymns are often referred to as a Dr. Watts, referring to the many hymns written by Isaac Watts that lend themselves to this method of call and response singing. Other hymns by Isaac Watts that have been used in long meter fashion would include "Come We That Love the Lord," "O God Our Help in Ages Past," and "Come, Holy Spirit, Heavenly Dove."

While long meter can still be heard in many churches throughout the country, it is waning in popularity and frequency of use for several reasons. First, fewer and fewer people are hearing this call and response approach to singing. It is a form of singing associated with being reared in the rural South; persons who were born and reared outside of that region may be unfamiliar with this kind of singing. Thus they do not know how to perform long meter songs, which allow that kind of singing to be passed on to the next generation. Second, with literacy no longer the major obstacle to the use of a hymnal, many people use the standard hymns and the standard tune, pitch, and rhythm. Many black church denominations publish and distribute their own hymnals without making any effort to preserve the melodies and rhythms of long meter music. Third and perhaps most important is the increased use of the modern gospel songs of such popular, contemporary song writers as **Richard Smallwood, Kirk Franklin, Andraé Crouch,** Donnie McClurken, and others. As the new songs gain in popularity among choirs and congregations, long meter singing may soon pass from the scene.

Bernice Johnson Reagon, ed., *We'll Understand It Better By and By;* Wyatt Tee Walker, *"Somebody's Calling My Name"* and *The Soul of Black Worship.*

☾ Nation of Islam

When **W. D. Fard** appeared in Detroit, Michigan, in 1930 claiming to have come from Mecca, Saudi Arabia, with a message of truth and freedom for black people in North America, the organization he formed was called the Nation of Islam. At the time, it was essentially one of the many cultic groups springing up in the urban centers of the North during the Great Migration and the Great Depression. During Fard's lifetime the movement sought to communicate the message that blacks in America were the lost tribe of Shabazz. He taught his followers that they had to abandon their allegiance to Christianity and embrace Islam as their true religion. He urged his followers to abandon their last names, calling them "slave names." He then assigned them the last name of X until a more appropriate Islamic name could be assigned. How-ever, he also taught a five-point doctrine that included the following:

- Black people were the original people on the earth.
- White people were a genetic accident created by a doctor named Yakub.
- White domination of the earth will last for 6,070 years and end in 1984.
- Fard's teachings will result in Christianity and Buddhism being swept away.
- Orthodox Islam will recognize the Nation of Islam as the true expression of the will of Allah.

These and other teachings were set down in two books, *The Secret Ritual of the Nation of Islam* and *Teaching for the Lost-Found Nation of Islam in a Mathematical Way.*

When Fard suddenly disappeared (some think that he was murdered) in June 1934, the leadership of the Nation of Islam fell to **Elijah Muhammad,** formerly Elijah Poole, who had been one of Fard's earliest and most ardent converts and supporters. At that time, the organization had approximately eight thousand members. Muhammad served in that position until his death in 1975. During that time he developed the Nation of Islam beyond its early cult status and into a major nationalist/separatist movement with a membership that may have reached as high as five hundred thousand nationally.

With headquarters in Chicago, Illinois, the Nation of Islam had adherents who met inside of buildings called Muhammad's Temple in every section of the country. The Nation operated the University of Islam, which was an alternative school for the children in the movement. Fard and Muhammad were imprisoned for failing to enroll their children in the public schools, preferring for

them that parochial education. They also owned and operated a string of restaurants, dry cleaners, barbershops, and bakeries. Their largest venture during the 1950s and 1960s was the operation of one-thousand-acre farms in Michigan and Georgia that provided jobs and wholesale goods for sale in the retail market. At the height of its influence in the early 1960s, the Nation of Islam was the embodiment of **Marcus Garvey**'s emphasis on black separatism and Booker T. Washington's focus on black economic self-sufficiency.

The Nation of Islam claimed most of its earliest converts from the slums of inner-city America and from the prison cells where "fishing" recruited persons for membership who would then affiliate with a local temple upon their release. That is how Elijah Muhammad recruited his most famous and most effective convert, **Malcolm X** (formerly Malcolm Little), in 1952. Much like the apostle Paul, Malcolm X traveled the country preaching the doctrines of Muhammad and establishing new Muhammad's Temples wherever he went.

The Nation of Islam came to national attention primarily through two events. The first was the 1959 television documentary *The Hate That Hate Produced,* hosted by Mike Wallace. The program was essentially television coverage of a Savior's Day event when the Nation of Islam honors the memory of its founder, Fard. The second event was publication of *The Black Muslims in America* (1961) by **C. Eric Lincoln.** Lincoln coined the phrase "black Muslims." National media coverage and the prominence of Malcolm X, who by 1964 was the second most vis-

ible public speaker in America after Barry Goldwater, meant that the Nation of Islam had become front-page news. Malcolm X broke away from the Nation of Islam in 1964 and in 1965 was assassinated by a group of persons that included a member of the Nation of Islam.

Following the death of Muhammad in 1975, leadership of the Nation of Islam fell to his son **Warithuddin (Wallace Deen) Muhammad.** He began almost immediately to transform the Nation from a black nationalist/separatist movement into an orthodox Muslim community. In 1976 he changed the name of the movement from Nation of Islam to the World Community of Al-Islam in the West. The name changed again in 1978 and became known as the American Muslim Mission. Virtually all of the ideology and theology taught by Fard and Elijah Muhammad was abandoned.

The fourth and present stage in the evolution of the Nation of Islam began on November 8, 1977. That is when **Louis Farrakhan,** minister of Muhammad's Temple #7 in New York City, broke away from Warithuddin Muhammad, objecting to the changes he was imposing on the organization. Farrakhan reclaimed the name Nation of Islam and restored much of the separatist/nationalist message that had been introduced by Fard and Muhammad in the 1930s. The former members of the Nation of Islam who remained followers of Warithuddin Muhammad have essentially merged into the wider orthodox Muslim community in the United States and have no organizational or theological connection to the movement that his father had led for forty-three years.

Mattias Gardell, *In the Name of Elijah Muhammad: Louis Farrakhan and the Nation of Islam;* C. Eric Lincoln, *The Black Muslims in America* and "The Muslim Mission in the Context of American Social History," in *African American Religion,* ed. Timothy E. Fulop and Albert J. Raboteau; Wallace D. Muhammad, "Self-Government in the New World," in *African American Religious History: A Documentary Witness,* 2d ed., ed. Milton C. Sernett; Gayraud S. Wilmore, *Black Religion and Black Radicalism;* Malcolm X and Alex Haley, *The Autobiography of Malcolm X.*

☯ National Baptist Convention of America (Boyd Convention)

In 1915, in a dispute over the ownership and control of the National Baptist Publishing Board, this convention was born from a division with the **National Baptist Convention, USA, Inc. (NBCUSA).** The question that divided black Baptists was neither doctrinal or theological. Rather, it was a matter of policy involving the leadership of the publishing board and the leadership of the convention at large: Does the publishing board belong to the convention, or is it an independent corporation?

A court ruling in Chicago, Illinois, in 1915 found that the publishing board should comply with the wishes of the NBCUSA. In response, the supporters of **Richard Henry Boyd** withdrew from the convention, and on September 9, 1915, at Salem Baptist Church of Chicago, the new convention was born. As Leon Fitts notes in *A History of Black Baptists,* the publishing board had been incorporated as a separate legal entity in August 1898. Thus no convention could claim control

of its operation, and its leaders could align themselves with any convention they chose. Thus Boyd aligned himself with the new National Baptist Convention of America.

While the convention was long referred to as the Boyd convention, Boyd never served as convention president. Instead, he and successive generations of his family have exercised influence over that convention through continued control of the publishing board. The continued influence of the Boyd family led to a split within the ranks of the National Baptist Convention of America. In 1989 a new body called the National Missionary Baptist Convention of America was formed. T. B. Boyd III was named chief executive officer of the National Baptist Publishing Board.

This practice of multiplication by division has plagued not only black Baptist congregations. It seems to be the central cause for the existence in 2001 of four separate and competing black Baptist denominations. The **Progressive National Baptist Convention (PNBC)** split from the NBCUSA in 1961. These four Baptist bodies, while born out of bitter controversy, vary in only modest ways in their structure and mission. All attempts to bring black Baptists under one organizational umbrella have failed, more as a result of stubborn leadership and institutional intransigence than as a result of any substantive theological or doctrinal differences.

It must be noted that the National Baptist Convention of America has continued to produce outstanding Sunday school materials under the leadership of its current president, E. Edward Jones, and Blanton Harper of the convention's Christian education board. Along with the standard curriculum of Bible studies and memory verses, this curriculum has added a section called Heritage House that incorporates on a weekly basis questions and answers based upon various aspects of black history. This curriculum serves primarily an adult and young adult group, but the board also produces materials for all ages. The commitment to producing excellent Christian education material that is relevant to a black church constituency is unchanged since the group's founding in 1915.

Theodore S. Boone, *The Split of the National Baptist Convention;* Leroy Fitts, *The History of Black Baptists;* C. Eric Lincoln and Lawrence W. Mamiya, *The Black Church in the African American Experience;* James Melvin Washington, *Frustrated Fellowship: The Black Baptist Quest for Social Power.*

☙ National Baptist Convention, USA, Inc. (NBCUSA)

Independent, nonplantation black Baptist churches began to emerge in the United States as early as the 1800s in Southern states such as Georgia and Virginia and in Northern cities such as Boston and New York. However, most attempts at organizing black churches beyond the level of local associations were unsuccessful, not least of all because of the realities of slavery and the general repression of most forms of religious organization among blacks as a result of the **Nat Turner** rebellion in 1831.

That began to change rapidly in the years following the Civil War. Several

attempts were made to organize the Baptist witness among black people in the North and the South. The Southern Baptist Convention (SBC) made it clear that it was not interested in or willing to allow any meaningful opportunities for black Baptists. It was also clear that the SBC would not advocate for the rights and protections of the freedmen during Reconstruction. As a result, black Baptists, who saw a national organization as a way to strengthen their advocacy for an improved quality of life for black people in America, needed to look elsewhere for a way to organize.

They began with the Consolidated American Baptist Missionary Convention in 1866. In 1873 the New England Baptist Missionary Convention was formed by some of the leading black Baptist pastors in the Northeast. In 1880 the Baptist Foreign Mission Convention was organized, replacing the now-defunct Consolidated Baptist Convention. Its focus was foreign missions in Africa. In 1886 the American National Baptist Convention was organized. This group sought to maintain cooperative relationships with various white Baptist bodies. In 1893 the National Baptist Educational Convention was founded in Washington, D.C., with a mission of trying to advocate and provide for an educated clergy among black Baptists.

On September 24, 1895, a group made a recommendation that a tripartite union between the National Baptist Educational Convention, the Baptist Foreign Mission Convention, and the American National Baptist Convention be enacted and that the new body be called the National Baptist Convention of the United States of America

(NBCUSA). Such a tripartite union had been proposed a year earlier that would have included The New England Missionary Baptist Convention and two other black Baptist bodies, but that partnership could not be established.

The NBCUSA was organized to advance all the initiatives that had been of particular interest to the various bodies that merged. Thus NBCUSA included a foreign mission board, a home mission board, an educational board, a Baptist young people's union board, and a publishing board. In 1900 a women's convention was added under the umbrella of the NBCUSA.

Elias Camp Morris became the first president of the convention and served until his death in 1922. He was followed by **Lacey Kirk (L. K.) Williams** (1922–1940), D. V. Jemison (1940–1952), **Joseph Harrison Jackson** (1953–1982), **Theodore Judson Jemison** (1982–1994), **Henry J. Lyons** (1994–1998), and William Shaw (1998–).

The convention underwent three divisions. In 1897 the Lott Carey Baptist Foreign Mission Convention emerged from the NBCUSA in a dispute over how to conduct foreign missions. The **National Baptist Convention of America** emerged in 1915 in a legal battle over the control of the publishing board. The **Progressive National Baptist Convention (PNBC)** was created in 1961 in a double controversy. First was the question of the tenure of the president of NBCUSA, who was accused of using unfair tactics to guarantee his reelection to office in the 1961 session. The second issue was the failure of the president of the NBCUSA to aggressively support the work of **Martin Luther King Jr.**

Despite these divisions and the crisis of confidence that hit the convention during the presidency of Lyons, who was sentenced to a prison term while serving in that office, the NBCUSA continues to be the largest of the non-Pentecostal black Baptist bodies. It has a headquarters in Nashville, Tennessee, and offers support to various colleges and seminaries across the country. It also has an impressive infrastructure of state conventions, regional Baptist associations, and local ministers' conferences.

Leroy Fitts, *A History of Black Baptists;* Lillian B. Horace and L. Venchael Booth, *Crowned with Glory and Honor: The Life of Rev. Lacey Kirk Williams;* Joseph H. Jackson, *A History of Christian Activism;* Thomas Kilgore Jr. with Jini Kilgore Ross, *A Servant's Journey: The Life and Work of Thomas Kilgore;* Peter J. Paris, *Black Leaders in Conflict* and *Black Religious Leaders;* James Melvin Washington, *Frustrated Fellowship.*

☻ National Conference of Black Churchmen (NCBC)

On July 31, 1966, a full-page statement called "Black Power" appeared in the *New York Times*. It had been drafted by Benjamin F. Payton of the National Council of Churches and signed by more than fifty of the leading black clergy in the country, most of them from the Northeast. It was the first significant challenge by black clergy to the southern-based, nonviolent leadership of **Martin Luther King Jr.** and the **Southern Christian Leadership Conference (SCLC)**. The ad hoc group that produced the document was called the

National Committee of Negro Churchmen. As its embrace of the concept of black power became more profound, the name of the group changed to the National Conference of Black Churchmen. It abandoned ad hoc status and became a formalized organization during a September 1967 conference in Washington, D.C., sponsored by the National Council of Churches.

NCBC played a substantive role in the formation of black caucuses in many predominantly white denominations, because it sought to foster increased collaboration in matters of social policy and political activism among the historically black denominations. NCBC also became a forum in which the ideas and arguments for **black theology** had their earliest hearing. **James H. Cone's** first book, *Black Theology and Black Power*, provided much of the material that the group debated for the next several years.

On July 4, 1970, NCBC issued a Black Declaration of Independence that roundly condemned the American government and white society for a string of offenses and acts of oppression directed against black people in America. It went so far as to threaten nonallegiance to the government if its demands were not addressed. The carefully worded language of the statement ended with this phrase: "We, therefore, the Black People of the United States of America ... declare that we shall be, and of Right ought to be, FREE AND INDEPENDENT FROM THE INJUSTICE, EXPLOITATIVE CONTROL, INSTITUTIONALIZED VIOLENCE AND RACISM OF WHITE AMERICA."

NCBC continued to meet throughout the 1970s and 1980s, but the group lost much of its focus after the initial debate about black power and black theology had subsided. Some attempts were made to establish contacts with black Christian leaders in Africa through a program called the Pan-African Skills Project. Members of NCBC did meet with leaders of the All-Africa Conference of Churches beginning in 1969. Papers from the 1971 conference were published in *Black Faith and Black Solidarity*.

National Conference of Black Churchmen, "Black Power Statement," in *African American Religious History: A Documentary Witness,* 2d ed., ed. Milton C. Sernett; Gayraud S. Wilmore and James H. Cone, eds., *Black Theology*.

☉ Pentecostalism

Pentecostalism is the movement that emerged out of the **holiness movement,** and it places primary emphasis on the experience of being baptized in the Holy Spirit and speaking in tongues, or glossolalia, as on the biblical day of Pentecost (Acts 2:1-13). Pentecostalism began in 1900 with Charles F. Parham, a white preacher in Topeka, Kansas. The roots of black Pentecostalism are traceable to **William Joseph Seymour,** the black Baptist preacher who had a Pentecostal experience and then made that doctrine the center of the **Azusa Street revival** in Los Angeles, California, between 1906 and 1908.

The theological controversy that attends this movement is the question of whether a person has to have a Pentecostal experience in order to give evidence of salvation. Pentecostalism can be viewed as a third step in the life of the believers who adhere to this doctrine: justification, sanctification, speaking in tongues.

Pentecostalism is the fastest-growing segment of the African American church. It is centered primarily in **The Church of God in Christ (COGIC),** which is now the largest black denomination in the country, with more than five million members. The movement is also rapidly expanding through the Full Gospel Baptist Church under Bishop **Paul Morton Sr.**

Iain MacRobert, "The Black Roots of Pentecostalism," in *African American Religion,* ed. Timothy E. Fulop and Albert J. Raboteau; Elsie W. Mason, "Bishop C. H. Mason and the Church of God in Christ," in *African American Religious History: A Documentary Witness,* 2d ed., ed. Milton C. Sernett.

☻ Progressive National Baptist Convention (PNBC)

On September 11, 1961, Rev. L. Venchael Booth of Zion Baptist Church of Cincinnati, Ohio, issued a call to disgruntled pastors within the **National Baptist Convention, USA, Inc. (NBCUSA)** to organize a new national convention. Booth and others wanted to address two issues of concern. One was the question of the length of tenure of the president of the NBCUSA and of the procedures by which a new president could be elected. The other was the refusal of the current president of the NBCUSA, **Joseph Harrison Jackson,** to lend the convention's support and prestige to **Martin Luther King Jr.** and the nonviolent direct action component of the **civil rights movement** that was

steadily building at that time.

Regarding the question of the tenure of the president of the NBCUSA and the procedures for an election, there had been attempts in 1960 and 1961 to defeat Jackson and replace him with **Gardner C. Taylor** of Brooklyn, New York. The 1960 convention held in Philadelphia, Pennsylvania, and the 1961 convention in Kansas City seemed evenly divided in support for Jackson and Taylor. After perceived voting irregularities, such as disqualifying certain delegates, stuffing the ballot boxes, and acts of voter intimidation, Jackson prevailed in both elections. In an apparent act of reprisal against the allies of Taylor, many officers within the convention were removed from their positions. Among those was King, who was then serving as vice president of the Congress of Christian Education.

Rev. L. Venchael Booth

The removal of King from his office points to the other sticking point within the leadership of the NBCUSA. Many of the pastors wanted the convention to take a more proactive position regarding the issue of civil rights. However, Jackson was extremely conservative in this area, preferring the more deliberate approach of the National Association for the Advancement of Colored People (NAACP) and the use of court challenges over the direct action and sometimes civil disobedience approach of King and the **Southern Christian Leadership Conference (SCLC)**. The removal of King from his office within the convention was viewed as having a double effect. It muted his voice within the convention, and it further distanced the convention from any identification with the civil rights movement.

On November 14–15, 1961, thirty-three clergy, representing twenty-two churches in fourteen states, met in response to the call from Booth, and the PNBC was born. The keynote speaker at the gathering in Cincinnati was **William Holmes Borders** of Atlanta, who had also been expelled from the NBCUSA. The presiding officer at the two-day session was J. Raymond Henderson of Los Angeles, California. The decision to form a new convention was decided by one vote. Following the decision to organize, **Timothy Moses (T. M.) Chambers** of California was elected as the first president of the PNBC. He served in that office from 1961 to 1967 and was succeeded by Taylor.

Following the initial presidency of Chambers, PNBC instituted a strict tenure rule that limited the president to two one-year terms. That eventually proved to be too restrictive, and the terms have now been extended to two two-year terms. Many of the leaders of the civil rights movement became active members of PNBC, thus establishing that convention as the primary Baptist witness for social justice in America in the second half of the twentieth century.

In terms of its organizational structure, PNBC appointed its first full-time general secretary in 1970 to oversee the work of the convention between annual sessions. That position was especially important given the short tenure of the president of the convention. A Baptist Foreign Mission Board was established in 1971 and supports missionary efforts in Haiti, Nicaragua, Grenada, and Nigeria. In 1971 the convention purchased the **Nannie Helen Burroughs** School in Washington, D.C., and that property now serves as the headquarters of PNBC. Christian education material is produced in partnership with David C. Cook Publishing Company. A journal called *Baptist Progress* is produced, and the *Progressive Hymnal* was first published in 1976. The convention also operates through a unified budget in which funds raised from all auxiliaries are accounted for through a single accounting procedure. That is another aspect of the progressive nature of PNBC.

It is a matter of some interest that the convention changed the date of its annual session from the week after the first Sunday in September to the week after the first Sunday in August. The September meeting date, still favored by NBCUSA, was a concession to the nature of black life in the rural South in 1895, when the

NBCUSA was initially organized. That week represented a break in the agricultural cycle, especially in places where cotton picking was the center of the economy. School for black children did not resume until after the cotton-picking season was over; thus that was the only week when a convention involving a largely rural black population could convene. That agricultural cycle no longer applied when PNBC was founded, and the August date seemed more practical in terms of family vacation and back-to-school schedules.

C. Eric Lincoln and Larry H. Mamiya, *The Black Church in the African American Experience;* Thomas Kilgore Jr. with Jini Kilgore Ross, *A Servant's Journey.*

☯ Santeria

One of the consequences of the encounter between West African people who were brought into Cuba and the Roman Catholic tradition that they encountered upon their arrival was the emergence of a distinctly African religion that continued to be practiced under the guise of Roman Catholic rituals and beliefs. That religion is called santeria, which means "the way of the saints," and it involves the veneration of the Orishas, the gods of the Yoruba people of West Africa.

In the Yoruba religion there are more than seventeen hundred Orishas, or divine spirits, that can be worshiped. Such blatant polytheism was disallowed by the Roman Catholic Church, whose influence in Cuba was strong during the slave era. In order to maintain their religious tradition of worshiping multiple Orishas, the Yoruba people gave the impression that they were honoring the three parts of the Trinity (Father, Son, and Holy Spirit). They also made use of the many saints of the Roman Catholic Church as objects through which they could appear to be faithful Catholics but were maintaining their links to their African past.

The practice of santeria involves four distinct principles. They are divination, sacrifice, the trance, and initiation. In divination one seeks a state of harmony with the gods that allows for enlightenment and even healing. That divination is brought on by the next two phases, sacrifice and the trance. Adherents of santeria frequently make live animal sacrifices to the object of their worship as a way of assuring their favor. The trance is a state of mind that is reached when the worshipers are involved in dancing and praying that results in an ecstatic state in which the celebrant appears to be physically possessed by the spirit of the Orisha that is being worshiped. In that ecstatic condition, the worshiper is able to reach a level of knowledge and serenity not available under any other circumstances. The final principle of santeria is initiation, the process by which a person joins the community by engaging in the sacrifice and the trance for the first time.

Although santeria began in Cuba, as Cuban people have left that island and spread out into places throughout North and South America the practice of santeria has accompanied them. Santeria has become a strong and visible influence in the United States. A 1993 U.S. Supreme Court decision upheld the ritual sacrifice of chickens, goats, and other animals as protected under the First Amendment of the Constitution. The items needed for the various kinds of sacrifices and other observances in santeria can be purchased in markets called botanicas. Those markets can be seen in many cities throughout the United States, but especially in Miami and New York City.

Joseph M. Murphy, *Santeria;* George Eaton Simpson, *Black Religions in the New World.*

☻ Southern Christian Leadership Conference (SCLC)

This civil rights organization was formed by a group of black clergy meeting at Ebenezer Baptist Church in Atlanta, Georgia, on January 10–11, 1957. The initial reason for forming the group was to coordinate the various demonstrations that were occurring throughout the South, most of them involving bus boycotts and the issue of equal access in public transportation. Thus the meeting in Atlanta was called The Southern Negro Leaders Conference on Transportation and Integration.

Bayard Rustin, who had been instrumental in helping to organize the bus boycott in Montgomery, Alabama (1955–1956), wrote seven working papers that became the basis for discussion at the conference. The group emerged with a determination to continue to engage in mass demonstrations that were meant to undermine the Jim Crow system of racial segregation in public accommodations. The name went through several changes, from Southern Negro Leaders Conference on Trans-

portation and Nonviolent Integration, to Southern Leaders Conference, and finally to Southern Christian Leadership Conference (SCLC).

The use of the word *Christian,* it was believed, would influence how whites would respond to the group, since at that time most of the Southern states were attempting to make the activities of the National Association for the Advancement of Colored People (NAACP) illegal. The notion of being a Christian organization was carried over into the mission statement of the group, which was "To Redeem the Soul of America." Through the use of boycotts, marches, and demonstrations, and through the use of sermons, prayers, and gospel singing, SCLC was a combination of the NAACP and the southern black church.

The original nine officers of SCLC were **Martin Luther King Jr.** of Montgomery, Alabama, president; C. K. Steele of Tallahassee, Florida, first vice president; A. L. Davis of New Orleans, Louisiana, second vice president; Samuel Williams of Atlanta, Georgia, third vice president; **Theodore Judson Jemison** of Baton Rouge, Louisiana, secretary; **Fred Lee Shuttlesworth** of Birmingham, Alabama, corresponding secretary; **Ralph David Abernathy** of Montgomery, Alabama, treasurer; **Kelly Miller Smith** of Nashville, Tennessee, chaplain; Lawrence Reddick (the only nonclergy) of Montgomery, Alabama, historian.

The best description of SCLC may be from Aldon D. Morris in *The Origins of the Civil Rights Movement,* who said,

"Thus, SCLC was anchored in the church, and probably could not have been otherwise. For it was these activist ministers who became the leaders and symbols of the mass bus boycotts, controlled the resource-filled churches of the black masses, had economic independence and flexible schedule, were members of ministerial alliances that spoke the same spiritual and financial language whether in Brooklyn or Birmingham, and who came to understand that there is power harnessed in an organization."

Two things were important about the operation of SCLC. The first was the charismatic leadership of King, whose presence in any community brought with him the national news media, thus making that city or town the center of national attention. Second, while the elected leaders of SCLC were southern, the fundraising base for their activities was as much in the North and far West as in the South. Harry Belafonte was as responsible as anyone for generating funds from New York and Los Angeles. In addition to Belafonte, other black entertainers who raised money for SCLC were Sammy Davis Jr., Nat "King" Cole, and **Mahalia Jackson.** In addition, the boxer Floyd Patterson and the white actor Marlon Brando were quite active in this area.

SCLC comprised a series of affiliate chapters and organizations. There were SCLC chapters in all of the southern states, as well as affiliated organizations like the Inter Civic Council (Florida), the Alabama Christian Movement for Human Rights, the Mobile Civil Association, the Petersburg Improvement Association (Virginia), and many others. **Wyatt Tee Walker** reports that by 1961 at least eighty affiliates were scattered throughout the country. The ability of King to mobilize the national media and the ability of the local

affiliates to mobilize the grassroots community made SCLC a formidable force during the **civil rights movement.**

It is important to note that SCLC was instrumental in the formation of a largely student-based movement known as the Student Nonviolent Coordinating Committee (SNCC) in 1960. That group was formed at a conference on the campus of Shaw University in Raleigh, North Carolina, April 15–17, 1960. It was convened by Ella Baker, who was at that time the executive director of SCLC. That group went on to take the lead role in most of the sit-ins and the Freedom Rides (1960–1961).

In 1961 SCLC developed Operation Breadbasket as the program that would challenge white-owned businesses to do more business in the black community. Under the threat of economic boycott, white companies were challenged to hire more black employees, promote blacks already in the company to higher positions in management, or purchase some of their products and services from black contractors and suppliers. It was through the work of Operation Breadbasket that **Jesse Jackson** became a national leader.

Beyond its original nine officers, SCLC produced many of the most outstanding black leaders of the next twenty to thirty years, including **Andrew J. Young,** Jackson, **Walter Edward Fauntroy,** C. T. Vivian, Walker, Hosea Williams, Joseph Lowery, James Bevel and Diane Bevel, and **Thomas Kilgore Jr.** The group continues, now under the leadership of Martin Luther King III. With **Alfred Sharpton**'s National Action Network, SCLC cosponsored a demonstration in August 2000 that was a reenactment of the 1963 March on

Washington, during which King Jr. delivered his "I Have a Dream" speech.

Taylor Branch, *Parting the Waters;* Adam Fairclough, *To Redeem the Soul of America;* Aldon D. Morris, *The Origins of the Civil Rights Movement.*

⊙ Spirituals

Over the several hundred years that black people have lived, labored, and languished in the United States, they have given expression to their experience in a series of musical forms. Among these are the blues, which emerged from the Mississippi Delta; jazz, which traveled from New Orleans to Chicago and New York; and spirituals, which began in the fields and slave quarters of the South and have reached around the world.

The content of spirituals was greatly influenced by the slaves' exposure to the Bible and the stories and characters in that book that seemed to speak to their condition. The manner in which the songs were structured and originally sung probably links them to the musical traditions of Africa, to call and response, and to African rhythmic patterns. The songs served five distinct purposes. First, they were work songs that established rhythms by which gang labor could be coordinated and the drudgery of the day could be eased. Second, they were songs of faith that were sung during religious services or as part of a time of personal devotion. Third, many of these songs were used as a form of coded communication among slaves. Some spirituals were sung as a way of signaling that an escape, perhaps by way of the Underground Railroad, was scheduled for that night. Songs such as "Steal Away to Jesus," "Swing Low, Sweet Chariot," "Deep River," "Wade in the Water," and "Get on Board, Little Children," were used in that fashion.

Many spirituals fit more precisely into a subcategory called sorrow songs, a term first used by **W. E. B. Du Bois.** These were laments that spoke of the despair and sense of abandonment that gripped many slaves. Some of the sorrow songs are "Sometimes I Feel Like a Motherless Child," "Nobody Knows the Trouble I've Seen," and "Give Me Jesus." In each case, the message was one of hopelessness and despair in the face of the present circumstance and a transference of hope into life after death. That concept, known as compensatory religion or pie in the sky, will be discussed later.

Finally, many of the spirituals were crafted to be protest songs, indicating that God did not will that black people should be slaves and that freedom from slavery was something they should

Many spirituals originated as work songs among slaves in the fields.

pray for and work for. Such songs as "Go Down, Moses," "Didn't My Lord Deliver Daniel," "O Mary, Don't You Weep, Don't You Moan," and "Over My Head" were used in that way. When work songs, church songs, coded messages, sorrow songs, and protest songs are added together, they constitute that large body of music known as the spirituals. Like jazz and the blues, the spirituals are an authentically American musical genre created by the experience of black slaves in the eighteenth and nineteenth centuries.

Two events must be considered in order to explain how the music of black slaves became known around the world. One is the emergence in 1871 of the Fisk Jubilee Singers. In an attempt to raise money for their fledgling university in Nashville, Tennessee, this chorale began giving concerts. Between 1871 and 1878 this group had raised more than $150,000 for Fisk University through concert appearances across the country and around the world. At the heart of the repertoire were the spirituals, which at that time were also called slave songs. It is not surprising that these songs would be featured so prominently, since many of the members of the Fisk Jubilee Singers had learned these songs while they had been slaves.

The other event that helped propel the spirituals as a musical genre was the *Symphony of the New World*, written by the Czech composer Antonin Dvorak after he traveled throughout America in 1892. In that symphony and in the interviews and other public comments he made about it, he brought to the attention of the world an American folk music that

had emerged from the experiences and imagination of black people who had lived in slavery. Among the spirituals that are echoed in *Symphony of the New World*, according to Dvorak's biographer, Paul Stefan-Gruenfeldt, are "Swing Low, Sweet Chariot," "Somebody's Knocking at Your Door," "Didn't My Lord Deliver Daniel," "Roll, Jordan, Roll," and "Seeking for a City." The one spiritual that is most widely associated with *Symphony of the New World* is "Going Home," which is the second movement of the symphony and is called *Largo*.

Three different scholarly interpretations of the spirituals have been offered over the last one hundred years. The first is from Du Bois in "Of the Sorrow Songs," in *The Souls of Black Folk* (1903), where he says, "This is the music of an unhappy people, of the children of disappointment; they tell of death and suffering and unvoiced longing toward a truer world, of misty wanderings and hidden ways." Despite his emphasis on the sorrow expressed in these songs, Du Bois also heard some glimmer of hope in these songs, as if the slaves were in despair but not defeated. He says, therefore, "Through all of the sorrow of the Sorrow Songs there breathes a hope—a faith in the ultimate justice of things."

A second scholarly assessment of the spirituals comes from **Benjamin Elijah Mays** in *The Negro's God* (1938). He speaks about black religion flowing out of the slave era as being centered around the compensatory idea. This means that since justice, freedom, and hope are denied to slaves in this life, God will compensate them with a better life in heaven after they die. Under this approach to the spirituals, the emphasis is on the many references to heaven or to things that will happen once one arrives. Consider such songs as "I Got Shoes," which has the recurring line "When I get to heaven, gonna put on my shoes, gonna walk all over God's heaven."

Dozens of songs fit into this compensatory category. They include such spirituals as "Heaven Bound Soldier," "Gonna Ride in the Chariot in the Morning," "In That Great Gettin' Up Morning," "Walk in Jerusalem Just Like John," "Walk Together, Children," and "Po' Mourner's Got a Home at Last." One of the songs with a compensatory theme was popularized by **Martin Luther King Jr.** in his "I Have a Dream" speech (1963), which ended with these words: "Free at last, free at last, thank God Almighty I'm free at last." These and other songs that employed the compensatory theme were meant to make slaves passive and accepting of their present condition. Rather than rebel against slavery, they lived in the hope that everything denied them in this life, and more, would be provided in the life to come.

The third scholarly reading of the spirituals is shared by a group of scholars including John Lovell Jr. *(Black Song: The Forge and the Flame, The Story of How the Afro-American Spiritual Was Hammered Out)*, Miles Mark Fisher *(Negro Slave Songs in the United States)*, **Howard Thurman** *(Deep River)*, and **James H. Cone** *(The Spirituals and the Blues)*. Fisher speaks for this group when he says, "The spirituals tell of how Negroes attempted to spread brotherhood by the sword, took flight to better territory when possible, became pacific in the United States, and laid hold upon another world as a last resort." In short, the spirituals were the method by which black slaves sought to interpret, explain, and respond to their predicament in America. The songs were a coping mechanism that served different purposes at different times. These songs gave them strength to face the present and faith to await the future.

In the preface to the two-volume collection *The Books of American Negro Spirituals* (1925), James Weldon Johnson says that his interest in the spirituals was first aroused when he read a poem by Paul Lawrence Dunbar, *O Black and Unknown Bard.* One section of that poem says:

> *Heart of what slave poured out*
> *such melody*
> *As "steal away to Jesus"?*
> *On its strains*
> *His spirit must have nightly*
> *floated free,*
> *Though still about his hands*
> *he felt his chains.*
> *Who heard great "Jordan Roll"?*
> *Whose starward eye*
> *Saw chariot "swing low"?*
> *And who was he*
> *That breathed that comforting*
> *melodic sigh,*
> *"Nobody knows de trouble I see"?*

The repertoire established and popularized by the Fisk Jubilee Singers has been carried on by many subsequent black performers. Singers such as Roland Hayes and Paul Robeson did concerts that consisted entirely of spirituals. Other concert singers from Marian Anderson to Jessye Norman made the spirituals an essential part of a far more diverse repertoire of songs. However, Norman has released several albums that feature only the spirituals. Together with Kathleen Battle, she performed in a classic concert at Carnegie Hall in New York City on March 18, 1990, as a tribute to Marian Anderson that was called Spirituals in Concert.

☯ Theological Education and the Black Church

Two questions have perplexed those black persons seeking ordination in the ministry of the black church. They have been whether to pursue theological education and where such an education was being made available, and later relevant, for black people and the churches they would serve.

As early as 1893, **Charles Harrison (C. H.) Mason** dropped out of Arkansas Baptist College, believing that its curriculum, which included the work of biblical criticism, would dampen his enthusiasm as a form of worship and also corrupt his commitment to a literal understanding of the Scriptures. Mason typifies an understanding of the role and worth of theological education that continues in many black churches: It is more important to have burning than it is to have learning. It cannot be overlooked, however, that **The Church of God in Christ (COGIC)** now supports a seminary as part of the **Interdenominational Theological Center (ITC)** in Atlanta, Georgia, named in honor of Mason.

The experience of such persons as **Howard Thurman** and **Mordecai Wyatt Johnson** raises the second important issue

in this area, namely, where a theological education could be acquired for those who sought such training. These men, and many others, were denied entrance to their seminary of first choice because until well into the twentieth century many theological seminaries would not admit black students. As a result, many of the historically black denominations began to organize theological seminaries. The list of such schools would include Payne Theological Seminary (African Methodist Episcopal) in 1891, Hood Theological Seminary (African Methodist Episcopal Zion) in 1910, the Virginia Baptist Seminary (later to be supported by the National Baptist Convention USA) in 1890, and the American Baptist Theological Seminary (NBCUSA) in 1913.

Through the efforts of white denominations other theological schools also began to emerge that were meant to serve and equip black students for ministry roles. They included Shaw University and Divinity School (American Baptist) in 1865, Virginia Union University and School of Theology (American Baptist) in 1898, and Howard University Divinity School (Congregational or United Church of Christ) in 1870.

The most ambitious attempt to provide theological education for persons seeking to do ministry in the black church is the **ITC**. This collaboration of six denominations has been in existence since 1958. Access to traditionally white theological schools has become less of an issue in the last forty years. However, the matter of a relevant curriculum for those doing ministry in the black church continues to be debated and is being creatively addressed by the increasing number of black scholars on those faculties.

Of greater concern is the continuing problem of persuading black clergy that a theological education is relevant, beneficial, or important. Johnson puts this problem in historical perspective. He observed in 1927, in his inaugural address as the first black president of Howard University, that "there are forty-seven thousand Negro churches in the United States and there are in the whole country today less than sixty college graduates getting ready to fill these pulpits." The problem may not be as severe as it was in 1927, but it continues to be a concern that must be addressed.

One of the factors may be the escalating cost of a theological education. To that end, the work of such funding agencies as the Rockefeller Brothers Protestant Fellowship Fund and the subsequent Fund for Theological Education must be acknowledged. So too must we acknowledge the leadership of persons such as C. Shelby Rooks Jr., Oscar McLeod, and Bishop William P. DeVeaux, who were pioneers in these two funding ventures.

"Charles Shelby Rooks," in *Major Black Religious Leaders Since 1940,* ed. Henry J. Young; C. Eric Lincoln and Larry H. Mamiya, *The Black Church in African American Experience;* Daniel A. Payne, *Sermons and Addresses and Recollections of Seventy Years.*

☻ Vodun

Between 1730 and 1790, when African slaves were being imported in large numbers into the Caribbean island of Haiti, those Africans brought with them religious beliefs and practices that were common in Senegal, Dahomey, and the Congo. When those traditional African practices encountered and in many instances blended with aspects of Roman Catholicism that was also practiced in Haiti, the resultant religion was called vodun, also known as voodoo.

This synthesis of religious practices occurred with differing results all over the Caribbean region. As Melville Herskovits argues, largely refuting the claims of **E. Franklin Frazier,** many aspects of African culture did survive the Middle Passage, the auction block, and centuries of slavery. It was made possible whenever and wherever the slave population greatly outnumbered the white population and where slaves born in Africa were regularly being introduced onto the plantations, bringing with them the living memory of religious practices from their homeland. At the turn of the eighteenth century, Haiti had a population of six thousand whites and fifty thousand black slaves, so Haiti was an ideal setting for this synthesis to occur.

Vodun is a religion that centers around the veneration of more than 150 African gods called Loa, symbolized by a snake. These gods are intermediaries for a supreme God, and they communicate the wishes of the worshipers to the supreme God, whose answer is likewise filtered through the loa. Over time the loa became identified with the many saints of the Roman Catholic Church, and by appearing to venerate an acceptable Catholic saint, African slaves could continue to practice a form of their traditional religion. The practice of vodun continues in Haiti and in many places throughout the

United States where Haitian immigrants have settled.

Two schools of vodun survived in Haiti, and they are known as *rada* and *petro*. George Eaton Simpson in *Black Religions in the New World* and Herskovits in *The Myth of the Negro Past* suggest that the rada followers came from places in Africa that were primarily Yoruban in influence. The petro followers came from other tribal groups in West and Central Africa. In both cases, the practice of the religion involved sacrifices and ecstatic dancing. As a way of appeasing the loa and endearing themselves to the supreme God, worshipers brought sacrifices of animals or birds. They also provided drink offerings of alcoholic beverages.

The worshipers also engage in the most energetic forms of dancing that, it is hoped, will result in being possessed by the spirit of the loa. Once under that possession, the worshiper enters a trancelike state, engages in violent behavior, or engages in acts of animal decapitation and sacrifice. The dancing and the sacrifices are important because they are the method by which one can win the favor of the loa. Failure to do so, it is believed, can result in a series of catastrophes, including crop failure, sickness, or the death of one's relatives.

An essential aspect of a vodun cult is the priest, who is believed to possess magical powers and who knows how to invoke spells and other mystical-magical practices. Much of the negative depiction of vodun in popular American culture is limited to the misunderstanding and the overstatement of the activities of the priest, often referred to as black magic. It is believed that vodun priests and priestesses can conjure the loa to bring a positive or negative result in someone's life. The loa can be conjured to effect wealth, sickness, love, personal revenge, or zombi, which involves the loa going to work in the spirits of those who are already dead. Much of the mythology affiliated with such terms as "root doctor" and "using roots on somebody" are traceable to this more sinister aspect of the practice of vodun. Writing in *Slave Religion*, Albert J. Raboteau suggests that these aspects of vodun are best understood under the category of hoo doo or conjuring, both of which involved a belief in the power of a certain person to manipulate certain aspects of vodun to visit some misfortune upon another person. However, it is a mistake to limit one's understanding of the religion solely to these punitive practices and beliefs.

Vodun first entered the United States as a result of the Louisiana Purchase in 1803 and the slave uprisings that resulted in white owners bringing their slaves from Haiti to New Orleans from 1800 to 1809. The Louisiana Purchase allowed French-owned Louisiana and the important port city of New Orleans to become an American possession. When the French abandoned Haiti after the slave uprisings led by Toussaint L'Ouverture, hundreds of white slave owners and thousands of former Haitian slaves migrated to New Orleans. By 1850 vodun had become a major religious cult in New Orleans, and the vodun priestesses Marie Laveau and her daughter Marie II were legitimate cult leaders in that city between 1830 and 1880. Vodun is practiced in the United States wherever large Haitian populations have settled.

That includes New Orleans, Miami, and New York City.

Beyond vodun and **santeria,** other African religions have blended with Roman Catholicism to create distinct religious practices. The most notable is Candomble, which developed in Brazil, and Shango, which emerged among slaves in Grenada and Trinidad. However, only vodun and santeria also took root in the United States and continue to be practiced by many African Americans in this country.

Herbert S. Klein, *African Slavery in Latin America and the Caribbean;* Bruce Jackson, "The Other Kind of Doctor: Conjure and Magic in Black American Folk Medicine," in *African American Religion,* ed. Timothy E. Fulop and Albert J. Raboteau; Albert J. Raboteau, *Slave Religion;* George Eaton Simpson, *Black Religions in the New World.*

☻ Womanist Theology

Womanist theology is a theological construct that seeks to reflect on liberation issues not only as they touch upon matters of race and ethnicity but also as they touch on the unique and continuing status and oppression of black women within the life of the wider American society, the black community in general, and within the life of the black religious community in particular.

The principal architects of womanist theology are theologians **Katie Cannon,** Emilie M. Townes, Cheryl Townsend Gilkes, and Jacqueline Grant, and biblical scholars Renita J. Weems and Clarice J. Martin. Womanist theology is a critique of feminism, which has considered the exploitation of women but with not much

sensitivity to the unique experience of black women. Thus feminism is charged with practicing a certain form of racism. At the same time, womanist theology is also a needed and long overdue critique on the **civil rights movement, black theology,** and all other forms of liberation theology that have neglected to address oppression born of gender and sexuality.

The substance of womanist theology preceded the use of the term by which that substance is described. The term *womanist* is drawn from the earlier colloquial expression common among African American mothers and their daughters known as being "womanish." When a daughter begins to act older than her age, asks questions that seem a bit too mature in their content, or begins to show too early an interest in boys, her mother or another adult woman will say, "You're acting so womanish."

Womanism as a social and political term was coined by novelist Alice Walker in *In Search of Our Mothers' Gardens* (1983). In its first usage the term sought to blend the historic issues of feminism in general and the unique issues that arise when one thinks about African American women. What does it mean to be a black woman, and what does Scripture communicate to black women as they seek their full humanity, whether in the context of their family life, their depictions in popular culture, or their access to power in the churches in which they constitute the large numerical majority?

Womanist theology is the effort by black women theologians and biblical scholars to think theologically about what Grant refers to as the "tri-dimensional experience" of oppression based upon race, gender, and class. Grant began to ask the question about the role of black women in the leadership of the black church in "Black Theology and the Black Woman," found in *Black Theology*. In that essay, which precedes the coining of the term "womanist theology," she says, "In examining Black theology it is necessary to make one of two assumptions: (1) either Black women have no place in the enterprise, or (2) Black men are capable of speaking for us. Both of these assumptions are false and need to be discarded." Grant's work laid the foundation for what would subsequently be called womanist theology.

Cheryl Townsend Gilkes

Not only does womanist theology offer a critique of black and other liberation theology efforts, but also it asks how it was possible that so much of the work of earlier Protestant theologians managed not to make these connections of race, class, or gender any sooner. This is the same question that **James H. Cone** and other black theology proponents asked of Paul Tillich, Karl Barth, Reinhold Niebuhr, and others.

Finally, womanism or womanist theology seeks to argue that traditional feminist theologians have reflected about being female from within the assumptions of white privilege. Womanist theology draws upon the inspiration of **Sojourner Truth** and her "Ain't I a Woman?" speech given in Akron, Ohio, in 1851. In so doing, womanist theology seeks to demonstrate that living as a black woman in America is a very different experience, inside and outside of the church, from living as a white woman. That is because black women bear the triple burdens of race (black), gender (female), and class (poverty). Womanist theology seeks to determine what the Christian gospel has to say to persons living under this tridimensional oppression and what it has to say to the persons who are responsible for maintaining that oppression.

Katie Cannon, *Black Womanist Ethics* and *Katie's Canon;* Cheryl Townsend Gilkes, *If It Wasn't for the Women;* Jacqueline Grant, "Black Theology and the Black Woman," in *Black Theology,* ed. James H. Cone and Gayraud S. Wilmore; Jacquelyn Grant, "Womanist Theology: Black Women's Experience As a Source for Doing Theology," in *Encyclopedia of African American Religions,* ed. Larry G. Murphy, J. Gordon Melton, and Gary L. Ward; C. Eric Lincoln and Lawrence W. Mamiya, "The Pulpit and the Pew: The Black Church and Women," in *The Black Church in the African American Experience;* Clarice J. Martin, "The Haustafeln (Household Codes)," in *Stony the Road We Trod,* ed. Cain Hope Felder; Emilie M. Townes, *In a Blaze of Glory;* Renita J. Weems, *Just a Sister Away.*   ◻

Timeline of African American Religious History

FROM THE EIGHTEENTH CENTURY TO THE PRESENT

1701

The Society for the Propagation of the Gospel in Foreign Parts is founded in England, thus beginning the work of evangelism among slaves in the West Indies and British North America.

1750

James Varick, one of the founders and the first bishop of the **African Methodist Episcopal Zion (AME Zion) Church,** is born near Newburgh, New York.

1753

Lemuel Haynes, a patriot in the Revolutionary War and a Congregational minister, is born in West Hartford, Connecticut.

1760

Richard Allen is born on February 14 in Philadelphia, Pennsylvania.

1763

John Chavis is born free in North Carolina.

1773

A Baptist church is established at Silver Bluff, South Carolina, and **George Liele** begins his preaching career at that church.

1778

George Liele leaves for Jamaica.

1780

Lott Carey is born in slavery in Virginia.

1787

The Free African Society is founded by **Richard Allen, Absalom Jones,** and William White in Philadelphia, Pennsylvania. Later that year, Allen and Jones lead a group of black worshipers out of the St. George Methodist Episcopal Church to protest the practice of segregation in seating in the church.

1788

Andrew Bryan establishes a Baptist church in Savannah, Georgia.

1793

The Bethel Church is founded by **Richard Allen** and his followers on July 17 in Philadelphia. It is the first congregation of what would become the **African Methodist Episcopal (AME) Church.**

1796
- The Zion Church is founded in New York City by **James Varick** after he and several other black members withdrew from the John Street Methodist Episcopal Church of New York. The church was incorporated in 1801.

1797
- Isabella Baumfree (**Sojourner Truth**) is born in slavery in Ulster County, New York.

1800
- **Nat Turner** is born into slavery in Southampton, Virginia.

1801
- **John Chavis** is appointed a missionary to the slaves by the Presbyterian General Synod.

1804
- **Jarena Lee** is converted and begins her unsanctioned preaching ministry in the **African Methodist Episcopal (AME) Church.**
- **Absalom Jones** is ordained a priest in the Episcopal Church.

1807
- The First African Presbyterian Church is founded in Philadelphia by John Gloucester.

1809
- Abyssinian Baptist Church is founded in New York. African Baptist churches are also founded in Boston and Philadelphia.

1811
- **Daniel A. Payne** is born to free parents in Charleston, South Carolina.

1812
- **John Jasper** is born in slavery in Virginia.

1815
- **Henry Highland Garnet** is born into slavery in Maryland.

1816
- **The African Methodist Episcopal (AME) Church** is formally organized.

1817
- Samuel Ringgold Ward is born in Maryland.

1818
- **Absalom Jones** dies.

1820
- **Daniel Coker** sails for Africa to do missionary work on behalf of the **African Methodist Episcopal (AME) Church.**

1821

- **The African Methodist Episcopal Zion (AME Zion) Church** is organized.
- **Lott Carey** and other colonists arrive in Sierra Leone and resettle in Liberia in 1822.

1822

- **James Varick** becomes the first bishop of the **African Methodist Episcopal Zion (AME Zion) Church.**
- **Morris Brown** flees from Charleston, South Carolina, after the Denmark Vesey uprising is uncovered. Much of the planning for the failed uprising took place in the AME Church in Charleston where Brown served as pastor.

1825

- **Richard Harvey Cain** is born free on April 12 in Virginia. He goes on to become the first black person to serve in the U.S. House of Representatives, representing South Carolina in two separate terms.

1826

- **Peter Williams Jr.** is ordained and installed as rector at St. Philip's Episcopal Church in New York City.

1829

- **Samuel Cornish** and John Russworm begin publishing *Freedom's Journal.*
- The Oblate Sisters of Providence, the first black religious order in the United States, is founded in Baltimore, Maryland.

1830

- **Daniel A. Payne** opens a school for free blacks in Charleston. It is closed by the state in 1835 in reaction to the **Nat Turner** rebellion.
- **James Augustine Healy,** the first African American Roman Catholic bishop, is born in Georgia.

1831

- The **Nat Turner** slave rebellion takes place.
- **James Walker Hood** is born. He is the **African Methodist Episcopal Zion (AME Zion) Church** bishop after whom Hood Theological Seminary is named.

1834

- **Henry McNeal Turner** is born in South Carolina.

1837

- Amanda Smith, an independent missionary who was denied ordination by the **African Methodist Episcopal (AME) Church,** is born in slavery in Maryland.

- The first National Negro Catholic Congress is held in Washington, D.C.
- **Samuel Cornish** begins publishing the *Weekly Advocate,* which later becomes the *Colored American.*

1838

- **John Chavis** dies on June 13

1839

- **John Jasper** is converted and begins his preaching ministry.

1841

- **James W. C. Pennington** releases *A Textbook on the Origin and History of the Colored People.*

1843

- Isabella Baumfree changes her name to **Sojourner Truth.**
- **Henry Highland Garnet** delivers a speech at the Negro Convention meeting in Buffalo, New York, calling upon slaves in the South to take up arms and overthrow the slave system. Many abolitionist leaders condemn the speech on the grounds that Garnet's appeal is too radical.
- **Richard Henry Boyd** is born in slavery in Mississippi.

1851

- **Sojourner Truth** delivers her famous "Ain't I a Woman?" speech at the Second Annual National Women's Suffrage Convention in Akron, Ohio.

1853

- **James W. C. Pennington** becomes the first president of the National Council of Colored People.

1854

- **James Augustine Healy** is ordained a Roman Catholic priest in Notre Dame Cathedral in Paris, France.

1855

- **James W. C. Pennington** is forcibly thrown from a horse-drawn streetcar in New York City. He sues the company and wins.

1856

- Wilberforce University in Ohio is founded by the **African Methodist Episcopal (AME) Church.**

1863

- **Henry McNeal Turner** becomes the first black chaplain in the U.S. army.
- **Daniel Payne** becomes president of Wilberforce; he is the first black to serve as a college president in American history.

1865

- **Henry Highland Garnet** becomes the first black person to speak before the U.S. Congress when he speaks to the House of Representatives about the meaning of the end of slavery.
- **Adam Clayton Powell Sr.** is born in Virginia.
- **Charles Price (C. P.) Jones** is born in Rome, Georgia.

1866

- George Alexander McGuire, founder and first bishop of the African Orthodox Church, is born in Antigua, British West Indies.
- **Charles Harrison (C. H.) Mason** is born in Tennessee.

1868

- **W. E. B. Du Bois** is born in Great Barrington, Massachusetts.

1869

- **Hiram R. Revels** is appointed by the Mississippi state legislature to serve in the U.S. Senate; in 1870 he is sworn in.

1870

- The **Colored (Christian) Methodist Episcopal (CME) Church** is founded in Jackson, Tennessee.

1871

- The Fisk Jubilee Singers begin singing Negro spirituals to raise money for the university.

1875

- **James Augustine Healy** becomes the first African American to serve as a Roman Catholic bishop. He is assigned to Portland, Maine.
- **Carter G. Woodson** is born.

1876

- A statue is erected in Philadelphia in honor of **Richard Allen.** It is the first statue erected in honor of an African American.

1878

- **Nannie Helen Burroughs** is born in Orange, Virginia.

1882

- Sometime between 1877 and 1883, George Baker (**Father Divine**) is born.

1883

- **Sojourner Truth** dies in Battle Creek, Michigan, on November 26.

1884

- The African Methodist Episcopal *Review* is founded.

1886

- Timothy Drew (**Noble Drew Ali**) is born in North Carolina.

1887

- **Marcus Garvey** is born in Jamaica, British West Indies.

1890

- Mordecai Wyatt Johnson is born in Paris, Tennessee.

1894

- E. Franklin Frazier is born in Baltimore, Maryland.

1895

- National Baptist Convention, USA, Inc. (NBCUSA) is founded.
- W. E. B. Du Bois receives a doctor of philosophy degree from Harvard.
- The African Methodist Episcopal Zion (AME Zion) Church ordains Julia Foote as a deacon.

1897

- Alexander Crummell cofounds the American Negro Academy.
- Elijah Poole (Elijah Muhammad) is born in Sandersville, Georgia.
- The Church of God in Christ (COGIC) is founded as a holiness movement.
- The Lott Carey Baptist Foreign Mission Convention is founded.
- The National Baptist Publishing Board is founded by Richard Henry Boyd.

1899

- Thomas A. Dorsey is born in Georgia.
- Edward Kennedy (Duke) Ellington is born in Washington, D.C.

1900

- Julia Foote is ordained an elder in the African Methodist Episcopal Zion (AME Zion) Church.

1901

- John Jasper dies in Richmond, Virginia, at the age of eighty-nine.
- Charles Albert Tindley releases his first hymn, "I'll Overcome Someday."

1906

- William Joseph Seymour begins the Azusa Street revival.

1907

- Charles Harrison (C. H.) Mason reorganizes The Church of God in Christ (COGIC) as a Pentecostal movement.

1908

- Adam Clayton Powell Jr. is born in New Haven, Connecticut.

1911

- Mahalia Jackson is born in New Orleans, Louisiana.

1913

- Noble Drew Ali begins the Moorish Science Temple.

1915

- Henry McNeal Turner dies in Canada.
- Clarence LaVaughn (C. L.) Franklin is born in Mississippi.

● Gospel singer Rosetta Tharpe is born in Cotton Plant, Arkansas.

● The **National Baptist Convention of America** is founded.

1916

● **Marcus Garvey** emigrates to the United States and establishes the Universal Negro Improvement Association (UNIA) in New York City.

1924

● George Alexander McGuire organizes the African Orthodox Church in New York City. The church was formed in protest over the refusal of the Episcopal Church to elevate black suffragan bishops to the level of diocesan bishop and refusal to allow black suffragans to vote in the House of Bishops. The consecration was performed by the archbishop of the American Catholic Church. The church was not formally incorporated in New York State until 1941. McGuire had formerly worked with **Marcus Garvey.**

1925

● **Marcus Garvey** begins a two-year prison sentence in Atlanta, Georgia, on a conviction for mail fraud. He is given an early release on the condition that he agrees to be deported to Jamaica.

1926

● **Ralph David Abernathy** is born in Alabama.

● **Mordecai Wyatt Johnson** is appointed president of Howard University.

1927

● James Weldon Johnson publishes *God's Trombones.*

1929

● **Martin Luther King Jr.** is born in Atlanta, Georgia.

1930

● **W. D. Fard** organizes the **Nation of Islam** in Detroit, Michigan.

1931

● **James Cleveland** is born in Chicago, Illinois.

1932

● **Andrew J. Young** is born in New Orleans, Louisiana.

● **Thomas A. Dorsey** writes "Precious Lord, Take My Hand" following the death of his wife and first child.

1933

● Louis Eugene Wolcott (**Louis Farrakhan**) is born.

1934

● **W. D. Fard** disappears, and **Elijah Muhammad** becomes the leader of the **Nation of Islam.**

1940

● **James H. Cone** is born in Fordyce, Arkansas.

● **Marcus Garvey** dies in London.

● **Lacey Kirk (L. K.) Williams** is killed in a plane crash
in Flint, Michigan.

1941

● **Benjamin Elijah Mays** becomes president of Morehouse College.

1942

● **Aretha Franklin** is born in Memphis, Tennessee, on March 25.

1944

● **Adam Clayton Powell Jr.** is elected to the U.S. House of
Representatives and is sworn in the next year.

1952

● **Albert Buford Cleage** opens The Shrine of the
Black Madonna in Detroit.

1953

● Bus boycott in Baton Rouge, Louisiana, lasts for six days and ends
most forms of segregation on that city's buses.

● **Howard Thurman** is appointed dean of the chapel
at Boston University.

● The radio broadcast sermons of **Clarence LaVaughn (C. L.)
Franklin** begin to be distributed by Chess Recording Company
of Chicago, Illinois.

1955

● The Montgomery bus boycott begins on December 1,
and **Martin Luther King Jr.** is elected president of the
Montgomery Improvement Association.

● **James Herman Robinson** becomes the first black preacher to
deliver the Lyman Beecher Lectures at Yale Divinity School.

1957

● The **Southern Christian Leadership Conference (SCLC)**
is founded in Atlanta, Georgia.

● The National Prayer Pilgrimage featuring **Martin Luther King Jr.**
as the speaker takes place in front of the Lincoln Memorial in
Washington, D.C.

1958

● The **Interdenominational Theological Center (ITC)** is
founded in Atlanta, Georgia.

1960

● **Mordecai Wyatt Johnson** retires as president of Howard University.

1961

● The **Progressive National Baptist Convention (PNBC)** is formed.

● **Adam Clayton Powell Jr.** becomes the chairman of the U.S. House
Education and Labor Committee.

● **C. Eric Lincoln** releases *Black Muslims in America*.

Mahalia Jackson sings at the inauguration of President John F. Kennedy.

1962

John Melville Burgess is consecrated as suffragan bishop of the Episcopal Church in Massachusetts. He is appointed bishop in 1969.

Martin de Porres is canonized by the Roman Catholic Church.

1963

Martin Luther King Jr. writes his "Letter from a Birmingham Jail."

The March on Washington takes place; 250,000 people gather to call upon the U.S. Congress to pass the civil rights bill.

W. E. B. Du Bois dies in Ghana on the day of the March on Washington.

Four black girls die in the bombing of the Sixteenth Street Baptist Church in Birmingham, Alabama.

The National Black Evangelical Association is founded.

1964

Martin Luther King Jr. wins the Nobel Prize for peace and is named Man of the Year by *Time*.

Malcolm X breaks away from the Nation of Islam and goes to Mecca.

1965

Malcolm X is assassinated in New York City.

Bloody Sunday occurs on March 7 in Selma, Alabama.

The march from Selma to Montgomery, Alabama, takes place (March 21–25).

Duke Ellington performs the first of his three sacred music concerts.

Harold Perry becomes the first black Roman Catholic bishop in the United States in the twentieth century. He is assigned to New Orleans.

Father Divine dies in Philadelphia.

1966

Maulana "Ron" Karenga creates the festival of **Kwanzaa.**

1968

Martin Luther King, Jr. is assassinated in Memphis, Tennessee.

1969

James H. Cone releases *Black Theology and Black Power.*

Thomas Kilgore Jr. becomes the first black president of the American Baptist Churches, USA.

1970

The Society for the Study of Black Religion is founded.

1971

Jesse Jackson forms Operation PUSH (People United to Save Humanity).

1972

- W. Sterling Carey becomes the first black president of the National Council of Churches.

1974

- **Katie Cannon** becomes the first black woman to be ordained by the Presbyterian Church.
- Lawrence Bottoms becomes the first black person to serve as moderator of the General Assembly of the United Presbyterian Church, now part of Presbyterian Church (U.S.A.).
- C. Shelby Rooks becomes president of Chicago Theological Seminary. He is the first black president of a predominantly white seminary.
- **Peter J. Gomes** is appointed the senior minister at the Memorial Church on the campus of Harvard University.

1975

- **Elijah Muhammad** dies and is succeeded by his son **Warithuddin (Wallace Deen) Muhammad,** who begins to shape the **Nation of Islam** into an orthodox Muslim community.

1976

- Thelma Adair is the first black woman to be elected moderator of the Presbyterian Church in the U.S., now part of the Presbyterian Church (U.S.A.).

1977

- **Benjamin Lawson Hooks** becomes executive director of the National Association for the Advancement of Colored People (NAACP).
- **Anna Pauline (Pauli) Murray** becomes the first black woman ordained to the priesthood of the Episcopal Church.
- **Andrew J. Young** is appointed United Nations ambassador by President Jimmy Carter. He is later elected mayor of Atlanta in 1981 and 1985.

1978

- **Louis Farrakhan** breaks away from **Warithuddin Muhammad** and begins to return the **Nation of Islam** to its separatist and nationalist origins.
- **John Hurst Adams** forms the **Congress of National Black Churches (CNBC).**

1982

- **Joseph Harrison Jackson** ends his term as president of the **National Baptist Convention, USA, Inc. (NBCUSA).** He is replaced by **Theodore Judson Jemison.**

1983

- The birthday of **Martin Luther King Jr.** is declared a national holiday.

1984

- **Leontine T. C. Kelly** becomes the first black woman to be elected bishop of a major denomination (United Methodist Church).
- Philip Cousins, an **African Methodist Episcopal (AME) Church** bishop, becomes president of the National Council of Churches.
- **Jesse Jackson** campaigns for the Democratic Party nomination for president of the United States. He will run again in 1988.

1986

- **Jesse Jackson** forms the Rainbow Coalition.
- Eugene A. Marino is named archbishop of Atlanta, Georgia. He is the first African American to become an archbishop.
- The National Missionary Baptist Convention is formed.

1989

- **Barbara Harris** is consecrated as the first African American female bishop of the Episcopal Church.
- Joan Salmon Campbell becomes the first African American female selected to be the moderator of the Presbyterian Church (U.S.A.).
- **James Alexander Forbes Jr.** is named pastor of Riverside Church in New York City.

1990

- George Stallings is consecrated a bishop of the African American Catholic Church (AACC). This is a splinter group from the Roman Catholic Church that believes the Catholic church is not working hard enough to meet the needs of its black members. Stallings was also the senior pastor of the Imani Church. AACC congregations in other cities are named after the seven principles of the festival of **Kwanzaa**. Stallings's consecration as bishop was sanctioned by Archbishop Richard W. Bridges of the American Independent Orthodox Church on the West Coast.

1991

- Vinton Anderson, an **African Methodist Episcopal (AME) Church** bishop, becomes the first African American president of the World Council of Churches.
- **William H. Gray III** becomes president of the United Negro College Fund.

1992

- **Albertina Walker** appears in the Steve Martin film *Leap of Faith*.
- **Leon Sullivan** receives the Presidential Medal of Freedom from George Bush.

1993

- **Paul Morton Sr.** organizes the Full Gospel Baptist Church and becomes the first bishop of this Pentecostal movement.

1995

- **Louis Farrakhan** convenes the Million Man March in Washington, D.C.

- **Katie Cannon** releases *Katie's Canon: Womanism and the Soul of the Black Community.*

1996

- **Kirk Franklin** wins his first Grammy award as Best Contemporary Gospel Artist.

1997

- **Suzan D. Johnson Cook** is named to the President's Initiative on Race and Reconciliation by President Bill Clinton.

1999

- **Henry Lyons,** president of the **National Baptist Conference, USA, Inc. (NBCUSA),** is convicted on multiple charges and begins serving a prison sentence.

2000

- **Vashti McKenzie** becomes the first woman to be consecrated as a bishop in the **African Methodist Episcopal (AME) Church.** She is assigned to the 18th District of the AME Church, which includes several countries in southern Africa.

- **Gardner C. Taylor** receives the Presidential Medal of Freedom from Bill Clinton.

- **Andrew J. Young** becomes president of the National Council of Churches.

2001

- **Alfred Sharpton** and **Walter Edward Fauntroy** convene a protest rally in Washington, D.C., to criticize the selection and inauguration of George W. Bush as president of the United States.

- **Alfred Sharpton** is sentenced to ninety days in prison for protesting the U.S. Navy practice of bombing on the Puerto Rican island of Vieques.

An Essential Bibliography

Allen, Richard. *The Life Experience and Gospel Labors of the Rt. Rev. Richard Allen.* Nashville: Abingdon, 1960.

Asante, Molefi Kete. *The Afrocentric Idea.* Philadelphia: Temple University Press, 1987; revised edition, 1998.

Bennett, Lerone, Jr. Pioneers in Protest. Chicago: Johnson Publishing Co., 1968.

Billingsley, Andrew. *Mighty Like a River: The Black Church and Social Reform.* New York: Oxford, 1999.

Boddie, Charles Emerson. *God's "Bad Boys."* Valley Forge, Pa.: Judson Press, 1972.

Bracey, John, August Meier, and Elliott Rudwick. *Black Nationalism in America.* New York: Bobbs-Merrill, 1970.

Branch, Taylor. *Parting the Waters: America in the King Years 1954–1963.* New York: Simon and Schuster, 1988.

Brotz, Howard. *Black Jews of Harlem.* New York: Schocken Books, 1970.

———— ed. *Negro Social and Political Thought 1850–1920.* New York: Basic Books, 1966; second edition published by New York: Simon and Schuster, 1998.

Burgess, John M. *Black Gospel/White Church.* San Francisco: HarperSanFrancisco, 1985.

Cannon, Katie. *Katie's Canon: Womanism and the Soul of the Black Community.* New York: Continuum, 1995.

Cleage, Albert B., Jr. *Black Christian Nationalism: New Directions for the Black Church.* New York: Morrow, 1972.

————. *The Black Messiah.* New York: Sheed and Ward, 1968.

Clemmons, Ithiel C. *Bishop C. H. Mason and the Roots of the Church of God in Christ.* Bakersfield, Calif.: Pneuma Life Publishing, 1996.

Collier-Thomas, Bettye. *Daughters of Thunder: Black Women Preachers and Their Sermons, 1850–1979.* San Francisco: Jossey-Bass Publishers, 1998.

Cone, James H. *Black Theology and Black Power.* New York: Seabury Press, 1969.

————. *A Black Theology of Liberation.* Philadelphia: Lippincott, 1970.

————. *God of the Oppressed.* New York: Seabury Press, 1975.

————. *Martin and Malcolm and America.* Maryknoll, N.Y.: Orbis, 1991.

————. *The Spirituals and the Blues.*

New York: Seabury Press, 1972.

Cook, Suzan D. Johnson. *Too Blessed to Be Stressed: Words of Wisdom for Women on the Move.* Nashville: Nelson, 1998.

Cowan, Tom, and Jack Maguire. *Timelines of African American History: 500 Years of Black Achievement.* New York: Perigee, 1994.

Cronon, Edmund David. *Black Moses.* Madison, Wisc.: University of Wisconsin Press, 1960.

Cushmeer, Bernard. *This Is the One: Messenger Elijah Muhammad.* Phoenix, Ariz.: Truth Publications, 1970.

Day, Richard Ellsworth. *Rhapsody in Black: The Life Story of John Jasper.* Philadelphia: Judson Press, 1953.

Du Bois, W. E. B. *The Souls of Black Folk.* New York: Fawcett, 1961.

Dyson, Michael Eric. *Beyond God and Gangsta Rap.* New York: Oxford University Press, 1996.

Essien-Udom, E. U. *Black Nationalism: A Search for an Identity in America.* New York: Dell Books, 1962.

Fairclough, Adam. *To Redeem the Soul of America: The Southern Christian Leadership Conference and Martin Luther King, Jr.* Athens, Ga.: University of Georgia Press, 1987.

Fauset, Arthur Huff. *Black Gods of the Metropolis: Negro Cults of the Urban North.* Philadelphia: University of Pennsylvania Press, 1971.

Felder, Cain Hope, ed. *Stony the Road We Trod: African American Biblical Interpretation.* Minneapolis: Fortress Press, 1991.

———. *Troubling the Biblical Waters: Race, Class and Family.* Maryknoll, N.Y.: Orbis, 1989.

Fitts, Leroy. *A History of Black Baptists.* Nashville: Broadman, 1985.

———. *Lott Carey: First Black Missionary to Africa.* Valley Forge, Pa.: Judson Press, 1978.

Floyd, Silas Xavier. *Life of Charles T. Walker, D.D.* 1902. New York: Negro Universities Press, 1969.

Franklin, John Hope, and August Meier, eds. *Black Leaders of the Twentieth Century.* Urbana: University of Illinois Press, 1982.

Franklin, V. P. *Telling Our Truths: Autobiography and the Making of the African American Intellectual Tradition.* New York: Scribner, 1995.

Frazier, E. Franklin. *The Negro Church in America,* and C. Eric Lincoln, *The Black Church Since Frazier.* New York: Schocken, 1974.

Fulop, Timothy E., and Albert J. Raboteau, eds. *African American Religion: Interpretive Essays in History and Culture.* New York: Routledge, 1997.

Gardell, Mattias. *In the Name of Elijah Muhammad.* Durham, N.C.: Duke University Press, 1996.

Garvey, Amy Jacques, ed. *Philosophy and Opinions of Marcus Garvey.* Portland: International Specialized Book Services, 1977.

Gates, Henry Louis, Jr. and Cornel West. *The African American Century: How Black Americans Have Shaped Our Century.* New York: The Free Press, 2000.

George, Carol V. R. *Segregated Sabbaths: Richard Allen and the Rise of Independent Black Chuches, 1760–1840.* New York: Oxford University Press, 1973.

Gilkes, Cheryl Townsend. *If It Wasn't for the Women*. Maryknoll, N.Y.: Orbis, 2001.

Halliburton, Warren J. *Historic Speeches of African Americans*. New York: F. Watts, 1993.

Hamilton, Charles V. *Adam Clayton Powell Jr.: The Political Biography of an American Dilemma*. New York: Atheneum, 1992.

———. *The Black Preacher in America*. New York: Morrow, 1972.

Harris, Michael W. *The Rise of Gospel Blues: The Music of Thomas Andrew Dorsey*. Cary, N.C.: Oxford University Press, 1994.

Hatcher, William Eldridge. *The Biography of John Jasper*. New York: Fleming H. Revel Co., 1900.

Higginbotham, Evelyn Brooks. *Righteous Discontent: The Women's Movement in the Black Baptist Church, 1880–1920*. Cambridge, Mass.: Harvard University Press, 1993.

Horace, Lillian B. *Crowned with Glory and Honor: The Life of Rev. Lacey Kirk Williams*. Hicksville, N.Y.: Exposition Press, 1978.

Jackson, Joseph H. *A Story of Christian Activism: The History of the National Baptist Convention, U.S.A., Inc.* Nashville: Townsend Press, 1980.

Jones, Bobby. *Touched by God: Black Gospel Greats Share Their Stories of Finding God*. New York: Pocket Books, 1998.

Jones, Ralph H. *Charles Albert Tindley: Prince of Preachers*. Nashville: Abingdon, 1982.

Katz, William Loren, ed. *An Address to the Slaves of the United States of America by Henry Highland Garnet*. New York: Arno Press/New York Times, 1969.

Kilgore, Thomas, Jr., with Jini Kilgore Ross. *A Servant's Journey: The Life and Work of Thomas Kilgore*. Valley Forge, Pa.: Judson Press, 1998.

King, Martin Luther, Jr. *Strength to Love*. Cleveland: William Collins, 1963.

———. *Stride Toward Freedom*. New York: Harper Perennial, 1958.

———. *Where Do We Go from Here?* New York: Bantam Books, 1967.

———. *Why We Can't Wait*. New York: Signet Books, 1964.

LaRue, Cleophus. *The Heart of Black Preaching*. Louisville: Westminster/John Knox Press, 2000.

Lincoln, C. Eric, ed. *The Black Experience in Religion*. Garden City, N.J.: Anchor Books, 1974.

———. *The Black Muslims in America*. Boston: Beacon, 1973; third edition published by Grand Rapids, Mich: Eerdmans and Trenton, N.J.: Africa World Press, 1993.

Lincoln, C. Eric, and Lawrence W. Mamiya. *The Black Church in the African American Experience*. Durham, N.C.: Duke University Press, 1990.

Litwack, Leon, and August Meier, eds. *Black Leaders of the Nineteenth Century*. Urbana: University of Illinois Press, 1991.

Low, W. Augustus, and Virgil A. Clift, eds. *Encyclopedia of Black America*. 1981. New York: Da Capo, 1984.

Magida, Arthur J. *Prophet of Rage: A Life of Louis Farrakhan and His Nation*. New York: Basic Books, 1996.

Massey, James Earl. *The Burdensome Joy of Preaching*. Nashville: Abingdon, 1997.

Mays, Benjamin E. *Born to Rebel: An Autobiography of Benjamin E. Mays*. New York: Scribner, 1971.

McKenzie, Vashti M. *Not Without a Struggle*. Cleveland: Pilgrim Press, 1996.

McMickle, Marvin A. *Living Water for Thirsty Souls: Unleashing the Power of Exegetical Preaching*. Valley Forge, Pa.: Judson Press, 2001.

———. *Preaching to the Black Middle Class*. Valley Forge, Pa.: Judson Press, 2000.

Meier, August. *Negro Thought in America: 1880–1915*. Ann Arbor, Mich.: University of Michigan Press, 1973.

Mitchell, Ella Pearson. *Those Preachin' Women*. Valley Forge, Pa.: Judson Press, 1985.

Mitchell, Henry H. *Black Preaching*. Nashville: Abingdon Press, 1990.

———. *The Recovery of Preaching*. New York: Harper & Row, 1977.

Morris, Aldon D. *The Origins of the Civil Rights Movement: Black Communities Organizing for Change*. New York: Free Press, 1984.

Moses, Wilson Jeremiah. *The Golden Age of Black Nationalism, 1850–1925*. New York: Oxford University Press, 1978; updated in 1988.

Muhammad, Elijah. *Message to the Blackman*. Chicago: Muhammad's Mosque No. 2, 1965.

Mullane, Deirdre, ed. *Crossing the Danger Water: Three Hundred Years of African American Writing*. Garden City, N.Y.: Doubleday, Anchor Books, 1993.

Murphy, Joseph M. *Santeria: African Spirits in America*. Boston: Beacon Press, 1993.

Murphy, Larry, J. Gordon Melton, and Gary Ward, eds. *Encyclopedia of African American Religions*. New York: Garland, 1993.

Ofari, Earl. *"Let Your Motto Be Resistance": The Life and Thought of Henry Highland Garnet*. Boston, Beacon Press, 1972.

Paris, Peter. *Black Leaders in Conflict*. New York: Pilgrim Press, 1978.

———. *Black Religious Leaders: Conflict in Unity*. Louisville, Ky.: Westminster/John Knox, 1991.

Payne, Daniel A. *Recollections of Seventy Years. 1888*. New York: Arno/New York Times, 1968.

Payne, Wardell J., ed. *Directory of African American Religious Bodies*. Washington, D.C.: Howard University Press, 1995.

Philpot, William M., ed. *Best Black Sermons*. Valley Forge, Pa.: Judson Press, 1972.

Ploski, Harry A., and Ernest Kaiser, eds. and comps. *The Negro Almanac*. New York: Bellwether Co., 1971.

Powell, Adam Clayton, Jr. *Adam by Adam: The Autobiography of Adam Clayton Powell Jr*. New York: Dial Press, 1971.

Quarles, Benjamin. *Black Abolitionists*. New York: Da Capo Press, 1969.

Raboteau, Albert J. *Slave Religion: The "Invisible Institution" in the Antebellum South*. New York: Oxford University Press, 1978.

Reagon, Bernice Johnson, ed. *We'll Understand It Better By and By: Pioneering African American Gospel*

Composers. Washington, D.C.: Smithsonian Institution Press, 1992.

Reynolds, Barbara. *Jesse Jackson: The Man, the Myth, the Movement.* Chicago: Nelson Hall, 1975.

Richardson, Harry V. Dark *Salvation: The Story of Methodism As It Developed among Blacks in America.* Garden City, N.Y.: Doubleday, Anchor Press, 1976.

Roberts, J. Deotis. *Africentric Christianity: A Theological Appraisal for Ministry.* Valley Forge, Pa.: Judson Press, 2000.

———. *A Black Political Theology.* Philadelphia: Westminster, 1974.

———. *Liberation and Reconciliation: A Black Theology.* Philadelphia: Westminster, 1971; revised edition, Maryknoll, N.Y.: Orbis, 1994.

Russell, Dick. *Black Genius and the American Experience.* New York: Carroll & Graf, 1998.

Sealey, Kelvin Shawn, ed. *Restoring Hope: Cornel West and Conversations on the Future of Black America.* Boston: Beacon Press, 1997.

Sernett, Milton C., ed. *African American Religious History: A Documentary Witness,* Second Edition. Durham, N.C.: Duke University Press, 1999.

———. *Bound for the Promised Land: African American Religion and the Great Migration.* Durham, N.C.: Duke University Press, 1997.

Simmons, Martha, and Frank A. Thomas, eds. *The African American Pulpit.* Winter 2000–2001.

Simpson, George Eaton. *Black Religions in the New World.* New York: Columbia University Press, 1978.

Sobel, Mechal. *Trabelin' On: The Slave Journey to an Afro-Baptist Faith.* Princeton, N.J.: Princeton University Press, 1988.

Southern, Eileen. *The Music of Black Americans: A History.* Second Edition. New York: Norton, 1983.

Sundquist, Eric J. *To Wake the Nations: Race in the Making of American Literature.* Cambridge, N.J.: Belknap, 1993.

Taylor, Gardner C. *How Shall They Preach?* Elgin, Ill.: Progressive Baptist Publishing House, 1977.

———. *The Words of Gardner Taylor.* Compiled by Edward L. Taylor. 6 vols. Valley Forge, Pa.: Judson Press, 1999–2002.

Thurman, Howard. *Jesus and the Disinherited.* Nashville: Abingdon, 1949.

———. *With Head and Heart: The Autobiography of Howard Thurman.* New York: Harcourt, Brace Jovanovich, 1979.

Titon, Jeff Todd, ed. *Give Me This Mountain: Life History and Selected Sermons of Reverend C. L. Franklin.* Baltimore: University of Illinois Press, 1989.

Townes, Emilie M. *In a Blaze of Glory: Womanist Spirituality as a Social Witness.* Nashville: Abingdon, 1995.

Walker, Wyatt Tee. *"Somebody's Calling My Name": Black Sacred Music and Social Change.* Valley Forge, Pa.: Judson Press, 1979.

Washington, James Melvin. *Conversations with God.* New York: Harper Perennial, 1994.

———. *Frustrated Fellowship: The Black Baptist Quest for Social Power.* Macon, Ga.: Mercer University Press, 1986.

Washington, Joseph R., Jr. *Black Religion.* Boston: Beacon Press, 1964.

———. *Black Sects and Cults.* Garden City, N.Y.: Doubleday, 1972.

Washington, Margaret, ed. *Narrative of Sojourner Truth.* Westminster, Md.: Vintage Books, 1993.

Watts, Jill. *God, Harlem U.S.A.: The Father Divine Story.* Berkeley, Calif.: University of California, 1992.

Weems, Renita J. *Just a Sister Away: A Womanist Vision of Women's Relationships in the Bible.* San Diego: LuraMedia, 1988.

Weisbrot, Robert. *Father Divine.* Boston: Beacon Press, 1983.

West, Cornel. *Prophetic Fragments.* Grand Rapids, Mich.: Eerdmans, 1988.

———. *Prophetic Reflections.* Monroe, Maine: Common Courage Press, 1993.

Williams, Juan. *Eyes on the Prize: America's Civil Rights Years, 1954–1965.* New York: Penguin, 1987.

Wilmore, Gayraud S. *Black Religion and Black Radicalism: An Examination of the Black Experience in Religion.* Garden City, N.Y.: Doubleday, 1972; third edition by Maryknoll, N.Y.: Orbis, 1998.

———, ed. *African American Religious Studies: An Introductory Anthology.* Durham, N.C.: Duke University Press, 1989.

Wilmore, Gayraud S., and James H. Cone, eds. *Black Theology: A Documentary History 1966–1979.* Maryknoll, N.Y.: Orbis, 1979; second edition, 1993.

Witter, Evelyn. *Mahalia Jackson.* Milford, Mich.: Mott Media, 1985.

Woodson, Carter G. *The History of the Negro Church.* Washington, D.C.: The Associated Publishers, 1972.

X, Malcolm, with Alex Haley. *The Autobiography of Malcolm X.* New York: Grove, 1965.

Young, Henry J. *Major Black Religious Leaders, 1755–1940.* Nashville: Abingdon, 1977.

———. *Major Black Religious Leaders Since 1940.* Nashville: Abingdon, 1979.

Index

⊙-⊙-⊙

Photo and Illustration Credits

⊙–⊙–⊙

Art by P. S. Duval, Philadelphia, permission of The New York Public Library / Schomburg Center for Research in Black Culture, 2

Photograph © by David Zadig, 19

Permission of The New York Public Library / Schomburg Center for Research in Black Culture, 20, 45, 103, 121, 132, 137, 141, 144, 158, 175, 178, 180, 208, 213

Permission of and © by Bettman / Corbis, 23, 126, 203, 218, 220, 234, 267

Photograph © by Raymond Linear, Baltimore, Maryland, 35

Photograph © by Jon Chase, Harvard NFWS Office, 61

Courtesy of T. D. Jakes Ministries, 65

Courtesy of Sixth Mount Zion Baptist Church, 66

Photograph © by Rodney L. Brown, 75

Courtesy of Abyssinian Baptist Church, New York City, 77

Photograph © by Butler Prestige, 93

Photograph © by Harris & Ewing, permission of The New York Public Library / Schomburg Center for Research in Black Culture, 104

Photograph © by Doug Knutson, 119

Photograph © by Gill Photographers, St. Albans, New York, 125

Photograph © by United Nations / Y. Nagata, permission of The New York Public Library / Schomburg Center for Research in Black Culture, 133

Engraving by J. Kearney, permission of The New York Public Library / Schomburg Center for Research in Black Culture, 140

Photograph © by Gaston Perry, permission of The New York Public Library / Schomburg Center for Research in Black Culture, 146

Permission of and © by Reuters NewMedia Inc. / Corbis, 159

Permission of and © by Flip Schulke / Corbis, 161

Photograph © by J. H. Preiter, permission of The New York Public Library / Schomburg Center for Research in Black Culture, 165

Photograph © by Karl Crutchfield Photo, 170

Art by K. S. Woerner, permission of The New York Public Library / Schomburg Center for Research in Black Culture, 191

Permission of and © by Reuters NewMedia Inc. / Corbis, 200

Permission of and © by Ted Williams / Corbis, 206

Photograph © by Atlantic Records, permission of The New York Public Library / Schomburg Center for Research in Black Culture, 209

Permission of and © by Hulton-Deutsch Collection / Corbis, 238

Permission of Ariel Skully / Corbis Stock Market, 248, 254